THE TYPE SPECIMEN BOOK

THE TYPE SPECIMEN BOOK

544 different typefaces
with over 3000 sizes
shown in complete alphabets

VNR VAN NOSTRAND REINHOLD COMPANY
New York Cincinnati Toronto London Melbourne

THE TYPE SPECIMEN BOOK
IS THE SPECIMEN BOOK OF
V & M TYPOGRAPHICAL, INC.
1652-60 McDONALD AVENUE,
BROOKLYN, N.Y. 11230
212-998-5520

Library of Congress Catalog Card Number 74-5951

ISBN 0-442-27915-9

Manufactured in the United States of America.

Cover Design: Howard S. Leiderman
Cover Photography: Joseph P. Manzella

Van Nostrand Reinhold Company Inc.
135 West 50th Street, New York, N.Y. 10020

16   15   14   13   12   11

Library of Congress Cataloging in Publication Data

V & M Typographical, Inc.
  The type specimen book.

  1. Printing—Specimens. I. Title.
Z250.V115   1974   686.2'24   74-5951
ISBN 0-442-27915-9

Airport Medium Condensed
18   Foundry 14 16 18 24

Akzidenz Grotesk
9   Linotype 6 8 9

Akzidenz Grotesk Bold
9   Linotype 6 8 9

Alternate Gothic No. 1
18   Foundry 10 12 14 18 24 30 36 48 60 72

Alternate Gothic No. 2
18   Foundry 18 24 30 36 42 48 60 72
                             Linotype 6 7 8 9 10 11 12 14

ALTERNATE GOTHIC ITALIC No. 2
Alternate Gothic Italic
30   Foundry 30

Alternate Gothic No. 3
18   Foundry 8 10 12 14 18 24 30 36 48 60 72
                      Linotype 6 8 9

Americana
18   Foundry 10 12 14 18 24 30 36 42

Americana Bold
14   Foundry 12 14 18 24 30 36 42 60

Americana Italic
14   Foundry 14 24

Antique No. 1
10   Linotype 8 9 10 14

Antique No. 1 Italic
10   Linotype 9 10

ANZEIGEN GROTESK
Anzeigen
48   Foundry 48 96

Arrighi
18   Foundry 18 22

Aster
12   Linotype 6 7 8 9 10 12 14

Aster Bold
12   Linotype 6 7 8 9 10 12 14

Aster Italic
12   Linotype 6 7 8 9 10 12 14

AUGUSTEA
18   Foundry 12 14 18 24

AUGUSTEA INLINE
AUGUSTEA
24   Foundry 24 42 48

Aurora Bold Condensed
16   Foundry 14 16 20 28 36 48

Aurora Condensed
20   Foundry 20 24 28 36 60

BANK GOTHIC CONDENSED LIGHT
BANK GOTHIC CONDENSE
18   Foundry 18 No. 39

Bank Script
18   Foundry 18 24 36 48

Baskerville
18 No. 2   Foundry 18 No. 1 2 24 30 36 48 60 72
                           Linotype 6 7 8 9 10 11 12 14 16

Baskerville Italic
18 No. 2   Foundry 18 No. 1 2
                           Linotype 6 7 8 9 10 11 12 14

Baskerville Bold
14   Foundry 30
                           Linotype 8 9 10 11 12 14

Baskerville Bold Italic
14   Linotype 8 9 10 11 12 14

Baskerville 353
18   Foundry 18 24 30 36

Baskerville Italic 3531
18   Foundry 18 24 30 36 48

Bauer Bodoni Roman
18   Foundry 16 18 24 30 42

Bauer Bodoni Bold
18   Foundry 18 30

Bauer Bodoni Bold Italic
16   Foundry 16 24 42

BAUER BODONI EXTRA BOLD
Bauer Bodoni
30   Foundry 30

BAUER BODONI EXTRA BOLD ITALIC
Bauer Bodoni Extra Bold
18   Foundry 14 18 24 30 42

Bauer Bodoni Italic
18   Foundry 16 18 24 30 42

BAUER BODONI TITLE
BAUER
42   Foundry 42 Caps only

Bell
18   Foundry 18 24 30 36

Bell Italic
18   Foundry 18 24 30

(AMERICAN)
Bembo
18   Foundry 18

(AMERICAN)
Bembo Italic
18   Foundry 14 18 24 36

(BRITISH)
Bembo
18   Foundry 8 10 18

(BRITISH)
Bembo Italic
14   Foundry 8 10 14

(BRITISH)
Bembo Bold
12   Foundry 8 12

Bernhard Cursive
24   Foundry 14 24 30 36 42 54

Bernhard Cursive Bold
24   Foundry 24 30 36 42 54

Bernhard Fashion
18   Foundry 18 24 30 36

Bernhard Modern Bold
18   Foundry 8 10 12 14 18 24 30 36 42 48

Bernhard Modern Bold Italic
18   Foundry 10 14 18 24 30 36

Bernhard Modern Italic
18   Foundry 12 18 24 30 36 42 48

Bernhard Modern Roman
18   Foundry 8 10 12 14 18 24 30 36 48 60

Bernhard Tango
18   Foundry 18 24 36 48 60

Beton Extrabold
18   Foundry 14 16 18 24 36 48

BETON OPEN
20   Foundry 20 24 30 36 48 Caps only

Bodoni
18   Foundry 14 18 24 30 36 42 48 60 72
                                      Linotype 6 7 8 9 10 12 14

Bodoni Italic
18   Foundry 14 18 24 30 36
                                      Linotype 6 7 8 9 10 12 14

Bodoni Bold
18   Foundry 12 14 42 72
Linotype 6 8 9 10 12 14
Ludlow 18 24 30 36 48

Bodoni Bold Italic
18   Foundry 12 14 72
Linotype 6 8 9 10 12 14
Ludlow 18 24 30 36 48

Bodoni Bold Condensed
18   Foundry 14 18 24 30 36 48 60

Bodoni Book
18   Foundry 18 24 30 36 42 48
Linotype 6 7 8 9 10 11 12 14

Bodoni Book Italic
18   Foundry 18 36
Linotype 6 7 8 9 10 11 12 14

Bodoni Campanile
18   Ludlow 14 18 24 36 48

Bodoni Open-face
24   Foundry 24 36

Bodoni Shaded
18   Foundry 14 18

Bodoni 175
18   Foundry 14 18 24 30 36

Bodoni Italic 1751 and 3751
18   Foundry 18 42

Bold Face No. 2
6   Linotype 6

BOLD FACE NUMBER SIX
10   Linotype 10 Caps only

Bon Aire
36   Foundry 36

Bookman
18   Foundry 14 18 24 30 36
Linotype 6 7 12

Bookman Italic
18   Foundry 18 36
Linotype 6 7 12

BROADWAY
18   Foundry 8 12 18

Brody
18   Foundry 18 24 30 36 48 60 72

Brush
24   Foundry 12 24 30 36 42 60

BULLETIN TYPEWRITER
Bulletin
18   Foundry 18 24

Bulmer Roman
18   Foundry 6 8 10 12 14 18 24 30 36 42 48

Bulmer Italic
18   Foundry 6 10 12 14 18 24 30 36 42 48

CARD ITALIC
10   Linotype 10 Caps only

Cairo
14   Intertype 6 8 10 12 14

Cairo Bold
14   Intertype 6 8 10 12 14

CAIRO BOLD ITALIC
10   Linotype 8 10 Caps only

Cairo Italic
14   Intertype 6 8 10 12 14

Cairo Medium
12   Intertype 6 8 10 12

Cairo Medium Italic
12   Intertype 6 8 10 12

Caledonia
14   Linotype 6 7 8 9 10 11 12 14

Caledonia Italic
14   Linotype 6 7 8 9 10 11 12 14

Caledonia Bold
12 — Linotype 6 7 8 9 10 11 12 14

Caledonia Bold Italic
12 — Linotype 6 7 8 9 10 11 12 14

CARTOON BOLD
18 — Foundry 14 18 24

Caslon
12 — Linotype 10 12 14

Caslon Italic
12 — Linotype 10 12 14

Caslon No. 3
14 — Linotype 14

Caslon No. 3 Italic
14 — Linotype 14

Caslon No. 4
18 — Linotype 18

Caslon Bold
18 — Foundry 18 24 30 36 42 48 60 72

Caslon Bold Italic
18 — Foundry 14 18 24 30 36

Caslon Bold Condensed
18 — Foundry 12 14 30 36 42 60
Ludlow 18

Caslon No. 540
18 — Foundry 12 14 with Small Caps 18 24 30 36 42 48 60 72 84

Caslon No. 540 Italic
18 — Foundry 10 14 18 24 30 36 42 48 60 72

Caslon Oldstyle No. 471
18 — Foundry 10 14 18 24 30 36 42 48

Caslon Oldstyle No. 471 Italic
14 — Foundry 14 18 24 30 36 42 48

Caslon Oldstyle No. 337
18 — Foundry 14 18 22 24 30 36 42 48

Caslon Oldstyle No. 3371 Italic
18 — Foundry 14 18 22 24 30 36 42 48

Caslon Openface
18 — Foundry 18 24 30 36

Centaur
18 — Foundry 14 16 18 24 30 36 48

Centaur Italic
18 — Foundry 18 48

Century Bold
18 — Foundry 18 24 30
Linotype 8 9 10 12 14

Century Bold Italic
18 — Foundry 18
Linotype 14

Century Bold Condensed
24 — Foundry 24 36

Century Expanded
18 — Foundry 10 18 24 30 48 60
Linotype 6 7 8 9 10 11 12 14

Century Expanded Italic
18 — Foundry 8 10 12 14 18 24 30 36 48
Linotype 6 7 8 9 10 11 12 14

Century Nova
14 — Foundry 14 24 48

Century Schoolbook
18 — Foundry 10 12 14 with Small caps 18 24 30 48

Century Schoolbook Italic
18 — Foundry 8 12 14 16 18 24 30 36

Century Schoolbook Bold
14 — Foundry 14 18 24 30 48

Cheltenham Bold
18 — Foundry 8 12 14 18 24 30 36
Ludlow 18

Cheltenham Bold Italic
14   Foundry 14 24 30

Cheltenham Bold Condensed
18   Foundry 10 12 14 18 30 36 60 72

Cheltenham Bold Extra Condensed
12   Foundry 12 24 30 36 84

CHELTENHAM BOLD EXTENDED
Cheltenham Bold
18   Foundry 14
Ludlow 18 24 30 36

Cheltenham Bold Outline
18   Foundry 18 24 30 36

Cheltenham Oldstyle
10   Foundry 8 10

CHELTENHAM OPEN
Cheltenham
42   Foundry 42 48

Cheltenham Wide No. 164
18   Foundry 12 14 18 24 30

Cheltenham Wide No. 164 Italic
14   Foundry 12 14 18 24 30

Cheltonian Bold
12   Intertype 12

Cheltonian Wide
12   Intertype 12

Chisel
30   Foundry 30 48 72

City Medium
24   Foundry 24-S

Clarendon Regular
18   Foundry 18 24 30 36 60

Clarendon Bold
18   Foundry 10 12 14 18 24 30 36 42 60 72

Clearface
18   Foundry 12 18 24 36

Clearface Italic
10   Foundry 10 12

Cloister Black
18   Foundry 14 18 24 36

Cloister Bold
30   Foundry 30

Cloister Bold Italic
30   Foundry 30

CLOISTER INITIALS

36   Foundry 36 48

Cochin No. 61
18   Foundry 18

Cochin Italic No. 611
18   Foundry 18 24 36

Columbia
18   Foundry 12 14 18 24-L

Columbia Italic
18   Foundry 18

COLUMNA
16   Foundry 16 28 36

COMMERCE GOTHIC LIGHT
12 No. 2   Ludlow 6 pt. No. 1 2 3 4   12 pt. No. 1 2 3 4

Commercial Script
18   Foundry 12 14 18 24 30 36 48

Comstock
18   Foundry 12 14 18 24 30 36

Cooper Black
18   Foundry 12 14 18 24 30 36 48

Cooper Black Italic
18   Foundry 12 14 18 24 36 48 72

COPPERPLATE GOTHIC BOLD
12 No. 46   Foundry 12 pt. No. 46 48   24 pt. No. 50

COPPERPLATE GOTHIC HEAVY
12 No. 26   Foundry 12 pt. No. 25 26 27 28
                              18 pt. No. 29 30
                              24 pt. No. 29 30

COPPERPLATE GOTHIC HEAVY CONDENSED
12 No. 15   Foundry 12 pt. No. 15 16 17 18

COPPERPLATE GOTHIC ITALIC
COPPERPLATE
18   Foundry 12 pt. No. 58   18 pt. No. 59 60

COPPERPLATE GOTHIC LIGHT
COPPERPLATE
18 No. 10   Foundry 6 pt. No. 1
                              18 pt. No. 10
                              24 pt. No. 10

COPPERPLATE GOTHIC LIGHT EXTENDED NO. 63
6   Foundry 6 pt. No. 63

COPPERPLATE GOTHIC LIGHT CONDENSED
COPPERPLATE GOTHIC LIGHT
12 No. 37   Foundry 12 pt. No. 36 37   18 pt. No. 39

COPPERPLATE GOTHIC HEAVY EXTENDED
COPPERPLATE GOTHIC
12 No. 76   Foundry—12 pt. No. 75 76 77 78
                              18 pt. No. 79 80
                              24 pt. No. 79 80

Coronet Bold
18   Ludlow 14 18 24 36 48

Coronet Light
18   Ludlow 14 18 24 36

Corvinus Bold
18   Foundry 12 14 18 24 30 36

Corvinus Light
18   Foundry 14 18 24 36

Corvinus Light Italic
16   Foundry 12 14 16 30

Corvinus Medium
18   Foundry 8 10 12 14 18 24 30 36 48 60

Corvinus Medium Italic
18   Foundry 12 14 18 24 36 48

Craw Clarendon
18   Foundry 8 10 12 14 18 24 30 36 48 60 72

Craw Clarendon Book
18   Foundry 8 10 14 18 24 30 36 48 60

CRAW CLARENDON CONDENSED
Craw Clarendon
30   Foundry 30 48 72

Craw Modern
18   Foundry 10 12 14 18 24 30 36

Craw Modern Bold
14   Foundry 10 12 14 18 24 30 36 48

Deepdene Roman
18   Foundry 12 14 16 18 24 30 36 48 60

Deepdene Italic
18   Foundry 12 14 18 24 30 36 48

DELPHIAN OPEN TITLE
DELPHIAN OPEN
24   Foundry 48
                     Ludlow 24 36

Delphin II
20   Foundry 10 14 20 48

DE VINNE OUTLINE
10   Linotype 10 Caps only

Dom Bold
18   Foundry 18 24 30 36 48 60 72

Dom Casual
18   Foundry 18 24 30 36 48 60 72

Dom Diagonal
18   Foundry 18 24 30 36 48 60 72

Dominante Roman
14   Foundry 14 28
                                                Linotype 8 9

Dominante Bold
9   Linotype 8 9

Dominante Italic
16   Foundry 16 28

Dominus
48   Foundry 48

Eden Bold
18   Ludlow 18 24 36

Eden Light
18   Ludlow 12 18 24 36

Egmont Medium
18   Foundry 18 24 30-S 30-L 36

Egmont Medium Italic
18   Foundry 18 24 30-S 30-L 36

EGYPTIAN EXPANDED
Egyp
36   Foundry 36

Egyptian Bold Condensed
18   Foundry 18 24 30 36 48

Electra
11   Linotype 7 8 9 10 11 12 14

Electra Bold
10   Linotype 8 9 10 11 12 14

Electra Bold Cursive
10   Linotype 8 9 10 11 12 14

Electra Cursive
11   Linotype 8 9 10 11 12 14

Electra Italic
11   Linotype 7 8 9 10 11 12 14

Elizabeth Italic
18   Foundry 10 12 14 16 18 24 30 36 48

Elizabeth Roman
18   Foundry 10 12 16 18 24 30 36 48

EMPIRE
36   Foundry 36 48 60 72 96

ENGRAVERS BOLD
12 No. 2   Foundry 12 pt. No. 1 2 3   18 pt. No. 1 2   24 36
                                                Ludlow 12 pt. No. 1

ENGRAVERS ROMAN
12 No. 42   Foundry 12 pt. No. 41 42 43   14 24

ENGRAVERS OLD ENGLISH
Engravers Old
36   Foundry 36

Eurostile Bold
10   Foundry 10 24-S 24-L

EUROSTILE BOLD CONDENSED
Eurostile Bold
36   Foundry 36

Eurostile Bold Extended
14   Foundry 6 8 10 12 14 18 24-S 24-L 30 36 48 72

Eurostile Extended
12 · Foundry 8 10 12 14 18 24-S 36

Eurostile Normal
10 · Foundry 6 8 10

Excelsior
6 · Linotype 5½ 6

Excelsior Italic
6 · Linotype 6

Excelsior Script Semi Bold
24 · Foundry 24

Fairfield
14 · Linotype 6 8 9 10 11 12 14

Fairfield Italic
14 · Linotype 6 8 9 10 11 12 14

Folio Bold
24 · Foundry 24

FOLIO BOLD CONDENSED ITALIC
Folio Bold Cond
42 · Foundry 42

Folio Demibold
30 · Foundry 30

Folio Extra Bold
18 · Foundry 14 16 18 30 42 54

Folio Light
18 · Foundry 14 16 18 24 54

Folio Medium
18 · Foundry 16 18 24 30 36 42 54 66

FOLIO MEDIUM CONDENSED
Folio Medium Cond
36 · Foundry 30 36 42 54

Folio Medium Extended
16 · Foundry 14 16 18 24 30 42 54

Fortuna Bold
16 · Foundry 14 16 24 30 36 54 60

Fortuna Bold Italic
16 · Foundry 16 24

Fortuna Extrabold
16 · Foundry 12 14 16 24 30 60

Fortuna Light
18 · Foundry 14 16 18 24 30 36 42 54 60

FORUM
30 · Foundry 30

FOURNIER
24 · Foundry 24

Franklin Gothic
18 · Foundry 6 8 10 12 14 18 24 30 36 42 48 60 72
Intertype 8 10
Ludlow 14 18

Franklin Gothic Condensed
18 · Foundry 6 8 10 12 14 18 24 30 36 42 48 60 72

FRANKLIN GOTHIC CONDENSED OUTLINE
FRANKLIN
48 · Foundry 48 Caps only

Franklin Gothic Extra Condensed
18 · Foundry 10 12 14 18 24 30 36 42 48 60 72 84

Franklin Gothic Italic
14 · Foundry 12 14 18 24 30
Intertype 8 10

Franklin Gothic Wide
14 · Foundry 6 8 10 12 14 18 24 30 36 42 48 60 72

Furtura Book
18   Foundry 18 30 36 48

Futura Demibold
16   Foundry 16 24 36
           Intertype 10 12

Futura Demibold Oblique
18   Foundry 18 24

Futura Black
20   Foundry 20 24 48

Futura Bold
18   Foundry 18 30

Futura Display
18   Foundry 14 18 24

Futura Light
18   Foundry 6 16 18 24 30 36 48 60 72

Futura Light Oblique
18   Foundry 18 24

Futura Medium
18   Foundry 8 18 24 30 48 60
           Intertype 10 12

Futura Medium Condensed
12   Foundry 12

GALLIA
18   Foundry 18 24 36

Garamond
18   Foundry 18 Caps only 30 36 48 60 72
           Intertype 6 7 8 9 10 11 12 14
           Ludlow 18 24 36

Garamond Italic
18   Foundry 16 24 30 36 42 48
           Intertype 6 7 8 9 10 11 12 14
           Ludlow 18 24 36

Garamond Bold
18   Foundry 16 30 36 42 60
           Ludlow 18 24 30 36 48

Garamond Bold Italic
18   Foundry 48
           Ludlow 18 24 30 36 48 60

Garamond No. 3
14   Linotype 6 8 9 10 11 12 14

Garamond Italic No. 3
14   Linotype 6 8 9 10 11 12 14

Garamond Bold No. 3
14   Linotype 6 8 10 12 14

Garamond Bold Italic No. 3
14   Linotype 6 8 10 12 14

Garamont Roman
18   Foundry 18 24 30 36 48 60 72

Garamont Italic
18   Foundry 18 24 30 36 72

Gillies Gothic Bold
18   Foundry 18 24 30

GLAMOUR BOLD

Glamour Bo
36   Foundry 36

Glamour Light
36   Foundry 36

GOLD RUSH
24   Foundry 24 Caps only

GOTHIC NO. THREE
5½   Linotype 5½ Caps only

GOTHIC CONDENSED NO. FOUR
5½   Linotype 5½ Caps only

Gothic No. 16
6   Linotype 6

Gothic No. 545
14   Foundry 14

Gothic Condensed No. 529
18   Foundry 18 36 42 60

GOTHIC OUTLINE TITLE No. 61
GOTHIC OUTLINE
24   Foundry 24 36 42 48 Caps only

Goudy Bold
18   Foundry 18 24 30 36 42 48
                          Ludlow 48

Goudy Bold Italic
18   Foundry 14 18 30 36

Goudy Handtool
18   Foundry 12 14 18 24 30 36 48

Goudy Handtool Italic
18   Foundry 14 18 24 30 36

Goudy Heavy
30   Foundry 30

Goudy Italic
18   Foundry 14 18 24 30 36

Goudy Light
18   Ludlow 6 8 10 12 14 18 24

Goudy Oldstyle
18   Foundry 14 18 24 30 36

Goudy Oldstyle Italic
14   Foundry 14

Goudy Open
18   Foundry 14 18 24 30 36

Goudy Open Italic
18   Foundry 18 24 30 36

Goudy Text
18   Foundry 18 36 60 72

Granjon
12   Linotype 8 9 10 11 12

Granjon Bold
12   Linotype 8 10 12

Granjon Italic
12   Linotype 8 9 10 11 12

Graphic Bold
18   Foundry 14 18 30 48

Grotesque No. 6
18   Foundry 12 18

Grotesque No. 8
24   Foundry 24 36 60 72

Grotesque No. 9
18   Foundry 8 10 12 14 18 24 36

Hauser Script
24   Ludlow 24

HEADLINE GOTHIC
HEADLINE
48   Foundry 48

Hellenic Wide
18   Foundry 10 12 14 18 24 30 42

Helvetica
18   Foundry 16 18 24-S 24-L 30 42 48 60
                          Linotype 6 7 8 9 10 11 12 14

Helvetica Italic
18   Foundry 16 18 24-S 24-L 30
                          Linotype 6 7 8 9 10 11 12 14

Helvetica Bold
18   Foundry 10 12 14 16 18 24-S 24-L 30 42 48 60

Helvetica Bold Compact Italic
14   Foundry 14 18 24 30

Helvetica Bold Condensed
18   Foundry 12 14 18 24-S 30 54

Helvetica Bold Extended
14 — Foundry 10 12 14 16 18 24-L 48

Helvetica Extra Bold Condensed
18 — Foundry 18 24 30 42 54 84

HELVETICA EXTRA BOLD EXTENDED
Helvetica Extra
18 — Foundry 10 12 14 16 18 24

Helvetica Regular Extended
14 — Foundry 14 16 18 48

Helvetica Regular Condensed
18 — Foundry 18

Helvetica Light
18 — Foundry 16 18 24-S 24-L 30 42 48
Linotype 6 7 8 9 10 11 12 14

Helvetica Light Italic
24 Small — Foundry 24-S
Linotype 6 7 8 9 10 11 12 14

Helvetica Medium
18 — Foundry 12 14 16 18 24-S 24-L 30 42 48 60 72
Linotype 6 7 8 9 10 11 12 14

Helvetica Medium Italic
18 — Foundry 18 24-S 24-L 30
Linotype 6 7 8 9 10 11 12 14

Horizon Light
30 — Foundry 30

HUXLEY VERTICAL
30 — Foundry 30 36 48 60

Imperial
12 — Intertype 12

Imperial Bold
12 — Intertype 12

Ionic No. 5
7 — Linotype 7

Ionic No. 5 Italic
7 — Linotype 7

Janson
18 — Foundry 14 18 24 30 36
Linotype 8 9 10 11 12 14

Janson Italic
18 — Foundry 18 24 30 36
Linotype 8 9 10 11 12 14

JIM CROW
24 — Foundry 24 Caps only

Karnak Black
18 — Ludlow 10 12 14 18 24

Karnak Black Condensed
18 — Ludlow 18

Karnak Light
18 — Ludlow 18

Karnak Medium
6 — Ludlow 6

Kaufmann Bold
18 — Foundry 18 36

Kennerly
18 — Foundry 10 12 14 18 24 36

Kennerly Italic
18 — Foundry 10 14 18 24 30

Keynote
18 — Foundry 18 24

Latin Bold
18 — Foundry 18 24 30 36 48

Latin Bold Condensed
24 — Foundry 10 12 24 30 36 72

Latin Elongated
18   Foundry 12 18 36

Latin Wide
12   Foundry 12 18

Legend
30   Foundry 30 48

LIBRA
18 Large   Foundry 12 18-S 18-L 24 30-S 30-L 36 48

LINING PLATE GOTHIC HEAVY
12 pt. No. 1   Ludlow 6 pt. No. 1 2 3 4   12 pt. No. 1 2 3 4

LINING PLATE GOTHIC HEAVY CONDENSED
6 pt. No. 4   Foundry 24 pt. No. 1
                                     Ludlow 6 pt. No. 1 2 3 4

Lightline Gothic
14   Foundry 14

LOMBARDIC INITIALS
LOMBARDIC
24   Foundry 24 48 60 72

Lucian
18   Foundry 14 18

Lucian Bold
14   Foundry 14 18 24 30 48

Lucian Italic
18   Foundry 14 18 20 24 30

Lydian
18   Foundry 10 12 14 18 24 30 36 48 60

Lydian Bold
18   Foundry 10 12 14 18 24 30 36

Lydian Bold Italic
18   Foundry 18 24 30 36

Lydian Cursive
18   Foundry 18 24 30 36 48

Lydian Italic
18   Foundry 10 12 14 18 24 30 36 48

MARBLE HEART
MARBLE
42   Foundry 42 Caps only

Medium Condensed Gothic
18   Ludlow 18 24 30 42

Melior
18   Foundry 10 12-S 12-L 14 18 24-S 24-L 30 36 48 60
                                     Linotype 6 7 8 9 10 12

Melior Italic
18   Foundry 14 18 24-S 24-L 48
                                     Linotype 6 7 8 9 10

Melior Bold Condensed
14   Foundry 12 14 24 36

Melior Semi-Bold
18   Foundry 10 12-S 12-L 18 24-S 24-L 36 60
                                     Linotype 6 7 8 9 10 12

Metropol 416
24   Ludlow 24

MICHELANGELO TITLING
16   Foundry 16 30

MICROGRAMMA
14   Foundry 12 14

MICROGRAMMA BOLD
12   Foundry 8 10 12 14 18 24 30B 36

MICROGRAMMA BOLD EXTENDED
8   Foundry 6 8 12 14 18 24 30A

MICROGRAMMA CONDENSED
10   Foundry 10

MICROGRAMMA EXTENDED
10   Foundry 6B 8 10 12

Mistral
18   Foundry 18 24-L 30 36 48

Modern No. 20
18   Foundry 14 18 24 30 36 48

Modern No. 20 Italic
18   Foundry 18 24 30

Monticello
14   Linotype 7 8 9 10 11 12 14

Monticello Italic
14   Linotype 7 8 9 10 11 12 14

MURRAY HILL BOLD
Murray Hill
36   Foundry 36

NEULAND
18   Foundry 14 18 24 30

New Caslon
18   Foundry 14 18 24 30 48

New Caslon Italic
18   Foundry 14 18 24 30 36 42

News Gothic
18   Foundry 6 8 10 12 14 18 24 30 36 42 48 72
    Linotype 6 8 9

News Gothic Bold
18   Foundry 6 10 12 14 18 24 30 36 42 48
    Linotype 6 8 9

News Gothic Bold Condensed
14   Linotype 6 7 8 9 10 11 12 14

News Gothic Condensed
18   Foundry 6 8 10 12 14 18 24 30 36 42 48 60 72
    Linotype 6 7 8 9 10 11 12 14

News Gothic Extra Condensed
18   Foundry 6 8 10 12 14 18 24 30 36 42 48 60 72

News Gothic Light
10   Linotype 8 9 10

News Gothic Light Italic
10   Linotype 8 9 10

Nicholas Cochin
18 No. 2   Foundry 14 18 No. 2 24 36

Nova Augustea
18   Foundry 12 18 24-S 36

Nubian
12   Foundry 12

NUMBER ELEVEN
5½   Linotype 5½ Caps only

Number Eighteen
14   Linotype 6 7 8 9 10 11 12 14

Number Twenty
14   Linotype 6 7 8 9 10 11 12 14

Number Twenty-one
8   Linotype 8 9 11

Number Twenty-one Italic
8   Linotype 8 9 11

OLD BOWERY
30   Foundry 30

𝔒𝔩𝔡 𝔈𝔫𝔤𝔩𝔦𝔰𝔥
18   Ludlow 8 10 12 14 18 24 30

OLD FACE OPEN
18   Foundry 14 18 24 30 42 48

Old Gothic Bold Italic
14   Foundry 10 14 60

Oldstyle No. 1
12   Linotype 6 7 8 9 10 11 12 14

Oldstyle No. 1 Italic
12   Linotype 6 7 8 9 10 11 12

Onyx
18   Foundry 18 24 30 42 48 60 72

Onyx Italic
48   Foundry 48

ORPLID
24   Foundry 24

Opticon
6   Linotype 6

Optima
18   Foundry 8-L 10 12-L 14 18 24-S 24-L 30 36 48
Linotype 6 7 8 9 10 12

Optima Italic
18   Foundry 12-L 14 18 24-S 24-L 30 36 48
Linotype 6 7 8 9 10

Optima Medium
12   Linotype 6 7 8 9 10 12

Optima Black
12   Linotype 6 7 8 9 10 12

Optima Semi-Bold
18   Foundry 10 12-L 14 18 24-S 24-L 30 36 48
Linotype 6 7 8 9 10 12

Pabst
14   Foundry 10 12 14

Pabst Extra Bold
14   Linotype 10 14

Pabst Extra Bold Italic
14   Linotype 10 14

Palatino
18   Foundry 10 12 14 18 20 24 30 42 54
Linotype 6 7 8 9 10 12

Palatino Italic
18   Foundry 10 12 14 18 20 24 30 42 54
Linotype 6 7 8 9 10 12

Palatino Semi-Bold
18   Foundry 14 18 20 24 30 42 54
Linotype 6 7 8 9 10 12

Park Avenue
36   Foundry 36

Peignot Medium
24   Foundry 14 24

Perpetua
18   Foundry 10 12 14 18 24 30 36 42 48 60 72

Perpetua Bold
18   Foundry 10 14 18 24 36

Perpetua Italic
18   Foundry 10 12 14 18 24 30 36 42 48

PERPETUA TITLING
18   Foundry 18 24 30 36 48 60 72

Post Roman Bold
18   Foundry 10-L 12 14-L 18 30 42 60

Post Roman Light
18   Foundry 14-S 14-L 18 24-S 24-L

Post Italic
14 Small   Foundry 14-S

Post Roman Medium
18   Foundry 12 14-S 14-L 18 24-S 24-L 30 42 48

Poster Bodoni
10   Linotype 10

Poster Bodoni Italic
10   Linotype 10

Primer
14   Linotype 6 7 8 9 10 11 12 14

Primer Italic
14   Linotype 6 7 8 9 10 11 12 14

PRISMA
24   Foundry 24 30 36

P. T. Barnum
18   Foundry 14 18 24 30 36

Radiant Bold
18   Foundry 14 18 36

Radiant Bold Condensed
14   Foundry 14

Record Gothic
10   Ludlow 10

Reiner Script
30-Large   Foundry 30-L 60

Repro Script
18   Foundry 18 36

REVERSE GOTHIC
REVERSE
24   Ludlow 24

ROMAN COMPRESSED NO. 3
Roman Compressed
30   Foundry 30 48

ROMANTIQUE NO. 5
ROMANTIQU
24   Foundry 24 36

Sans Serif Bold
18   Foundry 14 18 30 36

Sans Serif Extra Bold
24   Foundry 24

Sans Serif Light
18   Foundry 8 10 14 18 24 30 36 48

Sans Serif Light Italic
18   Foundry 18

SANS SERIF MEDIUM
Sans Serif
36   Foundry 36

Scotch Roman
18   Foundry 14 18 24 30 36

Scotch Italic
18   Foundry 14 18 24

SISTINA TITLING
16   Foundry 16 20 24 30 36

SOLEMNIS
18   Foundry 18 24 30 36 48 60

Spartan Black
18   Foundry 18 24 30 36 42 48 60 72 84
                                           Linotype 6 8 10 12 14

Spartan Black Condensed
18   Foundry 14 18 24 30 36 42 48 60 72

Spartan Black Italic
24   Foundry 24
                                        Linotype 6 8 10 12 14

Spartan Black Condensed Italic
18   Foundry 18 24 30 36 48 60

Spartan Book
18   Foundry 18 24
                                        Linotype 6 8 10 12 14

Spartan Book Condensed
14   Linotype 6 8 10 12 14

Spartan Extra Black
18   Foundry 18 24 30 36 42 48

Spartan Heavy
18   Foundry 18 24 30 36 60 72
                                            Linotype 6 8 10 12 14

Spartan Heavy Condensed
14   Linotype 6 8 10 12 14

Spartan Heavy Italic
18   Foundry 14 18 24 36 60
                                            Linotype 8 10 12 14

Spartan Medium
18   Foundry 18 24 30 36 48 72 84
                                            Linotype 6 8 9 10 11 12 14

Spartan Medium Condensed
24   Foundry 24

Spartan Medium Italic
18   Foundry 18 24 30
                                            Linotype 6 8 9 10 11 12 14

SPIRE
24   Foundry 24 48 72

Standard
18   Foundry 6 8 10 12 14 18 24-S 24-L 30 36 48

Standard Bold
18   Foundry 12 14 18 24-S 24-L 30

Standard Bold Condensed
18   Foundry 12 14 18 24-S 24-L 30 42 60 72

Standard Condensed
18   Foundry 14 18 24-S 24-L 60

Standard Extra-Bold Condensed
18   Foundry 18 24-S 24-L 30 42 48 60

STANDARD EXTRA BOLD EXTENDED
Standard Extra
24-Small   Foundry 24-S

Standard Italic
14   Foundry 14

Standard Light Condensed
18   Foundry 10 18

Standard Light Extended
10   Foundry 10 42

Standard Medium
18   Foundry 6 8 10 12 14 18 24-S 24-L 30 42 60 72

Standard Medium Condensed
18   Foundry 18 24-S 42 60 72

STANDARD MEDIUM EXTENDED
Standar
42   Foundry 42

Standard Medium Italic
14   Foundry 12 14

STENCIL
18   Foundry 18 24 30 36

Stradivarius
18   Foundry 18 48 84

Studio
18   Foundry 8 10 12 18 24-S 24-L 30 36 48

Studio Bold
18   Foundry 18 30

Stymie Black
24   Foundry 24 36

Stymie Bold
18   Foundry 14 Caps only 18 24 30 36 48 60

Stymie Bold Condensed
18   Foundry 12 14 18 24 30 60

Stymie Bold Italic
18   Foundry 18

Stymie Extra Bold
18   Foundry 18 24

STYMIE EXTRA BOLD ITALIC
Stymie Extra
24   Foundry 24

Stymie Bold Extra Condensed
18   Foundry 18

Stymie Light
18   Foundry 14 18 24 48

Stymie Light Italic
14   Foundry 14 24

Stymie Medium
14   Foundry 14 24 30 36

STYMIE MEDIUM CONDENSED
Stymie Medium
30   Foundry 30

STYMIE OPEN
24 pt. No. 1   Foundry 24 pt. No. 1   24 pt. No. 2   30 36 48

Tempo Bold
18   Ludlow 18 24 30 36 48

Tempo Bold Italic
18   Ludlow 18 24 30 36 48

Tempo Heavy
18   Ludlow 8 10 12 18 24 36

TEMPO HEAVY CONDENSED
Tempo Heavy
48   Ludlow 48

Tempo Medium
18   Ludlow 8 10 12 14 18 24

Tempo Medium Italic
10   Ludlow 10

THORNE SHADED
THORNE
24   Foundry 24 30 36 48

TIMES EXTENDED TITLING
TIMES EXTENDED
18   Foundry 14 18 24 30 36 48 60 72

TIMES HEAVY TITLING
18   Foundry 14 18 24 30 36 48 60 72

Times New Roman Bold
18   Foundry 14 18 24 30 36 42 48 60 72

TIMES NEW ROMAN BOLD ITALIC
Times New Roman Bold
18   Foundry 14 18 24 30 36 42 48 60 72

Times New Roman
18   Foundry 14 18 24 30 36 48 60 72

Times New Roman Italic
18   Foundry 14 18 24 30 36 48 60 72

Times Roman
14   Linotype 6 7 8 9 10 11 12 14

Times Roman Bold
14   Linotype 6 7 8 9 10 11 12 14

Times Roman Italic
14   Linotype 6 7 8 9 10 11 12 14

TIMES TITLING
18   Foundry 14 18 24 30 36 48 60 72

Torino Italic
18   Foundry 10 12 14 18 24-S 24-L 30

Torino Roman
18   Foundry 8 12 14 18 24-S 24-L 36 48

Tower
18   Foundry 18 48 60

Trade Gothic
9   Linotype 8 9

Trade Gothic Condensed
14   Linotype 6 7 8 9 10 11 12 14

Trade Gothic Bold
9   Linotype 8 9

Trade Gothic Bold Condensed
14   Linotype 6 7 8 9 10 11 12 14

Trade Gothic Light
10   Linotype 8 9 10

Trade Gothic Light Italic
10   Linotype 8 9 10

Trafton Script
36   Foundry 36 48 72

True Cut Caslon
22   Foundry 36 48
      Ludlow 22 30

TRUMP GRAVUR
TRUMP
36   Foundry 36 60

Trump Mediaeval
20   Foundry 12 20 24 28 36 48
      Linotype 6 7 8 9 10

Trump Mediaeval Bold
16   Foundry 16

Trump Mediaeval Italic
16   Foundry 12 14 16 20 24 28
      Linotype 6 7 8 9 10

Trump Mediaeval Medium
10   Linotype 6 8 9 10

Trylon
18   Foundry 18 24 36

Twentieth Century Light
18   Foundry 14 18 30

Twentieth Century Light Italic
18   Foundry 14 18 30

Typewriter
12   Linotype 10 12

Typewriter With Underscore
12   Linotype 10 12

Typo Script
18   Foundry 14 18 24 30

Typo Upright
18   Foundry 12 14 18 24 30

Ultra Bodoni
18   Foundry 8 12 14 18 24 30 36 42 48 60 72
      Linotype 10

Ultra Bodoni Italic
18   Foundry 8 10 12 14 18 24 30 36 42
      Linotype 10

ULTRA BODONI EXTRA CONDENSED
Ultra Bodoni Extra
24   Foundry 24 36 42

UMBRA
24   Ludlow 24 36 48

Univers No. 45
24 Large   Foundry 24-L 30 48

Univers No. 46
30   Foundry 30

Univers No. 55
18   Foundry 8 10 14 18 24-S 24-L 30

Univers No. 56
18   Foundry 10 12 14 18 24-S 24-L 30 36

Univers No. 57
18   Foundry 12 18 24-S 24-L 30

Univers No. 58
24-Small   Foundry 10 12 24-S 24-L 30

Univers No. 65
18   Foundry 8 10 12 14 18 24-S 24-L 30 36 48

Univers No. 66
18   Foundry 10 12 14 18 24-S 24-L 30 36

Univers No. 67
18   Foundry 10 18 24-S 24-L 30 36 48

Univers No. 68
18   Foundry 6 12 14 18

Univers No. 73
18   Foundry 10 12 14 18 24-L

Univers No. 75
18   Foundry 8 12 18 24-S 24-L 30 36

Univers No. 76
24-Large   Foundry 24-L 30

Vendome Bold Italic
24   Foundry 24 42

Vendome
10   Foundry 10

Venus Bold
14   Foundry 14 42 54

Venus Bold Condensed
18   Foundry 12 14 18 24 36

Venus Bold Extended
16   Foundry 8 10 12 14 16 18 24 30 36 42 54

Venus Bold Italic
18   Foundry 8 10 12 14 16 18 24 30 36

Venus Extrabold
12   Foundry 8 10 12

Venus Extrabold Condensed
18   Foundry 12 14 18

Venus Extrabold Extended
12   Foundry 8 10 12 14 16 18 24 30 36 42 54 66 84

Venus Light
18   Foundry 12 14 18 24

Venus Light Extended
18   Foundry 6 8 10 12 14 16 18 24 30 36

Venus Light Italic
18   Foundry 8 10 12 14 16 18 24

Venus Medium
18   Foundry 14 16 18 30

Venus Medium Extended
16   Foundry 6 8 10 12 14 16 18 24 30 36 42

Venus Medium Italic
18   Foundry 8 10 12 14 16 18 24

Verona
18   Foundry 18 30

Weiss Roman Bold
18   Foundry 14 18 24 30

WEISS INITIALS SERIES I
18   Foundry 18 24 30-S 30-L 42 54

WEISS INITIALS SERIES II
18   Foundry 14 18 24 30-S 30-L 42 66

WEISS INITIALS SERIES III
14   Foundry 14 18 30 42

Weiss Italic
18   Foundry 10 12 14 16 18 24 30 36
                         Intertype 8 9 10 11 12 14

Weiss Roman
18   Foundry 10 12 14 pt. with Small Caps 16 18 24 30 36 48 60
                       Intertype 8 9 10 11 12 14

WEISS ROMAN EXTRA BOLD
Weiss Roman Extra
24   Foundry 24 30

Windsor
18   Foundry 10 14 18 24 30 36 48

WINDSOR ELONGATED
Windsor Elo
60   Foundry 60

Windsor Light
24   Foundry 24

THE TYPE SPECIMEN BOOK

Airport Medium Condensed

ABCDEFGHIJKLMNOPQRSTUVWXYZ&
abcdefghijklmnopqrstuvwxyz
1234567890$

ABCDEFGHIJKLMNOPQRSTUVWXYZ&
abcdefghijklmnopqrstuvwxyz
1234567890$

ABCDEFGHIJKLMNOPQRSTUVWXYZ&
abcdefghijklmnopqrstuvwxyz
1234567890$

ABCDEFGHIJKLMNOPQRSTUVWXYZ&
abcdefghijklmnopqrstuvwxyz
1234567890$

Akzidenz Grotesk *(Must be leaded 1 point)*

The basic character in a type design is determined by the uniform design characteristics of all letters in the alphabet. However, this alone does not determine the standard of the type face and the quality of composition set with it. The appearance is something complex which forms itself out of many details, like form, proportion, ductus, rhythm etc. If everything harmonizes, the total result will be more than the sum of its components. The only reli able basis for the design in a type is a positive feeling for form and style. The basic character in a type design is determined by the uniform design

ABCDEFGHIJKLMNOPQRSTUVWXYZ&
abcdefghijklmnopqrstuvwxyz   1234567890$

The basic character in a type design is determined by the uni form design characteristics of all letters in the alphabet. How ever, this alone does not determine the standard of the type face and the quality of composition set with it. The appear ance is something complex which forms itself out of many details, like form, proportion, ductus, rhythm etc. If everything

ABCDEFGHIJKLMNOPQRSTUVWXYZ&
abcdefghijklmnopqrstuvwxyz   1234567890$

The basic character in a type design is determined by the uniform design characteristics of all letters in the alpha bet. However, this alone does not determine the standard of the type face and the quality of composition set with it. The appearance is something complex which forms it

ABCDEFGHIJKLMNOPQRSTUVWXYZ&
abcdefghijklmnopqrstuvwxyz   1234567890$

Akzidenz Grotesk Bold *(Must be leaded 1 point)*

The basic character in a type design is determined by the uniform design characteristics of all letters in the alphabet. However, this alone does not determine the standard of the type face and the quality of composition set with it. The appearance is something complex which forms itself out of many details, like form, proportion, ductus, rhythm etc. If everything harmonizes, the total result will be more than the sum of its components. The only reli able basis for the design in a type is a positive feeling for form and style. The basic character in a type design is determined by the uniform design

ABCDEFGHIJKLMNOPQRSTUVWXYZ&
abcdefghijklmnopqrstuvwxyz   1234567890$

The basic character in a type design is determined by the uni form design characteristics of all letters in the alphabet. How ever, this alone does not determine the standard of the type face and the quality of composition set with it. The appear ance is something complex which forms itself out of many details, like form, proportion, ductus, rhythm etc. If everything

ABCDEFGHIJKLMNOPQRSTUVWXYZ&
abcdefghijklmnopqrstuvwxyz   1234567890$

The basic character in a type design is determined by the uniform design characteristics of all letters in the alpha bet. However, this alone does not determine the standard of the type face and the quality of composition set with it. The appearance is something complex which forms it

ABCDEFGHIJKLMNOPQRSTUVWXYZ&
abcdefghijklmnopqrstuvwxyz   1234567890$

Alternate Gothic Italic No. 2

ABCDEFGHIJKLMNOPQRSTUVWXYZ&
abcdefghijklmnopqrstuvwxyz
1234567890$

Alternate Gothic No. 1

10 point Alternate Gothic No. 1 (Foundry)
ABCDEFGHIJKLMNOPQRSTUVWXYZ&
abcdefghijklmnopqrstuvwxyz
1234567890$

12 point Alternate Gothic No. 1 (Foundry)
ABCDEFGHIJKLMNOPQRSTUVWXYZ&
abcdefghijklmnopqrstuvwxyz
1234567890$

14 point Alternate Gothic No. 1 (Foundry)
ABCDEFGHIJKLMNOPQRSTUVWXYZ&
abcdefghijklmnopqrstuvwxyz
1234567890$

18 point Alternate Gothic No. 1 (Foundry)
ABCDEFGHIJKLMNOPQRSTUVWXYZ&
abcdefghijklmnopqrstuvwxyz
1234567890$

24 point Alternate Gothic No. 1 (Foundry)
ABCDEFGHIJKLMNOPQRSTUVWXYZ&
abcdefghijklmnopqrstuvwxyz
1234567890$

30 point Alternate Gothic No. 1 (Foundry)
ABCDEFGHIJKLMNOPQRSTUVWXYZ&
abcdefghijklmnopqrstuvwxyz
1234567890$

36 point Alternate Gothic No. 1 (Foundry)
ABCDEFGHIJKLMNOPQRSTUVWXYZ&
abcdefghijklmnopqrstuvwxyz
1234567890$

48 point Alternate Gothic No. 1 (Foundry)
ABCDEFGHIJKLMNOPQRSTUVWXYZ&
abcdefghijklmnopqrstuvwxyz
1234567890$

(Continued on Page 3)

60 point Alternate Gothic No. 1 (Foundry)

ABCDEFGHIJKLMNOPQRSTUVW
XYZ&
abcdefghijklmnopqrstuvwxyz
1234567890$

72 point Alternate Gothic No. 1 (Foundry)

ABCDEFGHIJKLMNOPQRST
UVWXYZ&
abcdefghijklmnopqrstuv
wxyz
1234567890$

Alternate Gothic No. 2

6 point Alternate Gothic No. 2 (Linotype)
The basic character in a type design is determined by the uniform design char
acteristics of all letters in the alphabet. However, this alone does not determine
the standard of the type face and the quality of composition set with it. The
appearance is something complex which forms itself out of many details, like
form, proportion, ductus, rhythm etc. If everything harmonizes, the total result
will be more than the sum of its components. The only reliable basis for the
design in a type is a positive feeling for form and style. The basic character
in a type design is determined by the uniform design characteristics of all

ABCDEFGHIJKLMNOPQRSTUVWXYZ&
abcdefghijklmnopqrstuvwxyz　　　　　　　　1234567890$

7 point Alternate Gothic No. 2 (Linotype)
The basic character in a type design is determined by the uniform design
characteristics of all letters in the alphabet. However, this alone does not
determine the standard of the type face and the quality of composition set
with it. The appearance is something complex which forms itself out of
many details, like form, proportion, ductus, rhythm etc. If everything har
monizes, the total result will be more than the sum of its components. The
only reliable basis for the design in a type is a positive feeling for form

ABCDEFGHIJKLMNOPQRSTUVWXYZ&
abcdefghijklmnopqrstuvwxyz　　　　　　　　1234567890$

8 point Alternate Gothic No. 2 (Linotype)
The basic character in a type design is determined by the uniform de
sign characteristics of all letters in the alphabet. However, this alone
does not determine the standard of the type face and the quality of
composition set with it. The appearance is something complex which
forms itself out of many details, like form, proportion, ductus, rhythm etc.
If everything harmonizes, the total result will be more than the sum of

ABCDEFGHIJKLMNOPQRSTUVWXYZ&
abcdefghijklmnopqrstuvwxyz　　　　　　　　1234567890$

9 point Alternate Gothic No. 2 (Linotype)
The basic character in a type design is determined by the uniform
design characteristics of all letters in the alphabet. However, this
alone does not determine the standard of the type face and the
quality of composition set with it. The appearance is something
complex which forms itself out of many details, like form, propor

ABCDEFGHIJKLMNOPQRSTUVWXYZ&
abcdefghijklmnopqrstuvwxyz　　　　　　　　1234567890$

10 point Alternate Gothic No. 2 (Linotype)
The basic character in a type design is determined by the uni
form design characteristics of all letters in the alphabet. However,
this alone does not determine the standard of the type face and
the quality of composition set with it. The appearance is some
thing complex which forms itself out of many details, like form,

ABCDEFGHIJKLMNOPQRSTUVWXYZ&
abcdefghijklmnopqrstuvwxyz　　　　　　　　1234567890$

11 point Alternate Gothic No. 2 (Linotype)
The basic character in a type design is determined by the
uniform design characteristics of all letters in the alphabet.
However, this alone does not determine the standard of the
type face and the quality of composition set with it. The ap

ABCDEFGHIJKLMNOPQRSTUVWXYZ&
abcdefghijklmnopqrstuvwxyz　　　　　　　　1234567890$

12 point Alternate Gothic No. 2 (Linotype)
The basic character in a type design is determined by the
uniform design characteristics of all letters in the alphabet.
However, this alone does not determine the standard of the
type face and the quality of composition set with it. The

ABCDEFGHIJKLMNOPQRSTUVWXYZ&
abcdefghijklmnopqrstuvwxyz　　　　　　　　1234567890$

14 point Alternate Gothic No. 2 (Linotype)
The basic character in a type design is determined
by the uniform design characteristics of all letters
in the alphabet. However, this alone does not deter

ABCDEFGHIJKLMNOPQRSTUVWXYZ&
abcdefghijklmnopqrstuvwxyz　　　　1234567890$

18 point Alternate Gothic No. 2 (Foundry)
ABCDEFGHIJKLMNOPQRSTUVWXYZ&
abcdefghijklmnopqrstuvwxyz
1234567890$

24 point Alternate Gothic No. 2 (Foundry)
ABCDEFGHIJKLMNOPQRSTUVWXYZ&
abcdefghijklmnopqrstuvwxyz
1234567890$

(Continued on Page 5)

30 point Alternate Gothic No. 2 (Foundry)

ABCDEFGHIJKLMNOPQRSTUVWXYZ&
abcdefghijklmnopqrstuvwxyz
1234567890$

36 point Alternate Gothic No. 2 (Foundry)

ABCDEFGHIJKLMNOPQRSTUVWXYZ&
abcdefghijklmnopqrstuvwxyz
1234567890$

42 point Alternate Gothic No. 2 (Foundry)

ABCDEFGHIJKLMNOPQRSTUVWXYZ&
abcdefghijklmnopqrstuvwxyz
1234567890$

48 point Alternate Gothic No. 2 (Foundry)

ABCDEFGHIJKLMNOPQRSTUVWXYZ
abcdefghijklmnopqrstuvwxyz&
1234567890$

(Continued on Page 6)

60 point Alternate Gothic No. 2 (Foundry)

ABCDEFGHIJKLMNOPQRS TUVWXYZ&
abcdefghijklmnopqrs tuvwxyz
1234567890$

72 point Alternate Gothic No. 2 (Foundry)

ABCDEFGHIJKLMNOPQ RSTUVWXYZ&
abcdefghijklmnopqrs tuvwxyz 1234567890$

Alternate Gothic No. 3

6 point Alternate Gothic No. 3 (Intertype)

The basic character in a type design is determined by the uniform de sign characteristics of all letters in the alphabet. However, this alone does not determine the standard of the type face and the quality of composition set with it. The appearance is something complex which forms itself out of many details, like form, proportion, ductus, rhythm etc. If everything harmonizes, the total result will be more than the sum of its components. The only reliable basis for the design in a type is a positive feeling for form and style. The basic character in a type design

ABCDEFGHIJKLMNOPQRSTUVWXYZ&
abcdefghijklmnopqrstuvwxyz   1234567890$

8 point Alternate Gothic No. 3 (Linotype)

The basic character in a type design is determined by the uni form design characteristics of all letters in the alphabet. How ever, this alone does not determine the standard of the type face and the quality of composition set with it. The appearance is something complex which forms itself out of many details, like form, proportion, ductus, rhythm etc. If everything har

ABCDEFGHIJKLMNOPQRSTUVWXYZ&
abcdefghijklmnopqrstuvwxyz   1234567890$

9 point Alternate Gothic No. 3 (Linotype)

The basic character in a type design is determined by the uniform design characteristics of all letters in the alpha bet. However, this alone does not determine the standard of the type face and the quality of composition set with it. The appearance is something complex which forms itself

ABCDEFGHIJKLMNOPQRSTUVWXYZ&
abcdefghijklmnopqrstuvwxyz   1234567890$

8 point Alternate Gothic No. 3 (Foundry)
ABCDEFGHIJKLMNOPQRSTUVWXYZ&
abcdefghijklmnopqrstuvwxyz
1234567890$

10 point Alternate Gothic No. 3 (Foundry)
ABCDEFGHIJKLMNOPQRSTUVWXYZ&
abcdefghijklmnopqrstuvwxyz
1234567890$

12 point Alternate Gothic No. 3 (Foundry)
ABCDEFGHIJKLMNOPQRSTUVWXYZ&
abcdefghijklmnopqrstuvwxyz
1234567890$

14 point Alternate Gothic No. 3 (Foundry)
ABCDEFGHIJKLMNOPQRSTUVWXYZ&
abcdefghijklmnopqrstuvwxyz
1234567890$

18 point Alternate Gothic No. 3 (Foundry)
ABCDEFGHIJKLMNOPQRSTUVWXYZ&
abcdefghijklmnopqrstuvwxyz
1234567890$

24 point Alternate Gothic No. 3 (Foundry)
ABCDEFGHIJKLMNOPQRSTUVWXYZ&
abcdefghijklmnopqrstuvwxyz
1234567890$

30 point Alternate Gothic No. 3 (Foundry)
ABCDEFGHIJKLMNOPQRSTUVWXYZ&
abcdefghijklmnopqrstuvwxyz
1234567890$

36 point Alternate Gothic No. 3 (Foundry)
ABCDEFGHIJKLMNOPQRSTUVWXYZ&
abcdefghijklmnopqrstuvwxyz
1234567890$

(Continued on Page 8)

48 point Alternate Gothic No. 3 (Foundry)

ABCDEFGHIJKLMNOPQRSTUV WXYZ&
abcdefghijklmnopqrstuvwxyz
1234567890$

60 point Alternate Gothic No. 3 (Foundry)

ABCDEFGHIJKLMNO PQRSTUVWXYZ&
abcdefghijklmno pqrstuvwxyz
1234567890$

(Continued on Page 9)

72 point Alternate Gothic No. 3 (Foundry)

ABCDEFGHIJKLMNOP
QRSTUVWXYZ&
abcdefghijklmnopqr
stuvwxyz
1234567890$

Americana

10 point Americana (Foundry)

ABCDEFGHIJKLMNOPQRSTUVWXYZ&
abcdefghijklmnopqrstuvwxyz
1234567890$

12 point Americana (Foundry)

ABCDEFGHIJKLMNOPQRSTUVWXYZ&
abcdefghijklmnopqrstuvwxyz
1234567890$

14 point Americana (Foundry)

ABCDEFGHIJKLMNOPQRSTUVWXYZ&
abcdefghijklmnopqrstuvwxyz
1234567890$

18 point Americana (Foundry)

ABCDEFGHIJKLMNOPQRSTUVWXYZ&
abcdefghijklmnopqrstuvwxyz
1234567890$

24 point Americana (Foundry)

ABCDEFGHIJKLMNOPQRSTUVWXYZ&
abcdefghijklmnopqrstuvwxyz
1234567890$

30 point Americana (Foundry)

ABCDEFGHIJKLMNOPQRSTUVW
XYZ&
abcdefghijklmnopqrstuvwxyz
1234567890$

(Continued on Page 11)

36 point Americana (Foundry)

ABCDEFGHIJKLMNOPQRS
TUVWXYZ&
abcdefghijklmnopqrstuv
wxyz
1234567890$

42 point Americana (Foundry)

ABCDEFGHIJKLMNOPQ
RSTUVWXYZ&
abcdefghijklmnopqrstuv
wxyz
1234567890$

Americana Bold

12 point Americana Bold (Foundry)

ABCDEFGHIJKLMNOPQRSTUVWXYZ&
abcdefghijklmnopqrstuvwxyz
1234567890$

14 point Americana Bold (Foundry)

ABCDEFGHIJKLMNOPQRSTUVWXYZ&
abcdefghijklmnopqrstuvwxyz
1234567890$

18 point Americana Bold (Foundry)

ABCDEFGHIJKLMNOPQRSTUVWXYZ&
abcdefghijklmnopqrstuvwxyz
1234567890$

24 point Americana Bold (Foundry)

ABCDEFGHIJKLMNOPQRSTUVWXYZ&
abcdefghijklmnopqrstuvwxyz
1234567890$

30 point Americana Bold (Foundry)

ABCDEFGHIJKLMNOPQRS
TUVWXYZ&
abcdefghijklmnopqrstuvwxyz
1234567890$

36 point Americana Bold (Foundry)

ABCDEFGHIJKLMNOPQRS
TUVWXYZ&
abcdefghijklmnopqrs
tuvwxyz
1234567890$

(Continued on page 13)

42 point Americana Bold (Foundry)

ABCDEFGHIJKLMNOP
QRSTUVWXYZ&
abcdefghijklmnopqrstu
vwxyz
1234567890$

60 point Americana Bold (Foundry)

ABCDEFGHIJK
LMNOPQRSTUV
WXYZ&
abcdefghijklmno
pqrstuvwxyz
1234567890$

Americana Italic

ABCDEFGHIJKLMNOPQRSTUVWXYZ&
abcdefghijklmnopqrstuvwxyz
1234567890$

ABCDEFGHIJKLMNOPQRSTUVWXYZ&
abcdefghijklmnopqrstuvwxyz
1234567890$

Antique No. 1

Antique No. 1 stems from the Old Style Antique series introduced by Miller and Richards, of Edinburgh, in the 1850's. It quickly became popular as a more satisfactory general-purpose face than the romans in vogue at the time with their "protracted hairlines and feeble serifs."

The basic character in a type design is determined by the uni form design characteristics of all letters in the alphabet. How ever, this alone does not determine the standard of the type face and the quality of composition set with it. The appearance is something complex which forms itself out of many details, like form, proportion, ductus, rhythm etc. If everything har

ABCDEFGHIJKLMNOPQRSTUVWXYZ&
abcdefghijklmnopqrstuvwxyz   1234567890$

The basic character in a type design is determined by the uniform design characteristics of all letters in the alphabet. However, this alone does not determine the standard of the type face and the quality of com position set with it. The appearance is something

ABCDEFGHIJKLMNOPQRSTUVWXYZ&
abcdefghijklmnopqrstuvwxyz   1234567890$

The basic character in a type design is determined by the uniform design char acteristics of all letters in the alphabet.

ABCDEFGHIJKLMNOPQRSTUV
WXYZ&   1234567890$
abcdefghijklmnopqrstuvwxyz

The basic character in a type design is determined by the uniform design characteristics of all letters in the alphabet. However, this alone does not determine the standard of the type face and the quality of composi tion set with it. The appearance is something complex

ABCDEFGHIJKLMNOPQRSTUVWXYZ&
abcdefghijklmnopqrstuvwxyz   1234567890$

Antique No. 1 Italic

The basic character in a type design is determined by the uniform design characteristics of all letters in the alphabet. However, this alone does not determine the standard of the type face and the quality of composi tion set with it. The appearance is something complex

ABCDEFGHIJKLMNOPQRSTUVWXYZ&
abcdefghijklmnopqrstuvwxyz   1234567890$

The basic character in a type design is determined by the uniform design characteristics of all letters in the alphabet. However, this alone does not determine the standard of the type face and the quality of com position set with it. The appearance is something

ABCDEFGHIJKLMNOPQRSTUVWXYZ&
abcdefghijklmnopqrstuvwxyz   1234567890$

Anzeigen Grotesk

48 point Anzeigen Grotesk (Foundry)

ABCDEFGHIJKLMNOPQRST
UVWXYZ&
abcdefghijklmnopqrstuv
wxyz
1234567890

(no dollar sign is made for this font)

96 point Anzeigen Grotesk (Foundry)

ABCDEFGHIJ
KLMNOPQRS
TUVWXYZ&

(lower case and figures continued on page 16)

96 point Anzeigen Grotesk (Foundry)

abcdefghijk
lmnopqrs
tuvwxyz
123456
7890

(no dollar sign is made for this font)

Arrighi *(Also known as Centaur Italic)*

ABCDEFGHIJKLMNOPQRSTUVWXYZ&
abcdefghijklmnopqrstuvwxyz
1234567890$

ABCDEFGHIJKLMNOPQRSTUVWXYZ&
abcdefghijklmnopqrstuvwxyz
1234567890$

Aster (Italian) *(Must be leaded 1 point)*

The basic character in a type design is determined by the uniform design characteristics of all letters in the alphabet. However, this alone does not determine the standard of the type face and the quality of composition set with it. The appearance is something complex which forms itself out of many details, like form, proportion, ductus, rhythm etc. If every thing harmonizes, the total result will be more than the sum of its components. The only reliable basis for the design in a type is a positive feeling for form and style. The basic character in a type design is de

ABCDEFGHIJKLMNOPQRSTUVWXYZ&
abcdefghijklmnopqrstuvwxyz 1234567890$
ABCDEFGHIJKLMNOPQRSTUVWXYZ

The basic character in a type design is determined by the uni form design characteristics of all letters in the alphabet. How ever, this alone does not determine the standard of the type face and the quality of composition set with it. The appearance is something complex which forms itself out of many details, like form, proportion, ductus, rhythm etc. If everything har monizes, the total result will be more than the sum of its

ABCDEFGHIJKLMNOPQRSTUVWXYZ&
abcdefghijklmnopqrstuvwxyz 1234567890$
ABCDEFGHIJKLMNOPQRSTUVWXYZ

The basic character in a type design is determined by the uniform design characteristics of all letters in the alpha bet. However, this alone does not determine the standard of the type face and the quality of composition set with it. The appearance is something complex which forms itself out of many details, like form, proportion, ductus, rhythm

ABCDEFGHIJKLMNOPQRSTUVWXYZ&
abcdefghijklmnopqrstuvwxyz 1234567890$
ABCDEFGHIJKLMNOPQRSTUVWXYZ

The basic character in a type design is determined by the uniform design characteristics of all letters in the alphabet. However, this alone does not determine the standard of the type face and the quality of composi tion set with it. The appearance is something complex

ABCDEFGHIJKLMNOPQRSTUVWXYZ&
abcdefghijklmnopqrstuvwxyz 1234567890$
ABCDEFGHIJKLMNOPQRSTUVWXYZ

The basic character in a type design is determined by the uniform design characteristics of all letters in the alphabet. However, this alone does not de termine the standard of the type face and the quality of composition set with it. The appearance is some

ABCDEFGHIJKLMNOPQRSTUVWXYZ&
abcdefghijklmnopqrstuvwxyz 1234567890$
ABCDEFGHIJKLMNOPQRSTUVWXYZ

The basic character in a type design is deter mined by the uniform design characteristics of all letters in the alphabet. However, this alone does not determine the standard of the

ABCDEFGHIJKLMNOPQRSTUVWXYZ&
abcdefghijklmnopqrstuvwxyz 1234567890$
ABCDEFGHIJKLMNOPQRSTUVWXYZ

The basic character in a type design is determined by the uniform design char acteristics of all letters in the alphabet.

ABCDEFGHIJKLMNOPQRSTUV
WXYZ& 1234567890$
abcdefghijklmnopqrstuvwxyz
ABCDEFGHIJKLMNOPQRSTUVWXYZ

Aster Bold (Italian)

6 point Aster Bold (Italian) Linotype

The basic character in a type design is determined by the uniform design characteristics of all letters in the alphabet. However, this alone does not determine the standard of the type face and the quality of composition set with it. The appearance is something complex which forms itself out of many details, like form, proportion, ductus, rhythm etc. If everything harmonizes, the total result will be more than the sum of its components. The only reliable basis for the design in a type is a positive feeling for

ABCDEFGHIJKLMNOPQRSTUVWXYZ&
abcdefghijklmnopqrstuvwxyz   1234567890$

7 point Aster Bold (Italian) Linotype

The basic character in a type design is determined by the uni form design characteristics of all letters in the alphabet. How ever, this alone does not determine the standard of the type face and the quality of composition set with it. The appearance is something complex which forms itself out of many details, like form, proportion, ductus, rhythm etc. If everything har

ABCDEFGHIJKLMNOPQRSTUVWXYZ&
abcdefghijklmnopqrstuvwxyz   1234567890$

8 point Aster Bold (Italian) Linotype

The basic character in a type design is determined by the uniform design characteristics of all letters in the alphabet. However, this alone does not determine the standard of the type face and the quality of composition set with it. The appearance is something complex which forms itself

ABCDEFGHIJKLMNOPQRSTUVWXYZ&
abcdefghijklmnopqrstuvwxyz   1234567890$

9 point Aster Bold (Italian) Linotype

The basic character in a type design is determined by the uniform design characteristics of all letters in the alphabet. However, this alone does not determine the standard of the type face and the quality of composi tion set with it. The appearance is something complex

ABCDEFGHIJKLMNOPQRSTUVWXYZ&
abcdefghijklmnopqrstuvwxyz   1234567890$

10 point Aster Bold (Italian) Linotype

The basic character in a type design is determined by the uniform design characteristics of all letters in the alphabet. However, this alone does not de termine the standard of the type face and the qual ity of composition set with it. The appearance of

ABCDEFGHIJKLMNOPQRSTUVWXYZ&
abcdefghijklmnopqrstuvwxyz   1234567890$

12 point Aster Bold (Italian) Linotype

The basic character in a type design is deter mined by the uniform design characteristics of all letters in the alphabet. However, this alone does not determine the standard of the

ABCDEFGHIJKLMNOPQRSTUVWXYZ&
abcdefghijklmnopqrstuvwxyz   1234567890$

14 point Aster Bold (Italian) Linotype

The basic character in a type design is determined by the uniform design char acteristics of all letters in the alphabet.

ABCDEFGHIJKLMNOPQRSTUV
WXYZ&   1234567890$
abcdefghijklmnopqrstuvwxyz

Aster Italic (Italian)

6 point Aster Italic (Italian) Linotype

The basic character in a type design is determined by the uniform design characteristics of all letters in the alphabet. However, this alone does not determine the standard of the type face and the quality of composi tion set with it. The appearance is something complex which forms itself out of many details, like form, proportion, ductus, rhythm etc. If every thing harmonizes, the total result will be more than the sum of its com ponents. The only reliable basis for the design in a type is a positive

ABCDEFGHIJKLMNOPQRSTUVWXYZ&
abcdefghijklmnopqrstuvwxyz   1234567890$

7 point Aster Italic (Italian) Linotype

The basic character in a type design is determined by the uni form design characteristics of all letters in the alphabet. How ever, this alone does not determine the standard of the type face and the quality of composition set with it. The appearance is something complex which forms itself out of many details, like form, proportion, ductus, rhythm etc. If everything har

ABCDEFGHIJKLMNOPQRSTUVWXYZ&
abcdefghijklmnopqrstuvwxyz   1234567890$

8 point Aster Italic (Italian) Linotype

The basic character in a type design is determined by the uniform design characteristics of all letters in the alpha bet. However, this alone does not determine the standard of the type face and the quality of composition set with it. The appearance is something complex which forms itself

ABCDEFGHIJKLMNOPQRSTUVWXYZ&
abcdefghijklmnopqrstuvwxyz   1234567890$

9 point Aster Italic (Italian) Linotype

The basic character in a type design is determined by the uniform design characteristics of all letters in the alphabet. However, this alone does not determine the standard of the type face and the quality of composi tion set with it. The appearance is something complex

ABCDEFGHIJKLMNOPQRSTUVWXYZ&
abcdefghijklmnopqrstuvwxyz   1234567890$

10 point Aster Italic (Italian) Linotype

The basic character in a type design is determined by the uniform design characteristics of all letters in the alphabet. However, this alone does not de termine the standard of the type face and the quality of composition set with it. The appearance is some

ABCDEFGHIJKLMNOPQRSTUVWXYZ&
abcdefghijklmnopqrstuvwxyz   1234567890$

12 point Aster Italic (Italian) Linotype

The basic character in a type design is deter mined by the uniform design characteristics of all letters in the alphabet. However, this alone does not determine the standard of the

ABCDEFGHIJKLMNOPQRSTUVWXYZ&
abcdefghijklmnopqrstuvwxyz   1234567890$

14 point Aster Italic (Italian) Linotype

The basic character in a type design is determined by the uniform design char acteristics of all letters in the alphabet.

ABCDEFGHIJKLMNOPQRSTUV
WXYZ&   1234567890$
abcdefghijklmnopqrstuvwxyz

Augustea

12 point Augustea, Caps only (Foundry)
ABCDEFGHIJKLMNOPQRSTUVWXYZ&   1234567890$

14 point Augustea, Caps only (Foundry)
ABCDEFGHIJKLMNOPQRSTUVWXYZ&   1234567890$

18 point Augustea, Caps only (Foundry)
ABCDEFGHIJKLMNOPQRSTUVWXYZ&   1234567890$

24 point Augustea, Caps only (Foundry)
ABCDEFGHIJKLMNOPQRSTUVWXYZ&
1234567890$

Augustea Inline

24 point Augustea Inline, Caps only (Foundry)
ABCDEFGHIJKLMNOPQRSTUVWXYZ&
1234567890$

42 point Augustea Inline, Caps only (Foundry)
ABCDEFGHIJKLMNO
PQRSTUVWXYZ&
1234567890$

48 point Augustea Inline, Caps only (Foundry)
ABCDEFGHIJKL
MNOPQRSTUV
WXYZ&
1234567890$

Aurora Bold Condensed

14 point Aurora Bold Condensed (Foundry)
ABCDEFGHIJKLMNOPQRSTUVWXYZ&
abcdefghijklmnopqrstuvwxyz 1234567890$

16 point Aurora Bold Condensed (Foundry)
ABCDEFGHIJKLMNOPQRSTUVWXYZ&
abcdefghijklmnopqrstuvwxz 1234567890$

20 point Aurora Bold Condensed (Foundry)
ABCDEFGHIJKLMNOPQRSTUVWXYZ&
abcdefghijklmnopqrstuvwxyz 1234567890$

28 point Aurora Bold Condensed (Foundry)
ABCDEFGHIJKLMNOPQRSTUVWXYZ&
abcdefghijklmnopqrstuvwxyz1234567890$

36 point Aurora Bold Condensed (Foundry)
ABCDEFGHIJKLMNOPQRSTUVWXYZ
abcdefghijklmnopqrstuvwxyz&
1234567890$

48 point Aurora Bold Condensed (Foundry)
ABCDEFGHIJKLMNOPQRST
UVWXYZ&
abcdefghijklmnopqrstuv
wxyz
1234567890$

Aurora Condensed *(Also known as Inserat Grotesque)*

20 point Aurora Condensed (Foundry)

ABCDEFGHIJKLMNOPQRSTUVWXYZ&
abcdefghijklmnopqrstuvwxyz
1234567890$

24 point Aurora Condensed (Foundry)

ABCDEFGHIJKLMNOPQRSTUVWXYZ&
abcdefghijklmnopqrstuvwxyz
1234567890$

28 point Aurora Condensed (Foundry)

ABCDEFGHIJKLMNOPQRSTUVWXYZ&
abcdefghijklmnopqrstuvwxyz
1234567890$

36 point Aurora Condensed (Foundry)

ABCDEFGHIJKLMNOPQRSTUVWXYZ&
abcdefghijklmnopqrstuvwxyz
1234567890$

60 point Aurora Condensed (Foundry)

ABCDEFGHIJKLMNOPQRSTUVWXYZ
abcdefghijklmnopqrstuvwxyz&
1234567890$

Bank Gothic Condensed Light

18 point No. 39 Bank Gothic Condensed Light Caps Only (Foundry)

ABCDEFGHIJKLMNOPQRSTUVWXYZ&
1234567890$

Bank Script

18 point Bank Script (Foundry)

ABCDEFGHIJKLMNOPQRSTUVWXYZ&
abcdefghijklmnopqrstuvwxyz 1234567890$

24 point Bank Script (Foundry)

ABCDEFGHIJKLMNOPQRS
TUVWXYZ&
abcdefghijklmnopqrstuvwxyz 1234567890$

36 point Bank Script (Foundry)

ABCDEFGHIJKLM
NOPQRSTUVWXYZ&
abcdefghijklmnopqrstuvwxyz 1234567890$

48 point Bank Script (Foundry)

ABCDEFGHIJ
KLMNOPQRSTU
VWXYZ& 1234567890$
abcdefghijklmnopqrstuvwxyz

Baskerville

6 point Baskerville (Linotype)

The basic character in a type design is determined by the uniform design characteristics of all letters in the alphabet. However, this alone does not determine the standard of the type face and the quality of composition set with it. The appearance is something complex which forms itself out of many details, like form, proportion, ductus, rhythm etc. If everything har monizes, the total result will be more than the sum of its components. The only reliable basis for the design in a type is a positive feeling for form and style. The basic character in a type design is determined by the uniform

ABCDEFGHIJKLMNOPQRSTUVWXYZ&
abcdefghijklmnopqrstuvwxyz   1234567890$

ABCDEFGHIJKLMNOPQRSTUVWXYZ

7 point Baskerville (Linotype)

The basic character in a type design is determined by the uniform design characteristics of all letters in the alphabet. However, this alone does not determine the standard of the type face and the quality of composition set with it. The appearance is something complex which forms itself out of many details, like form, proportion, ductus, rhythm etc. If everything harmonizes, the total result will be more than the sum of its components. The only reliable basis for the design in a type

ABCDEFGHIJKLMNOPQRSTUVWXY&
abcdefghijklmnopqrstuvwxyz   1234567890$

ABCDEFGHIJKLMNOPQRSTUVWXYZ

8 point Baskerville (Linotype)

The basic character in a type design is determined by the uni form design characteristics of all letters in the alphabet. However, this alone does not determine the standard of the type face and the quality of composition set with it. The appearance is some thing complex which forms itself out of many details, like form, proportion, ductus, rhythm etc. If everything harmonizes, the total

ABCDEFGHIJKLMNOPQRSTUVWXYZ&
abcdefghijklmnopqrstuvwxyz   1234567890$

ABCDEFGHIJKLMNOPQRSTUVWXYZ

9 point Baskerville (Linotype)

The basic character in a type design is determined by the uniform design characteristics of all letters in the alphabet. However, this alone does not determine the standard of the type face and the quality of composition set with it. The appearance is something complex which forms itself out of

ABCDEFGHIJKLMNOPQRSTUVWXYZ&
abcdefghijklmnopqrstuvwxyz   1234567890$

ABCDEFGHIJKLMNOPQRSTUVWXYZ

10 point Baskerville (Linotype)

The basic character in a type design is determined by the uniform design characteristics of all letters in the alpha bet. However, this alone does not determine the standard of the type face and the quality of composition set with it. The appearance is something complex which forms

ABCDEFGHIJKLMNOPQRSTUVWXYZ&
abcdefghijklmnopqrstuvwxyz   1234567890$

ABCDEFGHIJKLMNOPQRSTUVWXYZ

11 point Baskerville (Linotype)

The basic character in a type design is determined by the uniform design characteristics of all letters in the alphabet. However, this alone does not determine the standard of the type face and the quality of com

ABCDEFGHIJKLMNOPQRSTUVWXYZ&
abcdefghijklmnopqrstuvwxyz   1234567890$

ABCDEFGHIJKLMNOPQRSTUVWXYZ

12 point Baskerville (Linotype)

The basic character in a type design is determined by the uniform design characteristics of all letters in the alphabet. However, this alone does not de termine the standard of the type face and the

ABCDEFGHIJKLMNOPQRSTUVWXYZ&
abcdefghijklmnopqrstuvwxyz   1234567890$

ABCDEFGHIJKLMNOPQRSTUVWXYZ

14 point Baskerville (Linotype)

The basic character in a type design is deter mined by the uniform design characteristics of all letters in the alphabet. However, this

ABCDEFGHIJKLMNOPQRSTUV
WXYZ&   1234567890$
abcdefghijklmnopqrstuvwxyz

ABCDEFGHIJKLMNOPQRSTUVWXYZ

16 point Baskerville (Linotype)

The basic character in a type design is determined by the uniform design characteristics of all letters in the alphabet. However, this alone does not determine the standard of the

ABCDEFGHIJKLMNOPQRSTUV
WXYZ&   1234567890$
abcdefghijklmnopqrstuvwxyz

(Continued on Page 24)

18 point No. 1 Baskerville (Foundry)

ABCDEFGHIJKLMNOPQRSTUVWXYZ&
abcdefghijklmnopqrstuvwxyz
1234567890$

18 point No. 2 Baskerville (Foundry)

ABCDEFGHIJKLMNOPQRSTUVWXYZ&
abcdefghijklmnopqrstuvwxyz
1234567890$

24 point Baskerville (Foundry)

ABCDEFGHIJKLMNOPQRSTUVWXYZ&
abcdefghijklmnopqrstuvwxyz
1234567890$

30 point Baskerville (Foundry)

ABCDEFGHIJKLMNOPQRSTUV
WXYZ&
abcdefghijklmnopqrstuvwxyz
1234567890$

36 point Baskerville (Foundry)

ABCDEFGHIJKLMNOPQRST
UVWXYZ&
abcdefghijklmnopqrstuvwxyz
1234567890$

(Continued on Page 25)

48 point Baskerville (Foundry)

ABCDEFGHIJKLMNO
PQRSTUVWXYZ&
abcdefghijklmnopqrstuvw
xyz
1234567890$

60 point Baskerville (Foundry)

ABCDEFGHIJKL
MNOPQRSTUV
WXYZ&
abcdefghijklmnopqr
stuvwxyz
1234567890$

(Continued on Page 26)

(Continued from Page 25)

72 point Baskerville (Foundry)

ABCDEFGHIJ
KLMNOPQRS
TUVWXYZ&
abcdefghijklmn
opqrstuvwxyz
1234567890$

Baskerville Italic

6 point Baskerville Italic (Linotype)

The basic character in a type design is determined by the uniform design characteristics of all letters in the alphabet. However, this alone does not determine the standard of the type face and the quality of composition set with it. The appearance is something complex which forms itself out of many details, like form, proportion, ductus, rhythm etc. If everything harmonizes, the total result will be more than the sum of its components. The only reliable basis for the design in a type is a positive feeling for form

ABCDEFGHIJKLMNOPQRSTUVWXYZ&
abcdefghijklmnopqrstuvwxyz   *1234567890$*

7 point Baskerville Italic (Linotype)

The basic character in a type design is determined by the uniform design characteristics of all letters in the alphabet. However, this alone does not determine the standard of the type face and the quality of composition set with it. The appearance is something complex which forms itself out of many details, like form, proportion, ductus, rhythm etc. If everything harmonizes, the total result will be more than the sum of its components. The only reliable basis for the design in a type

ABCDEFGHIJKLMNOPQRSTUVWXY&
abcdefghijklmnopqrstuvwxyz   *1234567890$*

8 point Baskerville Italic (Linotype)

The basic character in a type design is determined by the uniform design characteristics of all letters in the alphabet. However, this alone does not determine the standard of the type face and the quality of composition set with it. The appearance is something complex which forms itself out of many details, like form, proportion, ductus, rhythm etc. If everything harmonizes, the total

ABCDEFGHIJKLMNOPQRSTUVWXYZ&
abcdefghijklmnopqrstuvwxyz   *1234567890$*

9 point Baskerville Italic (Linotype)

The basic character in a type design is determined by the uniform design characteristics of all letters in the alphabet. However, this alone does not determine the standard of the type face and the quality of composition set with it. The appearance is something complex which forms itself out of

ABCDEFGHIJKLMNOPQRSTUVWXYZ&
abcdefghijklmnopqrstuvwxyz   *1234567890$*

10 point Baskerville Italic (Linotype)

The basic character in a type design is determined by the uniform design characteristics of all letters in the alpha bet. However, this alone does not determine the standard of the type face and the quality of composition set with it. The appearance is something complex which forms

ABCDEFGHIJKLMNOPQRSTUVWXYZ&
abcdefghijklmnopqrstuvwxyz   *1234567890$*

11 point Baskerville Italic (Linotype)

The basic character in a type design is determined by the uniform design characteristics of all letters in the alphabet. However, this alone does not determine

ABCDEFGHIJKLMNOPQRSTUVWXYZ&
abcdefghijklmnopqrstuvwxyz   *1234567890$*

12 point Baskerville Italic (Linotype)

The basic character in a type design is determined by the uniform design characteristics of all letters in the alphabet. However, this alone does not de

ABCDEFGHIJKLMNOPQRSTUVWXYZ&
abcdefghijklmnopqrstuvwxyz   *1234567890$*

14 point Baskerville Italic (Linotype)

The basic character in a type design is deter mined by the uniform design characteristics of all letters in the alphabet. However, this

ABCDEFGHIJKLMNOPQRSTUV WXYZ&   *1234567890$*
abcdefghijklmnopqrstuvwxyz

18 point No. 1 Baskerville Italic (Foundry)

ABCDEFGHIJKLMNOPQRSTUVWXYZ&
abcdefghijklmnopqrstuvwxyz
1234567890$

18 point No. 2 Baskerville Italic (Foundry)

ABCDEFGHIJKLMNOPQRSTUVWXYZ&
abcdefghijklmnopqrstuvwxyz
1234567890$

8 point Baskerville Bold (Linotype)

The basic character in a type design is determined by the uni form design characteristics of all letters in the alphabet. How ever, this alone does not determine the standard of the type face and the quality of composition set with it. The appearance is something complex which forms itself out of many details, like form, proportion, ductus, rhythm etc. If everything harmonizes,

ABCDEFGHIJKLMNOPQRSTUVWXYZ&
abcdefghijklmnopqrstuvwxyz   1234567890$

9 point Baskerville Bold (Linotype)

The basic character in a type design is determined by the uniform design characteristics of all letters in the alphabet. However, this alone does not determine the standard of the type face and the quality of composition set with it. The appearance is something complex which forms itself out of

ABCDEFGHIJKLMNOPQRSTUVWXYZ&
abcdefghijklmnopqrstuvwxyz   1234567890$

10 point Baskerville Bold (Linotype)

The basic character in a type design is determined by the uniform design characteristics of all letters in the alphabet. However, this alone does not determine the standard of the type face and the quality of composition set with it. The appearance is something complex which

ABCDEFGHIJKLMNOPQRSTUVWXYZ&
abcdefghijklmnopqrstuvwxyz   1234567890$

11 point Baskerville Bold (Linotype)

The basic character in a type design is determined by the uniform design characteristics of all letters in the alphabet. However, this alone does not determine the standard of the type face and the quality

ABCDEFGHIJKLMNOPQRSTUVWXYZ&
abcdefghijklmnopqrstuvwxyz   1234567890$

12 point Baskerville Bold (Linotype)

The basic character in a type design is determined by the uniform design characteristics of all letters in the alphabet. However, this alone does not determine the standard of the type face and the

ABCDEFGHIJKLMNOPQRSTUVWXYZ&
abcdefghijklmnopqrstuvwxyz   1234567890$

14 point Baskerville Bold (Linotype)

The basic character in a type design is de termined by the uniform design character istics of all letters in the alphabet. However,

ABCDEFGHIJKLMNOPQRSTUVW
XYZ&   1234567890$
abcdefghijklmopqrstuvwxyz

30 point Baskerville Bold (Foundry)

ABCDEFGHIJKLMNOPQRSTUVWXYZ&
abcdefghijklmnopqrstuvwxyz
1234567890$

Baskerville Bold Italic

The basic character in a type design is determined by the uni form design characteristics of all letters in the alphabet. How ever, this alone does not determine the standard of the type face and the quality of composition set with it. The appearance is something complex which forms itself out of many details, like form, proportion, ductus, rhythm etc. If everything harmonizes,
ABCDEFGHIJKLMNOPQRSTUVWXYZ&
abcdefghijklmnopqrstuvwxyz   1234567890$

The basic character in a type design is determined by the uniform design characteristics of all letters in the alphabet. However, this alone does not determine the standard of the type face and the quality of composition set with it. The appearance is something complex which forms itself out of
ABCDEFGHIJKLMNOPQRSTUVWXYZ&
abcdefghijklmnopqrstuvwxyz   1234567890$

The basic character in a type design is determined by the uniform design characteristics of all letters in the alphabet. However, this alone does not determine the standard of the type face and the quality of composition set with it. The appearance is something complex which
ABCDEFGHIJKLMNOPQRSTUVWXYZ&
abcdefghijklmnopqrstuvwxyz   1234567890$

The basic character in a type design is determined by the uniform design characteristics of all letters in the alphabet. However, this alone does not deter mine the standard of the type face and the quality
ABCDEFGHIJKLMNOPQRSTUVWXYZ&
abcdefghijklmnopqrstuvwxyz   1234567890$

The basic character in a type design is determined by the uniform design characteristics of all letters in the alphabet. However, this alone does not de termine the standard of the type face and the
ABCDEFGHIJKLMNOPQRSTUVWXYZ&
abcdefghijklmnopqrstuvwxyz   1234567890$

The basic character in a type design is de termined by the uniform design character istics of all letters in the alphabet. However,
ABCDEFGHIJKLMNOPQRSTUVW XYZ&   1234567890$
abcdefghijklmopqrstuvwxyz

Baskerville 353

ABCDEFGHIJKLMNOPQRSTUVWXYZ&
abcdefghijklmnopqrstuvwxyz
1234567890$ 1234567890

ABCDEFGHIJKLMNOPQRSTUVWXYZ&
1234567890$ abcdefghijklmnopqrstuvwxyz   1234567890

ABCDEFGHIJKLMNOPQRSTUVWXYZ&
abcdefghijklmnopqrstuvwxyz
1234567890$ 1234567890

(Continued on Page 30)

36 point Baskerville 353 (Foundry)

ABCDEFGHIJKLMNOPQRSTUVW XYZ&

abcdefghijklmnopqrstuvwxyz

1234567890$ 1234567890

Baskerville Italic 3531

18 point Baskerville Italic 3531 (Foundry)

ABCDEFGHIJKLMNOPQRSTUVWXYZ&
abcdefghijklmnopqrstuvwxyz
1234567890$

24 point Baskerville Italic 3531 (Foundry)

ABCDEFGHIJKLMNOPQRSTUVWXYZ&
abcdefghijklmnopqrstuvwxyz
1234567890$ 1234567890

30 point Baskerville Italic 3531 (Foundry)

ABCDEFGHIJKLMNOPQRSTUVWXYZ&
abcdefghijklmnopqrstuvwxyz
1234567890$

36 point Baskerville Italic 3531 (Foundry)

ABCDEFGHIJKLMNOPQRS
TUVWXYZ&
abcdefghijklmnopqrstuvwxyz
1234567890$

(Continued on Page 31)

(Continued from Page 30)

48 point Baskerville Italic 3531 (Foundry)

ABCDEFGHIJKLMNOPQR
STUVWXYZ&
abcdefghijklmnopqrstuvwxyz
1234567890$

Bauer Bodoni Roman

16 point Bauer Bodoni Roman (Foundry)

ABCDEFGHIJKLMNOPQRSTUVWXYZ&
abcdefghijklmnopqrstuvwxyz
1234567890$

18 point Bauer Bodoni Roman (Foundry)

ABCDEFGHIJKLMNOPQRSTUVWXYZ&
abcdefghijklmnopqrstuvwxyz
1234567890$

24 point Bauer Bodoni Roman (Foundry)

ABCDEFGHIJKLMNOPQRSTUVWXYZ&
abcdefghijklmnopqrstuvwxyz
1234567890$

(Continued on Page 32)

(Continued from Page 31)

30 point Bauer Bodoni Roman (Foundry)

ABCDEFGHIJKLMNOPQRSTUVWXYZ&
abcdefghijklmnopqrstuvwxyz
1234567890$

42 point Bauer Bodoni Roman (Foundry)

ABCDEFGHIJKLMNOPQRSTUV
WXYZ&
abcdefghijklmnopqrstuvwxyz
1234567890$

Bauer Bodoni Bold

18 point Bauer Bodoni Bold (Foundry)

ABCDEFGHIJKLMNOPQRSTUVWXYZ&
abcdefghijklmnopqrstuvwxyz
1234567890$

30 point Bauer Bodoni Bold (Foundry)

ABCDEFGHIJKLMNOPQRSTUVWXYZ
abcdefghijklmnopqrstuvwxyz&
1234567890$

Bauer Bodoni Bold Italic

16 point Bauer Bodoni Bold Italic (Foundry)

ABCDEFGHIJKLMNOPQRSTUVWXYZ&
abcdefghijklmnopqrstuvwxyz
1234567890$

24 point Bauer Bodoni Bold Italic (Foundry)

ABCDEFGHIJKLMNOPQRSTUVWXYZ&
abcdefghijklmnopqrstuvwxyz
1234567890$

42 point Bauer Bodoni Bold Italic (Foundry)

ABCDEFGHIJKLMNOPQRS
TUVWXYZ&
abcdefghijklmnopqrstuvwxyz
1234567890$

Bauer Bodoni Extra Bold

30 point Bauer Bodoni Extra Bold (Foundry)

ABCDEFGHIJKLMNOPQRSTUVWXYZ
abcdefghijklmnopqrstuvwxyz&
1234567890$

Bauer Bodoni Extra Bold Italic

14 point Bauer Bodoni Extra Bold Italic (Foundry)

ABCDEFGHIJKLMNOPQRSTUVWXYZ&
abcdefghijklmnopqrstuvwxyz
1234567890$

18 point Bauer Bodoni Extra Bold Italic (Foundry)

ABCDEFGHIJKLMNOPQRSTUVWXYZ&
abcdefghijklmnopqrstuvwxyz
1234567890$

24 point Bauer Bodoni Extra Bold Italic (Foundry)

ABCDEFGHIJKLMNOPQRSTUVWXYZ&
abcdefghijklmnopqrstuvwxyz
1234567890$

30 point Bauer Bodoni Extra Bold Italic (Foundry)

ABCDEFGHIJKLMNOPQRSTUVW
XYZ&
abcdefghijklmnopqrstuvwxyz
1234567890$

42 point Bauer Bodoni Extra Bold Italic (Foundry)

ABCDEFGHIJKLMNOPQR
STUVWXYZ&
abcdefghijklmnopqrstuv
wxyz
1234567890$

Bauer Bodoni Italic

16 point Bauer Bodoni Italic (Foundry)
ABCDEFGHIJKLMNOPQRSTUVWXYZ&
abcdefghijklmnopqrstuvwxyz
1234567890$

18 point Bauer Bodoni Italic (Foundry)
ABCDEFGHIJKLMNOPQRSTUVWXYZ&
abcdefghijklmnopqrstuvwxyz
1234567890$

24 point Bauer Bodoni Italic (Foundry)
ABCDEFGHIJKLMNOPQRSTUVWXYZ&
abcdefghijklmnopqrstuvwxyz
1234567890$

30 point Bauer Bodoni Italic (Foundry)
ABCDEFGHIJKLMNOPQRSTUVWXYZ&
abcdefghijklmnopqrstuvwxyz 1234567890$

42 point Bauer Bodoni Italic (Foundry)
ABCDEFGHIJKLMNOPQRS
TUVWXYZ& 1234567890$
abcdefghijklmnopqrstuvwxyz

Bauer Bodoni Title

42 point Bauer Bodoni Title, Caps only (Foundry)
ABCDEFGHIJKLMNO
PQRSTUVWXYZ&
1234567890$

Bell
The Englishman John Bell (1745-1831) was responsible for the original cutting of this Type design.

18 point Bell (Foundry)

ABCDEFGHIJKLMNOPQRSTUVWXYZ&
abcdefghijklmnopqrstuvwxyz 1234567890$

24 point Bell (Foundry)

ABCDEFGHIJKLMNOPQRSTUVWXYZ&
abcdefghijklmnopqrstuvwxyz 1234567890$

30 point Bell (Foundry)

ABCDEFGHIJKLMNOPQRSTUVW
XYZ&
abcdefghijklmnopqrstuvwxyz 1234567890$

36 point Bell (Foundry)

ABCDEFGHIJKLMNOPQRSTU
VWXYZ& 1234567890$
abcdefghijklmnopqrstuvwxyz

Bell Italic

18 point Bell Italic (Foundry)

ABCDEFGHIJKLMNOPQRSTUVWXYZ&
abcdefghijklmnopqrstuvwxyz 1234567890$

24 point Bell Italic (Foundry)

ABCDEFGHIJKLMNOPQRSTUVWXYZ&
abcdefghijklmnopqrstuvwxyz 1234567890$

30 point Bell Italic (Foundry)

ABCDEFGHIJKLMNOPQRSTUV
WXYZ& 1234567890$
abcdefghijklmnopqrstuvwxyz

Bembo (American)

18 point Bembo, American (Foundry)

ABCDEFGHIJKLMNOPQRSTUVWXYZ&
abcdefghijklmnopqrstuvwxyz
1234567890$

Bembo Italic (American)

14 Bembo Italic, American (Foundry)

ABCDEFGHIJKLMNOPQRSTUVWXYZ&
abcdefghijklmnopqrstuvwxyz
1234567890$

18 Bembo Italic, American (Foundry)

ABCDEFGHIJKLMNOPQRSTUVWXYZ&
abcdefghijklmnopqrstuvwxyz
1234567890$

24 Bembo Italic, American (Foundry)

ABCDEFGHIJKLMNOPQRSTUVWXYZ&
abcdefghijklmnopqrstuvwxyz
1234567890$

36 Bembo Italic, American (Foundry)

ABCDEFGHIJKLMNOPQRSTUVW
1234567890   XYZ&   1234567890$
abcdefghijklmnopqrstuvwxyz

Bembo (British)

8 point Bembo, British (Foundry)

ABCDEFGHIJKLMNOPQRSTUVWXYZ&
abcdefghijklmnopqrstuvwxyz
1234567890$

10 point Bembo, British (Foundry)

ABCDEFGHIJKLMNOPQRSTUVWXYZ&
abcdefghijklmnopqrstuvwxyz
1234567890$

18 point Bembo, British (Foundry)

ABCDEFGHIJKLMNOPQRSTUVWXYZ&
abcdefghijklmnopqrstuvwxyz
1234567890$

Bembo Italic (British)

ABCDEFGHIJKLMNOPQRSTUVWXYZ&
abcdefghijklmnopqrstuvwxyz
1234567890$

ABCDEFGHIJKLMNOPQRSTUVWXYZ&
abcdefghijklmnopqrstuvwxyz
1234567890$

ABCDEFGHIJKLMNOPQRSTUVWXYZ&
abcdefghijklmnopqrstuvwxyz
1234567890$

Bembo Bold (British)

ABCDEFGHIJKLMNOPQRSTUVWXYZ&
abcdefghijklmnopqrstuvwxyz
1234567890$

ABCDEFGHIJKLMNOPQRSTUVWXYZ&
abcdefghijklmnopqrstuvwxyz
1234567890$

Bernhard Cursive

ABCDEFGHIJKLMNOPQRSTUVWXYZ&
abcdefghijklmnopqrstuvwxyz
1234567890$

ABCDEFGHIJKLMNOPQRSTUVWXYZ&
abcdefghijklmnopqrstuvwxyz
1234567890$

ABCDEFGHIJKLMNOPQRSTUV
WXYZ&
abcdefghijklmnopqrstuvwxyz
1234567890$

ABCDEFGHIJKLMNOPQRST
UVWXYZ&
abcdefghijklmnopqrstuvwxyz
1234567890$

(Continued on Page 39)

Bernhard Cursive

(Continued from Page 38)

42 point Bernhard Cursive (Foundry)

ABCDEFGHIJKLMNOP
QRSTUVWXYZ&

abcdefghijklmnopqrstuvwxyz   1234567890$

54 point Bernhard Cursive (Foundry)

ABCDEFGHIJKL
MNOPQRSTUVW
XYZ&   1234567890$

abcdefghijklmnopqrstuvwxyz

Bernhard Cursive Bold

24 point Bernhard Cursive Bold (Foundry)

ABCDEFGHIJKLMNOPQRSTUVWXYZ&

abcdefghijklmnopqrstuvwxyz

1234567890$

30 point Bernhard Cursive Bold (Foundry)

ABCDEFGHIJKLMNOPQRSTUV
WXYZ&   1234567890$

abcdefghijklmnopqrstuvwxyz

(Continued on Page 40)

36 point Bernhard Cursive Bold (Foundry)

ABCDEFGHIJKLMNOPQRST
UVWXYZ&   1234567890$

abcdefghijklmnopqrstuvwxyz

42 point Bernhard Cursive Bold (Foundry)

ABCDEFGHIJKLMNOP
QRSTUVWXYZ&

abcdefghijklmnopqrstuvwxyz

1234567890$

54 point Bernhard Cursive Bold (Foundry)

ABCDEFGHIJKL
MNOPQRSTUVW
XYZ&

abcdefghijklmnopqrstuvwxyz

1234567890$

Bernhard Fashion

18 point Bernhard Fashion (Foundry)

ABCDEFGHIJKLMNOPQRSTUVWXYZ&
abcdefghijklmnopqrstuvwxyz
1234567890$

24 point Bernhard Fashion (Foundry)

ABCDEFGHIJKLMNOPQRSTUVWXYZ
abcdefghijklmnopqrstuvwxyz&
1234567890$

30 point Bernhard Fashion (Foundry)

ABCDEFGHIJKLMNOPQRSTUV
WXYZ&
abcdefghijklmnopqrstuvwxyz
1234567890$

36 point Bernhard Fashion (Foundry)

ABCDEFGHIJKLMNOPQR
STUVWXYZ&
abcdefghijklmnopqrstuvwxyz
1234567890$

Bernhard Modern Bold

8 point Bernhard Modern Bold (Foundry)
8 point Bernhard Modern Bold (Foundry)
ABCDEFGHIJKLMNOPQRSTUVWXYZ&
abcdefghijklmnopqrstuvwxyz
1234567890$

10 point Bernhard Modern Bold (Foundry)
ABCDEFGHIJKLMNOPQRSTUVWXYZ&
abcdefghijklmnopqrstuvwxyz
1234567890$

12 point Bernhard Modern Bold (Foundry)
ABCDEFGHIJKLMNOPQRSTUVWXYZ&
abcdefghijklmnopqrstuvwxyz
1234567890$

14 point Bernhard Modern Bold (Foundry)
ABCDEFGHIJKLMNOPQRSTUVWXYZ&
abcdefghijklmnopqrstuvwxyz
1234567890$

18 point Bernhard Modern Bold (Foundry)
ABCDEFGHIJKLMNOPQRSTUVWXYZ&
abcdefghijklmnopqrstuvwxyz
1234567890$

24 point Bernhard Modern Bold (Foundry)
ABCDEFGHIJKLMNOPQRSTUVWXYZ&
abcdefghijklmnopqrstuvwxyz
1234567890$

30 point Bernhard Modern Bold (Foundry)
ABCDEFGHIJKLMNOPQRSTUVWXYZ&
abcdefghijklmnopqrstuvwxyz
1234567890$

36 point Bernhard Modern Bold (Foundry)
ABCDEFGHIJKLMNOPQRSTUV
WXYZ&
abcdefghijklmnopqrstuvwxyz
1234567890$

(Continued on Page 43)

42 point Bernhard Modern Bold (Foundry)

ABCDEFGHIJKLMNOPQRS
TUVWXYZ&
abcdefghijklmnopqrstuvwxyz
1234567890$

48 point Bernhard Modern Bold (Foundry)

ABCDEFGHIJKLMNOP
QRSTUVWXYZ&
abcdefghijklmnopqrstuv
wxyz
1234567890$

Bernhard Modern Bold Italic

10 point Bernhard Modern Bold Italic (Foundry)

ABCDEFGHIJKLMNOPQRSTUVWXYZ&
abcdefghijklmnopqrstuvwxyz
1234567890$

14 point Bernhard Modern Bold Italic (Foundry)

ABCDEFGHIJKLMNOPQRSTUVWXYZ&
abcdefghijklmnopqrstuvwxyz
1234567890$

18 point Bernhard Modern Bold Italic (Foundry)

ABCDEFGHIJKLMNOPQRSTUVWXYZ&
abcdefghijklmnopqrstuvwxyz
1234567890$

24 point Bernhard Modern Bold Italic (Foundry)

ABCDEFGHIJKLMNOPQRSTUVWXYZ&
abcdefghijklmnopqrstuvwxyz
1234567890$

30 point Bernhard Modern Bold Italic (Foundry)

ABCDEFGHIJKLMNOPQRSTUVWXYZ
abcdefghijklmnopqrstuvwxyz&
1234567890$

36 point Bernhard Modern Bold Italic (Foundry)

ABCDEFGHIJKLMNOPQRSTUV
WXYZ&
abcdefghijklmnopqrstuvwxyz
1234567890$

Bernhard Modern Italic

12 point Bernhard Modern Italic (Foundry)

ABCDEFGHIJKLMNOPQRSTUVWXYZ&
abcdefghijklmnopqrstuvwxyz
1234567890$

18 point Bernhard Modern Italic (Foundry)

ABCDEFGHIJKLMNOPQRSTUVWXYZ&
abcdefghijklmnopqrstuvwxyz
1234567890$

24 Point Bernhard Modern Italic (Foundry)

ABCDEFGHIJKLMNOPQRSTUVWXYZ&
abcdefghijklmnopqrstuvwxyz
1234567890$

30 point Bernhard Modern Italic (Foundry)

ABCDEFGHIJKLMNOPQRSTUVWXYZ&
abcdefghijklmnopqrstuvwxyz
1234567890$

36 point Bernhard Modern Italic (Foundry)

ABCDEFGHIJKLMNOPQRSTUV
WXYZ&
abcdefghijklmnopqrstuvwxyz
1234567890$

(Continued on Page 46)

(Continued from Page 45)

42 point Bernhard Modern Italic (Foundry)

ABCDEFGHIJKLMNOPQRST
UVWXYZ&
abcdefghijklmnopqrstuvwxyz
1234567890$

48 point Bernhard Modern Italic (Foundry)

ABCDEFGHIJKLMNOPQ
RSTUVWXYZ&
abcdefghijklmnopqrstuvwxyz
1234567890$

Bernhard Modern Roman

8 point Bernhard Modern Roman (Foundry)
ABCDEFGHIJKLMNOPQRSTUVWXYZ&
abcdefghijklmnopqrstuvwxyz
1234567890$

10 point Bernhard Modern Roman (Foundry)
ABCDEFGHIJKLMNOPQRSTUVWXYZ&
abcdefghijklmnopqrstuvwxyz
1234567890$

12 point Bernhard Modern Roman (Foundry)
ABCDEFGHIJKLMNOPQRSTUVWXYZ&
abcdefghijklmnopqrstuvwxyz
1234567890$

14 point Bernhard Modern Roman (Foundry)
ABCDEFGHIJKLMNOPQRSTUVWXYZ&
abcdefghijklmnopqrstuvwxyz
1234567890$

18 point Bernhard Modern Roman (Foundry)
ABCDEFGHIJKLMNOPQRSTUVWXYZ&
abcdefghijklmnopqrstuvwxyz
1234567890$

24 point Bernhard Modern Roman (Foundry)
ABCDEFGHIJKLMNOPQRSTUVWXYZ&
abcdefghijklmnopqrstuvwxyz
1234567890$

30 point Bernhard Modern Roman (Foundry)
ABCDEFGHIJKLMNOPQRSTUVWXYZ&
abcdefghijklmnopqrstuvwxyz
1234567890$

36 point Bernhard Modern Roman
ABCDEFGHIJKLMNOPQRSTUV
WXYZ&
abcdefghijklmnopqrstuvwxyz
1234567890$

(Continued on Page 48)

48 point Bernhard Modern Roman (Foundry)

ABCDEFGHIJKLMNOPQR
STUVWXYZ&
abcdefghijklmnopqrstuvwxyz
1234567890$

60 point Bernhard Modern Roman (Foundry)

ABCDEFGHIJKLMN
OPQRSTUVWXYZ&
abcdefghijklmnopqrstuv
wxyz
1234567890$

Bernhard Tango

18 point Bernhard Tango (Foundry)

ABCDEFGHIJKLMNOPQRSTUVWXYZ&
abcdefghijklmnopqrstuvwxyz
1234567890$

24 point Bernhard Tango (Foundry)

ABCDEFGHIJKLMNOPQRSTUVWXYZ&
abcdefghijklmnopqrstuvwxyz
1234567890$

36 point Bernhard Tango (Foundry)

ABCDEFGHIJKLMNOPQRSTUV
WXYZ&
abcdefghijklmnopqrstuvwxyz
1234567890$

48 point Bernhard Tango (Foundry)

ABCDEFGHIJKLMNOPQ
RSTUVWXYZ&
abcdefghijklmnopqrstuvwxyz
1234567890$

(Continued on Page 50)

60 point Bernhard Tango (Foundry)

ABCDEFGHIJKLMN
OPQRSTUVWXYZ
abcdefghijklmnopqrstuvwxyz
&1234567890$

Beton Extrabold

14 point Beton Extrabold (Foundry)

ABCDEFGHIJKLMNOPQRSTUVWXYZ&
abcdefghijklmnopqrstuvwxyz
1234567890$

16 point Beton Extrabold (Foundry)

ABCDEFGHIJKLMNOPQRSTUVWXYZ&
abcdefghijklmnopqrstuvwxyz
1234567890$

18 point Beton Extrabold (Foundry)

ABCDEFGHIJKLMNOPQRSTUVWXYZ&
abcdefghijklmnopqrstuvwxyz
1234567890$

(Continued on Page 51)

(Continued from Page 50)

24 point Beton Extrabold (Foundry)

ABCDEFGHIJKLMNOPQRSTUVWXYZ&
abcdefghijklmnopqrstuvwxyz
1234567890$

36 point Beton Extrabold (Foundry)

ABCDEFGHIJKLMNOPQRS
TUVWXYZ&
abcdefghijklmnopqrstuv
wxyz
1234567890$

48 point Beton Extrabold (Foundry)

ABCDEFGHIJKLMN
OPQRSTUVWXYZ&
abcdefghijklmnopqrs
tuvwxyz
1234567890$

Beton Open

20 point Beton Open (Foundry)

ABCDEFGHIJKLMNOPQRSTUVWXYZ&
1234567890$

24 point Beton Open (Foundry)

ABCDEFGHIJKLMNOPQRST
UVWXYZ&
1234567890$

30 point Beton Open, Caps only (Foundry)

ABCDEFGHIJKLMNOPQRST
UVWXYZ&
1234567890$

36 point Beton Open, Caps only (Foundry)

ABCDEFGHIJKLMNOP
QRSTUVWXYZ&
1234567890$

48 Beton Open, Cap font (Foundry)

ABCDEFGHIJKL
MNOPQRSTUV
WXYZ&
1234567890$

6 point Bodoni (Linotype)

The basic character in a type design is determined by the uniform design charac teristics of all letters in the alphabet. But, this alone does not determine the standards of the type face and the quality of composition set with it. The appear ance is something complex which forms itself out of many details, like form, pro portion, ductus, rhythm etc. If all harmonizes, the total result will be more than the sum of its components. The only reliable basis for the design in a type is a sure feeling for form and style. The basic character in a type design is determined by the uniform design characteristics of all letters in the alphabet. But, this alone

ABCDEFGHIJKLMNOPQRSTUVWXYZ&
abcdefghijklmnopqrstuvwxyz   1234567890$

7 point Bodoni (Linotype)

The basic character in a type design is determined by the uniform de sign characteristics of all letters in the alphabet. However, this alone does not determine the standard of the type face and the quality of composition set with it. The appearance is something complex which forms itself out of many details, like form, proportion, ductus, rhythm etc. If everything harmonizes, the total result will be more than the sum of its components. The only reliable basis for the design in a type is a

ABCDEFGHIJKLMOPQRSTUVWXYZ&
abcdefghijklmnopqrstuvwxyz   1234567890$
ABCDEFGHIJKLMNOPQRSTUVWXYZ

8 point Bodoni (Linotype)

The basic character in a type design is determined by the uniform design characteristics of all letters in the alphabet. However, this alone does not determine the standard of the type and the quality of composition set with it. The appearance is something complex which forms itself out of many details, like form, proportion, ductus, rhythm etc. If everything harmonizes, the total result will

ABCDEFGHIJKLMNOPQRSTUVWXYZ&
abcdefghijklmnopqrstuvwxyz   1234567890$
ABCDEFGHIJKLMNOPQRSTUVWXYZ

9 point Bodoni (Linotype)

The basic character in a type design is determined by the uniform design characteristics of all letters in the alphabet. However, this alone does not determine the standard of the type face and the quality of composition set with it. The appearance is something complex which forms itself out of

ABCDEFGHIJKLMNOPQRSTUVWXYZ&
abcdefghijklmnopqrstuvwxyz   1234567890$
ABCDEFGHIJKLMNOPQRSTUVWXYZ

10 point Bodoni (Linotype)

The basic character in a type design is determined by the uniform design characteristics of all letters in the alphabet. However, this alone does not determine the standard of the type face and the quality of composition set with it. The appearance is something complex which

ABCDEFGHIJKLMNOPQRSTUVWXYZ&
abcdefghijklmnopqrstuvwxyz   1234567890$
ABCDEFGHIJKLMNOPQRSTUVWXYZ

12 point Bodoni (Linotype)

The basic character in a type design is determined by the uniform design characteristics of all letters in the alphabet. However, this alone does not de termine the standard of the type face and the qual

ABCDEFGHIJKLMNOPQRSTUVWXYZ&
abcdefghijklmnopqrstuvwxyz   1234567890$
ABCDEFGHIJKLMNOPQRSTUVWXYZ

14 point Bodoni (Linotype)

The basic character in a type design is deter mined by the uniform design characteristics of all letters in the alphabet. However, this alone

ABCDEFGHIJKLMNOPQRSTUVWXYZ&
abcdefghijklmnopqrstuvwxyz   1234567890$
ABCDEFGHIJKLMNOPQRSTUVWXYZ

14 point Bodoni (Foundry)

ABCDEFGHIJKLMNOPQRSTUVWXYZ&
abcdefghijklmnopqrstuvwxyz
1234567890$

18 point Bodoni (Foundry)

ABCDEFGHIJKLMNOPQRSTUVWXYZ&
abcdefghijklmnopqrstuvwxyz
1234567890$

24 point Bodoni (Foundry)

ABCDEFGHIJKLMNOPQRSTUVWXYZ&
abcdefghijklmnopqrstuvwxyz
1234567890$

(Continued on Page 54)

30 point Bodoni (Foundry)

ABCDEFGHIJKLMNOPQRSTUVWXYZ&
abcdefghijklmnopqrstuvwxyz
1234567890$

36 point Bodoni (Foundry)

ABCDEFGHIJKLMNOPQRSTUV
WXYZ&
abcdefghijklmnopqrstuvwxyz
1234567890$

42 point Bodoni (Foundry)

ABCDEFGHIJKLMNOPQRSTUV
WXYZ&
abcdefghijklmnopqrstuvwxyz
1234567890$

(Continued on page 55)

48 point Bodoni (Foundry)

ABCDEFGHIJKLMNOPQRS
TUVWXYZ&
abcdefghijklmnopqrstuvwxyz
1234567890$

60 point Bodoni (Foundry)

ABCDEFGHIJKLMNO
PQRSTUVWXYZ&
abcdefghijklmnopqrst
uvwxyz
1234567890$

(Continued on Page 56)

(Continued from Page 55)

72 point Bodoni (Foundry)

ABCDEFGHIJKLM NOPQRSTUV WXYZ&

abcdefghijklmnopqr
stuvwxyz
1234567890$

Bodoni Italic

(Continued on Page 58)

(Continued from Page 57)

30 point Bodoni Italic (Foundry)

ABCDEFGHIJKLMNOPQRSTUVWXYZ&
abcdefghijklmnopqrstuvwxyz
1234567890$

36 point Bodoni Italic (Foundry)

ABCDEFGHIJKLMNOPQRSTUV
WXYZ&
abcdefghijklmnopqrstuvwxyz
1234567890$

Bodoni Bold

6 point Bodoni Bold (Linotype)

The basic character in a type design is determined by the uniform design characteristics of all letters in the alphabet. However, this alone does not determine the standard of the type face and the quality of composition set with it. The appearance is something complex which forms itself out of many details, like form, proportion, ductus, rhythm etc. If everything har monizes, the total result will be more than the sum of its components. The only reliable basis for the design in a type is a positive feeling for form and style. The basic character in a type design is determined by the uni

ABCDEFGHIJKLMNOPQRSTUVWXYZ&
abcdefghijklmnopqrstuvwxyz   1234567890$
ABCDEFGHIJKLMNOPQRSTUVWXYZ

8 point Bodoni Bold (Linotype)

The basic character in a type design is determined by the uniform design characteristics of all letters in the alphabet. However, this alone does not determine the standard of the type face and the quality of composition set with it. The ap pearance is something complex which forms itself out of many details, like form, proportion, ductus, rhythm etc. If

ABCDEFGHIJKLMNOPQRSTUVWXYZ&
abcdefghijklmnopqrstuvwxyz   1234567890$
ABCDEFGHIJKLMNOPQRSTUVWXYZ

9 point Bodoni Bold (Linotype)

The basic character in a type design is determined by the uniform design characteristics of all letters in the alphabet. However, this alone does not determine the standard of the type face and the quality of composition set with it. The appearance is something complex which

ABCDEFGHIJKLMNOPQRSTUVWXYZ&
abcdefghijklmnopqrstuvwxyz   1234567890$
ABCDEFGHIJKLMNOPQRSTUVWXYZ

10 point Bodoni Bold (Linotype)

The basic character in a type design is determined by the uniform design characteristics of all letters in the alphabet. However, this alone does not determine the standard of the type face and the quality of com

ABCDEFGHIJKLMNOPQRSTUVWXYZ&
abcdefghijklmnopqrstuvwxyz   1234567890$

12 point Bodoni Bold (Linotype)

The basic character in a type design is deter mined by the uniform design characteristics of all letters in the alphabet. However, this alone

ABCDEFGHIJKLMNOPQRSTUVWXYZ&
abcdefghijklmnopqrstuvwxyz   1234567890$
ABCDEFGHIJKLMNOPQRSTUVWXYZ

14 point Bodoni Bold (Linotype)

The basic character in a type design is deter mined by the uniform design characteris tics of all letters in the alphabet. However,

ABCDEFGHIJKLMNOPQRSTUVWXYZ&
abcdefghijklmnopqrstuvwxyz
1234567890$
ABCDEFGHIJKLMNOPQRSTUVWXYZ

(Continued on Page 59)

Bodoni Bold

(Continued from Page 58)

12 point Bodoni Bold (Foundry)

ABCDEFGHIJKLMNOPQRSTUVWXYZ&
abcdefghijklmnopqrstuvwxyz
1234567890$

14 point Bodoni Bold (Foundry)

ABCDEFGHIJKLMNOPQRSTUVWXYZ&
abcdefghijklmnopqrstuvwxyz
1234567890$

18 point Bodoni Bold (Ludlow)

ABCDEFGHIJKLMNOPQRSTUVWXYZ&
abcdefghijklmnopqrstuvwxyz
1234567890$

24 point Bodoni Bold (Ludlow)

ABCDEFGHIJKLMNOPQRSTUVWXYZ&
abcdefghijklmnopqrstuvwxyz
1234567890$

30 point Bodoni Bold (Ludlow)

ABCDEFGHIJKLMNOPQRSTUVWXYZ&
abcdefghijklmnopqrstuvwxyz
1234567890$

(Continued on Page 60)

(Continued from Page 59)

36 point Bodoni Bold (Ludlow)

ABCDEFGHIJKLMNOPQRST UVWXYZ& abcdefghijklmnopqrstuvwxyz 1234567890$

42 point Bodoni Bold (Foundry)

ABCDEFGHIJKLMNOPQRST UVWXYZ& abcdefghijklmnopqrstuvwxyz 1234567890$

48 point Bodoni Bold (Ludlow)

ABCDEFGHIJKLMNOPQ RSTUVWXYZ& abcdefghijklmnopqrstuv wxyz 1234567890$

(Continued on Page 61)

72 point Bodoni Bold (Foundry)

ABCDEFGHIJKL
MNOPQRSTUVW
XYZ&
abcdefghijklmno
pqrstuvwxyz
1234567890$

Bodoni Bold Italic

6 point Bodoni Bold Italic (Linotype)

The basic character in a type design is determined by the uniform design characteristics of all letters in the alphabet. However, this alone does not determine the standard of the type face and the quality of composition set with it. The appearance is something complex which forms itself out of many details, like form, proportion, ductus, rhythm etc. If everything har monizes, the total result will be more than the sum of its components. The only reliable basis for the design in a type is a positive feeling for form and style. The basic character in a type design is determined by the uni

ABCDEFGHIJKLMNOPQRSTUVWXYZ&
abcdefghijklmnopqrstuvwxyz   *1234567890$*

---

8 point Bodoni Bold Italic (Linotype)

The basic character in a type design is determined by the uniform design characteristics of all letters in the alphabet. However, this alone does not determine the standard of the type face and the quality of composition set with it. The ap pearance is something complex which forms itself out of many details, like form, proportion, ductus, rhythm etc. If

ABCDEFGHIJKLMNOPQRSTUVWXYZ&
abcdefghijklmnopqrstuvwxyz   *1234567890$*

---

9 point Bodoni Bold Italic (Linotype)

The basic character in a type design is determined by the uniform design characteristics of all letters in the alphabet. However, this alone does not determine the standard of the type face and the quality of composition set with it. The appearance is something complex which

ABCDEFGHIJKLMNOPQRSTUVWXYZ&
abcdefghijklmnopqrstuvwxyz   *1234567890$*

---

10 point Bodoni Bold Italic (Linotype)

The basic character in a type design is determined by the uniform design characteristics of all letters in the alphabet. However, this alone does not determine the standard of the type face and the quality of com position set with it. The appearance is something

ABCDEFGHIJKLMNOPQRSTUVWXYZ&
abcdefghijklmnopqrstuvwxyz   *1234567890$*

---

12 point Bodoni Bold Italic (Linotype)

The basic character in a type design is deter mined by the uniform design characteristics of all letters in the alphabet. However, this alone does not determine the standard of the type face

ABCDEFGHIJKLMNOPQRSTUVWXYZ&
abcdefghijklmnopqrstuvwxyz   *1234567890$*

---

14 point Bodoni Bold Italic (Linotype)

The basic character in a type design is deter mined by the uniform design characteris tics of all letters in the alphabet. However,

ABCDEFGHIJKLMNOPQRSTUVWXYZ&
abcdefghijklmnopqrstuvwxyz
1234567890$

---

12 point Bodoni Bold Italic (Foundry)

ABCDEFGHIJKLMNOPQRSTUVWXYZ&
abcdefghijklmnopqrstuvwxyz
1234567890$

---

14 point Bodoni Bold Italic (Foundry)

ABCDEFGHIJKLMNOPQRSTUVWXYZ&
abcdefghijklmnopqrstuvwxyz
1234567890$

---

18 point Bodoni Bold Italic (Ludlow)

ABCDEFGHIJKLMNOPQRSTUVWXYZ&
abcdefghijklmnopqrstuvwxyz
1234567890$

---

24 point Bodoni Bold Italic (Ludlow)

ABCDEFGHIJKLMNOPQRSTUVWXYZ&
abcdefghijklmnopqrstuvwxyz
1234567890$

(Continued on Page 63)

(Continued from Page 62)

30 point Bodoni Bold Italic (Ludlow)

ABCDEFGHIJKLMNOPQRSTUV
WXYZ&
abcdefghijklmnopqrstuvwxyz
1234567890$

36 point Bodoni Bold Italic (Ludlow)

ABCDEFGHIJKLMNOPQRSTU
VWXYZ&
abcdefghijklmnopqrstuvwxyz
1234567890$

48 point Bodoni Bold Italic (Ludlow)

ABCDEFGHIJKLMNOP
QRSTUVWXYZ&
abcdefghijklmnopqrstu
vwxyz
1234567890$

(Continued on Page 64)

72 point Bodoni Bold Italic (Foundry)

ABCDEFGHIJKL

MNOPQRSTUVW

XYZ&

abcdefghijklmno

pqrstuvwxyz

1234567890$

Bodoni Bold Condensed

14 point Bodoni Bold Condensed (Foundry)

ABCDEFGHIJKLMNOPQRSTUVWXYZ&
abcdefghijklmnopqrstuvwxyz
1234567890$

18 point Bodoni Bold Condensed (Foundry)

ABCDEFGHIJKLMNOPQRSTUVWXYZ&
abcdefghijklmnopqrstuvwxyz
1234567890$

24 point Bodoni Bold Condensed (Foundry)

ABCDEFGHIJKLMNOPQRSTUVWXYZ&
abcdefghijklmnopqrstuvwxyz
1234567890$

30 point Bodoni Bold Condensed (Foundry)

ABCDEFGHIJKLMNOPQRSTUVWXYZ&
abcdefghijklmnopqrstuvwxyz
1234567890$

36 point Bodoni Bold Condensed (Foundry)

ABCDEFGHIJKLMNOPQRSTUVWXYZ&
abcdefghijklmnopqrstuvwxyz
1234567890$

(Continued on Page 66)

48 point Bodoni Bold Condensed (Foundry)

ABCDEFGHIJKLMNOPQRSTUV WXYZ&
abcdefghijklmnopqrstuvwxyz
1234567890$

60 point Bodoni Bold Condensed (Foundry)

ABCDEFGHIJKLMNOPQR STUVWXYZ&
abcdefghijklmnopqrstuv wxyz
1234567890$

Bodoni Book

6 point Bodoni Book (Linotype)

The basic character in a type design is determined by the uniform design characteristics of all letters in the alphabet. However, this alone does not determine the standard of the type face and the quality of composition set with it. The appearance is something complex which forms itself out of many details, like form, proportion, ductus, rhythm etc. If everything harmonizes, the total result will be more than the sum of its components. The only reliable basis for the design in a type is a positive feeling for form and style. The basic character in a type design

ABCDEFGHIJKLMNOPQRSTUVWXYZ&
abcdefghijklmnopqrstuvwxyz 1234567890$
ABCDEFGHIJKLMNOPQRSTUVWXYZ

7 point Bodoni Book (Linotype)

The basic character in a type design is determined by the uniform design characteristics of all letters in the alphabet. However, this alone does not determine the standard of the type face and the quality of composition set with it. The appearance is something complex which forms itself out of many details, like form, proportion, ductus, rhythm etc. If everything harmonizes, the total result will be more than the sum of its components. The only reliable basis for the design in a type is a positive feeling for form and style.

ABCDEFGHIJKLMNOPQRSTUVWXYZ&
abcdefghijklmnopqrstuvwxyz 1234567890$
ABCDEFGHIJKLMNOPQRSTUVWXYZ

8 point Bodoni Book (Linotype)

The basic character in a type design is determined by the uniform design characteristics of all letters in the alphabet. However, this alone does not determine the standard of the type face and the quality of composition set with it. The appearance is something complex which forms itself out of many details, like form, proportion, ductus, rhythm etc. If everything harmonizes, the total result will be

ABCDEFGHIJKLMNOPQRSTUVWXYZ&
abcdefghijklmnopqrstuvwxyz 1234567890$
ABCDEFGHIJKLMNOPQRSTUVWXYZ

9 point Bodoni Book (Linotype)

The basic character in a type design is determined by the uniform design characteristics of all letters in the alphabet. However, this alone does not determine the standard of the type face and the quality of composition set with it. The appearance is something complex which forms itself out of many details,

ABCDEFGHIJKLMNOPQRSTUVWXYZ&
abcdefghijklmnopqrstuvwxyz 1234567890$
ABCDEFGHIJKLMNOPQRSTUVWXYZ

10 point Bodoni Book (Linotype)

The basic character in a type design is determined by the uniform design characteristics of all letters in the alphabet. However, this alone does not determine the standard of the type face and the quality of composition set with it. The appearance is something complex which forms itself out of

ABCDEFGHIJKLMNOPQRSTUVWXYZ&
abcdefghijklmnopqrstuvwxyz 1234567890$
ABCDEFGHIJKLMNOPQRSTUVWXYZ

11 point Bodoni Book (Linotype)

The basic character in a type design is determined by the uniform design characteristics of all letters in the alpha bet. However, this alone does not determine the standard of the type face and the quality of composition set with

ABCDEFGHIJKLMNOPQRSTUVWXYZ&
abcdefghijklmnopqrstuvwxyz 1234567890$
ABCDEFGHIJKLMNOPQRSTUVWXYZ

12 point Bodoni Book (Linotype)

The basic character in a type design is determined by the uniform design characteristics of all letters in the alphabet. However, this alone does not determine the standard of the type face and the quality of composi

ABCDEFGHIJKLMNOPQRSTUVWXYZ&
abcdefghijklmnopqrstuvwxyz 1234567890$
ABCDEFGHIJKLMNOPQRSTUVWXYZ

14 point Bodoni Book (Linotype)

The basic character in a type design is deter mined by the uniform design characteristics of all letters in the alphabet. However, this alone

ABCDEFGHIJKLMNOPQRSTUVWXYZ&
abcdefghijklmnopqrstuvwxyz 1234567890$
ABCDEFGHIJKLMNOPQRSTUVWXYZ

18 point Bodoni Book (Foundry)

ABCDEFGHIJKLMNOPQRSTUVWXYZ&
abcdefghijklmnopqrstuvwxyz
1234567890$

24 point Bodoni Book (Foundry)

ABCDEFGHIJKLMNOPQRSTUVWXYZ&
abcdefghijklmnopqrstuvwxyz
1234567890$

(Continued on Page 68)

30 point Bodoni Book (Foundry)

ABCDEFGHIJKLMNOPQRSTUVWXYZ&
abcdefghijklmnopqrstuvwxyz
1234567890$

36 point Bodoni Book (Foundry)

ABCDEFGHIJKLMNOPQRSTUVWXYZ
abcdefghijklmnopqrstuvwxyz&
1234567890$

42 point Bodoni Book (Foundry)

ABCDEFGHIJKLMNOPQRSTUV
WXYZ&
abcdefghijklmnopqrstuvwxyz
1234567890$

48 point Bodoni Book (Foundry)

ABCDEFGHIJKLMNOPQRST
UVWXYZ&
abcdefghijklmnopqrstuvwxyz
1234567890$

Bodoni Book Italic

6 point Bodoni Book Italic (Linotype)

The basic character in a type design is determined by the uniform design characteristics of all letters in the alphabet. However, this alone does not determine the standard of the type face and the quality of composition set with it. The appearance is something complex which forms itself out of many details, like form, proportion, ductus, rhythm etc. If everything harmonizes, the total result will be more than the sum of its components. The only reliable basis for the design in a type is a positive feeling for form and style. The basic character in a type design

ABCDEFGHIJKLMNOPQRSTUVWXYZ&
abcdefghijklmnopqrstuvwxyz   1234567890$

7 point Bodoni Book Italic (Linotype)

The basic character in a type design is determined by the uniform design characteristics of all letters in the alphabet. However, this alone does not determine the standard of the type face and the quality of composition set with it. The appearance is something complex which forms itself out of many details, like form, proportion, ductus, rhythm etc. If everything harmonizes, the total result will be more than the sum of its components. The only re

ABCDEFGHIJKLMNOPQRSTUVWXYZ&
abcdefghijklmnopqrstuvwxyz   1234567890$

8 point Bodoni Book Italic (Linotype)

The basic character in a type design is determined by the uniform design characteristics of all letters in the alphabet. However, this alone does not determine the standard of the type face and the quality of composition set with it. The appearance is something complex which forms itself out of many details, like form, proportion,

ABCDEFGHIJKLMNOPQRSTUVWXYZ&
abcdefghijklmnopqrstuvwxyz   1234567890$

9 point Bodoni Book Italic (Linotype)

The basic character in a type design is determined by the uniform design characteristics of all letters in the alphabet. However, this alone does not determine the standard of the type face and the quality of composition set with it. The appearance is something complex which forms itself out of many details,

ABCDEFGHIJKLMNOPQRSTUVWXYZ&
abcdefghijklmnopqrstuvwxyz   1234567890$

10 point Bodoni Book Italic (Linotype)

The basic character in a type design is determined by the uniform design characteristics of all letters in the alphabet. However, this alone does not determine the standard of the type face and the quality of composition set with it. The appearance is something complex which forms itself out of

ABCDEFGHIJKLMNOPQRSTUVWXYZ&
abcdefghijklmnopqrstuvwxyz   1234567890$

11 point Bodoni Book Italic (Linotype)

The basic character in a type design is determined by the uniform design characteristics of all letters in the alphabet. However, this alone does not determine the standard of the type face and the quality of composition set with

ABCDEFGHIJKLMNOPQRSTUVWXYZ&
abcdefghijklmnopqrstuvwxyz   1234567890$

12 point Bodoni Book Italic (Linotype)

The basic character in a type design is determined by the uniform design characteristics of all letters in the alphabet. However, this alone does not determine the standard of the type face and the quality of composi

ABCDEFGHIJKLMNOPQRSTUVWXYZ&
abcdefghijklmnopqrstuvwxyz   1234567890$

14 point Bodoni Book Italic (Linotype)

The basic character in a type design is determined by the uniform design characteristics of all letters in the alphabet. However, this alone

ABCDEFGHIJKLMNOPQRSTUVWXYZ&
abcdefghijklmnopqrstuvwxyz   1234567890$

18 point Bodoni Book Italic (Foundry)

ABCDEFGHIJKLMNOPQRSTUVWXYZ&
abcdefghijklmnopqrstuvwxyz
1234567890$

36 point Bodoni Book Italic (Foundry)

ABCDEFGHIJKLMNOPQRSTUVWXYZ
abcdefghijklmnopqrstuvwxyz&
1234567890$

Bodoni Campanile

ABCDEFGHIJKLMNOPQRSTUVWXYZ&
abcdefghijklmnopqrstuvwxyz
1234567890$

ABCDEFGHIJKLMNOPQRSTUVWXYZ&
abcdefghijklmnopqrstuvwxyz
1234567890$

ABCDEFGHIJKLMNOPQRSTUVWXYZ&
abcdefghijklmnopqrstuvwxyz
1234567890$

ABCDEFGHIJKLMNOPQRSTUVWXYZ&
abcdefghijklmnopqrstuvwxyz
1234567890$

ABCDEFGHIJKLMNOPQRSTUVWXYZ&
abcdefghijklmnopqrstuvwxyz
1234567890$

Bodoni Open-face

24 point Bodoni Open-face (Foundry)

ABCDEFGHIJKLMNOPQRSTUVWXYZ&
abcdefghijklmnopqrstuvwxyz
1234567890$

36 point Bodoni Open-face (Foundry)

ABCDEFGHIJKLMNOPQRSTUV
WXYZ&
abcdefghijklmnopqrstuvwxyz
1234567890$

Bodoni Shaded

14 point Bodoni Shaded (Foundry)

ABCDEFGHIJKLMNOPQRSTUVWXYZ&
abcdefghijklmnopqrstuvwxyz
1234567890$

18 point Bodoni Shaded (Foundry)

ABCDEFGHIJKLMNOPQRSTUVWXYZ&
abcdefghijklmnopqrstuvwxyz
1234567890$

Bold Face No. 2

6 point Bold Face No. 2 (Linotype)

The basic character in a type design is determined by the uniform design characteristics of all letters in the alphabet. However, this alone does not determine the standard of the type face and the quality of composition set with it. The appearance is something complex which forms itself out of many details, like form, proportion, ductus, rhythm etc. If everything harmonizes, the total result will be more than the sum of its components. The only reliable basis for the design in a type is a positive feeling for form and

ABCDEFGHIJKLMNOPQRSTUVWXYZ&
abcdefghijklmnopqrstuvwxyz   1234567890$

14 point Bodoni 175 (Foundry)

ABCDEFGHIJKLMNOPQRSTUVWXYZ&
abcdefghijklmnopqrstuvwxyz
1234567890$

18 point Bodoni 175 (Foundry)

ABCDEFGHIJKLMNOPQRSTUVWXYZ&
abcdefghijklmnopqrstuvwxyz
1234567890$

24 point Bodoni 175 (Foundry)

ABCDEFGHIJKLMNOPQRSTUVWXYZ&
abcdefghijklmnopqrstuvwxyz
1234567890$

30 point Bodoni 175 (Foundry)

ABCDEFGHIJKLMNOPQRSTUV
WXYZ&
abcdefghijklmnopqrstuvwxyz
1234567890$

36 point Bodoni 175 (Foundry)

ABCDEFGHIJKLMNOPQRST
UVWXYZ&
abcdefghijklmnopqrstuvwxyz
1234567890$

Bodoni Italic 1751 and 3751

ABCDEFGHIJKLMNOPQRSTUVWXYZ&
abcdefghijklmnopqrstuvwxyz
1234567890$

ABCDEFGHIJKLMNOPQRSTU
VWXYZ&
abcdefghijklmnopqrstuvwxyz
1234567890$

Bon Aire

ABCDEFGHIJKLMNOPQRSTUV
WXYZ&
abcdefghijklmnopqrstuvwxyz
1234567890$

6 point Bookman (Linotype)

The basic character in a type design is determined by the uniform design characteristics of all letters in the alphabet. However, this alone does not determine the standard of the type face and the quality of composition set with it. The appearance is something complex which forms itself out of many details, like form, proportion, ductus, rhythm etc. If everything har monizes, the total result will be more than the sum of its components. The only reliable basis for the design in a type is a positive feeling for

ABCDEFGHIJKLMNOPQRSTUVWXYZ&
abcdefghijklmnopqrstuvwxyz　　　1234567890$
ABCDEFGHIJKLMNOPQRSTUVWXYZ

7 point Bookman (Linotype)

The basic character in a type design is determined by the uniform design characteristics of all letters in the alphabet. However, this alone does not determine the standard of the type face and the quality of composition set with it. The appearance is something complex which forms itself out of many details, like form, proportion, ductus, rhythm etc. If everything harmonizes, the total result will be more

ABCDEFGHIJKLMNOPQRSTUVWXYZ&
abcdefghijklmnopqrstuvwxyz　　　1234567890$
ABCDEFGHIJKLMNOPQRSTUVWXYZ

12 point Bookman (Linotype)

The basic character in a type design is deter mined by the uniform design characteristics of all letters in the alphabet. However, this alone does not determine the standard of the type face

ABCDEFGHIJKLMNOPQRSTUVWXYZ&
abcdefghijklmnopqrstuvwxyz　　1234567890$
ABCDEFGHIJKLMNOPQRSTUVWXYZ

14 point Bookman (Foundry)

ABCDEFGHIJKLMNOPQRSTUV
WXYZ&
abcdefghijklmnopqrstuvwxyz
1234567890$

18 point Bookman (Foundry)

ABCDEFGHIJKLMNOPQRSTUVWXYZ&
abcdefghijklmnopqrstuvwxyz　　1234567890$

24 point Bookman (Foundry)

ABCDEFGHIJKLMNOPQRSTUVW
XYZ&
abcdefghijklmnopqrstuvwxyz
1234567890$

30 point Bookman (Foundry)

ABCDEFGHIJKLMNOPQRSTUV
WXYZ&
abcdefghijklmnopqrstuvwxyz
1234567890$

36 point Bookman (Foundry)

ABCDEFGHIJKLMNOPQRS
TUVWXYZ&
abcdefghijklmnopqrstuvwxyz
1234567890$

Bookman Italic

6 point Bookman Italic (Linotype)

The basic character in a type design is determined by the uniform design characteristics of all letters in the alphabet. However, this alone does not determine the standard of the type face and the quality of composition set with it. The appearance is something complex which forms itself out of many details, like form, proportion, ductus, rhythm etc. If everything harmonizes, the total result will be more than the sum of its components. The only reliable basis for the design in a type is a positive feeling for form and style. The basic character in a type design is determined by the

ABCDEFGHIJKLMNOPQRSTUVWXYZ&
abcdefghijklmnopqrstuvwxyz   *1234567890$*

7 point Bookman Italic (Linotype)

The basic character in a type design is determined by the uniform design characteristics of all letters in the alphabet. However, this alone does not determine the standard of the type face and the quality of composition set with it. The appearance is something complex which forms itself out of many details, like form, proportion, ductus, rhythm etc. If everything harmonizes, the total result will be more than the sum of its components. The only reliable basis for the design in a

ABCDEFGHIJKLMNOPQRSTUVWXYZ&
abcdefghijklmnopqrstuvwxyz   *1234567890$*

12 point Bookman Italic (Linotype)

The basic character in a type design is determined by the uniform design characteristics of all letters in the alphabet. However, this alone does not determine the standard of the type face and the quality of composition set with it. The appearance is something com

ABCDEFGHIJKLMNOPQRSTUVWXYZ&
abcdefghijklmnopqrstuvwxyz   *1234567890$*

18 point Bookman Italic (Foundry)

ABCDEFGHIJKLMNOPQRSTUVWXYZ&
abcdefghijklmnopqrstuvwxyz
1234567890$

36 point Bookman Italic (Foundry)

ABCDEFGHIJKLMNOPQR
STUVWXYZ&
abcdefghijklmnopqrstuvwxyz
1234567890$

Broadway

8 point Broadway, Cap font (Foundry)

ABCDEFGHIJKLMNOPQRSTUVWXYZ&
1234567890$

12 point Broadway, Cap font (Foundry)

ABCDEFGHIJKLMNOPQRSTUVWXYZ&
1234567890$

18 point Broadway, Cap font (Foundry)

ABCDEFGHIJKLMNOPQRSTUVWXYZ&
1234567890$

Brody

18 point Brody (Foundry)

ABCDEFGHIJKLMNOPQRSTUVWXYZ&
abcdefghijklmnopqrstuvwxyz
1234567890$

24 point Brody (Foundry)

ABCDEFGHIJKLMNOPQRSTUVWXYZ&
abcdefghijklmnopqrstuvwxyz
1234567890$

30 point Brody (Foundry)

ABCDEFGHIJKLMNOPQRSTUVWXYZ&
abcdefghijklmnopqrstuvwxyz
1234567890$

36 point Brody (Foundry)

ABCDEFGHIJKLMNOPQRSTUVWXYZ&
abcdefghijklmnopqrstuvwxyz
1234567890$

48 point Brody (Foundry)

ABCDEFGHIJKLMNOPQRST
UVWXYZ
abcdefghijklmnopqrstuvwxyz
1234567890$

(Continued on Page 77)

60 point Brody (Foundry)

ABCDEFGHIJKLMNOP
QRSTUVWXYZ&
abcdefghijklmnopqrstuv
wxyz
1234567890$

72 point Brody (Foundry)

ABCDEFGHIJKLM
NOPQRSTUVWXYZ
abcdefghijklmnopqrstu
vwxyz& 1234567890$

12 point Brush (Foundry)

ABCDEFGHIJKLMNOP2RSTUVWXYZ&
abcdefghijklmnopqrstuvwxyz
1234567890$

24 point Brush (Foundry)

ABCDEFGHIJKLMNOP2RSTUVWXYZ&
abcdefghijklmnopqrstuvwxyz
1234567890$

30 point Brush (Foundry)

ABCDEFGHIJKLMNOP2RSTUV
WXYZ&
abcdefghijklmnopqrstuvwxyz
1234567890$

36 point Brush (Foundry)

ABCDEFGHIJKLMNOP2RST
UVWXYZ&
abcdefghijklmnopqrstuvwxyz
1234567890$

42 point Brush (Foundry)

ABCDEFGHIJKLMNOP2
RSTUVWXYZ&
abcdefghijklmnopqrstuvwxyz
1234567890$

(Continued on Page 79)

Brush

60 point Brush (Foundry)

ABCDEFGHIJKL
MNOPQRSTUVW
XYZ&
abcdefghijklmnopqrstuv
wxyz
1234567890$

Bulletin Typewriter

18 point Bulletin Typewriter (Foundry)

ABCDEFGHIJKLMNOPQRSTUVWXYZ&
abcdefghijklmnopqrstuvwxyz
1234567890$

24 point Bulletin Typewriter (Foundry)

ABCDEFGHIJKLMNOPQRSTUVWXYZ&
abcdefghijklmnopqrstuvwxyz
1234567890$

Bulmer Roman

6 point Bulmer Roman (Foundry)
ABCDEFGHIJKLMNOPQRSTUVWXYZ&
abcdefghijklmnopqrstuvwxyz
1234567890$

8 point Bulmer Roman (Foundry)
ABCDEFGHIJKLMNOPQRSTUVWXYZ&
abcdefghijklmnopqrstuvwxyz
1234567890$

10 point Bulmer Roman (Foundry)
ABCDEFGHIJKLMNOPQRSTUVWXYZ&
abcdefghijklmnopqrstuvwxyz
1234567890$

12 point Bulmer Roman (Foundry)
ABCDEFGHIJKLMNOPQRSTUVWXYZ&
abcdefghijklmnopqrstuvwxyz
1234567890$

14 point Bulmer Roman (Foundry)
ABCDEFGHIJKLMNOPQRSTUVWXYZ&
abcdefghijklmnopqrstuvwxyz
1234567890$

18 point Bulmer Roman (Foundry)
ABCDEFGHIJKLMNOPQRSTUVWXYZ&
abcdefghijklmnopqrstuvwxyz
1234567890$

24 point Bulmer Roman (Foundry)
ABCDEFGHIJKLMNOPQRSTUVWXYZ&
abcdefghijklmnopqrstuvwxyz
1234567890$

30 point Bulmer Roman (Foundry)
ABCDEFGHIJKLMNOPQRSTUVWXYZ&
abcdefghijklmnopqrstuvwxyz
1234567890$

36 point Bulmer Roman (Foundry)
ABCDEFGHIJKLMNOPQRSTUV
WXYZ&
abcdefghijklmnopqrstuvwxyz
1234567890$

(Continued on Page 81)

42 point Bulmer Roman (Foundry)

ABCDEFGHIJKLMNOPQRST
UVWXYZ&
abcdefghijklmnopqrstuvwxyz
1234567890$

48 point Bulmer Roman (Foundry)

ABCDEFGHIJKLMNOPQRS
TUVWXYZ&
abcdefghijklmnopqrstuvwxyz
1234567890$

Bulmer Italic

6 point Bulmer Italic (Foundry)
ABCDEFGHIJKLMNOPQRSTUVWXYZ&
abcdefghijklmnopqrstuvwxyz
1234567890$

12 point Bulmer Italic (Foundry)
ABCDEFGHIJKLMNOPQRSTUVWXYZ&
abcdefghijklmnopqrstuvwxyz
1234567890$

10 point Bulmer Italic (Foundry)
ABCDEFGHIJKLMNOPQRSTUVWXYZ&
abcdefghijklmnopqrstuvwxyz
1234567890$

14 point Bulmer Italic (Foundry)
ABCDEFGHIJKLMNOPQRSTUV WXYZ&
abcdefghijklmnopqrstuvwxyz
1234567890$

(Continued on Page 82)

(Continued from Page 81)

18 point Bulmer Italic (Foundry)

ABCDEFGHIJKLMNOPQRSTUVWXYZ&
abcdefghijklmnopqrstuvwxyz
1234567890$

24 point Bulmer Italic (Foundry)

ABCDEFGHIJKLMNOPQRSTUVWXYZ&
abcdefghijklmnopqrstuvwxyz
1234567890$

30 point Bulmer Italic (Foundry)

ABCDEFGHIJKLMNOPQRSTUVWXYZ&
abcdefghijklmnopqrstuvwxyz
1234567890$

36 point Bulmer Italic (Foundry)

ABCDEFGHIJKLMNOPQRSTUV
WXYZ&
abcdefghijklmnopqrstuvwxyz
1234567890$

42 point Bulmer Italic (Foundry)

ABCDEFGHIJKLMNOPQRSTUV
WXYZ&
abcdefghijklmnopqrstuvwxyz
1234567890$

(Continued on Page 83)

48 point Bulmer Italic (Foundry)

ABCDEFGHIJKLMNOPQRST
UVWXYZ&
abcdefghijklmnopqrstuvwxyz
1234567890$

Cairo

6 point Cairo (Intertype)

The basic character in a type design is determined by the uniform design characteristics of all letters in the alphabet. However, this alone does not determine the standard of the type face and the quality of composition set with it. The appearance is something complex which forms itself out

ABCDEFGHIJKLMNOPQRSTUVWXYZ&
abcdefghijklmnopqrstuvwxyz   1234567890$

8 point Cairo (Intertype)

The basic character in a type design is determined by the uni form design characteristics of all letters in the alphabet. How ever, this alone does not determine the standard of the type face and the quality of composition set with it. The appearance

ABCDEFGHIJKLMNOPQRSTUVWXYZ&
abcdefghijklmnopqrstuvwxyz   1234567890$

10 point Cairo (Intertype)

The basic character in a type design is determined by the uniform design characteristics of all letters in the alphabet. However, this alone does not determine the

ABCDEFGHIJKLMNOPQRSTUVWXYZ&
abcdefghijklmnopqrstuvwxyz   1234567890$

12 point Cairo (Intertype)

The basic character in a type design is deter mined by the uniform design characteristics

ABCDEFGHIJKLMNOPQRSTUVWXYZ&
abcdefghijklmnopqrstuvwxyz   1234567890$

14 point Cairo (Intertype)

The basic character in a type design is determined by the uniform design char

ABCDEFGHIJKLMNOPQRSTUV
WXYZ&   1234567890$
abcdefghijklmnopqrstuvwxyz

Cairo Bold

6 point Cairo Bold (Intertype)

The basic character in a type design is determined by the uniform design characteristics of all letters in the alphabet. However, this alone does not determine the standard of the type face and the quality of composition set with it. The appearance is something complex which forms itself out

ABCDEFGHIJKLMNOPQRSTUVWXYZ&
abcdefghijklmnopqrstuvwxyz   1234567890$

8 point Cairo Bold (Intertype)

The basic character in a type design is determined by the uni form design characteristics of all letters in the alphabet. How ever, this alone does not determine the standard of the type face and the quality of composition set with it. The appearance

ABCDEFGHIJKLMNOPQRSTUVWXYZ&
abcdefghijklmnopqrstuvwxyz   1234567890$

10 point Cairo Bold (Intertype)

The basic character in a type design is determined by the uniform design characteristics of all letters in the alphabet. However, this alone does not determine the

ABCDEFGHIJKLMNOPQRSTUVWXYZ&
abcdefghijklmnopqrstuvwxyz   1234567890$

12 point Cairo Bold (Intertype)

The basic character in a type design is deter mined by the uniform design characteristics

ABCDEFGHIJKLMNOPQRSTUVWXYZ&
abcdefghijklmnopqrstuvwxyz   1234567890$

14 point Cairo Bold (Intertype)

The basic character in a type design is determined by the uniform design char

ABCDEFGHIJKLMNOPQRSTUV
WXYZ&   1234567890$
abcdefghijklmnopqrstuvwxyz

Cario Italic

The basic character in a type design is determined by the uniform de
sign characteristics of all letters in the alphabet. However, this alone
does not determine the standard of the type face and the quality of
composition set with it. The appearance is something complex which
forms itself out of many details, like form, proportion, ductus, rhythm etc.

ABCDEFGHIJKLMNOPQRSTUVWXYZ&
abcdefghijklmnopqrstuvwxyz   1234567890$

The basic character in a type design is determined by the uni
form design characteristics of all letters in the alphabet. How
ever, this alone does not determine the standard of the type

ABCDEFGHIJKLMNOPQRSTUVWXYZ&
abcdefghijklmnopqrstuvwxyz   1234567890$

The basic character in a type design is determined by
the uniform design characteristics of all letters in the
alphabet. However, this alone does not determine the

ABCDEFGHIJKLMNOPQRSTUVWXYZ&
abcdefghijklmnopqrstuvwxyz   1234567890$

The basic character in a type design is deter
mined by the uniform design characteristics
of all letters in the alphabet. However, this
alone does not determine the standard of the

ABCDEFGHIJKLMNOPQRSTUVWXYZ&
abcdefghijklmnopqrstuvwxyz   1234567890$

The basic character in a type design is
determined by the uniform design char
acteristics of all letters in the alphabet.

ABCDEFGHIJKLMNOPQRSTUV
WXYZ&   1234567890$
abcdefghijklmnopqrstuvwxyz

Cairo Medium (Small caps are available)

The basic character in a type design is determined by the uniform design
characteristics of all letters in the alphabet. However, this alone does not
determine the standard of the type face and the quality of composition
set with it. The appearance is something complex which forms itself out
of many details, like form, proportion, ductus, rhythm etc. If everything

ABCDEFGHIJKLMNOPQRSTUVWXYZ&
abcdefghijklmnopqrstuvwxyz   1234567890$

The basic character in a type design is determined by the uniform
design characteristics of all letters in the alphabet. However, this
alone does not determine the standard of the type face and the

ABCDEFGHIJKLMNOPQRSTUVWXYZ&
abcdefghijklmnopqrstuvwxyz   1234567890$

The basic character in a type design is determined by
the uniform design characteristics of all letters in the
alphabet. However, this alone does not determine the

ABCDEFGHIJKLMNOPQRSTUVWXYZ&
abcdefghijklmnopqrstuvwxyz   1234567890$

The basic character in a type design is deter
mined by the uniform design characteristics of
all letters in the alphabet. However, this alone
does not determine the standard of the type

ABCDEFGHIJKLMNOPQRSTUVWXYZ&
abcdefghijklmnopqrstuvwxyz   1234567890$

Cairo Medium Italic

The basic character in a type design is determined by the uniform design
characteristics of all letters in the alphabet. However, this alone does not
determine the standard of the type face and the quality of composition
set with it. The appearance is something complex which forms itself out
of many details, like form, proportion, ductus, rhythm etc. If everything

ABCDEFGHIJKLMNOPQRSTUVWXYZ&
abcdefghijklmnopqrstuvwxyz   1234567890$

The basic character in a type design is determined by the uniform
design characteristics of all letters in the alphabet. However, this
alone does not determine the standard of the type face and the

ABCDEFGHIJKLMNOPQRSTUVWXYZ&
abcdefghijklmnopqrstuvwxyz   1234567890$

The basic character in a type design is determined by
the uniform design characteristics of all letters in the
alphabet. However, this alone does not determine the

ABCDEFGHIJKLMNOPQRSTUVWXYZ&
abcdefghijklmnopqrstuvwxyz   1234567890$

The basic character in a type design is deter
mined by the uniform design characteristics of
all letters in the alphabet. However, this alone
does not determine the standard of the type

ABCDEFGHIJKLMNOPQRSTUVWXYZ&
abcdefghijklmnopqrstuvwxyz   1234567890$

Caledonia *(Long descenders set 1 point leaded)*

6 point Caledonia (Linotype)
The basic character in a type design is determined by the uniform design characteristics of all letters in the alphabet. However, this alone does not determine the standard of the type face and the quality of composition set with it. The appearance is something complex which forms itself out of many
ABCDEFGHIJKLMNOPQRSTUVWXYZ&
abcdefghijklmnopqrstuvwxyz   1234567890$
ABCDEFGHIJKLMNOPQRSTUVWXYZ

7 point Caledonia (Linotype)
The basic character in a type design is determined by the uniform de sign characteristics of all letters in the alphabet. However, this alone does not determine the standard of the type face and the quality of composition set with it. The appearance is something complex which
ABCDEFGHIJKLMNOPQRSTUVWXYZ&
abcdefghijklmnopqrstuvwxyz   1234567890$
ABCDEFGHIJKLMNOPQRSTUVWXYZ

8 point Caledonia (Linotype)
The basic character in a type design is determined by the uniform design characteristics of all letters in the alphabet. However, this alone does not determine the standard of the type face and the
ABCDEFGHIJKLMNOPQRSTUVWXYZ&
abcdefghijklmnopqrstuvwxyz   1234567890$
ABCDEFGHIJKLMNOPQRSTUVWXYZ

9 point Caledonia (Linotype)
The basic character in a type design is determined by the uniform design characteristics of all letters in the alphabet. However, this alone does not determine the standard of the
ABCDEFGHIJKLMNOPQRSTUVWXYZ&
abcdefghijklmnopqrstuvwxyz   1234567890$
ABCDEFGHIJKLMNOPQRSTUVWXYZ

10 point Caledonia (Linotype)
The basic character in a type design is determined by the uniform design characteristics of all letters in the alpha bet. However, this alone does not determine the standard
ABCDEFGHIJKLMNOPQRSTUVWXYZ&
abcdefghijklmnopqrstuvwxyz   1234567890$
ABCDEFGHIJKLMNOPQRSTUVWXYZ

11 point Caledonia (Linotype)
The basic character in a type design is determined by the uniform design characteristics of all letters in the
ABCDEFGHIJKLMNOPQRSTUVWXYZ&
abcdefghijklmnopqrstuvwxyz   1234567890$
ABCDEFGHIJKLMNOPQRSTUVWXYZ

12 point Caledonia (Linotype)
The basic character in a type design is determined by the uniform design characteristics of all letters
ABCDEFGHIJKLMNOPQRSTUVWXYZ&
abcdefghijklmnopqrstuvwxyz   1234567890$
ABCDEFGHIJKLMNOPQRSTUVWXYZ

14 point Caledonia (Linotype)
The basic character in a type design is de termined by the uniform design character
ABCDEFGHIJKLMNOPQRSTUV
WXYZ&   1234567890$
abcdefghijklmnopqrstuvwxyz
ABCDEFGHIJKLMNOPQRSTUVWXYZ

Caledonia Italic

6 point Caledonia Italic (Linotype)
The basic character in a type design is determined by the uniform design characteristics of all letters in the alphabet. However, this alone does not determine the standard of the type face and the quality of composition set with it. The appearance is something complex which forms itself out of many details, like form, proportion, ductus, rhythm etc. If everything harmonizes, the total result will be more than the sum of its components. The only re
ABCDEFGHIJKLMNOPQRSTUVWXYZ&
abcdefghijklmnopqrstuvwxyz   1234567890$

7 point Caledonia Italic (Linotype)
The basic character in a type design is determined by the uniform de sign characteristics of all letters in the alphabet. However, this alone does not determine the standard of the type face and the quality of composition set with it. The appearance is something complex which forms itself out of many details, like form, proportion, ductus, rhythm
ABCDEFGHIJKLMNOPQRSTUVWXYZ&
abcdefghijklmnopqrstuvwxyz   1234567890$

8 point Caledonia Italic (Linotype)
The basic character in a type design is determined by the uniform design characteristics of all letters in the alphabet. However, this alone does not determine the standard of the type face and the quality of composition set with it. The appearance is something
ABCDEFGHIJKLMNOPQRSTUVWXYZ&
abcdefghijklmnopqrstuvwxyz   1234567890$

9 point Caledonia Italic (Linotype)
The basic character in a type design is determined by the uniform design characteristics of all letters in the alphabet. However, this alone does not determine the standard of the
ABCDEFGHIJKLMNOPQRSTUVWXYZ&
abcdefghijklmnopqrstuvwxyz   1234567890$

10 point Caledonia Italic (Linotype)
The basic character in a type design is determined by the uniform design characteristics of all letters in the alpha bet. However, this alone does not determine the standard
ABCDEFGHIJKLMNOPQRSTUVWXYZ&
abcdefghijklmnopqrstuvwxyz   1234567890$

11 point Caledonia Italic (Linotype)
The basic character in a type design is determined by the uniform design characteristics of all letters in the
ABCDEFGHIJKLMNOPQRSTUVWXYZ&
abcdefghijklmnopqrstuvwxyz   1234567890$

12 point Caledonia Italic (Linotype)
The basic character in a type design is determined by the uniform design characteristics of all letters
ABCDEFGHIJKLMNOPQRSTUVWXYZ&
abcdefghijklmnopqrstuvwxyz   1234567890$

14 point Caledonia Italic (Linotype)
The basic character in a type design is de termined by the uniform design character
ABCDEFGHIJKLMNOPQRSTUV
WXYZ&   1234567890$
abcdefghijklmnopqrstuvwxyz

Caledonia Bold *(Long descenders set 1 point leaded)*

6 point Caledonia Bold (Linotype)
The basic character in a type design is determined by the uniform design characteristics of all letters in the alphabet. However, this alone does not determine the standard of the type face and the quality of composition set with it. The appearance is something complex which forms itself out

ABCDEFGHIJKLMNOPQRSTUVWXYZ&
abcdefghijklmnopqrstuvwxyz 1234567890$
ABCDEFGHIJKLMNOPQRSTUVWXYZ

7 point Caledonia Bold (Linotype)
The basic character in a type design is determined by the uniform design characteristics of all letters in the alphabet. However, this alone does not determine the standard of the type face and the quality

ABCDEFGHIJKLMNOPQRSTUVWXYZ&
abcdefghijklmnopqrstuvwxyz 1234567890$
ABCDEFGHIJKLMNOPQRSTUVWXYZ

8 point Caledonia Bold (Linotype)
The basic character in a type design is determined by the uniform design characteristics of all letters in the alphabet. However, this alone does not determine the standard of the type face and the

ABCDEFGHIJKLMNOPQRSTUVWXYZ&
abcdefghijklmnopqrstuvwxyz 1234567890$
ABCDEFGHIJKLMNOPQRSTUVWXYZ

9 point Caledonia Bold (Linotype)
The basic character in a type design is determined by the uniform design characteristics of all letters in the alphabet. However, this alone does not determine the standard of the

ABCDEFGHIJKLMNOPQRSTUVWXYZ&
abcdefghijklmnopqrstuvwxyz 1234567890$
ABCDEFGHIJKLMNOPQRSTUVWXYZ

10 point Caledonia Bold (Linotype)
The basic character in a type design is determined by the uniform design characteristics of all letters in the alphabet. However, this alone does not determine the

ABCDEFGHIJKLMNOPQRSTUVWXYZ&
abcdefghijklmnopqrstuvwxyz 1234567890$
ABCDEFGHIJKLMNOPQRSTUVWXYZ

11 point Caledonia Bold (Linotype)
The basic character in a type design is determined by the uniform design characteristics of all letters in

ABCDEFGHIJKLMNOPQRSTUVWXYZ&
abcdefghijklmnopqrstuvwxyz 1234567890$
ABCDEFGHIJKLMNOPQRSTUVWXYZ

12 point Caledonia Bold (Linotype)
The basic character in a type design is determined by the uniform design characteristics of all letters

ABCDEFGHIJKLMNOPQRSTUVWXYZ&
abcdefghijklmnopqrstuvwxyz 1234567890$
ABCDEFGHIJKLMNOPQRSTUVWXYZ

14 point Caledonia Bold (Linotype)
The basic character in a type design is de termined by the uniform design character
ABCDEFGHIJKLMNOPQRSTUV
WXYZ& 1234567890$
abcdefghijklmnopqrstuvwxyz
ABCDEFGHIJKLMNOPQRSTUVWXYZ

Caledonia Bold Italic

6 point Caledonia Bold Italic (Linotype)
The basic character in a type design is determined by the uniform design characteristics of all letters in the alphabet. However, this alone does not determine the standard of the type face and the quality of composition set with it. The appearance is something complex which forms itself out of many details, like form, proportion, ductus, rhythm etc. If everything harmonizes, the total result will be more than the sum of its compon

ABCDEFGHIJKLMNOPQRSTUVWXYZ&
abcdefghijklmnopqrstuvwxyz 1234567890$

7 point Caledonia Bold Italic (Linotype)
The basic character in a type design is determined by the uniform design characteristics of all letters in the alphabet. However, this alone does not determine the standard of the type face and the quality of composition set with it. The appearance is something complex which forms itself out of many details, like form, proportion, ductus,

ABCDEFGHIJKLMNOPQRSTUVWXYZ&
abcdefghijklmnopqrstuvwxyz 1234567890$

8 point Caledonia Bold Italic (Linotype)
The basic character in a type design is determined by the uniform design characteristics of all letters in the alphabet. However, this alone does not determine the standard of the type face and the quality of composition set with it. The appearance is something

ABCDEFGHIJKLMNOPQRSTUVWXYZ&
abcdefghijklmnopqrstuvwxyz 1234567890$

9 point Caledonia Bold Italic (Linotype)
The basic character in a type design is determined by the uniform design characteristics of all letters in the alphabet. However, this alone does not determine the standard of the

ABCDEFGHIJKLMNOPQRSTUVWXYZ&
abcdefghijklmnopqrstuvwxyz 1234567890$

10 point Caledonia Bold Italic (Linotype)
The basic character in a type design is determined by the uniform design characteristics of all letters in the alphabet. However, this alone does not determine the

ABCDEFGHIJKLMNOPQRSTUVWXYZ&
abcdefghijklmnopqrstuvwxyz 1234567890$

11 point Caledonia Bold Italic (Linotype)
The basic character in a type design is determined by the uniform design characteristics of all letters in

ABCDEFGHIJKLMNOPQRSTUVWXYZ&
abcdefghijklmnopqrstuvwxyz 1234567890$

12 point Caledonia Bold Italic (Linotype)
The basic character in a type design is determined by the uniform design characteristics of all letters

ABCDEFGHIJKLMNOPQRSTUVWXYZ&
abcdefghijklmnopqrstuvwxyz 1234567890$

14 point Caledonia Bold Italic (Linotype)
The basic character in a type design is de termined by the uniform design character
ABCDEFGHIJKLMNOPQRSTUV
WXYZ& 1234567890$
abcdefghijklmnopqrstuvwxyz

Cartoon Bold

14 point Cartoon Bold, Cap font (Foundry)

ABCDEFGHIJKLMNOPQRSTUVWXYZ&
1234567890$

18 point Cartoon Bold, Cap font (Foundry)

ABCDEFGHIJKLMNOPQRSTUVWXYZ&
1234567890$

24 point Cartoon Bold, Cap font (Foundry)

ABCDEFGHIJKLMNOPQRSTUV
WXYZ&
1234567890$

Caslon No. 3

14 point Caslon No. 3 (Linotype)

The basic character in a type design is determined by the uniform design char acteristics of all letters in the alphabet.

ABCDEFGHIJKLMNOPQRSTU
VWXYZ& 1234567890$
abcdefghijklmnopqrstuvwxyz
ABCDEFGHIJKLMNOPQRSTUVWXYZ

Caslon No. 3 Italic

14 point Caslon No. 3 Italic (Linotype)

The basic character in a type design is determined by the uniform design char acteristics of all letters in the alphabet.

ABCDEFGHIJKLMNOPQRSTU
VWXYZ& 1234567890$
abcdefghijklmnopqrstuvwxyz

Caslon No. 4

18 point Caslon No. 4 (Linotype)

The basic character in a type design is deter mined by the uniform design characteristics of all letters in the alphabet. However, this alone

ABCDEFGHIJKLMNOPQRSTUVWXYZ&
abcdefghijklmnopqrstuvwxyz
1234567890$

18 point Caslon Bold (Foundry)

ABCDEFGHIJKLMNOPQRSTUVWXYZ&
abcdefghijklmnopqrstuvwxyz
1234567890$

24 point Caslon Bold (Foundry)

ABCDEFGHIJKLMNOPQRSTUVWXYZ&
abcdefghijklmnopqrstuvwxyz
1234567890$

30 point Caslon Bold (Foundry)

ABCDEFGHIJKLMNOPQRST
UVWXYZ&
abcdefghijklmnopqrstuvwxyz
1234567890$

36 point Caslon Bold (Foundry)

ABCDEFGHIJKLMNOPQR
STUVWXYZ&
abcdefghijklmnopqrstuvwxyz
1234567890$

42 point Caslon Bold (Foundry)

ABCDEFGHIJKLMNO
PQRSTUVWXYZ&
abcdefghijklmnopqr
stuvwxyz 1234567890$

(Continued on Page 89)

(Continued from Page 88)

48 point Caslon Bold (Foundry)

ABCDEFGHIJKLMN
OPQRSTUVWXYZ&
abcdefghijklmnopqrst
uvwxyz
1234567890$

60 point Caslon Bold (Foundry)

ABCDEFGHIJK
LMNOPQRSTU
VWXYZ&
abcdefghijklmno
pqrstuvwxyz
1234567890$

(Continued on Page 90)

72 point Caslon Bold (Foundry)

ABCDEFGHI
JKLMNOPQ
RSTUV
WXYZ&
abcdefghijkl
mnopqrstuv
wxyz
1234567890$

Caslon Bold Italic

14 point Caslon Bold Italic (Foundry)

ABCDEFGHIJKLMNOPQRSTUVWXYZ&
abcdefghijklmnopqrstuvwxyz
1234567890$

18 point Caslon Bold Italic (Foundry)

ABCDEFGHIJKLMNOPQRSTUVWXYZ&
abcdefghijklmnopqrstuvwxyz
1234567890$

24 point Caslon Bold Italic (Foundry)

ABCDEFGHIJKLMNOPQRSTU
VWXYZ&
abcdefghijklmnopqrstuvwxyz
1234567890$

30 point Caslon Bold Italic (Foundry)

ABCDEFGHIJKLMNOPQRSTU
VWXYZ&
abcdefghijklmnopqrstuvwxyz
1234567890$

36 point Caslon Bold Italic (Foundry)

ABCDEFGHIJKLMNOPQ
RSTUVWXYZ&
abcdefghijklmnopqrstuv
wxyz
1234567890$

Caslon Bold Condensed

12 point Caslon Bold Condensed (Foundry)
ABCDEFGHIJKLMNOPQRSTUVWXYZ&
abcdefghijklmnopqrstuvwxyz
1234567890$

14 point Caslon Bold Condensed (Foundry)
ABCDEFGHIJKLMNOPQRSTUVWXYZ&
abcdefghijklmnopqrstuvwxyz
1234567890$

18 point Caslon Bold Condensed (Ludlow)
ABCDEFGHIJKLMNOPQRSTUVWXYZ&
abcdefghijklmnopqrstuvwxyz
1234567890$

30 point Caslon Bold Condensed (Foundry)
ABCDEFGHIJKLMNOPQRSTUVWXYZ&
abcdefghijklmnopqrstuvwxyz
1234567890$

36 point Caslon Bold Condensed (Foundry)
ABCDEFGHIJKLMNOPQRSTUVW
XYZ&
abcdefghijklmnopqrstuvwxyz
1234567890$

42 point Caslon Bold Condensed (Foundry)
ABCDEFGHIJKLMNOPQRSTU
VWXYZ&
abcdefghijklmnopqrstuvwxyz
1234567890$

(Continued on Page 93)

Caslon Bold Condensed

(Continued from Page 92)

60 point Caslon Bold Condensed (Foundry)

ABCDEFGHIJKLMN OPQRSTUVWXYZ& abcdefghijklmnopqr stuvwxyz 1234567890$

Caslon No. 540

12 point Caslon No. 540 with Small Caps (Foundry)

ABCDEFGHIJKLMNOPQRSTUVWXYZ&
abcdefghijklmnopqrstuvwxyz
1234567890$
ABCDEFGHIJKLMNOPQRSTUVWXYZ&

14 Point Caslon No. 540 with Small Caps (Foundry)

ABCDEFGHIJKLMNOPQRSTUVWXYZ&
abcdefghijklmnopqrstuvwxyz
1234567890$
ABCDEFGHIJKLMNOPQRSTUVWXYZ&

18 point Caslon No. 540 (Foundry)

ABCDEFGHIJKLMNOPQRSTUVWXYZ&
abcdefghijklmnopqrstuvwxyz
1234567890$

(Continued on Page 94)

24 point Caslon No. 540 (Foundry)

ABCDEFGHIJKLMNOPQRSTUVWXYZ&
abcdefghijklmnopqrstuvwxyz
1234567890$

30 point Caslon No. 540 (Foundry)

ABCDEFGHIJKLMNOPQRSTUV
WXYZ&
abcdefghijklmnopqrstuvwxyz
1234567890$

36 point Caslon No. 540 (Foundry)

ABCDEFGHIJKLMNOPQRS
TUVWXYZ&
abcdefghijklmnopqrstuvwxyz
1234567890$

42 point Caslon No. 540 (Foundry)

ABCDEFGHIJKLMNO
PQRSTUVWXYZ&
abcdefghijklmnopqrstuvw
xyz
1234567890$

(Continued on Page 95)

(Continued from Page 94)

48 point Caslon No. 540 (Foundry)

ABCDEFGHIJKLM
NOPQRSTUVWXYZ
abcdefghijklmnopqrstuv
wxyz&
1234567890$

60 point Caslon No. 540 (Foundry)

ABCDEFGHIJK
LMNOPQRSTU
VWXYZ&
abcdefghijklmnopq
rstuvwxyz
1234567890$

(Continued on Page 96)

(Continued from Page 95)

72 point Caslon No. 540 (Foundry)

ABCDEFGH
IJKLMNOP
QRSTUVW
XYZ&
abcdefghijklm
nopqrstuvwxyz
1234567890$

(Continued on Page 97)

84 point Caslon No. 540 (Foundry)

ABCDEFGH
IJKLMNOP
QRSTUVW
XYZ& abcde
fghijklmno
pqrstuvwxyz
1234567890$

Caslon No. 540 Italic

10 point Caslon No. 540 Italic (Foundry)
ABCDEFGHIJKLMNOPQRSTUVWXYZ& abcdefghijklmnopqrstuvwxyz 1234567890$

14 point Caslon No. 540 Italic (Foundry)
ABCDEFGHIJKLMNOPQRSTUVWXYZ&
abcdefghijklmnopqrstuvwxyz 1234567890$

18 point Caslon No. 540 Italic (Foundry)
ABCDEFGHIJKLMNOPQRSTUVWXYZ&
abcdefghijklmnopqrstuvwxyz 1234567890$

24 point Caslon No. 540 Italic (Foundry)
ABCDEFGHIJKLMNOPQRSTUVWXYZ
abcdefghijklmnopqrstuvwxyz& 1234567890$

30 point Caslon No. 540 Italic (Foundry)
ABCDEFGHIJKLMNOPQR
STUVWXYZ& 1234567890$
abcdefghijklmnopqrstuvwxyz

36 point Caslon No. 540 Italic (Foundry)
ABCDEFGHIJKLMNOPQR
STUVWXYZ& 1234567890$
abcdefghijklmnopqrstuvwxyz

42 point Caslon No. 540 Italic (Foundry)
ABCDEFGHIJKLMNOP
QRSTUVWXYZ&
abcdefghijklmnopqrstuvwxyz
1234567890$

(Continued on Page 99)

(Continued from Page 98)

48 point Caslon No. 540 Italic (Foundry)

ABCDEFGHIJKLMN
OPQRSTUVWXYZ&
abcdefghijklmnopqrstuv
wxyz
1234567890$

60 point Caslon No. 540 Italic (Foundry)

ABCDEFGHIJKL
MNOPQRSTUVW
XYZ&
abcdefghijklmnopqrstu
vwxyz
1234567890$

(Continued on Page 100)

72 point Caslon No. 540 Italic (Foundry)

ABCDEFGHIJ
KLMNOPQR
STUVWXYZ&
abcdefghijklmnopq
rstuvwxyz
1234567890$

Caslon Oldstyle No. 471 *(Font contains some Alternate Characters)*

10 point Caslon Oldstyle No. 471 (Foundry)
ABCDEFGHIJKLMNOPQRSTUVWXYZ&
abcdefghijklmnopqrstuvwxyz
1234567890$

14 point Caslon Oldstyle No. 471 (Foundry)
ABCDEFGHIJKLMNOPQRSTUVWXYZ
abcdefghijklmnopqrstuvwxyz&
1234567890$

18 point Caslon Oldstyle No. 471 (Foundry)
ABCDEFGHIJKLMNOPQRSTUVWXYZ&
abcdefghijklmnopqrstuvwxyz
1234567890$

24 point Caslon Oldstyle No. 471 (Foundry)
ABCDEFGHIJKLMNOPQRSTUVWXYZ&
abcdefghijklmnopqrstuvwxyz
1234567890$

30 point Caslon Oldstyle No. 471 (Foundry)
ABCDEFGHIJKLMNOPQRSTUVWXYZ&
abcdefghijklmnopqrstuvwxyz
1234567890$

36 point Caslon Oldstyle No. 471 (Foundry)
ABCDEFGHIJKLMNOPQRSTUV
WXYZ&
abcdefghijklmnopqrstuvwxyz
1234567890$

42 point Caslon Oldstyle No. 471 (Foundry)
ABCDEFGHIJKLMNOPQR
STUVWXYZ&
abcdefghijklmnopqrstuvwxyz
1234567890$

(Continued on Page 102)

48 point Caslon Oldstyle No. 471 (Foundry)

ABCDEFGHIJKLMNOP QRSTUVWXYZ& abcdefghijklmnopqrstuv wxyz 1234567890$

Caslon Oldstyle No. 471 Italic

14 point Caslon Oldstyle No. 471 Italic (Foundry)

ABCDEFGHIJKLMNOPQRSTUVWXYZ&
abcdefghijklmnopqrstuvwxyz
1234567890$

SWASH

A B C D E F G H J K K L M N O P R S T U W Y
ε k v w z QU ɛt ɡr

18 point Caslon Oldstyle No. 471 Italic (Foundry)

ABCDEFGHIJKLMNOPQRSTUVWXYZ&
abcdefghijklmnopqrstuvwxyz
1234567890$

SWASH

A B C D E F G G H H J K K L L M N O P Q R S T U
W Y ε k v w z ɛt ɡr

(Continued on Page 103)

(Continued from Page 102)

24 point Caslon Oldstyle No. 471 Italic (Foundry)

ABCDEFGHIJKLMNOPQRSTUVWXYZ&
abcdefghijklmnopqrstuvwxyz
1234567890$

SWASH

A B C D E F F G H H J K K L L M
N O P Q S T U V W Y e k v w z ct gy

30 point Caslon Oldstyle No. 471 Italic (Foundry)

ABCDEFGHIJKLMNOPQRSTUVWXYZ
abcdefghijklmnopqrstuvwxyz&
1234567890$

SWASH

A B C D E F G G H H J K K L L M
N O P Q R S T U V W Y e k v w z gy

36 point Caslon Oldstyle No. 471 Italic (Foundry)

ABCDEFGHIJKLMNOPQRST
UVWXYZ&
abcdefghijklmnopqrstuvwxyz
1234567890$

SWASH

A B C G D E G H J L L M P Q
R S T U V W Y h ct

(Continued on Page 104)

42 point Caslon Oldstyle No. 471 Italic (Foundry)

ABCDEFGHIJKLMNOPQR
STUVWXYZ&
abcdefghijklmnopqrstuvwxyz
1234567890$

SWASH

ABCGDEF FGHHJ
K K L L M N O P Q R S
TUWY e h k v w z ct gy

48 point Caslon Oldstyle No. 471 Italic (Foundry)

ABCDEFGHIJKLMNOPQ
RSTUVWXYZ&
abcdefghijklmnopqrstuvwxyz
1234567890$

SWASH

JQTYhct

Caslon Oldstyle No. 337 *(Font contains some Alternate Characters)*

14 point Caslon Oldstyle No. 337 (Foundry)

ABCDEFGHIJKLMNOPQRSTUVWXYZ&
abcdefghijklmnopqrstuvwxyz
1234567890$

18 point Caslon Oldstyle No. 337 (Foundry)

ABCDEFGHIJKLMNOPQRSTUVWXYZ&
abcdefghijklmnopqrstuvwxyz
1234567890$

22 point Caslon Oldstyle No. 337 (Foundry)

ABCDEFGHIJKLMNOPQRSTUVWXYZ&
abcdefghijklmnopqrstuvwxyz
1234567890$

24 point Caslon Oldstyle No. 337 (Foundry)

ABCDEFGHIJKLMNOPQRSTUVWXYZ&
abcdefghijklmnopqrstuvwxyz
1234567890$

30 point Caslon Oldstyle No. 337 (Foundry)

ABCDEFGHIJKLMNOPQRSTUVWXYZ&
abcdefghijklmnopqrstuvwxyz
1234567890$

(Continued on Page 106)

36 point Caslon Oldstyle No. 337 (Foundry)

ABCDEFGHIJKLMNOPQRSTUV
WXYZ&
abcdefghijklmnopqrstuvwxyz
1234567890$

42 point Caslon Oldstyle No. 337 (Foundry)

ABCDEFGHIJKLMNOPQRS
TUVWXYZ&
abcdefghijklmnopqrstuvwxyz
1234567890$

48 point Caslon Oldstyle No. 337 (Foundry)

ABCDEFGHIJKLMNOP
QRSTUVWXYZ&
abcdefghijklmnopqrstuv
wxyz
1234567890$

Caslon Oldstyle No. 3371 Italic *(Font contains some Alternate Characters)*

14 point Caslon Oldstyle No. 3371 Italic (Foundry)

ABCDEFGHIJKLMNOPQRSTUVWXYZ& abcdefghijklmnopqrstuvwxyz 1234567890$

SWASH

A B C D E G J K L M N P R T U W Y h k ct

18 point Caslon Oldstyle No. 3371 Italic (Foundry)

ABCDEFGHIJKLMNOPQRSTUVWXYZ&

abcdefghijklmnopqrstuvwxyz 1234567890$

SWASH

A B C D E G J L M N P Q R T U W Y k v w z &

22 point Caslon Oldstyle No. 3371 Italic (Foundry)

ABCDEFGHIJKLMNOPQRSTUVWXYZ&
abcdefghijklmnopqrstuvwxyz
1234567890$

SWASH

A B C D E J P Q R T Y

24 point Caslon Oldstyle No. 3371 Italic (Foundry)

ABCDEFGHIJKLMNOPQRSTUVWXYZ&
abcdefghijklmnopqrstuvwxyz
1234567890$

SWASH

A B C D E G J K L M N P Q R T W Y
k v w z ct &

30 point Caslon Oldstyle No. 3371 Italic (Foundry)

ABCDEFGHIJKLMNOPQRSTUVWXYZ
abcdefghijklmnopqrstuvwxyz&
1234567890$

SWASH

A B C D E G J K L M N P Q R T U W Y
k v w z ct &

(Continued on Page 108)

36 point Caslon Oldstyle No. 3371 Italic (Foundry)

ABCDEFGHIJKLMNOPQR
STUVWXYZ& *1234567890$*
abcdefghijklmnopqrstuvwxyz
ABCDEGJKLMNPR
TUWYvwzct&

42 point Caslon Oldstyle No. 3371 Italic (Foundry)

ABCDEFGHIJKLMNOPQRS
TUVWXYZ&
abcdefghijklmnopqrstuvwxyz
1234567890$

48 point Caslon Oldstyle No. 3371 Italic (Foundry)

ABCDEFGHIJKLMNO
PQRSTUVWXYZ&
abcdefghijklmnopqrstuvwxyz
1234567890$

Caslon Openface

18 point Caslon Openface (Foundry)

ABCDEFGHIJKLMNOPQRSTUVWXYZ&
abcdefghijklmnopqrstuvwxyz
1234567890$

24 point Caslon Openface (Foundry)

ABCDEFGHIJKLMNOPQRSTUVWXYZ
abcdefghijklmnopqrstuvwxyz&
1234567890$

30 point Caslon Openface (Foundry)

ABCDEFGHIJKLMNOPQRSTU
VWXYZ&
abcdefghijklmnopqrstuvwxyz
1234567890$

36 point Caslon Openface (Foundry)

ABCDEFGHIJKLMNOP
QRSTUVWXYZ&
abcdefghijklmnopqrstuvwxyz
1234567890$

14 point Centaur (Foundry)
ABCDEFGHIJKLMNOPQRSTUVWXYZ&
abcdefghijklmnopqrstuvwxyz
1234567890$

16 point Centaur (Foundry)
ABCDEFGHIJKLMNOPQRSTUVWXYZ
abcdefghijklmnopqrstuvwxyz&
1234567890$

18 point Centaur (Foundry)
ABCDEFGHIJKLMNOPQRSTUVWXYZ&
abcdefghijklmnopqrstuvwxyz
1234567890$

24 point Centaur (Foundry)
ABCDEFGHIJKLMNOPQRSTUVWXYZ&
abcdefghijklmnopqrstuvwxyz
1234567890$

30 point Centaur (Foundry)
ABCDEFGHIJKLMNOPQRSTUVWXYZ&
abcdefghijklmnopqrstuvwxyz
1234567890$

36 point Centaur (Foundry)
ABCDEFGHIJKLMNOPQRSTUV
WXYZ&
abcdefghijklmnopqrstuvwxyz
1234567890$

48 point Centaur (Foundry)
ABCDEFGHIJKLMNOPQR
STUVWXYZ&
abcdefghijklmnopqrstuvwxyz
1234567890$

Centaur Italic *(Also known as Arrighi)*

18 point Centaur Italic (Foundry)

ABCDEFGHIJKLMNOPQRSTUVWXYZ&
abcdefghijklmnopqrstuvwxyz
1234567890$

48 point Centaur Italic (Foundry)

ABCDEFGHIJKLMNOPQ
RSTUVWXYZ&
abcdefghijklmnopqrstuvwxyz
1234567890$

Century Bold

8 point Century Bold (Linotype)

The basic character in a type design is determined by the uni
form design characteristics of all letters in the alphabet. How
ever, this alone does not determine the standard of the type
face and the quality of composition set with it. The appear
ance is something complex which forms itself out of many
details, like form, proportion, ductus, rhythm etc. If everything

ABCDEFGHIJKLMNOPQRSTUVWXYZ&
abcdefghijklmnopqrstuvwxyz   1234567890$

9 point Century Bold (Linotype)

The basic character in a type design is determined by
the uniform design characteristics of all letters in the
alphabet. However, this alone does not determine the
standard of the type face and the quality of composi
tion set with it. The appearance is something complex

ABCDEFGHIJKLMNOPQRSTUVWXYZ&
abcdefghijklmnopqrstuvwxyz   1234567890$

10 point Century Bold (Linotype)

The basic character in a type design is determined
by the uniform design characteristics of all letters
in the alphabet. However, this alone does not deter
mine the standard of the type face and the quality
of composition set with it. The appearance is some

ABCDEFGHIJKLMNOPQRSTUVWXYZ&
abcdefghijklmnopqrstuvwxyz   1234567890$

12 point Century Bold (Linotype)

The basic character in a type design is deter
mined by the uniform design characteristics
of all letters in the alphabet. However, this
alone does not determine the standard of the

ABCDEFGHIJKLMNOPQRSTUVWXYZ&
abcdefghijklmnopqrstuvwxyz   1234567890$

14 point Century Bold (Linotype)

The basic character in a type design is
determined by the uniform design
characteristics of all letters in the al

ABCDEFGHIJKLMNOPQRSTU
VWXYZ&   1234567890$
abcdefghijklmnopqrstuvwxyz

(Continued on Page 112)

(Continued from Page 111)

18 point Century Bold (Foundry)

ABCDEFGHIJKLMNOPQRSTUVWXYZ&
abcdefghijklmnopqrstuvwxyz 1234567890$

24 point Century Bold (Foundry)

ABCDEFGHIJKLMNOPQRSTUVWXYZ&
abcdefghijklmnopqrstuvwxyz 1234567890$

30 point Century Bold (Foundry)

ABCDEFGHIJKLMNOPQRSTUVWXYZ
abcdefghijklmnopqrstuvwxyz&
1234567890$

Century Bold Italic

14 point Century Bold Italic (Linotype)

The basic character in a type design is determined by the uniform design characteristics of all letters in the al

ABCDEFGHIJKLMNOPQRSTU VWXYZ& 1234567890$ abcdefghijklmnopqrstuvwxyz

18 point Century Bold Italic (Foundry)

ABCDEFGHIJKLMNOPQR STUVWXYZ& abcdefghijklmnopqrstuvwxyz 1234567890$

Century Bold Condensed

24 point Century Bold Condensed (Foundry)

ABCDEFGHIJKLMNOPQRSTUVWXYZ&
abcdefghijklmnopqrstuvwxyz 1234567890$

36 point Century Bold Condensed (Foundry)

ABCDEFGHIJKLMNOPQRSTUVWXYZ&
abcdefghijklmnopqrstuvwxyz 1234567890$

Century Expanded

6 point Century Expanded (Linotype)
The basic character in a type design is determined by the uniform design characteristics of all letters in the alphabet. However, this alone does not determine the standard of the type face and the quality of composition set with it. The appearance is something complex which forms itself out of many details, like form, proportion, ductus, rhythm etc. If everything har monizes, the total result will be more than the sum of its components. The only reliable basis for the design in a type is a positive feeling for form and style. The basic character in a type design is determined by the uni

ABCDEFGHIJKLMNOPQRSTUVWXYZ&
abcdefghijklmnopqrstuvwxyz   1234567890$
ABCDEFGHIJKLMNOPQRSTUVWXYZ

7 point Century Expanded (Linotype)
The basic character in a type design is determined by the uniform design characteristics of all letters in the alphabet. However, this alone does not determine the standard of the type face and the quality of composition set with it. The appearance is something complex which forms itself out of many details, like form, propor tion, ductus, rhythm etc. If everything harmonizes, the total result will be more than the sum of its components. The only reliable

ABCDEFGHIJKLMNOPQRSTUVWXYZ&
abcdefghijklmnopqrstuvwxyz   1234567890$
ABCDEFGHIJKLMNOPQRSTUVWXYZ

8 point Century Expanded (Linotype)
The basic character in a type design is determined by the uniform design characteristics of all letters in the alphabet. However, this alone does not determine the standard of the type face and the quality of composition set with it. The appearance is something complex which forms itself out of many details, like form, proportion, ductus, rhythm etc. If

ABCDEFGHIJKLMNOPQRSTUVWXYZ&
abcdefghijklmnopqrstuvwxyz   1234567890$
ABCDEFGHIJKLMNOPQRSTUVWXYZ

9 point Century Expanded (Linotype)
The basic character in a type design is determined by the uniform design characteristics of all letters in the alpha bet. However, this alone does not determine the standard of the type face and the quality of composition set with it. The appearance is something complex which forms

ABCDEFGHIJKLMNOPQRSTUVWXYZ&
abcdefghijklmnopqrstuvwxyz   1234567890$
ABCDEFGHIJKLMNOPQRSTUVWXYZ

10 point Century Expanded (Linotype)
The basic character in a type design is determined by the uniform design characteristics of all letters in the alphabet. However, this alone does not deter mine the standard of the type face and the quality of composition set with it. The appearance is some

ABCDEFGHIJKLMNOPQRSTUVWXYZ&
abcdefghijklmnopqrstuvwxyz   1234567890$
ABCDEFGHIJKLMNOPQRSTUVWXYZ

11 point Century Expanded (Linotype)
The basic character in a type design is determined by the uniform design characteristics of all letters in the alphabet. However, this alone does not de termine the standard of the type face and the

ABCDEFGHIJKLMNOPQRSTUVWXYZ&
abcdefghijklmnopqrstuvwxyz   1234567890$
ABCDEFGHIJKLMNOPQRSTUVWXYZ

12 point Century Expanded (Linotype)
The basic character in a type design is deter mined by the uniform design characteristics of all letters in the alphabet. However, this alone does not determine the standard of the

ABCDEFGHIJKLMNOPQRSTUVWXYZ&
abcdefghijklmnopqrstuvwxyz   1234567890$
ABCDEFGHIJKLMNOPQRSTUVWXYZ

14 point Century Expanded (Linotype)
The basic character in a type design is determined by the uniform design char acteristics of all letters in the alphabet.

ABCDEFGHIJKLMNOPQRSTU
VWXYZ&   1234567890$
abcdefghijklmnopqrstuvwxyz
ABCDEFGHIJKLMNOPQRSTUVWXYZ

10 point Century Expanded (Foundry)
ABCDEFGHIJKLMNOPQRSTUVWXYZ&
abcdefghijklmnopqrstuvwxyz
1234567890$

18 point Century Expanded (Foundry)
ABCDEFGHIJKLMNOPQ
RSTUVWXYZ&
abcdefghijklmnopqrstuvwxyz
1234567890$

(Continued on Page 114)

24 point Century Expanded (Foundry)

ABCDEFGHIJKLMNOPQRSTUVWXYZ&
abcdefghijklmnopqrstuvwxyz
1234567890$

30 point Century Expanded (Foundry)

ABCDEFGHIJKLMNOPQRSTUV
WXYZ&
abcdefghijklmnopqrstuvwxyz
1234567890$

48 point Century Expanded (Foundry)

ABCDEFGHIJKLMNO
PQRSTUVWXYZ&
abcdefghijklmnopqrstuv
wxyz
1234567890$

(Continued on Page 115)

(Continued from Page 114)

60 point Century Expanded (Foundry)

ABCDEFGHIJKL
MNOPQRSTUVW
XYZ&
abcdefghijklmnopqr
stuvwxyz
1234567890$

Century Expanded Italic

6 point Century Expanded Italic (Linotype)

The basic character in a type design is determined by the uniform design characteristics of all letters in the alphabet. However, this alone does not determine the standard of the type face and the quality of composition set with it. The appearance is something complex which forms itself out of many details, like form, proportion, ductus, rhythm etc. If everything harmonizes, the total·result will be more than the sum of its components. The only reliable basis for the design in a type is a positive feeling for form and style. The basic character in a type design is determined by the uni

ABCDEFGHIJKLMNOPQRSTUVWXYZ&
abcdefghijklmnopqrstuvwxyz   *1234567890$*

7 point Century Expanded Italic (Linotype)

The basic character in a type design is determined by the uniform design characteristics of all letters in the alphabet. However, this alone does not determine the standard of the type face and the quality of composition set with it. The appearance is something complex which forms itself out of many details, like form, proportion, ductus, rhythm etc. If everything harmonizes, the total result will be more than the sum of its components. The only reliable

ABCDEFGHIJKLMNOPQRSTUVWXYZ&
abcdefghijklmnopqrstuvwxyz   *1234567890$*

8 point Century Expanded Italic (Linotype)

The basic character in a type design is determined by the uniform design characteristics of all letters in the alphabet. However, this alone does not determine the standard of the type face and the quality of composition set with it. The appearance is something complex which forms itself out of many details, like form, proportion, ductus, rhythm etc. If

ABCDEFGHIJKLMNOPQRSTUVWXYZ&
abcdefghijklmnopqrstuvwxyz   *1234567890$*

9 point Century Expanded Italic (Linotype)

The basic character in a type design is determined by the uniform design characteristics of all letters in the alphabet. However, this alone does not determine the standard of the type face and the quality of composition set with it. The appearance is something complex which forms

ABCDEFGHIJKLMNOPQRSTUVWXYZ&
abcdefghijklmnopqrstuvwxyz   *1234567890$*

10 point Century Expanded Italic (Linotype)

The basic character in a type design is determined by the uniform design characteristics of all letters in the alphabet. However, this alone does not determine the standard of the type face and the quality of composition set with it. The appearance is some

ABCDEFGHIJKLMNOPQRSTUVWXYZ&
abcdefghijklmnopqrstuvwxyz   *1234567890$*

11 point Century Expanded Italic (Linotype)

The basic character in a type design is determined by the uniform design characteristics of all letters in the alphabet. However, this alone does not de termine the standard of the type face and the

ABCDEFGHIJKLMNOPQRSTUVWXYZ&
abcdefghijklmnopqrstuvwxyz   *1234567890$*

12 point Century Expanded Italic (Linotype)

The basic character in a type design is deter mined by the uniform design characteristics of all letters in the alphabet. However, this alone does not determine the standard of the

ABCDEFGHIJKLMNOPQRSTUVWXYZ&
abcdefghijklmnopqrstuvwxyz   *1234567890$*

14 point Century Expanded Italic (Linotype)

The basic character in a type design is determined by the uniform design char acteristics of all letters in the alphabet.

ABCDEFGHIJKLMNOPQRSTU VWXYZ&   *1234567890$*
abcdefghijklmnopqrstuvwxyz

8 point Century Expanded Italic (Foundry)

ABCDEFGHIJKLMNOPQRSTUVWXYZ&
abcdefghijklmnopqrstuvwxyz   *1234567890$*

10 point Century Expanded Italic (Foundry)

ABCDEFGHIJKLMNOPQRSTUVWXYZ&
abcdefghijklmnopqrstuvwxyz   *1234567890$*

12 point Century Expanded Italic (Foundry)

ABCDEFGHIJKLMNOPQRSTUVWXYZ&
abcdefghijklmnopqrstuvwxyz   *1234567890$*

14 point Century Expanded Italic (Foundry)

ABCDEFGHIJKLMNOPQRST UVWXYZ&
abcdefghijklmnopqrstuvwxyz
1234567890$

18 point Century Expanded Italic (Foundry)

ABCDEFGHIJKLMNOPQRSTUVWXYZ&
abcdefghijklmnopqrstuvwxyz
1234567890$

(Continued on Page 117)

(Continued from Page 116)

24 point Century Expanded Italic (Foundry)

ABCDEFGHIJKLMNOPQRSTUVWXYZ&
abcdefghijklmnopqrstuvwxyz
1234567890$

30 point Century Expanded Italic (Foundry)

ABCDEFGHIJKLMNOPQRSTUV
WXYZ&
abcdefghijklmnopqrstuvwxyz
1234567890$

36 point Century Expanded Italic (Foundry)

ABCDEFGHIJKLMNOPQRS
TUVWXYZ&
abcdefghijklmnopqrstuvwxyz
1234567890$

48 point Century Expanded Italic (Foundry)

ABCDEFGHIJKLMNO
PQRSTUVWXYZ&
abcdefghijklmnopqrstuv
wxyz
1234567890$

Century Nova

ABCDEFGHIJKLMNOPQRSTUVWXYZ&
abcdefghijklmnopqrstuvwxyz
1234567890$

ABCDEFGHIJKLMNOPQRSTUVWXYZ&
abcdefghijklmnopqrstuvwxyz
1234567890$

ABCDEFGHIJKLMNOPQRS
TUVWXYZ&
abcdefghijklmnopqrstuvwxyz
1234567890$

Century Schoolbook

ABCDEFGHIJKLMNOPQRSTUVWXYZ&
abcdefghijklmnopqrstuvwxyz
1234567890$

ABCDEFGHIJKLMNOPQRSTUVWXYZ&
abcdefghijklmnopqrstuvwxyz
1234567890$

ABCDEFGHIJKLMNOPQRSTUVWXYZ&
abcdefghijklmnopqrstuvwxyz
1234567890$
ABCDEFGHIJKLMNOPQRSTUVWXYZ&

ABCDEFGHIJKLMNOPQRSTUVWXYZ&
abcdefghijklmnopqrstuvwxyz
1234567890$

ABCDEFGHIJKLMNOPQRSTUVWXYZ&
abcdefghijklmnopqrstuvwxyz
1234567890$

(Continued on Page 119)

30 point Century Schoolbook (Foundry)

ABCDEFGHIJKLMNOPQRSTUV
WXYZ&
abcdefghijklmnopqrstuvwxyz
1234567890$

48 point Century Schoolbook (Foundry)

ABCDEFGHIJKLMNO
PQRSTUVWXYZ&
abcdefghijklmnopqrstu
vwxyz
1234567890$

Century Schoolbook Italic

8 point Century Schoolbook Italic (Foundry)
*ABCDEFGHIJKLMNOPQRSTUVWXYZ&
abcdefghijklmnopqrstuvwxyz
1234567890$*

12 point Century Schoolbook Italic (Foundry)
*ABCDEFGHIJKLMNOPQRSTUVWXYZ&
abcdefghijklmnopqrstuvwxyz
1234567890$*

14 point Century Schoolbook Italic (Foundry)
*ABCDEFGHIJKLMNOPQRSTUVWXYZ&
abcdefghijklmnopqrstuvwxyz   1234567890$*

16 point Century Schoolbook Italic (Foundry)
*ABCDEFGHIJKLMNOPQRSTUVWXYZ&
abcdefghijklmnopqrstuvwxyz   1234567890$*

(Continued on Page 120)

18 point Century Schoolbook Italic (Foundry)

ABCDEFGHIJKLMNOPQRSTUVWXYZ&
abcdefghijklmnopqrstuvwxyz
1234567890$

24 point Century Schoolbook Italic (Foundry)

ABCDEFGHIJKLMNOPQRSTUVWXYZ&
abcdefghijklmnopqrstuvwxyz
1234567890$

30 point Century Schoolbook Italic (Foundry)

ABCDEFGHIJKLMNOPQRSTUV
WXYZ&
abcdefghijklmnopqrstuvwxyz
1234567890$

36 point Century Schoolbook Italic (Foundry)

ABCDEFGHIJKLMNOPQRS
TUVWXYZ&
abcdefghijklmnopqrstuvwxyz
1234567890$

Century Schoolbook Bold

14 point Century Schoolbook Bold (Foundry)
ABCDEFGHIJKLMNOPQRSTUVWXYZ&
abcdefghijklmnopqrstuvwxyz
1234567890$

18 point Century Schoolbook Bold (Foundry)
ABCDEFGHIJKLMNOPQRSTUVWXYZ&
abcdefghijklmnopqrstuvwxyz
1234567890$

24 point Century Schoolbook Bold (Foundry)
ABCDEFGHIJKLMNOPQRSTUVWXYZ&
abcdefghijklmnopqrstuvwxyz
1234567890$

30 point Century Schoolbook Bold (Foundry)
ABCDEFGHIJKLMNOPQRSTUV
WXYZ&
abcdefghijklmnopqrstuvwxyz
1234567890$

48 point Century Schoolbook Bold (Foundry)
ABCDEFGHIJKLMN
OPQRSTUVWXYZ&
abcdefghijklmnopqrs
tuvwxyz
1234567890$

8 point Cheltenham Bold (Foundry)
ABCDEFGHIJKLMNOPQRSTUVWXYZ&
abcdefghijklmnopqrstuvwxyz
1234567890$

12 point Cheltenham Bold (Foundry)
ABCDEFGHIJKLMNOPQRSTUVWXYZ&
abcdefghijklmnopqrstuvwxyz
1234567890$

14 point Cheltenham Bold (Foundry)
ABCDEFGHIJKLMNOPQRSTUVWXYZ&
abcdefghijklmnopqrstuvwxyz
1234567890$

18 point Cheltenham Bold (Foundry)
ABCDEFGHIJKLMNOPQRSTUVWXYZ&
abcdefghijklmnopqrstuvwxyz
1234567890$

18 point Cheltenham Bold (Ludlow)
ABCDEFGHIJKLMNOPQRSTUVWXYZ&
abcdefghijklmnopqrstuvwxyz
1234567890$

24 point Cheltenham Bold (Foundry)
ABCDEFGHIJKLMNOPQRSTUVWXYZ&
abcdefghijklmnopqrstuvwxyz
1234567890$

30 point Cheltenham Bold (Foundry)
ABCDEFGHIJKLMNOPQRSTUVWXYZ
abcdefghijklmnopqrstuvwxyz&
1234567890$

36 point Cheltenham Bold (Foundry)
ABCDEFGHIJKLMNOPQRSTUV
WXYZ&
abcdefghijklmnopqrstuvwxyz
1234567890$

Cheltenham Bold Italic

14 point Cheltenham Bold Italic (Foundry)

ABCDEFGHIJKLMNOPQRSTUVWXYZ&
abcdefghijklmnopqrstuvwxyz
1234567890$

24 point Cheltenham Bold Italic (Foundry)

ABCDEFGHIJKLMNOPQRSTUVWXYZ&
abcdefghijklmnopqrstuvwxyz
1234567890$

30 point Cheltenham Bold Italic (Foundry)

ABCDEFGHIJKLMNOPQRSTUV
WXYZ&
abcdefghijklmnopqrstuvwxyz
1234567890$

Cheltenham Bold Condensed

10 point Cheltenham Bold Condensed (Foundry)

ABCDEFGHIJKLMNOPQRSTUVWXYZ&
abcdefghijklmnopqrstuvwxyz
1234567890$

12 point Cheltenham Bold Condensed (Foundry)

ABCDEFGHIJKLMNOPQRSTUVWXYZ&
abcdefghijklmnopqrstuvwxyz
1234567890$

14 point Cheltenham Bold Condensed (Foundry)

ABCDEFGHIJKLMNOPQRSTUVWXYZ&
abcdefghijklmnopqrstuvwxyz
1234567890$

18 point Chentenham Bold Condensed (Foundry)

ABCDEFGHIJKLMNOPQRSTUVWXYZ&
abcdefghijklmnopqrstuvwxyz
1234567890$

(Continued on Page 124)

30 point Cheltenham Bold Condensed (Foundry)

ABCDEFGHIJKLMNOPQRSTUVWXYZ&
abcdefghijklmnopqrstuvwxyz
1234567890$

36 point Cheltenham Bold Condensed (Foundry)

ABCDEFGHIJKLMNOPQRSTUVWXYZ&
abcdefghijklmnopqrstuvwxyz
1234567890$

60 point Cheltenham Bold Condensed (Foundry)

ABCDEFGHIJKLMNOP
QRSTUVWXYZ&
abcdefghijklmnopqrstuv
wxyz
1234567890$

(Continued on Page 125)

Cheltanham Bold Condensed

(Continued from Page 124)

72 point Cheltenham Bold Condensed (Foundry)

ABCDEFGHIJKLMN
OPQRSTUVWXYZ&
abcdefghijklmnopqrst
uvwxyz
1234567890$

Cheltenham Bold Extra Condensed

12 point Cheltenham Bold Extra Condensed (Foundry)

ABCDEFGHIJKLMNOPQRSTUVWXYZ&
abcdefghijklmnopqrstuvwxyz
1234567890$

24 point Cheltenham Bold Extra Condensed (Foundry)

ABCDEFGHIJKLMNOPQRSTUVWXYZ&
abcdefghijklmnopqrstuvwxyz
1234567890$

(Continued on Page 126)

30 point Cheltenham Bold Extra Condensed (Foundry)

ABCDEFGHIJKLMNOPQRSTUVWXYZ&
abcdefghijklmnopqrstuvwxyz
1234567890$

36 point Cheltenham Bold Extra Condensed (Foundry)

ABCDEFGHIJKLMNOPQRSTUVWXYZ&
abcdefghijklmnopqrstuvwxyz   1234567890$

84 point Cheltenham Bold Extra Condensed (Foundry)

ABCDEFGHIJKLMNOP
QRSTUVWXYZ&
abcdefghijklmnopqrstu
vwxyz
1234567890$

Cheltenham Bold Extended

14 point Cheltenham Bold Extended (Foundry)

ABCDEFGHIJKLMNOPQRSTUVWXYZ&
abcdefghijklmnopqrstuvwxyz
1234567890$

18 point Cheltenham Bold Extended (Ludlow)

ABCDEFGHIJKLMNOPQRSTUVWXYZ&
abcdefghijklmnopqrstuvwxyz
1234567890$

24 point Cheltenham Bold Extended (Ludlow)

ABCDEFGHIJKLMNOPQRST
UVWXYZ&
abcdefghijklmnopqrstuvwxyz
1234567890$

30 point Cheltenham Bold Extended (Ludlow)

ABCDEFGHIJKLMNOPQRST
UVWXYZ&
abcdefghijklmnopqrstuvwxyz
1234567890$

36 point Cheltenham Bold Extended (Ludlow)

ABCDEFGHIJKLMNOPQ
RSTUVWXYZ&
abcdefghijklmnopq
rstuvwxyz
1234567890$

Cheltenham Bold Outline *(Font contains some Alternate Characters)*

18 point Cheltenham Bold Outline (Foundry)

ABCDEFGHIJKLMNOPQRSTUVWXYZ&
abcdefghijklmnopqrstuvwxyz
1234567890$

24 point Cheltenham Bold Outline (Foundry)

ABCDEFGHIJKLMNOPQRSTUVWXYZ&
abcdefghijklmnopqrstuvwxyz
1234567890$

30 point Cheltenham Bold Outline (Foundry)

ABCDEFGHIJKLMNOPQRSTUVWXYZ
abcdefghijklmnopqrstuvwxyz&
1234567890$

36 point Cheltenham Bold Outline (Foundry)

ABCDEFGHIJKLMNOPQRST
UVWXYZ&
abcdefghijklmnopqrstuvwxyz
1234567890$

Cheltenham Oldstyle

8 point Cheltenham Oldstyle (Foundry)

ABCDEFGHIJKLMNOPQRSTUVWXYZ&
abcdefghijklmnopqrstuvwxyz
1234567890$

10 point Cheltenham Oldstyle (Foundry)

ABCDEFGHIJKLMNOPQRSTUVWXYZ&
abcdefghijklmnopqrstuvwxyz
1234567890$

Cheltenham Open

42 point Cheltenham Open (Foundry)

ABCDEFGHIJKLMNOPQ
RSTUVWXYZ&
abcdefghijklmnopqrstuvwxyz
1234567890$

48 point Cheltenham Open (Foundry)

ABCDEFGHIJKLMNOP
QRSTUVWXYZ&
abcdefghijklmnopqrst
uvwxyz
1234567890$

Cheltonian Bold

12 point Cheltonian Bold (Intertype)

**The basic character in a type design is determined
by the uniform design characteristics of all letters
in the alphabet. However, this alone does not de
termine the standard of the type face and the**

**ABCDEFGHIJKLMNOPQRSTUVWXYZ&
abcdefghijklmnopqrstuvwxyz 1234567890$**

Cheltonian Wide

12 point Cheltonian Wide (Intertype)

The basic character in a type design is determined
by the uniform design characteristics of all letters
in the alphabet. However, this alone does not de
termine the standard of the type face and the

ABCDEFGHIJKLMNOPQRSTUVWXYZ&
abcdefghijklmnopqrstuvwxyz 1234567890$

Cheltenham Wide No. 164

12 point Cheltenham Wide No. 164 (Foundry)
ABCDEFGHIJKLMNOPQRSTUVWXYZ&
abcdefghijklmnopqrstuvwxyz
1234567890$

14 point Cheltenham Wide No. 164 (Foundry)
ABCDEFGHIJKLMNOPQRSTUVWXYZ&
abcdefghijklmnopqrstuvwxyz
1234567890$

18 point Cheltenham Wide No. 164 (Foundry)
ABCDEFGHIJKLMNOPQRSTUVWXYZ&
abcdefghijklmnopqrstuvwxyz
1234567890$

24 point Chentenham Wide No.164 (Foundry)
ABCDEFGHIJKLMNOPQRSTUVWXYZ&
abcdefghijklmnopqrstuvwxyz
1234567890$

30 point Cheltenham Wide No. 164 (Foundry)
ABCDEFGHIJKLMNOPQRSTUVWXYZ
abcdefghijklmnopqrstuvwxyz&
1234567890$

Cheltenham Wide No. 164 Italic

12 point Cheltenham Wide No. 164 Italic (Foundry)
ABCDEFGHIJKLMNOPQRSTUVWXYZ&
abcdefghijklmnopqrstuvwxyz
1234567890$

14 point Cheltenham Wide No. 164 Italic (Foundry)
ABCDEFGHIJKLMNOPQRSTUVWXYZ&
abcdefghijklmnopqrstuvwxyz
1234567890$

18 point Cheltenham Wide No. 164 Italic (Foundry)
ABCDEFGHIJKLMNOPQRSTUVWXYZ&
abcdefghijklmnopqrstuvwxyz
1234567890$

24 point Cheltenham Wide No. 164 Italic (Foundry)
ABCDEFGHIJKLMNOPQRSTUVWXYZ&
abcdefghijklmnopqrstuvwxyz
1234567890$

(Continued on Page 131)

30 point Cheltenham Wide No. 164 Italic (Foundry)

ABCDEFGHIJKLMNOPQRSTU
VWXYZ&
abcdefghijklmnopqrstuvwxyz
1234567890$

Chisel

30 point Chisel (Foundry)

ABCDEFGHIJKLMNOPQRSTUVWXYZ&
abcdefghijklmnopqrstuvwxyz
1234567890$

48 point Chisel (Foundry)

ABCDEFGHIJKLMNOP
QRSTUVWXYZ&
abcdefghijklmnopqrstu
vwxyz
1234567890$

(Continued on Page 132)

V & M TYPOGRAPHICAL, INCORPORATED |

(Continued from Page 131)

72 point Chisel (Foundry)

ABCDEFGHIJK
LMNOPQRSTU
VWXYZ&
abcdefghijklmn
opqrstuvwxyz
1234567890$

City Medium

24 point City Medium small (Foundry)

ABCDEFGHIJKLMNOPQRSTUVWXYZ&
abcdefghijklmnopqrstuvwxyz
1234567890$

Clarendon Regular

18 point Clarendon Regular (Foundry)

ABCDEFGHIJKLMNOPQRSTUVWXYZ&
abcdefghijklmnopqrstuvwxyz
1234567890$

24 point Clarendon Regular (Foundry)

ABCDEFGHIJKLMNOPQRSTUVWXYZ&
abcdefghijklmnopqrstuvwxyz
1234567890$

30 point Clarendon Regular (Foundry)

ABCDEFGHIJKLMNOPQRSTUVWXYZ
abcdefghijklmnopqrstuvwxyz&
1234567890$

36 point Clarendon Regular (Foundry)

ABCDEFGHIJKLMNOPQRST
UVWXYZ&
abcdefghijklmnopqrstuvwxyz
1234567890$

(Continued on Page 134)

60 point Clarendon Regular (Foundry)

ABCDEFGHIJKL MNOPQRSTUV WXYZ&

abcdefghijklmno
pqrstuvwxyz
1234567890$

Clarendon Bold

10 point Clarendon Bold (Foundry)
**ABCDEFGHIJKLMNOPQRSTUVWXYZ&
abcdefghijklmnopqrstuvwxyz
1234567890$**

12 point Clarendon Bold (Foundry)
**ABCDEFGHIJKLMNOPQRSTUVWXYZ
abcdefghijklmnopqrstuvwxyz&
1234567890$**

14 point Clarendon Bold (Foundry)
**ABCDEFGHIJKLMNOPQRSTUVWXYZ&
abcdefghijklmnopqrstuvwxyz
1234567890$**

18 point Clarendon Bold (Foundry)
**ABCDEFGHIJKLMNOPQRSTUVWXYZ&
abcdefghijklmnopqrstuvwxyz
1234567890$**

24 point Clarendon Bold (Foundry)
**ABCDEFGHIJKLMNOPQRSTUVWXYZ&
abcdefghijklmnopqrstuvwxyz
1234567890$**

30 point Clarendon Bold (Foundry)
**ABCDEFGHIJKLMNOPQRSTUV
WXYZ&
abcdefghijklmnopqrstuvwxyz
1234567890$**

36 point Clarendon Bold (Foundry)
**ABCDEFGHIJKLMNOPQRS
TUVWXYZ&
abcdefghijklmnopqrstuvwxyz
1234567890$**

(Continued on Page 136)

(Continued from Page 135)

42 point Clarendon Bold (Foundry)

ABCDEFGHIJKLMNO
PQRSTUVWXYZ&
abcdefghijklmnopqrst
uvwxyz
1234567890$

60 point Clarendon Bold (Foundry)

ABCDEFGHIJKL
MNOPQRSTUV
WXYZ&
abcdefghijklmno
pqrstuvwxyz
1234567890$

(Continued on Page 137)

72 point Clarendon Bold (Foundry)

ABCDEFGHIJ
KLMNOPQRS
TUVWXYZ&
abcdefghijkl
mnopqrstuv
wxyz
1234567890$

Clearface

ABCDEFGHIJKLMNOPQRSTUVWXYZ&
abcdefghijklmnopqrstuvwxyz
1234567890$

ABCDEFGHIJKLMNOPQRSTUVWXYZ&
abcdefghijklmnopqrstuvwxyz
1234567890$

ABCDEFGHIJKLMNOPQRSTUVWXYZ&
abcdefghijklmnopqrstuvwxyz
123456790$

ABCDEFGHIJKLMNOPQRST
UVWXYZ&
abcdefghijklmnopqrstuvwxyz
1234567890$

Clearface Italic

ABCDEFGHIJKLMNOPQRSTUVWXYZ&
abcdefghijklmnopqrstuvwxyz
1234567890$

ABCDEFGHIJKLMNOPQRSTUVWXYZ&
abcdefghijklmnopqrstuvwxyz
1234567890$

Cloister Black

14 point Cloister Black (Foundry)

ABCDEFGHIJKLMNOPQRSTUVWXYZ&
abcdefghijklmnopqrstuvwxyz
1234567890$

18 point Cloister Black (Foundry)

ABCDEFGHIJKLMNOPQRSTUVWXYZ&
abcdefghijklmnopqrstuvwxyz
1234567890$

24 point Cloister Black (Foundry)

ABCDEFGHIJKLMNOPQRSTUVWXYZ&
abcdefghijklmnopqrstuvwxyz
1234567890$

36 point Cloister Black (Foundry)

ABCDEFGHIJKLMNOPQ
RSTUVWXYZ&
abcdefghijklmnopqrstuvwxyz
1234567890$

Cloister Bold

30 point Cloister Bold (Foundry)

ABCDEFGHIJKLMNOPQRSTUVWXYZ&
abcdefghijklmnopqrstuvwxyz
1234567890$

Cloister Bold Italic

30 point Cloister Bold Italic (Foundry)

ABCDEFGHIJKLMNOPQRSTUVWXYZ&
abcdefghijklmnopqrstuvwxyz
1234567890$

Cloister Initials

36 point Cloister Initials, Cap font (Foundry)

Color Block

48 point Cloister Initials, Cap font (Foundry)

Color Block

Cochin No. 61

18 point Cochin No. 61 (Foundry)

ABCDEFGHIJKLMNOPQRSTUVWXYZ&
abcdefghijklmnopqrstuvwxyz
1234567890$

Cochin Italic No. 611

18 point Cochin Italic No. 611 (Foundry)

ABCDEFGHIJKLMNOPQRSTUVWXYZ&
abcdefghijklmnopqrstuvwxyz
1234567890$

24 point Cochin Italic No. 611 (Foundry)

ABCDEFGHIJKLMNOPQRSTUVWXYZ&
abcdefghijklmnopqrstuvwxyz
1234567890$

36 point Cochin Italic No. 611 (Foundry)

ABCDEFGHIJKLMNOPQRS
TUVWXYZ&
abcdefghijklmnopqrstuvwxyz
1234567890$

Columbia

12 point Columbia (Foundry)

ABCDEFGHIJKLMNOPQRSTUVWXYZ&
abcdefghijklmnopqrstuvwxyz
1234567890$

14 point Columbia (Foundry)

ABCDEFGHIJKLMNOPQRSTUVWXYZ&
abcdefghijklmnopqrstuvwxyz
1234567890$

18 point Columbia (Foundry)

ABCDEFGHIJKLMNOPQRSTUVWXYZ&
abcdefghijklmnopqrstuvwxyz
1234567890$

24 point Columbia large (Foundry)

ABCDEFGHIJKLMNOPQRSTUVWXYZ&
abcdefghijklmnopqrstuvwxyz
1234567890$

Columbia Italic

18 point Columbia Italic (Foundry)

ABCDEFGHIJKLMNOPQRSTUVWXYZ&
abcdefghijklmnopqrstuvwxyz
1234567890$

Columna *(Also known as Contura)*

16 point Columna, Cap font (Foundry)

ABCDEFGHIJKLMNOPQRSTUVWXYZ&
1234567890$

28 point Columna, Cap font (Foundry)

ABCDEFGHIJKLMNOPQRST
UVWXYZ&
1234567890

(no dollar sign is made for this font)

36 point Columna, Cap font (Foundry)

ABCDEFGHIJKLMNOP
QRSTUVWXYZ&
1234567890

(no dollar sign is made for this font)

Commerce Gothic Light

6 point Commerce Gothic Light No. 1, Cap font (Ludlow)

ABCDEFGHIJKLMNOPQRSTUVWXYZ&　1234567890$

6 point Commerce Gothic Light No. 2, Cap font (Ludlow)

ABCDEFGHIJKLMNOPQRSTUVWXYZ&　1234567890$

6 point Commerce Gothic Light No. 3, Cap font (Ludlow)

ABCDEFGHIJKLMNOPQRSTUVWXYZ&　1234567890$

6 point Commerce Gothic Light No. 4, Cap font (Ludlow)

ABCDEFGHIJKLMNOPQRSTUVWXYZ&
1234567890$

12 point Commerce Gothic Light No.1, Cap font (Ludlow)

ABCDEFGHIJKLMNOPQRSTUVWXYZ&
1234567890$

12 point Commerce Gothic Light No. 2, Cap font (Ludlow)

ABCDEFGHIJKLMNOPQRSTUVWXYZ&
1234567890$

12 point Commerce Gothic Light No. 3, Cap font (Ludlow)

ABCDEFGHIJKLMNOPQRSTUV
WXYZ&　1234567890$

12 point Commerce Gothic Light No. 4, Cap font (Ludlow)

ABCDEFGHIJKLMNOPQRST
UVWXYZ&　1234567890$

Commercial Script

Comstock

12 point Comstock (Foundry)

ABCDEFGHIJKLMNOPQRSTUVWXYZ&
abcdefghijklmnopqrstuvwxyz
1234567890$

14 point Comstock (Foundry)

ABCDEFGHIJKLMNOPQRSTUVWXYZ&
abcdefghijklmnopqrstuvwxyz
1234567890$

18 point Comstock (Foundry)

ABCDEFGHIJKLMNOPQRSTUVWXYZ&
abcdefghijklmnopqrstuvwxyz
1234567890$

24 point Comstock (Foundry)

ABCDEFGHIJKLMNOPQRSTUVWXYZ&
abcdefghijklmnopqrstuvwxyz
1234567890$

30 point Comstock (Foundry)

ABCDEFGHIJKLMNOPQRST
UVWXYZ&
abcdefghijklmnopqrstuvwxyz
1234567890$

36 point Comstock (Foundry)

ABCDEFGHIJKLMNOPQ
RSTUVWXYZ&
abcdefghijklmnopqrstuv
wxyz
1234567890$

Cooper Black

12 point Cooper Black (Foundry)

ABCDEFGHIJKLMNOPQRSTUVWXYZ&
abcdefghijklmnopqrstuvwxyz
1234567890$

14 point Cooper Black (Foundry)

ABCDEFGHIJKLMNOPQRSTUVWXYZ&
abcdefghijklmnopqrstuvwxyz
1234567890$

18 point Cooper Black (Foundry)

ABCDEFGHIJKLMNOPQRSTUVWXYZ&
abcdefghijklmnopqrstuvwxyz
1234567890$

24 point Cooper Black (Foundry)

ABCDEFGHIJKLMNOPQRSTUVWXYZ
abcdefghijklmnopqrstuvwxyz&
1234567890$

30 point Cooper Black (Foundry)

ABCDEFGHIJKLMNOPQRST
UVWXYZ&
abcdefghijklmnopqrstuvwxyz
1234567890$

36 point Cooper Black (Foundry)

ABCDEFGHIJKLMNO
PQRSTUVWXYZ&
abcdefghijklmnopqrst
uvwxyz
1234567890$

(Continued on Page 146)

(Continued from Page 145)

48 point Cooper Black (Foundry)

ABCDEFGHIJKLM NOPQRSTUVW XYZ& abcdefghijklmno pqrstuvwxyz 1234567890$

Swash for Cooper Black and Cooper Black Italic

18 point

ABEFGMNPRY

24 point

ABDEFGMNPRTY

30 point

ABDEFGMNPRTY

36 point

ABDEFGMNPRTY

Cooper Black Italic

12 point Cooper Black Italic (Foundry)

ABCDEFGHIJKLMNOPQRSTUVWXYZ&
abcdefghijklmnopqrstuvwxyz
1234567890$

14 point Cooper Black Italic (Foundry)

ABCDEFGHIJKLMNOPQRSTUVWXYZ&
abcdefghijklmnopqrstuvwxyz
1234567890$

18 point Cooper Black Italic (Foundry)

ABCDEFGHIJKLMNOPQRSTUVWXYZ&
abcdefghijklmnopqrstuvwxyz
1234567890$

24 point Cooper Black Italic (Foundry)

ABCDEFGHIJKLMNOPQRSTUVWXYZ&
abcdefghijklmnopqrstuvwxyz
1234567890$

36 point Cooper Black Italic (Foundry)

ABCDEFGHIJKLMNO
PQRSTUVWXYZ&
abcdefghijklmnopqrstuv
wxyz
1234567890$

(Continued on Page 148)

Cooper Black Italic

(Continued from Page 147)

48 point Cooper Black Italic (Foundry)

ABCDEFGHIJKLM NOPQRSTUVWXYZ abcdefghijklmnopq rstuvwxyz& 1234567890$

(Continued on Page 149)

Copperplate Gothic Heavy Condensed

12 point Copperplate Gothic Heavy Condensed No. 15,
Cap font (Foundry)

ABCDEFGHIJKLMNOPQRSTUVWXYZ&
1234567890$

12 point Copperplate Gothic Heavy Condensed No. 17,
Cap font (Foundry)

ABCDEFGHIJKLMNOPQRSTUVWXYZ&
1234567890$

12 point Copperplate Gothic Heavy Condensed No. 16,
Cap font (Foundry)

ABCDEFGHIJKLMNOPQRSTUVWXYZ&
1234567890$

12 point Copperplate Gothic Heavy Condensed No. 18,
Cap font (Foundry)

ABCDEFGHIJKLMNOPQRSTUVWXYZ
&1234567890$

Copperplate Gothic Italic

12 point Copperplate Gothic Italic No. 58, Cap font (Foundry)

ABCDEFGHIJKLMNOPQRSTUVWXYZ& 1234567890$

18 point Copperplate Gothic Italic No. 59, Cap font (Foundry)

ABCDEFGHIJKLMNOPQRSTUVWXYZ&
1234567890$

18 point Copperplate Gothic Italic No. 60, Cap font (Foundry)

ABCDEFGHIJKLMNOPQRSTUVWXYZ&
1234567890$

72 point Cooper Black Italic (Foundry)

ABCDEFGHI
JKLMNOPQR
STUVWXYZ
abcdefghijkl
mnopqrstuv
wxyz&
1234567890$

Copperplate Gothic Light Extended

6 point Copperplate Gothic Light Extended No. 63, Cap font
ABCDEFGHIJKLMNOPQRSTUVWXYZ&   1234567890$

Copperplate Gothic Bold

12 point Copperplate Gothic Bold No. 46, Cap font (Foundry)

ABCDEFGHIJKLMNOPQRSTUVWXYZ& 1234567890$

12 point Copperplate Gothic Bold No. 48, Cap font (Foundry)

ABCDEFGHIJKLMNOPQRSTUVWXYZ& 1234567890$

24 point Copperplate Gothic Bold No. 50, Cap font (Foundry)

ABCDEFGHIJKLMNOPQRS TUVWXYZ& 1234567890$

Copperplate Gothic Heavy

12 point Copperplate Gothic Heavy No. 25, Cap font (Foundry)

ABCDEFGHIJKLMNOPQRSTUVWXYZ& 1234567890$

12 point Copperplate Gothic Heavy No. 26, Cap font (Foundry)

ABCDEFGHIJKLMNOPQRSTUVWXYZ& 1234567890$

12 point Copperplate Gothic Heavy No. 27, Cap font (Foundry)

ABCDEFGHIJKLMNOPQRSTUVWXYZ& 1234567890$

12 point Copperplate Gothic Heavy No. 28, Cap font (Foundry)

ABCDEFGHIJKLMNOPQRSTUVWXYZ& 1234567890$

18 point Copperplate Gothic Heavy No. 29, Cap font (Foundry)

ABCDEFGHIJKLMNOPQRSTUVWXYZ& 1234567890$

18 point Copperplate Gothic Heavy No. 30, Cap font (Foundry)

ABCDEFGHIJKLMNOPQRSTUVWXYZ& 1234567890$

24 point Copperplate Gothic Heavy No. 29, Cap font (Foundry)

ABCDEFGHIJKLMNOPQRSTUVWXYZ &1234567890$

24 point Copperplate Gothic Heavy No. 30, Cap font (Foundry)

ABCDEFGHIJKLMNOPQRST UVWXYZ& 1234567890$

Copperplate Gothic Heavy Extended

12 point Copperplate Gothic Heavy Extended No. 75,
Cap font (Foundry)

ABCDEFGHIJKLMNOPQRSTUV
WXYZ&
1234567890$

12 point Copperplate Gothic Heavy Extended No. 77,
Cap font (Foundry)

ABCDEFGHIJKLMNOPQ
RSTUVWXYZ&
1234567890$

12 point Copperplate Gothic Heavy Extended No. 76,
Cap font (Foundry)

ABCDEFGHIJKLMNOPQRSTU
VWXYZ&
1234567890$

12 point Copperplate Gothic Heavy Extended No. 78,
Cap font (Foundry)

ABCDEFGHIJKLMN
OPQRSTUVWXYZ&
1234567890$

18 point Copperplate Gothic Heavy Extended No. 79, Cap font (Foundry)

ABCDEFGHIJKLMNOPQRSTUVWXYZ&
1234567890$

18 point Copperplate Gothic Heavy Extended No. 80, Cap font (Foundry)

ABCDEFGHIJKLMNOPQRST
UVWXYZ&
1234567890$

24 point Copperplate Gothic Heavy Extended No. 79, Cap font (Foundry)

ABCDEFGHIJKLMNOPQRST
UVWXYZ&
1234567890$

24 point Copperplate Gothic Heavy Extended No. 80, Cap font (Foundry)

ABCDEFGHIJKLMNO
PQRSTUVWXYZ&
1234567890$

Copperplate Gothic Light Condensed

12 point Copperplate Gothic Light Condensed No. 36,
Cap font (Foundry)

ABCDEFGHIJKLMNOPQRSTUVWXYZ&
1234567890$

18 point Copperplate Gothic Light Condensed No. 39,
Cap font (Foundry)

ABCDEFGHIJKLMNOPQRST
UVWXYZ&
1234567890$

12 point Copperplate Gothic Light Condensed No. 37,
Cap font (Foundry)

ABCDEFGHIJKLMNOPQRSTUVWXYZ&
1234567890$

Copperplate Gothic Light

6 point Copperplate Gothic Light No. 1, Cap font (Foundry)

ABCDEFGHIJKLMNOPQRSTUVWXYZ&
1234567890$

18 point Copperplate Gothic Light No. 10, Cap font (Foundry)

ABCDEFGHIJKLMNOPQRSTUVWXYZ&
1234567890$

24 point Copperplate Gothic Light No. 10, Cap font (Foundry)

ABCDEFGHIJKLMNOPQRST
UVWXYZ&
1234567890$

Coronet Light

14 point Coronet Light (Ludlow)

ABCDEFGHIJKLMNOPQRSTUVWXYZ&
abcdefghijklmnopqrstuvwxyz
1234567890$

18 point Coronet Light (Ludlow)

ABCDEFGHIJKLMNOPQRSTUVWXYZ&
abcdefghijklmnopqrstuvwxyz
1234567890$

24 point Coronet Light (Ludlow)

ABCDEFGHIJKLMNOPQRSTUVWXYZ&
abcdefghijklmnopqrstuvwxyz
1234567890$

36 point Coronet Light (Ludlow)

ABCDEFGHIJKLMNOPQRSTUV
WXYZ&
abcdefghijklmnopqrstuvwxyz
1234567890$

Coronet Bold

14 point Coronet Bold (Ludlow)

ABCDEFGHIJKLMNOPQRSTUVWXYZ&
abcdefghijklmnopqrstuvwxyz
1234567890$

18 point Coronet Bold (Ludlow)

ABCDEFGHIJKLMNOPQRSTUVWXYZ&
abcdefghijklmnopqrstuvwxyz
1234567890$

24 point Coronet Bold (Ludlow)

ABCDEFGHIJKLMNOPQRSTUVWXYZ&
abcdefghijklmnopqrstuvwxyz
1234567890$

36 point Coronet Bold (Ludlow)

ABCDEFGHIJKLMNOPQRSTU
VWXYZ&
abcdefghijklmnopqrstuvwxyz
1234567890$

48 point Coronet Bold (Ludlow)

ABCDEFGHIJKLMNOP
QRSTUVWXYZ&
abcdefghijklmnopqrstuvwxyz
1234567890$

Corvinus Light

14 point Corvinus Light (Foundry)
ABCDEFGHIJKLMNOPQRSTUVWXYZ&
abcdefghijklmnopqrstuvwxyz
1234567890$

18 point Corvinus Light (Foundry)
ABCDEFGHIJKLMNOPQRSTUVWXYZ
abcdefghijklmnopqrstuvwxyz&
1234567890$

24 point Corvinus Light (Foundry)
ABCDEFGHIJKLMNOPQRSTUVWXYZ&
abcdefghijklmnopqrstuvwxyz
1234567890$

36 point Corvinus Light (Foundry)
ABCDEFGHIJKLMNOPQRST
UVWXYZ&
abcdefghijklmnopqrstuvwxyz
1234567890$

Corvinus Light Italic

12 point Corvinus Light Italic (Foundry)
ABCDEFGHIJKLMNOPQRSTUVWXYZ&
abcdefghijklmnopqrstuvwxyz
1234567890$
ALTERNATE LETTERS
A E G K M N Th v w

14 point Corvinus Light Italic (Foundry)
ABCDEFGHIJKLMNOPQRSTUVWXYZ&
abcdefghijklmnopqrstuvwxyz
1234567890$
ALTERNATE LETTERS
A E G K M N Th v w

16 point Corvinus Light Italic (Foundry)
ABCDEFGHIJKLMNOPQRSTUVWXYZ&
ALTERNATE LETTERS
abcdefghijklmnopqrstuvwxyz   1234567890$
A E G K M N Th v w

30 point Corvinus Light Italic (Foundry)
ABCDEFGHIJKLMNOPQRSTUVWXYZ&
abcdefghijklmnopqrstuvwxyz   1234567890$
ALTERNATE LETTERS
A E G K M N Th v w

Corvinus Medium

8 point Corvinus Medium (Foundry)
ABCDEFGHIJKLMNOPQRSTUVWXYZ&
abcdefghijklmnopqrstuvwxyz
1234567890$

12 point Corvinus Medium (Foundry)
ABCDEFGHIJKLMNOPQRSTUVWXYZ&
abcdefghijklmnopqrstuvwxyz
1234567890$

10 point Corvinus Medium (Foundry)
ABCDEFGHIJKLMNOPQRSTUVWXYZ&
abcdefghijklmnopqrstuvwxyz
1234567890$

14 point Corvinus Medium (Foundry)
ABCDEFGHIJKLMNOPQRSTUVWXYZ&
abcdefghijklmnopqrstuvwxyz
1234567890$

18 point Corvinus Medium (Foundry)
ABCDEFGHIJKLMNOPQRSTUVWXYZ&
abcdefghijklmnopqrstuvwxyz
1234567890$

24 point Corvinus Medium (Foundry)
ABCDEFGHIJKLMNOPQRSTUVWXYZ&
abcdefghijklmnopqrstuvwxyz
1234567890$

30 point Corvinus Medium (Foundry)
ABCDEFGHIJKLMNOPQRSTUVWXYZ&
abcdefghijklmnopqrstuvwxyz
1234567890$

36 point Corvinus Medium (Foundry)
ABCDEFGHIJKLMNOPQRST
UVWXYZ&
abcdefghijklmnopqrstuvwxyz
1234567890$

(Continued on Page 156)

(Continued from Page 155)

48 point Corvinus Medium (Foundry)

ABCDEFGHIJKLMNO
PQRSTUVWXYZ&
abcdefghijklmnopqrstuv
wxyz
1234567890$

60 point Corvinus Medium (Foundry)

ABCDEFHGIJKLMN
OPQRSTUVWXYZ&
abcdefghijklmnopq
rstuvwxyz
1234567890$

Corvinus Medium Italic

ABCDEFGHIJKLMNOPQRSTUVWXYZ&
abcdefghijklmnopqrstuvwxyz
1234567890$

ALTERNATE LETTERS

A E G K M N Th v w

ABCDEFGHIJKLMNOPQRSTUVWXYZ&
abcdefghijklmnopqrstuvwxyz
1234567890$

ALTERNATE LETTERS

A E G K M N Th v w

ABCDEFGHIJKLMNOPQRSTUVWXYZ&
abcdefghijklmnopqrstuvwxyz
1234567890$

ALTERNATE LETTERS

A E G K M N Th v w

ABCDEFGHIJKLMNOPQRSTUVWXYZ&
abcdefghijklmnopqrstuvwxyz
1234567890$

ALTERNATE LETTERS

A E G K M N Th v w

ABCDEFGHIJKLMNOPQRSTUV
WXYZ&
abcdefghijklmnopqrstuvwxyz
1234567890$

ALTERNATE LETTERS

A E G K M N Th v w

(Continued on Page 158)

48 point Corvinus Medium Italic (Foundry)

ABCDEFGHIJKLMNOPQRS
TUVWXYZ&
abcdefghijklmnopqrstuv
wxyz
1234567890$

ALTERNATE LETTERS

A E G K M N Th v w

Corvinus Bold

12 point Corvinus Bold (Foundry)
ABCDEFGHIJKLMNOPQRSTUVWXYZ&
abcdefghijklmnopqrstuvwxyz
1234567890$

14 point Corvinus Bold (Foundry)
ABCDEFGHIJKLMNOPQRSTUVWXYZ&
abcdefghijklmnopqrstuvwxyz
1234567890$

18 point Corvinus Bold (Foundry)
ABCDEFGHIJKLMNOPQRSTUVWXYZ&
abcdefghijklmnopqrstuvwxyz
1234567890$

24 point Corvinus Bold (Foundry)
ABCDEFGHIJKLMNOPQRSTUVWXYZ&
abcdefghijklmnopqrstuvwxyz
1234567890$

30 point Corvinus Bold (Foundry)
ABCDEFGHIJKLMNOPQRSTUVWXYZ&
abcdefghijklmnopqrstuvwxyz
1234567890$

36 point Corvinus Bold (Foundry)
ABCDEFGHIJKLMNOPQRST
UVWXYZ&
abcdefghijklmnopqrstuvwxyz
1234567890$

Craw Clarendon

8 point Craw Clarendon (Foundry)
ABCDEFGHIJKLMNOPQRSTUVWXYZ&
abcdefghijklmnopqrstuvwxyz
1234567890$

10 point Craw Clarendon (Foundry)
ABCDEFGHIJKLMNOPQRSTUVWXYZ&
abcdefghijklmnopqrstuvwxyz
1234567890$

12 point Craw Clarendon (Foundry)
ABCDEFGHIJKLMNOPQRSTUVWXYZ&
abcdefghijklmnopqrstuvwxyz
1234567890$

14 point Craw Clarendon (Foundry)
ABCDEFGHIJKLMNOPQRSTUVWXYZ&
abcdefghijklmnopqrstuvwxyz
1234567890$

18 point Craw Clarendon (Foundry)
ABCDEFGHIJKLMNOPQRSTUVWXYZ&
abcdefghijklmnopqrstuvwxyz
1234567890$

24 point Craw Clarendon (Foundry)
ABCDEFGHIJKLMNOPQRSTUVWXYZ
abcdefghijklmnopqrstuvwxyz&
1234567890$

30 point Craw Clarendon (Foundry)
ABCDEFGHIJKLMNOPQRST
UVWXYZ&
abcdefghijklmnopqrstuvwxyz
1234567890$

36 point Craw Clarendon (Foundry)
ABCDEFGHIJKLMNOPQR
STUVWXYZ&
abcdefghijklmnopqrst
uvwxyz
1234567890$

(Continued on Page 161)

(Continued from Page 160)

48 point Craw Clarendon (Foundry)

ABCDEFGHIJKLMN
OPQRSTUVWXYZ&
abcdefghijklmnopqrs
tuvwxyz
1234567890$

60 point Craw Clarendon (Foundry)

ABCDEFGHIJK
LMNOPQRSTUV
WXYZ&
abcdefghijklmno
pqrstuvwxyz
1234567890$

(Continued on Page 162)

(Continued from Page 161)

72 point Craw Clarendon (Foundry)

ABCDEFGHI
JKLMNOPQR
STUVWXYZ&
abcdefghijk
lmnopqrstuv
wxyz
1234567890$

Craw Clarendon Book

8 point Craw Clarendon Book (Foundry)
ABCDEFGHIJKLMNOPQRSTUVWXYZ&
abcdefghijklmnopqrstuvwxyz
1234567890$

10 point Craw Clarendon Book (Foundry)
ABCDEFGHIJKLMNOPQRSTUVWXYZ&
abcdefghijklmnopqrstuvwxyz
1234567890$

14 point Craw Clarendon Book (Foundry)
ABCDEFGHIJKLMNOPQRSTUVWXYZ&
abcdefghijklmnopqrstuvwxyz
1234567890$

18 point Craw Clarendon Book (Foundry)
ABCDEFGHIJKLMNOPQRSTUVWXYZ&
abcdefghijklmnopqrstuvwxyz
1234567890$

24 point Craw Clarendon Book (Foundry)
ABCDEFGHIJKLMNOPQRSTUVWXYZ&
abcdefghijklmnopqrstuvwxyz
1234567890$

30 point Craw Clarendon Book (Foundry)
ABCDEFGHIJKLMNOPQRST
UVWXYZ&
abcdefghijklmnopqrstuvwxyz
1234567890$

36 point Craw Clarendon Book (Foundry)
ABCDEFGHIJKLMNOPQ
RSTUVWXYZ&
abcdefghijklmnopqrst
uvwxyz
1234567890$

(Continued on Page 164)

48 point Craw Clarendon Book (Foundry)

ABCDEFGHIJKLMN
OPQRSTUVWXYZ&
abcdefghijklmnopqrs
tuvwxyz
1234567890$

60 point Craw Clarendon Book (Foundry)

ABCDEFGHIJKL
MNOPQRSTUV
WXYZ&
abcdefghijklmno
pqrstuvwxyz
1234567890$

Craw Clarendon Condensed

30 point Craw Clarendon Condensed (Foundry)

ABCDEFGHIJKLMNOPQRSTUVWXYZ&
abcdefghijklmnopqrstuvwxyz
1234567890$

48 point Craw Clarendon Condensed (Foundry)

ABCDEFGHIJKLMNOPQRSTUV
WXYZ&
abcdefghijklmnopqrstuvwxyz
1234567890$

72 point Craw Clarendon Condensed (Foundry)

ABCDEFGHIJKLMNO
PQRSTUVWXYZ& ab
cdefghijklmnopqrst
uvwxyz1234567890$

10 point Craw Modern (Foundry)
ABCDEFGHIJKLMNOPQRSTUVWXYZ&
abcdefghijklmnopqrstuvwxyz   1234567890$

12 point Craw Modern (Foundry)
ABCDEFGHIJKLMNOPQRSTUVWXYZ&
abcdefghijklmnopqrstuvwxyz   1234567890$

14 point Craw Modern (Foundry)
ABCDEFGHIJKLMNOPQRSTUVWXYZ&
abcdefghijklmnopqrstuvwxyz   1234567890$

18 point Craw Modern (Foundry)
ABCDEFGHIJKLMNOPQRSTUVWXYZ&
abcdefghijklmnopqrstuvwxyz 1234567890$

24 point Craw Modern (Foundry)
ABCDEFGHIJKLMNOPQRST
UVWXYZ&
abcdefghijklmnopqrstuvwxyz
1234567890$

30 point Craw Modern (Foundry)
ABCDEFGHIJKLMNOP
QRSTUVWXYZ&
abcdefghijklmnopqrstuv
wxyz
1234567890$

36 point Craw Modern (Foundry)
ABCDEFGHIJKLMN
OPQRSTUVWXYZ&
abcdefghijklmnopqrs
tuvwxyz
1234567890$

Craw Modern Bold

10 point Craw Modern Bold (Foundry)

ABCDEFGHIJKLMNOPQRSTUVWXYZ&
abcdefghijklmnopqrstuvwxyz
1234567890$

12 point Craw Modern Bold (Foundry)

ABCDEFGHIJKLMNOPQRSTUVWXYZ&
abcdefghijklmnopqrstuvwxyz
1234567890$

14 point Craw Modern Bold (Foundry)

ABCDEFGHIJKLMNOPQRSTUVWXYZ&
abcdefghijklmnopqrstuvwxyz
1234567890$

18 point Craw Modern Bold (Foundry)

ABCDEFGHIJKLMNOPQRSTUVWXYZ&
abcdefghijklmnopqrstuvwxyz
1234567890$

24 point Craw Modern Bold (Foundry)

ABCDEFGHIJKLMNOPQRST
UVWXYZ&
abcdefghijklmnopqrstuv
wxyz
1234567890$

30 point Craw Modern Bold (Foundry)

ABCDEFGHIJKLMNOP
QRSTUVWXYZ&
abcdefghijklmnopqrs
tuvwxyz
1234567890$

(Continued on Page 168)

36 point Craw Modern Bold (Foundry)

ABCDEFGHIJKLMN
OPQRSTUVWXYZ&
abcdefghijklmno
pqrstuvwxyz
1234567890$

48 point Craw Modern Bold (Foundry)

ABCDEFGHIJ
KLMNOPQRS
TUVWXYZ&
abcdefghijkl
mnopqrstu
vwxyz
1234567890$

Deepdene Roman

12 point Deepdene Roman (Foundry)
ABCDEFGHIJKLMNOPQRSTUVWXYZ&
abcdefghijklmnopqrstuvwxyz
1234567890$

14 point Deepdene Roman (Foundry)
ABCDEFGHIJKLMNOPQRSTUVWXYZ&
abcdefghijklmnopqrstuvwxyz
1234567890$

16 point Deepdene Roman (Foundry)
ABCDEFGHIJKLMNOPQRSTUVWXYZ&
abcdefghijklmnopqrstuvwxyz
1234567890$

18 point Deepdene Roman (Foundry)
ABCDEFGHIJKLMNOPQRSTUVWXYZ&
abcdefghijklmnopqrstuvwxyz
1234567890$

24 point Deepdene Roman (Foundry)
ABCDEFGHIJKLMNOPQRSTUVWXYZ&
abcdefghijklmnopqrstuvwxyz
1234567890$

30 point Deepdene Roman (Foundry)
ABCDEFGHIJKLMNOPQRSTUVWXYZ&
abcdefghijklmnopqrstuvwxyz
1234567890$

36 point Deepdene Roman (Foundry)
ABCDEFGHIJKLMNOPQRSTUV
WXYZ&
abcdefghijklmnopqrstuvwxyz
1234567890$

(Continued on Page 170)

48 point Deepdene Roman (Foundry)

ABCDEFGHIJKLMNOPQRS
TUVWXYZ&
abcdefghijklmnopqrstuvwxyz
1234567890$

60 point Deepdene Roman (Foundry)

ABCDEFGHIJKLMN
OPQRSTUVWXYZ&
abcdefghijklmnopqrstuv
wxyz
1234567890$

Deepdene Italic *(Font contains some Alternate Characters)*

12 point Deepdene Italic (Foundry)
ABCDEFGHIJKLMNOPQRSTUVWXYZ&
abcdefghijklmnopqrstuvwxyz
1234567890$

14 point Deepdene Italic (Foundry)
ABCDEFGHIJKLMNOPQRSTUVWXYZ&
abcdefghijklmnopqrstuvwxyz
1234567890$

18 point Deepdene Italic (Foundry)
ABCDEFGHIJKLMNOPQRSTUVWXYZ&
abcdefghijklmnopqrstuvwxyz
1234567890$

24 point Deepdene Italic (Foundry)
ABCDEFGHIJKLMNOPQRSTUVWXYZ&
abcdefghijklmnopqrstuvwxyz
1234567890$

30 point Deepdene Italic (Foundry)
ABCDEFGHIJKLMNOPQRSTUVWXYZ&
abcdefghijklmnopqrstuvwxyz
1234567890$

36 point Deepdene Italic (Foundry)
ABCDEFGHIJKLMNOPQRSTUV
WXYZ&
abcdefghijklmnopqrstuvwxyz
1234567890$

(Continued on Page 172)

(Continued from Page 171)

48 point Deepdene Italic (Foundry)

ABCDEFGHIJKLMNOPQRST
UVWXYZ&
abcdefghijklmnopqrstuvwxyz
1234567890$

Delphian Open Title

24 point Delphian Open Title, Cap font (Ludlow)

ABCDEFGHIJKLMNOPQRSTUVWXYZ&
1234567890$

36 point Delphian Open Title, Cap font (Ludlow)

ABCDEFGHIJKLMNOPQRSTU
VWXYZ&
1234567890$

48 point Delphian Open Title, Cap font (Foundry)

ABCDEFGHIJKLMNO
PQRSTUVWXYZ&
1234567890$

Delphin II

10 point Delphin II (Foundry)

ABCDEFGHIJKLMNOPQRSTUVWXYZ&
abcdefghijklmnopqrstuvwxyz
1234567890$

14 point Delphin II (Foundry)

ABCDEFGHIJKLMNOPQRSTUVWXYZ&
abcdefghijklmnopqrstuvwxyz
1234567890$

20 point Delphin II (Foundry)

ABCDEFGHIJKLMNOPQRSTUVWXYZ&
abcdefghijklmnopqrstuvwxyz
1234567890$

48 point Delphin II (Foundry)

ABCDEFGHIJKLMNOPQRST
UVWXYZ&
abcdefghijklmnopqrstuvwxyz
1234567890$

Dom Bold

18 point Dom Bold (Foundry)

ABCDEFGHIJKLMNOPQRSTUVWXYZ&
abcdefghijklmnopqrstuvwxyz
1234567890$

24 point Dom Bold (Foundry)

ABCDEFGHIJKLMNOPQRSTUVWXYZ&
abcdefghijklmnopqrstuvwxyz
1234567890$

30 point Dom Bold (Foundry)

ABCDEFGHIJKLMNOPQRSTUVWXYZ&
abcdefghijklmnopqrstuvwxyz
1234567890$

36 point Dom Bold (Foundry)

ABCDEFGHIJKLMNOPQRSTUVWXYZ&
abcdefghijklmnopqrstuvwxyz
1234567890$

48 point Dom Bold (Foundry)

ABCDEFGHIJKLMNOPQRSTUV
WXYZ&
abcdefghijklmnopqrstuvwxyz
1234567890$

(Continued on Page 175)

(Continued from Page 174)

60 point Dom Bold (Foundry)

ABCDEFGHIJKLMNOPQRST
UVWXYZ&
abcdefghijklmnopqrstuvwxyz
1234567890$

72 point Dom Bold (Foundry)

ABCDEFGHIJKLMNOPQ
RSTUVWXYZ&
abcdefghijklmnopqrstuv
wxyz
1234567890$

Dom Casual

18 point Dom Casual (Foundry)

ABCDEFGHIJKLMNOPQRSTUVWXYZ&
abcdefghijklmnopqrstuvwxyz
1234567890$

24 point Dom Casual (Foundry)

ABCDEFGHIJKLMNOPQRSTUVWXYZ&
abcdefghijklmnopqrstuvwxyz
1234567890$

30 point Dom Casual (Foundry)

ABCDEFGHIJKLMNOPQRSTUVWXYZ&
abcdefghijklmnopqrstuvwxyz
1234567890$

36 point Dom Casual (Foundry)

ABCDEFGHIJKLMNOPQRSTUVWXYZ&
abcdefghijklmnopqrstuvwxyz
1234567890$

48 point Dom Casual (Foundry)

ABCDEFGHIJKLMNOPQRSTUVWXYZ
abcdefghijklmnopqrstuvwxyz&
1234567890$

(Continued on Page 177)

60 point Dom Casual (Foundry)

ABCDEFGHIJKLMNOPQRSTU
VWXYZ&
abcdefghijklmnopqrstuvwxyz
1234567890$

72 point Dom Casual (Foundry)

ABCDEFGHIJKLMNOPQ
RSTUVWXYZ&
abcdefghijklmnopqrstuvwxyz
1234567890$

Dom Diagonal

ABCDEFGHIJKLMNOPQRSTUVWXYZ&
abcdefghijklmnopqrstuvwxyz
1234567890$

ABCDEFGHIJKLMNOPQRSTUVWXYZ&
abcdefghijklmnopqrstuvwxyz
1234567890$

ABCDEFGHIJKLMNOPQRSTUVWXYZ&
abcdefghijklmnopqrstuvwxyz
1234567890$

ABCDEFGHIJKLMNOPQRSTUVWXYZ&
abcdefghijklmnopqrstuvwxyz
1234567890$

ABCDEFGHIJKLMNOPQRSTUVWXYZ
abcdefghijklmnopqrstuvwxyz&
1234567890$

(Continued on Page 179)

60 point Dom Diagonal (Foundry)

ABCDEFGHIJKLMNOPQRST
UVWXYZ&
abcdefghijklmnopqrstuvwxyz
1234567890$

72 point Dom Diagonal (Foundry)

ABCDEFGHIJKLMNOPQ
RSTUVWXYZ&
abcdefghijklmnopqrstuv
wxyz
1234567890$

Dominante Roman *(Must be leaded 1 point)*

8 point Dominante Roman (Linotype)
The basic character in a type design is determined by the uni form design characteristics of all letters in the alphabet. How ever, this alone does not determine the standard of the type face and the quality of composition set with it. The appearance is something complex which forms itself out of many details, like form, proportion, ductus, rhythm etc. If everything har

ABCDEFGHIJKLMNOPQRSTUVWXYZ&
abcdefghijklmnopqrstuvwxyz 1234567890$

9 point Dominante Roman (Linotype)
The basic character in a type design is determined by the uniform design characteristics of all letters in the alphabet. However, this alone does not determine the standard of the type face and the quality of composition set with it. The appearance is something complex which

ABCDEFGHIJKLMNOPQRSTUVWXYZ&
abcdefghijklmnopqrstuvwxyz 1234567890$

14 point Dominante Roman (Foundry)
ABCDEFGHIJKLMNOPQRSTUVWXYZ&
abcdefghijklmnopqrstuvwxyz
1234567890$

28 point Dominante Roman (Foundry)
ABCDEFGHIJKLMNOPQRSTUVWXYZ
abcdefghijklmnopqrstuvwxyz&
1234567890$

Dominante Bold *(Must be leaded 1 point)*

8 point Dominante Bold (Linotype)
The basic character in a type design is determined by the uni form design characteristics of all letters in the alphabet. How ever, this alone does not determine the standard of the type face and the quality of composition set with it. The appearance is something complex which forms itself out of many details, like form, proportion, ductus, rhythm etc. If everything har

ABCDEFGHIJKLMNOPQRSTUVWXYZ&
abcdefghijklmnopqrstuvwxyz 1234567890$

9 point Dominante Bold (Linotype)
The basic character in a type design is determined by the uniform design characteristics of all letters in the alphabet. However, this alone does not determine the standard of the type face and the quality of composition set with it. The appearance is something complex which

ABCDEFGHIJKLMNOPQRSTUVWXYZ&
abcdefghijklmnopqrstuvwxyz 1234567890$

Dominante Italic

ABCDEFGHIJKLMNOPQRSTUVWXYZ&
abcdefghijklmnopqrstuvwxyz
1234567890$

ABCDEFGHIJKLMNOPQRSTUVWXYZ
abcdefghijklmnopqrstuvwxyz&
1234567890$

Dominus

ABCDEFGHIJKLMN
OPQRSTUVWXYZ&
abcdefghijklmnopqrst
uvwxyz
1234567890$

Eden Light

12 point Eden Light (Ludlow)
ABCDEFGHIJKLMNOPQRSTUVWXYZ&   abcdefghijklmnopqrstuvwxyz   1234567890$

18 point Eden Light (Ludlow)
ABCDEFGHIJKLMNOPQRSTUVWXYZ&
abcdefghijklmnopqrstuvwxyz   1234567890$

24 point Eden Light (Ludlow)
ABCDEFGHIJKLMNOPQRSTUVWXYZ&
abcdefghijklmnopqrstuvwxyz   1234567890$

36 point Eden Light (Ludlow)
ABCDEFGHIJKLMNOPQRSTUVWXYZ&
abcdefghijklmnopqrstuvwxyz
1234567890$

Eden Bold

18 point Eden Bold (Ludlow)
ABCDEFGHIJKLMNOPQRSTUVWXYZ&
abcdefghijklmnopqrstuvwxyz   1234567890$

24 point Eden Bold (Ludlow)
ABCDEFGHIJKLMNOPQRSTUVWXYZ&
abcdefghijklmnopqrstuvwxyz   1234567890$

36 point Eden Bold (Ludlow)
ABCDEFGHIJKLMNOPQRSTUVWXYZ
abcdefghijklmnopqrstuvwxyz&
1234567890$

Egmont Medium

18 point Egmont Medium (Foundry)

ABCDEFGHIJKLMNOPQRSTUVWXYZ&
abcdefghijklmnopqrstuvwxyz
1234567890$

24 point Egmont Medium (Foundry)

ABCDEFGHIJKLMNOPQRSTUVWXYZ&
abcdefghijklmnopqrstuvwxyz
1234567890$

30 point Egmont Medium small (Foundry)

ABCDEFGHIJKLMNOPQRSTUVWXYZ&
abcdefghijklmnopqrstuvwxyz
1234567890$

30 point Egmont Medium large (Foundry)

ABCDEFGHIJKLMNOPQRSTUV
WXYZ&
abcdefghijklmnopqrstuvwxyz
1234567890$

36 point Egmont Medium (Foundry)

ABCDEFGHIJKLMNOPQRST
UVWXYZ&
abcdefghijklmnopqrstuvwxyz
1234567890$

18 point Egmont Medium Italic (Foundry)

ABCDEFGHIJKLMNOPQRSTUVWXYZ&
abcdefghijklmnopqrstuvwxyz
1234567890$

24 point Egmont Medium Italic (Foundry)

ABCDEFGHIJKLMNOPQRSTUVWXYZ&
abcdefghijklmnopqrstuvwxyz
1234567890$

30 point Egmont Medium Italic small (Foundry)

ABCDEFGHIJKLMNOPQRSTUVWXYZ&
abcdefghijklmnopqrstuvwxyz
1234567890$

30 point Egmont Medium Italic large (Foundry)

ABCDEFGHIJKLMNOPQRSTUV
WXYZ&
abcdefghijklmnopqrstuvwxyz
1234567890$

36 point Egmont Medium Italic (Foundry)

ABCDEFGHIJKLMNOPQRST
UVWXYZ&
abcdefghijklmnopqrstuvwxyz
1234567890$

Egyptian Bold Condensed

18 point Egyptian Bold Condensed (Foundry)

ABCDEFGHIJKLMNOPQRSTUVWXYZ&
abcdefghijklmnopqrstuvwxyz
1234567890$

24 point Egyptian Bold Condensed (Foundry)

ABCDEFGHIJKLMNOPQRSTUVWXYZ&
abcdefghijklmnopqrstuvwxyz
1234567890$

30 point Egyptian Bold Condensed (Foundry)

ABCDEFGHIJKLMNOPQRSTUVWXYZ&
abcdefghijklmnopqrstuvwxyz
1234567890$

36 point Egyptian Bold Condensed (Foundry)

ABCDEFGHIJKLMNOPQRSTUVWXYZ&
abcdefghijklmnopqrstuvwxyz
1234567890$

48 point Egyptian Bold Condensed (Foundry)

ABCDEFGHIJKLMNOPQRSTUV
WXYZ&
abcdefghijklmnopqrstuvwxyz
1234567890$

Egyptian Expanded

36 point Egyptian Expanded

ABCDEFG
HIJKLMN
OPQRSTU
VWXYZ&
abcdefghijk
lmnopqrst
uvwxyz123
4567890$

Electra Bold

8 point Electra Bold (Linotype)

The basic character in a type design is determined by the uniform design characteristics of all letters in the alphabet. However, this alone does not determine the standard of the type face and the quality of composition set with it. The appearance is something complex which forms itself out of many details, like form, pro

ABCDEFGHIJKLMNOPQRSTUVWXYZ&
abcdefghijklmnopqrstuvwxyz   1234567890$
ABCDEFGHIJKLMNOPQRSTUVWXYZ

9 point Electra Bold (Linotype)

The basic character in a type design is determined by the uniform design characteristics of all letters in the alphabet. However, this alone does not determine the standard of the type face and the quality of composition set with it. The

ABCDEFGHIJKLMNOPQRSTUVWXYZ&
abcdefghijklmnopqrstuvwxyz   1234567890$
ABCDEFGHIJKLMNOPQRSTUVWXYZ

10 point Electra Bold (Linotype)

The basic character in a type design is determined by the uniform design characteristics of all letters in the alpha bet. However, this alone does not determine the standard of the type face and the quality of composition set with

ABCDEFGHIJKLMNOPQRSTUVWXYZ&
abcdefghijklmnopqrstuvwxyz   1234567890$
ABCDEFGHIJKLMNOPQRSTUVWXYZ

11 point Electra Bold (Linotype)

The basic character in a type design is determined by the uniform design characteristics of all letters in the alphabet. However, this alone does not determine the

ABCDEFGHIJKLMNOPQRSTUVWXYZ&
abcdefghijklmnopqrstuvwxyz   1234567890$
ABCDEFGHIJKLMNOPQRSTUVWXYZ

12 point Electra Bold (Linotype)

The basic character in a type design is determined by the uniform design characteristics of all letters

ABCDEFGHIJKLMNOPQRSTUVWXYZ&
abcdefghijklmnopqrstuvwxyz   1234567890$
ABCDEFGHIJKLMNOPQRSTUVWXYZ

14 point Electra Bold (Linotype)

The basic character in a type design is deter mined by the uniform design characteristics

ABCDEFGHIJKLMNOPQRSTU
VWXYZ&   1234567890$
abcdefghijklmnopqrstuvwxyz
ABCDEFGHIJKLMNOPQRSTUVWXYZ

Electra
(Long descenders set 1 point leaded)

7 point Electra (Linotype)
The basic character in a type design is determined by the uniform design characteristics of all letters in the alphabet. However, this alone does not determine the standard of the type face and the quality of composition set with it. The appearance is something complex which forms itself out

ABCDEFGHIJKLMNOPQRSTUVWXYZ&
abcdefghijklmnopqrstuvwxyz   1234567890$
ABCDEFGHIJKLMNOPQRSTUVWXYZ

8 point Electra (Linotype)
The basic character in a type design is determined by the uniform design characteristics of all letters in the alphabet. However, this alone does not determine the standard of the type face and the quality of composition set with it. The appearance is something

ABCDEFGHIJKLMNOPQRSTUVWXYZ&
abcdefghijklmnopqrstuvwxyz   1234567890$
ABCDEFGHIJKLMNOPQRSTUVWXYZ

9 point Electra (Linotype)
The basic character in a type design is determined by the uniform design characteristics of all letters in the alphabet. However, this alone does not determine the standard of the

ABCDEFGHIJKLMNOPQRSTUVWXYZ&
abcdefghijklmnopqrstuvwxyz   1234567890$
ABCDEFGHIJKLMNOPQRSTUVWXYZ

10 point Electra (Linotype)
The basic character in a type design is determined by the uniform design characteristics of all letters in the alphabet. However, this alone does not determine the standard of the type face and the quality of composition set with it.

ABCDEFGHIJKLMNOPQRSTUVWXYZ&
abcdefghijklmnopqrstuvwxyz   1234567890$
ABCDEFGHIJKLMNOPQRSTUVWXYZ

11 point Electra (Linotype)
The basic character in a type design is determined by the uniform design characteristics of all letters in the alphabet. However, this alone does not determine the

ABCDEFGHIJKLMNOPQRSTUVWXYZ&
abcdefghijklmnopqrstuvwxyz   1234567890$
ABCDEFGHIJKLMNOPQRSTUVWXYZ

12 point Electra (Linotype)
The basic character in a type design is determined by the uniform design characteristics of all letters in the alphabet. However, this alone does not de

ABCDEFGHIJKLMNOPQRSTUVWXYZ&
abcdefghijklmnopqrstuvwxyz   1234567890$
ABCDEFGHIJKLMNOPQRSTUVWXYZ

14 point Electra (Linotype)
The basic character in a type design is deter mined by the uniform design characteristics of

ABCDEFGHIJKLMNOPQRSTU
VWXYZ&   1234567890$
abcdefghijklmnopqrstuvwxyz
ABCDEFGHIJKLMNOPQRSTUVWXYZ

Electra Italic
(Long descenders set 1 point leaded)

7 point Electra Italic (Linotype)
The basic character in a type design is determined by the uniform design characteristics of all letters in the alphabet. However, this alone does not determine the standard of the type face and the quality of composition set with it. The appearance is something complex which forms itself out of many details, like form, proportion, ductus, rhythm etc. If everything

ABCDEFGHIJKLMNOPQRSTUVWXYZ&
abcdefghijklmnopqrstuvwxyz   1234567890$

8 point Electra Italic (Linotype)
The basic character in a type design is determined by the uniform design characteristics of all letters in the alphabet. However, this alone does not determine the standard of the type face and the quality of composition set with it. The appearance is something

ABCDEFGHIJKLMNOPQRSTUVWXYZ&
abcdefghijklmnopqrstuvwxyz   1234567890$

9 point Electra Italic (Linotype)
The basic character in a type design is determined by the uniform design characteristics of all letters in the alphabet. However, this alone does not determine the standard of the type face and the quality of composition set with it. The ap

ABCDEFGHIJKLMNOPQRSTUVWXYZ&
abcdefghijklmnopqrstuvwxyz   1234567890$

10 point Electra Italic (Linotype)
The basic character in a type design is determined by the uniform design characteristics of all letters in the alphabet. However, this alone does not determine the standard of the type face and the quality of composition set with it. The appearance is something complex which forms itself

ABCDEFGHIJKLMNOPQRSTUVWXYZ&
abcdefghijklmnopqrstuvwxyz   1234567890$

11 point Electra Italic (Linotype)
The basic character in a type design is determined by the uniform design characteristics of all letters in the alphabet. However, this alone does not determine the standard of the type face and the quality of composi

ABCDEFGHIJKLMNOPQRSTUVWXYZ&
abcdefghijklmnopqrstuvwxyz   1234567890$

12 point Electra Italic (Linotype)
The basic character in a type design is determined by the uniform design characteristics of all letters in the alphabet. However, this alone does not de termine the standard of the type face and the qual

ABCDEFGHIJKLMNOPQRSTUVWXYZ&
abcdefghijklmnopqrstuvwxyz   1234567890$

14 point Electra Italic (Linotype)
The basic character in a type design is deter mined by the uniform design characteristics of all letters in the alphabet. However, this alone

ABCDEFGHIJKLMNOPQRSTU
VWXYZ&   1234567890$
abcdefghijklmnopqrstuvwxyz

Electra Cursive *(Long descenders set 1 point leaded)*

8 point Electra Cursive (Linotype)

The basic character in a type design is determined by the uniform design characteristics of all letters in the alphabet. However, this alone does not determine the standard of the type face and the quality of composition set with it. The appearance is something complex which forms itself out of many details, like form, propor tion, rhythm etc. If everything harmonizes, the total result will be

ABCDEFGHIJKLMNOPQRSTUVWXYZ&
abcdefghijklmnopqrstuvwxyz   1234567890$

9 point Electra Cursive (Linotype)

The basic character in a type design is determined by the uniform design characteristics of all letters in the alphabet. However, this alone does not determine the standard of the type face and the quality of composition set with it. The ap pearance is something complex which forms itself out of

ABCDEFGHIJKLMNOPQRSTUVWXYZ&
abcdefghijklmnopqrstuvwxyz   1234567890$

10 point Electra Cursive (Linotype)

The basic character in a type design is determined by the uniform design characteristics of all letters in the alpha bet. However, this alone does not determine the standard of the type face and the quality of composition set with it. The appearance is something complex which forms

ABCDEFGHIJKLMNOPQRSTUVWXYZ&
abcdefghijklmnopqrstuvwxyz   1234567890$

11 point Electra Cursive (Linotype)

The basic character in a type design is determined by the uniform design characteristics of all letters in the al phabet. However, this alone does not determine the standard of the type face and the quality of composi

ABCDEFGHIJKLMNOPQRSTUVWXYZ&
abcdefghijklmnopqrstuvwxyz   1234567890$

12 point Electra Cursive (Linotype)

The basic character in a type design is determined by the uniform design characteristics of all letters in the alphabet. However, this alone does not de termine the standard of the type face and the quality

ABCDEFGHIJKLMNOPQRSTUVWXYZ&
abcdefghijklmnopqrstuvwxyz   1234567890$

14 point Electra Cursive (Linotype)

The basic character in a type design is deter mined by the uniform design characteristics of all letters in the alphabet. However, this

ABCDEFGHIJKLMNOPQRSTU
VWXYZ&   1234567890$
abcdefghijklmnopqrstuvwxyz

Electra Bold Cursive *(Long descenders set 1 point leaded)*

8 point Electra Bold Cursive (Linotype)

The basic character in a type design is determined by the uniform design characteristics of all letters in the alphabet. However, this alone does not determine the standard of the type face and the quality of composition set with it. The appearance is something complex which forms itself out of many details, like form, pro portion, ductus, rhythm etc. If everything harmonizes, the total

ABCDEFGHIJKLMNOPQRSTUVWXYZ&
abcdefghijklmnopqrstuvwxyz   1234567890$

9 point Electra Bold Cursive (Linotype)

The basic character in a type design is determined by the uniform design characteristics of all letters in the alphabet. However, this alone does not determine the standard of the type face and the quality of composition set with it. The appearance is something complex which forms itself out of

ABCDEFGHIJKLMNOPQRSTUVWXYZ&
abcdefghijklmnopqrstuvwxyz   1234567890$

10 point Electra Bold Cursive (Linotype)

The basic character in a type design is determined by the uniform design characteristics of all letters in the alpha bet. However, this alone does not determine the standard of the type face and the quality of composition set with it. The appearance is something complex which forms

ABCDEFGHIJKLMNOPQRSTUVWXYZ&
abcdefghijklmnopqrstuvwxyz   1234567890$

11 point Electra Bold Cursive (Linotype)

The basic character in a type design is determined by the uniform design characteristics of all letters in the alphabet. However, this alone does not determine the standard of the type face and the quality of composi

ABCDEFGHIJKLMNOPQRSTUVWXYZ&
abcdefghijklmnopqrstuvwxyz   1234567890$

12 point Electra Bold Cursive (Linotype)

The basic character in a type design is determined by the uniform design characteristics of all letters in the alphabet. However, this alone does not de termine the standard of the type face and the qual

ABCDEFGHIJKLMNOPQRSTUVWXYZ&
abcdefghijklmnopqrstuvwxyz   1234567890$

14 point Electra Bold Cursive (Linotype)

The basic character in a type design is deter mined by the uniform design characteristics of all letters in the alphabet. However, this

ABCDEFGHIJKLMNOPQRSTU
VWXYZ&   1234567890$
abcdefghijklmnopqrstuvwxyz

Elizabeth Roman

ABCDEFGHIJKLMNOPQRSTUVWXYZ&
abcdefghijklmnopqrstuvwxyz
1234567890$

ABCDEFGHIJKLMNOPQRSTUVWXYZ&
abcdefghijklmnopqrstuvwxyz
1234567890$

ABCDEFGHIJKLMNOPQRSTUVWXYZ&
abcdefghijklmnopqrstuvwxyz
1234567890$

ABCDEFGHIJKLMNOPQRSTUVWXYZ&
abcdefghijklmnopqrstuvwxyz
1234567890$

ABCDEFGHIJKLMNOPQRSTUVWXYZ&
abcdefghijklmnopqrstuvwxyz
1234567890$

ABCDEFGHIJKLMNOPQRSTUVWXYZ&
abcdefghijklmnopqrstuvwxyz
1234567890$

ABCDEFGHIJKLMNOPQRST
UVWXYZ&
abcdefghijklmnopqrstuvwxyz
1234567890$

(Continued on Page 190)

(Continued from Page 189)

48 point Elizabeth Roman (Foundry)

ABCDEFGHIJKLMNOPQR
STUVWXYZ&
abcdefghijklmnopqrstuvwxyz
1234567890$

Elizabeth Italic

10 point Elizabeth Italic (Foundry)

ABCDEFGHIJKLMNOPQRSTUVWXYZ&
abcdefghijklmnopqrstuvwxyz
1234567890$

12 point Elizabeth Italic (Foundry)

ABCDEFGHIJKLMNOPQRSTUVWXYZ&
abcdefghijklmnopqrstuvwxyz
1234567890$

14 point Elizabeth Italic (Foundry)

ABCDEFGHIJKLMNOPQRSTUVWXYZ&
abcdefghijklmnopqrstuvwxyz
1234567890$

16 point Elizabeth Italic (Foundry)

ABCDEFGHIJKLMNOPQRSTUVWXYZ&
abcdefghijklmnopqrstuvwxyz
1234567890$

18 point Elizabeth Italic (Foundry)

ABCDEFGHIJKLMNOPQRSTUVWXYZ&
abcdefghijklmnopqrstuvwxyz
1234567890$

SWASH

A B D E F G H I K L M N P R T W Z k

24 point Elizabeth Italic (Foundry)

ABCDEFGHIJKLMNOPQRSTUVWXYZ&
abcdefghijklmnopqrstuvwxyz
1234567890$

SWASH

A A B D E F G H I K L M N P R T W Z k

(Continued on Page 191)

30 point Elizabeth Italic (Foundry)

ABCDEFGHIJKLMNOPQRSTUVWXYZ&
abcdefghijklmnopqrstuvwxyz
1234567890$

36 point Elizabeth Italic (Foundry)

ABCDEFGHIJKLMNOPQRSTU
VWXYZ&
abcdefghijklmnopqrstuvwxyz
1234567890$

SWASH

C A B D E F G H I K L M N
P R T W Z k

48 point Elizabeth Italic (Foundry)

ABCDEFGHIJKLMNOPQR
STUVWXYZ&
abcdefghijklmnopqrstuvwxyz
1234567890$

36 point Empire, Cap font (Foundry)

ABCDEFGHIJKLMNOPQRSTUVWXYZ&
1234567890$

48 point Empire, Cap font (Foundry)

ABCDEFGHIJKLMNOPQRSTUVWXYZ&
1234567890$

60 point Empire, Cap font (Foundry)

ABCDEFGHIJKLMNOPQRSTUVWXYZ&
1234567890$

72 point Empire, Cap font (Foundry)

ABCDEFGHIJKLMNOPQRSTUVWXYZ&
1234567890$

(Continued on Page 193)

Empire

96 point Empire, Cap font (Foundry)

ABCDEFGHIJKLMNOPQRSTUV
WXYZ&
1234567890$

Engravers Roman

12 point Engravers Roman No. 41, Cap font (Foundry)

ABCDEFGHIJKLMNOPQRSTUVWXYZ&
1234567890$

12 point Engravers Roman No. 42, Cap font (Foundry)

ABCDEFGHIJKLMNOPQRSTUVWXYZ&
1234567890$

12 point Engravers Roman No. 43, Cap font (Foundry)

ABCDEFGHIJKLMNOPQRSTUVWXYZ&
1234567890$

14 point Engravers Roman, Cap font (Foundry)

ABCDEFGHIJKLMNOPQRSTUVWXYZ&
1234567890$

24 point Engravers Roman, Cap font (Foundry)

ABCDEFGHIJKLMNOPQRSTU
VWXYZ&
1234567890$

Engravers Bold

Engravers Old English

36 point Engravers Old English (Foundry)

ABCDEFGHIJKLMNOPQRS
TUVWXYZ&
abcdefghijklmnopqrstuvwxyz
1234567890$

Eurostile Bold

10 point Eurostile Bold (Foundry)

ABCDEFGHIJKLMNOPQRSTUVWXYZ&
abcdefghijklmnopqrstuvwxyz
1234567890$

24 point Eurostile Bold Small (Foundry)

ABCDEFGHIJKLMNOPQRSTUVWXYZ&
abcdefghijklmnopqrstuvwxyz
1234567890$

24 point Eurostile Bold Large (Foundry)

ABCDEFGHIJKLMNOPQRSTUVWXYZ&
abcdefghijklmnopqrstuvwxyz
1234567890$

Eurostile Bold Condensed

36 point Eurostile Bold Condensed (Foundry)

ABCDEFGHIJKLMNOPQRSTUVWXYZ&
abcdefghijklmnopqrstuvwxyz
1234567890$

Eurostile Extended

ABCDEFGHIJKLMNOPQRSTUVWXYZ&
abcdefghijklmnopqrstuvwxyz
1234567890$

ABCDEFGHIJKLMNOPQRSTUVWXYZ&
abcdefghijklmnopqrstuvwxyz
1234567890$

ABCDEFGHIJKLMNOPQRSTUVWXYZ&
abcdefghijklmnopqrstuvwxyz
1234567890$

ABCDEFGHIJKLMNOPQRSTUVWXYZ&
abcdefghijklmopqrstuvwxyz
1234567890$

ABCDEFGHIJKLMNOPQRSTUVWXYZ&
abcdefghijklmnopqrstuvwxyz
1234567890$

ABCDEFGHIJKLMNOPQRSTUVWXYZ
abcdefghijklmnopqrstuvwxyz&
1234567890$

ABCDEFGHIJKLMNO
PQRSTUVWXYZ&
abcdefghijklmnopqrstu
vwxyz
1234567890$

Eurostile Bold Extended

6 point Eurostile Bold Extended (Foundry)
ABCDEFGHIJKLMNOPQRSTUVWXYZ&
abcdefghijklmnopqrstuvwxyz
1234567890$

8 point Eurostile Bold Extended (Foundry)
ABCDEFGHIJKLMNOPQRSTUVWXYZ&
abcdefghijklmnopqrstuvwxyz
1234567890$

10 point Eurostile Bold Extended (Foundry)
ABCDEFGHIJKLMNOPQRSTUVWXYZ&
abcdefghijklmnopqrstuvwxyz
1234567890$

12 point Eurostile Bold Extended (Foundry)
ABCDEFGHIJKLMNOPQRSTUVWXYZ&
abcdefghijklmnopqrstuvwxyz
1234567890$

14 point Eurostile Bold Extended (Foundry)
ABCDEFGHIJKLMNOPQRSTUVWXYZ&
abcdefghijklmnopqrstuvwxyz
1234567890$

18 point Eurostile Bold Extended (Foundry)
ABCDEFGHIJKLMNOPQRSTUVWXYZ&
abcdefghijklmnopqrstuvwxyz
1234567890$

24 point Eurostile Bold Extended small (Foundry)
ABCDEFGHIJKLMNOPQRSTUV
WXYZ&
abcdefghijklmnopqrstuvwxyz
1234567890$

24 point Eurostile Bold Extended large (Foundry)
ABCDEFGHIJKLMNOPQRS
TUVWXYZ&
abcdefghijklmnopqrstuvwxyz
1234567890$

(Continued on Page 198)

30 point Eurostile Bold Extended (Foundry)

ABCDEFGHIJKLMNO
PQRSTUVWXYZ&
abcdefghijklmnopqrstu
vwxyz 1234567890$

36 point Eurostile Bold Extended (Foundry)

ABCDEFGHIJKLMN
OPQRSTUVWXYZ&
abcdefghijklmnopq
rstuvwxyz
1234567890$

48 point Eurostile Bold Extended (Foundry)

ABCDEFGHIJ
KLMNOPQRS
TUVWXYZ&
abcdefghijklmn
opqrstuvwxyz
1234567890$

(Continued on Page 199)

Eurostile Bold Extended

(Continued from Page 198)

72 point Eurostile Bold Extended (Foundry)

ABCDEF GHIJKLM NOPQRS TUV WXYZ&

(Lower case and figures Continued on Page 200)

Eurostile Normal

6 point Eurostile Normal (Foundry)
ABCDEFGHIJKLMNOPQRSTUVWXYZ&
abcdefghijklmnopqrstuvwxyz
1234567890$

8 point Eurostile Normal (Foundry)
ABCDEFGHIJKLMNOPQRSTVUWXYZ&
abcdefghijklmnopqrstuvwxyz
1234567890$

10 point Eurostile Normal (Foundry)
ABCDEFGHIJKLMNOPQRSTUVWXYZ&
abcdefghijklmnopqrstuvwxyz
1234567890$

(Continued from Page 199)

72 point Eurostile Bold Extended (Foundry)

abcdefghi
jklmnopqr
stuvwxyz
123456
7890$

Excelsior

5½ point Excelsior, Caps only (Linotype)

THE BASIC CHARACTER IN A TYPE DESIGN IS DETERMINED BY THE UNIFORM DESIGN CHARACTERISTICS OF ALL LETTERS IN THE ALPHABET. HOWEVER, THIS ALONE DOES NOT DETERMINE THE STANDARD OF THE TYPE FACE AND THE QUALITY OF COM POSITION SET WITH IT. THE APPEARANCE IS SOMETHING COM PLEX WHICH FORMS ITSELF OUT OF MANY DETAILS, LIKE FORM, PROPORTION DUCTUS, RHYTHM ETC. IF EVERYTHING HARMO NIZES, THE TOTAL RESULT WILL BE MORE THAN THE SUM OF ITS COMPONENTS. THE ONLY RELIABLE BASIS FOR THE DESIGN

ABCDEFGHIJKLMNOPQRSTUVWXYZ&

6 point Excelsior (Linotype)

The basic character in a type design is determined by the uniform design characteristics of all letters in the alphabet. However, this alone does not determine the standard of the type face and the quality of composition set with it. The appearance is something complex which forms itself out of many details, like form, propor tion, ductus, rhythm etc. If everything harmonizes, the total result will be more than the sum of its components. The only reliable basis for the design in a type is a positive feeling for form and

ABCDEFGHIJKLMNOPQRSTUVWXYZ&
abcdefghijklmnopqrstuvwxyz
1234567890$

Excelsior Italic

Excelsior Script Semi Bold

24 point Excelsior Script Semi Bold (Foundry)

ABCDEFGHIJKLMNOPQRSTUV
WXYJ&
abcdefghijklmnopqrstuvwxyz
1234567890$

Folio Bold

24 point Folio Bold (Foundry)

ABCDEFGHIJKLMNOPQRSTUVWXYZ&
abcdefghijklmnopqrstuvwxyz
1234567890$

Folio Demibold

30 point Folio Demibold (Foundry)

ABCDEFGHIJKLMNOPQRSTUVWXYZ&
abcdefghijklmnopqrstuvwxyz
1234567890$

Fairfield

6 point Fairfield (Linotype)
The basic character in a type design is determined by the uniform design characteristics of all letters in the alphabet. However, this alone does not determine the standard of the type face and the quality of composition set with it. The appearance is something complex which forms itself out of many details, like form, proportion, ductus, rhythm etc. If everything har monizes, the total result will be more than the sum of its components. The only reliable basis for the design in a type is a positive feeling for form

ABCDEFGHIJKLMNOPQRSTUVWXYZ&
abcdefghijklmnopqrstuvwxyz 1234568790$
ABCDEFGHIJKLMNOPQRSTUVWXYZ

8 point Fairfield (Linotype)
The basic character in a type design is determined by the uniform design characteristics of all letters in the alphabet. However, this alone does not determine the standard of the type face and the quality of composition set with it. The appearance is something complex which forms itself out of many details, like form, propor

ABCDEFGHIJKLMNOPQRSTUVWXYZ&
abcdefghijklmnopqrstuvwxyz 1234567890$
ABCDEFGHIJKLMNOPQRSTUVWXYZ

9 point Fairfield (Linotype)
The basic character in a type design is determined by the uni form design characteristics of all letters in the alphabet. How ever, this alone does not determine the standard of the type face and the quality of composition set with it. The appearance

ABCDEFGHIJKLMNOPQRSTUVWXYZ&
abcdefghijklmnopqrstuvwxyz 1234567890$
ABCDEFGHIJKLMNOPQRSTUVWXYZ

10 point Fairfield (Linotype)
The basic character in a type design is determined by the uniform design characteristics of all letters in the alphabet. However, this alone does not determine the standard of the type face and the quality of composition set with it. The

ABCDEFGHIJKLMNOPQRSTUVWXYZ&
abcdefghijklmnopqrstuvwxyz 1234567890$
ABCDEFGHIJKLMNOPQRSTUVWXYZ

11 point Fairfield (Linotype)
The basic character in a type design is determined by the uniform design characteristics of all letters in the alphabet. However, this alone does not determine the

ABCDEFGHIJKLMNOPQRSTUVWXYZ&
abcdefghijklmnopqrstuvwxyz 1234567890$
ABCDEFGHIJKLMNOPQRSTUVWXYZ

12 point Fairfield (Linotype)
The basic character in a type design is determined by the uniform design characteristics of all letters in the alphabet. However, this alone does not determine the

ABCDEFGHIJKLMNOPQRSTUVWXYZ&
abcdefghijklmnopqrstuvwxyz 1234567890$
ABCDEFGHIJKLMNOPQRSTUVWXYZ

14 point Fairfield (Linotype)
The basic character in a type design is deter mined by the uniform design characteristics of

ABCDEFGHIJKLMNOPQRSTUVWXYZ
abcdefghijklmnopqrstuvwxyz& 1234567890$
ABCDEFGHIJKLMNOPQRSTUVWXYZ

Fairfield Italic

6 point Fairfield Italic (Linotype)
The basic character in a type design is determined by the uniform design characteristics of all letters in the alphabet. However, this alone does not determine the standard of the type face and the quality of composition set with it. The appearance is something complex which forms itself out of many details, like form, proportion, ductus, rhythm etc. If everything har monizes, the total result will be more than the sum of its components. The only reliable basis for the design in a type is a positive feeling for form and style. The basic character in a type design is determined by the uniform

ABCDEFGHIJKLMNOPQRSTUVWXYZ&
abcdefghijklmnopqrstuvwxyz 1234567890$

8 point Fairfield Italic (Linotype)
The basic character in a type design is determined by the uniform design characteristics of all letters in the alphabet. However, this alone does not determine the standard of the type face and the quality of composition set with it. The appearance is something complex which forms itself out of many details, like form, propor tion, ductus, rhythm etc. If everything harmonizes, the total result

ABCDEFGHIJKLMNOPQRSTUVWXYZ&
abcdefghijklmnopqrstuvwxyz 1234567890$

9 point Fairfield Italic (Linotype)
The basic character in a type design is determined by the uni form design characteristics of all letters in the alphabet. How ever, this alone does not determine the standard of the type face and the quality of composition set with it. The appearance is something complex which forms itself out of many details,

ABCDEFGHIJKLMNOPQRSTUVWXYZ&
abcdefghijklmnopqrstuvwxyz 1234567890$

10 point Fairfield Italic (Linotype)
The basic character in a type design is determined by the uniform design characteristics of all letters in the alphabet. However, this alone does not determine the standard of the type face and the quality of composition set with it. The appearance is something complex which forms itself out of

ABCDEFGHIJKLMNOPQRSTUVWXYZ&
abcdefghijklmnopqrstuvwxyz 1234567890$

11 point Fairfield Italic (Linotype)
The basic character in a type design is determined by the uniform design characteristics of all letters in the alphabet. However, this alone does not determine the standard of the type face and the quality of composition

ABCDEFGHIJKLMNOPQRSTUVWXYZ&
abcdefghijklmnopqrstuvwxyz 1234567890$

12 point Fairfield Italic (Linotype)
The basic character in a type design is determined by the uniform design characteristics of all letters in the alphabet. However, this alone does not determine the standard of the type face and the quality of composi

ABCDEFGHIJKLMNOPQRSTUVWXYZ&
abcdefghijklmnopqrstuvwxyz 1234567890$

14 point Fairfield Italic (Linotype)
The basic character in a type design is deter mined by the uniform design characteristics of all letters in the alphabet. However, this alone

ABCDEFGHIJKLMNOPQRSTUVWXYZ
abcdefghijklmnopqrstuvwxyz& 1234567890$

Folio Bold Condensed Italic

42 point Folio Bold Condensed Italic (Foundry)

ABCDEFGHIJKLMNOPQRSTUVWXYZ&
abcdefghijklmnopqrstuvwxyz
1234567890$

Folio Light

14 point Folio Light (Foundry)

ABCDEFGHIJKLMNOPQRSTUVWXYZ&
abcdefghijklmnopqrstuvwxyz
1234567890$

16 point Folio Light (Foundry)

ABCDEFGHIJKLMNOPQRSTUVWXYZ&
abcdefghijklmnopqrstuvwxyz
1234567890$

18 point Folio Light (Foundry)

ABCDEFGHIJKLMNOPQRSTUVWXYZ&
abcdefghijklmnopqrstuvwxyz
1234567890$

24 point Folio Light (Foundry)

ABCDEFGHIJKLMNOPQRSTUVWXYZ&
abcdefghijklmnopqrstuvwxyz
1234567890$

(Continued on Page 204)

(Continued from Page 203)

54 point Folio Light (Foundry)

ABCDEFGHIJKLMNO PQRSTUVWXYZ& abcdefghijklmnopqrst uvwxyz 1234567890$

Folio Extra Bold

14 point Folio Extra Bold (Foundry)

**ABCDEFGHIJKLMNOPQRSTUVWXYZ&
abcdefghijklmnopqrstuvwxyz
1234567890$**

16 point Folio Extra Bold (Foundry)

**ABCDEFGHIJKLMNOPQRSTUVWXYZ&
abcdefghijklmnopqrstuvwxyz
1234567890$**

18 point Folio Extra Bold (Foundry)

**ABCDEFGHIJKLMNOPQRSTUVWXYZ&
abcdefghijklmnopqrstuvwxyz
1234567890$**

(Continued on Page 205)

30 point Folio Extra Bold (Foundry)

ABCDEFGHIJKLMNOPQRSTUVWXYZ&
abcdefghijklmnopqrstuvwxyz
1234567890$

42 point Folio Extra Bold (Foundry)

ABCDEFGHIJKLMNOPQ
RSTUVWXYZ&
abcdefghijklmnopqrs
tuvwxyz
1234567890$

54 point Folio Extra Bold (Foundry)

ABCDEFGHIJKLMN
OPQRSTUVWXYZ&
abcdefghijklmno
pqrstuvwxyz
1234567890$

Folio Medium

16 point Folio Medium (Foundry)

ABCDEFGHIJKLMNOPQRSTUVWXYZ&
abcdefghijklmnopqrstuvwxyz
1234567890$

18 point Folio Medium (Foundry)

ABCDEFGHIJKLMNOPQRSTUVWXYZ&
abcdefghijklmnopqrstuvwxyz
1234567890$

24 point Folio Medium (Foundry)

ABCDEFGHIJKLMNOPQRSTUVWXYZ&
abcdefghijklmnopqrstuvwxyz
1234567890$

30 point Folio Medium (Foundry)

ABCDEFGHIJKLMNOPQRSTUVWXYZ&
abcdefghijklmnopqrstuvwxyz
1234567890$

36 point Folio Medium (Foundry)

ABCDEFGHIJKLMNOPQRSTUV
WXYZ&
abcdefghijklmnopqrstuvwxyz
1234567890$

(Continued on Page 207)

42 point Folio Medium (Foundry)

ABCDEFGHIJKLMNOPQR
STUVWXYZ&
abcdefghijklmnopqrstuvwxyz
1234567890$

54 point Folio Medium (Foundry)

ABCDEFGHIJKLMN
OPQRSTUVWXYZ&
abcdefghijklmnopqrs
tuvwxyz
1234567890$

(Continued on Page 208)

66 point Folio Medium (Foundry)

ABCDEFGHIJKL
MNOPQRSTUV
WXYZ&
abcdefghijklmnop
qrstuvwxyz
1234567890$

Folio Medium Condensed

30 point Folio Medium Condensed (Foundry)

ABCDEFGHIJKLMNOPQRSTUVWXYZ&
abcdefghijklmnopqrstuvwxyz
1234567890$

36 point Folio Medium Condensed (Foundry)

ABCDEFGHIJKLMNOPQRSTUVWXYZ&
abcdefghijklmnopqrstuvwxyz
1234567890$

42 point Folio Medium Condensed (Foundry)

ABCDEFGHIJKLMNOPQRSTUVWXYZ&
abcdefghijklmnopqrstuvwxyz
1234567890$

54 point Folio Medium Condensed (Foundry)

ABCDEFGHIJKLMNOPQRST
UVWXYZ&
abcdefghijklmnopqrstuvwxyz
1234567890$

14 point Folio Medium Extended (Foundry)

ABCDEFGHIJKLMNOPQRSTUVWXYZ&
abcdefghijklmnopqrstuvwxyz
1234567890$

16 point Folio Medium Extended (Foundry)

ABCDEFGHIJKLMNOPQRSTUVWXYZ&
abcdefghijklmnopqrstuvwxyz
1234567890$

18 point Folio Medium Extended (Foundry)

ABCDEFGHIJKLMNOPQRSTUVWXYZ&
abcdefghijklmnopqrstuvwxyz
1234567890$

24 point Folio Medium Extended (Foundry)

ABCDEFGHIJKLMNOPQRSTUVWXYZ&
abcdefghijklmnopqrstuvwxyz
1234567890$

30 point Folio Medium Extended (Foundry)

ABCDEFGHIJKLMNOPQRSTUVWXYZ
abcdefghijklmnopqrstuvwxyz&
1234567890$

42 point Folio Medium Extended (Foundry)

ABCDEFGHIJKLMNOPQ
RSTUVWXYZ&
abcdefghijklmnopqrstu
vwxyz
1234567890$

(Continued on Page 211)

54 point Folio Medium Extended (Foundry)

ABCDEFGHIJKLM NOPQRSTUV WXYZ& abcdefghijklmnop qrstuvwxyz 1234567890$

Fortuna Bold Italic

16 point Fortuna Bold Italic (Foundry)

*ABCDEFGHIJKLMNOPQRSTUVWXYZ&
abcdefghijklmnopqrstuvwxyz
1234567890$*

24 point Fortuna Bold Italic (Foundry)

*ABCDEFGHIJKLMNOPQRSTUVWXYZ&
abcdefghijklmnopqrstuvwxyz
1234567890$*

Fortuna Bold

14 point Fortuna Bold (Foundry)

ABCDEFGHIJKLMNOPQRSTUVWXYZ&
abcdefghijklmnopqrstuvwxyz
1234567890$

16 point Fortuna Bold (Foundry)

ABCDEFGHIJKLMNOPQRSTUVWXYZ&
abcdefghijklmnopqrstuvwxyz
1234567890$

24 point Fortuna Bold (Foundry)

ABCDEFGHIJKLMNOPQRSTU
VWXYZ&
abcdefghijklmnopqrstuvwxyz
1234567890$

30 point Fortuna Bold (Foundry)

ABCDEFGHIJKLMNOPQRST
UVWXYZ&
abcdefghijklmnopqrstuvwxyz
1234567890$

36 point Fortuna Bold (Foundry)

ABCDEFGHIJKLMNOPQ
RSTUVWXYZ&
abcdefghijklmnopqrstuv
wxyz
1234567890$

(Continued on Page 213)

54 point Fortuna Bold (Foundry)

ABCDEFGHIJK
LMNOPQRSTU
VWXYZ&
abcdefghijklmno
pqrstuvwxyz
1234567890$

(Continued on Page 214)

60 point Fortuna Bold (Foundry)

ABCDEFGH
IJKLMNOP
QRSTUV
WXYZ&
abcdefghijkl
mnopqrst
uvwxyz
1234567890$

Fortuna Light

14 point Fortuna Light (Foundry)

ABCDEFGHIJKLMNOPQRSTUVWXYZ&
abcdefghijklmnopqrstuvwxyz
1234567890$

16 point Fortuna Light (Foundry)

ABCDEFGHIJKLMNOPQRSTUVWXYZ&
abcdefghijklmnopqrstuvwxyz
1234567890$

18 point Fortuna Light (Foundry)

ABCDEFGHIJKLMNOPQRSTUVWXYZ&
abcdefghijklmnopqrstuvwxyz
1234567890$

24 point Fortuna Light (Foundry)

ABCDEFGHIJKLMNOPQRSTUVWXYZ
abcdefghijklmnopqrstuvwxyz&
1234567890$

30 point Fortuna Light (Foundry)

ABCDEFGHIJKLMNOPQRST
UVWXYZ&
abcdefghijklmnopqrstuvwxyz
1234567890$

36 point Fortuna Light (Foundry)

ABCDEFGHIJKLMNOPQR
STUVWXYZ&
abcdefghijklmnopqrstuvwxyz
1234567890$

(Continued on Page 216)

(Continued from Page 215)

42 point Fortuna Light (Foundry)

ABCDEFGHIJKLMNO
PQRSTUVWXYZ&
abcdefghijklmnopqrst
uvwxyz
1234567890$

54 point Fortuna Light (Foundry)

ABCDEFGHIJKL
MNOPQRST
UVWXYZ&
abcdefghijklmnopq
rstuvwxyz
1234567890$

(Continued on Page 217)

(Continued from Page 216)

60 point Fortuna Light (Foundry)

ABCDEFGHIJ
KLMNOPQRS
TUVWXYZ&
abcdefghijklmn
opqrstuvwxyz
1234567890$

Fortuna Extrabold

12 point Fortuna Extrabold (Foundry)

ABCDEFGHIJKLMNOPQRSTUVWXYZ&
abcdefghijklmnopqrstuvwxyz
1234567890$

14 point Fortuna Extrabold (Foundry)

ABCDEFGHIJKLMNOPQRSTUVWXYZ&
abcdefghijklmnopqrstuvwxyz
1234567890$

16 point Fortuna Extrabold (Foundry)

ABCDEFGHIJKLMNOPQRSTUVWXYZ&
abcdefghijklmnopqrstuvwxyz
1234567890$

24 point Fortuna Extrabold (Foundry)

ABCDEFGHIJKLMNOPQRST
UVWXYZ&
abcdefghijklmnopqrstuvwxyz
1234567890$

30 point Fortuna Extrabold (Foundry)

ABCDEFGHIJKLMNOPQ
RSTUVWXYZ&
abcdefghijklmnopqrst
uvwxyz
1234567890$

(Continued on Page 219)

Fortuna Extrabold

(Continued from Page 218)

60 point Fortuna Extrabold (Foundry)

ABCDEFG
HIJKLMN
OPQRST
UVWXYZ&
abcdefghij
klmnopqrs
tuvwxyz
1234567
890$

Forum

30 point Forum, Cap font (Foundry)

ABCDEFGHIJKLMNOPQRST
UVWXYZ&
1234567890

(no dollar sign is made for this font)

Fournier

24 point Fournier, Cap font (Foundry)

ABCDEFGHIJKLMNOPQRSTU
VWXYZ&

Franklin Gothic

8 point Franklin Gothic (Intertype)

The basic character in a type design is determined by
the uniform design characteristics of all letters in the
alphabet. However, this alone does not determine the
standard of the type face and the quality of composi
tion set with it. The appearance is something complex
which forms itself out of many details, like form, pro

ABCDEFGHIJKLMNOPQRSTUVWXYZ&
abcdefghijklmnopqrstuvwxyz   1234567890$

10 point Franklin Gothic (Intertype)

The basic character in a type design is de
termined by the uniform design characteris
tics of all letters in the alphabet. However,
this alone does not determine the standard of
the type face and the quality of composition

ABCDEFGHIJKLMNOPQRSTUVWXYZ&
abcdefghijklmnopqrstuvwxyz   1234567890$

6 point Franklin Gothic (Foundry)
ABCDEFGHIJKLMNOPQRSTUVWXYZ&
abcdefghijklmnopqrstuvwxyz
1234567890$

8 point Franklin Gothic (Foundry)
ABCDEFGHIJKLMNOPQRSTUVWXYZ&
abcdefghijklmnopqrstuvwxyz
1234567890$

10 point Franklin Gothic (Foundry)
ABCDEFGHIJKLMNOPQRSTUVWXYZ&
abcdefghijklmnopqrstuvwxyz
1234567890$

12 point Franklin Gothic (Foundry)
ABCDEFGHIJKLMNOPQRSTUVWXYZ&
abcdefghijklmnopqrstuvwxyz
1234567890$

14 point Franklin Gothic (Foundry)
ABCDEFGHIJKLMNOPQRSTUVWXYZ&
abcdefghijklmnopqrstuvwxyz   1234567890$

14 point Franklin Gothic (Ludlow)
ABCDEFGHIJKLMNOPQRSTUVWXYZ&
abcdefghijklmnopqrstuvwxyz   1234567890$

18 point Franklin Gothic (Ludlow)
ABCDEFGHIJKLMNOPQRSTUVWXYZ&
abcdefghijklmnopqrstuvwxyz   1234567890$

(Continued on Page 221)

(Continued from Page 220)

18 point Franklin Gothic (Foundry)

ABCDEFGHIJKLMNOPQRSTUVWXYZ&
abcdefghijklmnopqrstuvwxyz
1234567890$

24 point Franklin Gothic (Foundry)

ABCDEFGHIJKLMNOPQRSTUVWXYZ&
abcdefghijklmnopqrstuvwxyz
1234567890$

30 point Franklin Gothic (Foundry)

ABCDEFGHIJKLMNOPQRSTUV
WXYZ&
abcdefghijklmnopqrstuvwxyz
1234567890$

36 point Franklin Gothic (Foundry)

ABCDEFGHIJKLMNOPQRST
UVWXYZ&
abcdefghijklmnopqrstuvwxyz
1234567890$

42 point Franklin Gothic (Foundry)

ABCDEFGHIJKLMNO
PQRSTUVWXYZ&
abcdefghijklmnopqrst
uvwxyz 1234567890$

(Continued on Page 222)

(Continued from Page 221)

48 point Franklin Gothic (Foundry)

ABCDEFGHIJKLMNO
PQRSTUVWXYZ&
abcdefghijklmnopqrst
uvwxyz
1234567890$

60 point Franklin Gothic (Foundry)

ABCDEFGHIJKLM
NOPQRSTUV
WXYZ&
abcdefghijklmnop
qrstuwxyz
1234567890$

(Continued on Page 223)

72 point Franklin Gothic (Foundry)

ABCDEFGHIJK
LMNOPQRST
UVWXYZ&
abcdefghijkl
mnopqrst
uvwxyz
1234567890$

Franklin Gothic Condensed

6 point Franklin Gothic Condensed (Foundry)
ABCDEFGHIJKLMNOPQRSTUVWXYZ&
abcdefghijklmnopqrstuvwxyz
1234567890$

8 point Franklin Gothic Condensed (Foundry)
ABCDEFGHIJKLMNOPQRSTUVWXYZ&
abcdefghijklmnopqrstuvwxyz
1234567890$

10 point Franklin Gothic Condensed (Foundry)
ABCDEFGHIJKLMNOPQRSTUVWXYZ&
abcdefghijklmnopqrstuvwxyz
1234567890$

12 point Franklin Gothic Condensed (Foundry)
ABCDEFGHIJKLMNOPQRSTUVWXYZ&
abcdefghijklmnopqrstuvwxyz
1234567890$

14 point Franklin Gothic Condensed (Foundry)
ABCDEFGHIJKLMNOPQRSTUVWXYZ&
abcdefghijklmnopqrstuvwxyz
1234567890$

18 point Franklin Gothic Condensed (Foundry)
ABCDEFGHIJKLMNOPQRSTUVWXYZ&
abcdefghijklmnopqrstuvwxyz
1234567890$

24 Franklin Gothic Condensed (Foundry)
ABCDEFGHIJKLMNOPQRSTUVWXYZ&
abcdefghijklmnopqrstuvwxyz
1234567890$

30 point Franklin Gothic Condensed (Foundry)
ABCDEFGHIJKLMNOPQRSTUVWXYZ&
abcdefghijklmnopqrstuvwxyz
1234567890$

(Continued on Page 225)

36 point Franklin Gothic Condensed (Foundry)

ABCDEFGHIJKLMNOPQRSTUVWXYZ
abcdefghijklmnopqrstuvwxyz&
1234567890$

42 point Franklin Gothic Condensed (Foundry)

ABCDEFGHIJKLMNOPQRSTU
VWXYZ&
abcdefghijklmnopqrstuvwxyz
1234567890$

48 point Franklin Gothic Condensed (Foundry)

ABCDEFGHIJKLMNOPQRS
TUVWXYZ&
abcdefghijklmnopqrstuv
wxyz
1234567890$

(Continued on Page 226)

Franklin Gothic Condensed

60 point Franklin Gothic Condensed (Foundry)

ABCDEFGHIJKLMNO
PQRSTUVWXYZ&
abcdefghijklmnopqrs
tuvwxyz
1234567890$

(Continued on Page 227)

Franklin Gothic Condensed Outline

48 point Franklin Gothic Condensed Outline, Cap font (Foundry)

ABCDEFGHIJKLMNOPQRS
TUVWXYZ&
1234567890$

226

72 point Franklin Gothic Condensed (Foundry)

ABCDEFGHIJKL MNOPQRSTUV WXYZ& abcdefghijklmno pqrstuvwxyz 1234567890$

Franklin Gothic Extra Condensed

10 point Franklin Gothic Extra Condensed (Foundry)
ABCDEFGHIJKLMNOPQRSTUVWXYZ&
abcdefghijklmnopqrstuvwxyz
1234567890$

12 point Franklin Gothic Extra Condensed (Foundry)
ABCDEFGHIJKLMNOPQRSTUVWXYZ&
abcdefghijklmnopqrstuvwxyz
1234567890$

14 point Franklin Gothic Extra Condensed (Foundry)
ABCDEFGHIJKLMNOPQRSTUVWXYZ&
abcdefghijklmnopqrstuvwxyz
1234567890$

18 point Franklin Gothic Extra Condensed (Foundry)
ABCDEFGHIJKLMNOPQRSTUVWXYZ&
abcdefghijklmnopqrstuvwxyz
1234567890$

24 point Franklin Gothic Extra Condensed (Foundry)
ABCDEFGHIJKLMNOPQRSTUVWXYZ&
abcdefghijklmnopqrstuvwxyz
1234567890$

30 point Franklin Gothic Extra Condensed (Foundry)
ABCDEFGHIJKLMNOPQRSTUVWXYZ&
abcdefghijklmnopqrstuvwxyz
1234567890$

36 point Franklin Gothic Extra Condensed (Foundry)
ABCDEFGHIJKLMNOPQRSTUVWXYZ&
abcdefghijklmnopqrstuvwxyz
1234567890$

42 point Franklin Gothic Extra Condensed (Foundry)
ABCDEFGHIJKLMNOPQRSTUVWXYZ&
abcdefghijklmnopqrstuvwxyz
1234567890$

(Continued on Page 229)

48 point Franklin Gothic Extra Condensed (Foundry)

ABCDEFGHIJKLMNOPQRSTUV WXYZ&
abcdefghijklmnopqrstuvwxyz
1234567890$

60 point Franklin Gothic Extra Condensed (Foundry)

ABCDEFGHIJKLMNOPQRST UVWXYZ&
abcdefghijklmnopqrst uvwxyz
1234567890$

(Continued on Page 230)

(Continued from Page 229)

72 point Franklin Gothic Extra Condensed (Foundry)

ABCDEFGHIJKLMNOP
QRSTUVWXYZ&
abcdefghijklmnopqrs
tuvwxyz
1234567890$

(Continued on Page 231)

(Continued from Page 230)

84 point Franklin Gothic Extra Condensed (Foundry)

ABCDEFGHIJKLMNO
PQRSTUVWXYZ&
abcdefghijklmno
pqrstuvwxyz
1234567890$

V & M TYPOGRAPHICAL, INCORPORATED

Franklin Gothic Italic

8 point Franklin Gothic Italic (Intertype)

The basic character in a type design is determined by the uniform design characteristics of all letters in the alphabet. However, this alone does not determine the standard of the type face and the quality of composition set with it. The appearance is something complex which forms itself out of many details, like form, pro

ABCDEFGHIJKLMNOPQRSTUVWXYZ&
abcdefghijklmnopqrstuvwxyz   1234567890$

10 point Franklin Gothic Italic (Intertype)

The basic character in a type design is de termined by the uniform design characteris tics of all letters in the alphabet. However, this alone does not determine the standard of the type face and the quality of composition

ABCDEFGHIJKLMNOPQRSTUVWXYZ&
abcdefghijklmnopqrstuvwxyz   1234567890$

12 point Franklin Gothic Italic (Foundry)

ABCDEFGHIJKLMNOPQRSTUVWXYZ&
abcdefghijklmnopqrstuvwxyz
1234567890$

14 point Franklin Gothic Italic (Foundry)

ABCDEFGHIJKLMNOPQRSTUVWXYZ&
abcdefghijklmnopqrstuvwxyz
1234567890$

18 point Franklin Gothic Italic (Foundry)

ABCDEFGHIJKLMNOPQRSTUVWXYZ&
abcdefghijklmnopqrstuvwxyz
1234567890$

24 point Franklin Gothic Italic (Foundry)

ABCDEFGHIJKLMNOPQRSTUVWXYZ&
abcdefghijklmnopqrstuvwxyz
1234567890$

30 point Franklin Gothic Italic (Foundry)

ABCDEFGHIJKLMNOPQRSTUV WXYZ&
abcdefghijklmnopqrstuvwxyz
1234567890$

Franklin Gothic Wide

10 point Franklin Gothic Wide (Foundry)
ABCDEFGHIJKLMNOPQRSTUVWXYZ&
abcdefghijklmnopqrstuvwxyz
1234567890$

12 point Franklin Gothic Wide (Foundry)
ABCDEFGHIJKLMNOPQRSTUVWXYZ&
abcdefghijklmnopqrstuvwxyz
1234567890$

14 point Franklin Gothic Wide (Foundry)
ABCDEFGHIJKLMNOPQRSTUVWXYZ&
abcdefghijklmnopqrstuvwxyz
1234567890$

18 point Franklin Gothic Wide (Foundry)
ABCDEFGHIJKLMNOPQRSTUVWXYZ&
abcdefghijklmnopqrstuvwxyz
1234567890$

24 point Franklin Gothic Wide (Foundry)
ABCDEFGHIJKLMNOPQRSTUV
WXYZ&
abcdefghijklmnopqrstuvwxyz
1234567890$

30 point Franklin Gothic Wide (Foundry)
ABCDEFGHIJKLMNOPQRST
UVWXYZ&
abcdefghijklmnopqrstuvwxyz
1234567890$

(Continued on Page 234)

(Continued from Page 233)

36 point Franklin Gothic Wide (Foundry)

ABCDEFGHIJKLMNO
PQRSTUVWXYZ&
abcdefghijklmnopqrst
uvwxyz
1234567890$

42 point Franklin Gothic Wide (Foundry)

ABCDEFGHIJKLMN
OPQRSTUVWXYZ&
abcdefghijklmnopqrs
tuvwxyz
1234567890$

48 point Franklin Gothic Wide (Foundry)

ABCDEFGHIJKLM
NOPQRSTUV
WXYZ&

(Continued on Page 235)

48 point Franklin Gothic Wide (Foundry)

abcdefghijklmno
pqrstuvwxyz
1234567890$

60 point Franklin Gothic Wide (Foundry)

ABCDEFGHIJ
KLMNOPQRS
TUVWXYZ&
abcdefghijkl
mnopqrstuv
wxyz
1234567890$

(Continued on page 236)

(Continued from Page 235)

72 point Franklin Gothic Wide (Foundry)

ABCDEFGH
IJKLMNOP
QRSTUV
WXYZ&
abcdefghijkl
mnopqrstuv
wxyz 123
4567890$

Futura Black

20 point Futura Black (Foundry)

ABCDEFGHIJKLMNOPQRSTUVWXYZ&
abcdefghijklmnopqrstuvwxyz
1234567890$

24 point Futura Black (Foundry)

ABCDEFGHIJKLMNOPQRSTUVWXYZ&
abcdefghijklmnopqrstuvwxyz
1234567890$

48 point Futura Black (Foundry)

ABCDEFGHIJKLMNOP
QRSTUVWXYZ&
abcdefghijklmnopqrst
UVWXYZ
1234567890$

Futura Book

ABCDEFGHIJKLMNOPQRSTUVWXYZ&
abcdefghijklmnopqrstuvwxyz
1234567890$

ABCDEFGHIJKLMNOPQRSTUVWXYZ&
abcdefghijklmnopqrstuvwxyz
1234567890$

ABCDEFGHIJKLMNOPQRSTUV
WXYZ&
abcdefghijklmnopqrstuvwxyz
1234567890$

ABCDEFGHIJKLMNOPQRST
UVWXYZ&
abcdefghijklmnopqrstuv
wxyz
1234567890$

Futura Bold

18 point Futura Bold (Foundry)

ABCDEFGHIJKLMNOPQRSTUVWXYZ&
abcdefghijklmnopqrstuvwxyz
1234567890$

30 point Futura Bold (Foundry)

ABCDEFGHIJKLMNOPQRSTUV
WXYZ&
abcdefghijklmnopqrstuvwxyz
1234567890$

Futura Display

14 point Futura Display (Foundry)

ABCDEFGHIJKLMNOPQRSTUVWXYZ&
abcdefghijklmnopqrstuvwxyz
1234567890$

18 point Futura Display (Foundry)

ABCDEFGHIJKLMNOPQRSTUVWXYZ&
abcdefghijklmnopqrstuvwxyz
1234567890$

24 point Futura Display (Foundry)

ABCDEFGHIJKLMNOPQRSTUVWXYZ&
abcdefghijklmnopqrstuvwxyz
1234567890$

Futura Demibold

The basic character in a type design is determined by the uniform design characteristics of all letters in the alphabet. However, this alone does not determine the standard of the type face and the quality of composition set with it. The appearance is something complex which forms itself

ABCDEFGHIJKLMNOPQRSTUVWXYZ&
abcdefghijklmnopqrstuvwxyz   1234567890$

The basic character in a type design is determined by the uniform design characteristics of all letters in the alphabet. However, this alone does not determine the standard of the type face and the

ABCDEFGHIJKLMNOPQRSTUVWXYZ&
abcdefghijklmnopqrstuvwxyz   1234567890$

ABCDEFGHIJKLMNOPQRSTUVWXYZ&
abcdefghijklmnopqrstuvwxyz
1234567890$

ABCDEFGHIJKLMNOPQRSTUVWXYZ&
abcdefghijklmnopqrstuvwxyz
1234567890$

ABCDEFGHIJKLMNOPQRSTUV
WXYZ&
abcdefghijklmnopqrstuvwxyz
1234567890$

Futura Demibold Oblique

18 point Futura Demibold Oblique (Foundry)

ABCDEFGHIJKLMNOPQRSTUVWXYZ&
abcdefghijklmnopqrstuvwxyz
1234567890$

24 point Futura Demibold Oblique (Foundry)

ABCDEFGHIJKLMNOPQRSTUVWXYZ&
abcdefghijklmnopqrstuvwxyz
1234567890$

Futura Light

6 point Futura Light (Foundry)

ABCDEFGHIJKLMNOPQRSTUVWXYZ&
abcdefghijklmnopqrstuvwxyz
1234567890$

16 point Futura Light (Foundry)

ABCDEFGHIJKLMNOPQRSTUVWXYZ&
abcdefghijklmnopqrstuvwxyz
1234567890$

18 point Futura Light (Foundry)

ABCDEFGHIJKLMNOPQRSTUVWXYZ&
abcdefghijklmnopqrstuvwxyz
1234567890$

24 point Futura Light (Foundry)

ABCDEFGHIJKLMNOPQRSTUVWXYZ&
abcdefghijklmnopqrstuvwxyz
1234567890$

30 point Futura Light (Foundry)

ABCDEFGHIJKLMNOPQRSTUVWXYZ&
abcdefghijklmnopqrstuvwxyz
1234567890$

(Continued on Page 242)

(Continued from Page 241)

36 point Futura Light (Foundry)

ABCDEFGHIJKLMNOPQRSTUV
WXYZ&
abcdefghijklmnopqrstuvwxyz
1234567890$

48 point Futura Light (Foundry)

ABCDEFGHIJKLMNOPQRS
TUVWXYZ&
abcdefghijklmnopqrstuv
wxyz 1234567890$

60 point Futura Light (Foundry)

ABCDEFGHIJKLMNO
PQRSTUVWXYZ&
abcdefghijklmnopqrstu
vwxyz 1234567890$

(Continued on Page 243)

72 point Futura Light (Foundry)

ABCDEFGHIJKLMN
OPQRSTUVWXYZ
abcdefghijklmnopq
rstuvwxyz&
1234567890$

Futura Light Oblique

18 point Futura Oblique Light (Foundry)

ABCDEFGHIJKLMNOPQRSTUVWXYZ&
abcdefghijklmnopqrstuvwxyz
1234567890$

24 Futura Oblique Light (Foundry)

ABCDEFGHIJKLMNOPQRSTUVWXYZ&
abcdefghijklmnopqrstuvwxyz
1234567890$

Futura Medium Condensed

ABCDEFGHIJKLMNOPQRSTUVWXYZ&
abcdefghijklmnopqrstuvwxyz
1234567890$

Futura Medium

The basic character in a type design is determined by the uniform design characteristics of all letters in the alphabet. However, this alone does not determine the standard of the type face and the quality of composition set with it. The appearance is something complex which forms itself

ABCDEFGHIJKLMNOPQRSTUVWXYZ&
abcdefghijklmnopqrstuvwxyz   1234567890$

The basic character in a type design is determined by the uniform design characteristics of all letters in the alphabet. However, this alone does not determine the standard of the type face and the

ABCDEFGHIJKLMNOPQRSTUVWXYZ&
abcdefghijklmnopqrstuvwxyz   1234567890$

ABCDEFGHIJKLMNOPQRSTUVWXYZ&
abcdefghijklmnopqrstuvwxyz
1234567890$

ABCDEFGHIJKLMNOPQRSTUVWXYZ&
abcdefghijklmnopqrstuvwxyz
1234567890$

ABCDEFGHIJKLMNOPQRSTUVWXYZ&
abcdefghijklmnopqrstuvwxyz
1234567890$

ABCDEFGHIJKLMNOPQRSTUVWXYZ&
abcdefghijklmnopqrstuvwxyz
1234567890$

(Continued on Page 245)

48 point Futura Medium (Foundry)

ABCDEFGHIJKLMNOPQRS
TUVWXYZ&
abcdefghijklmnopqrstuv
wxyz
1234567890$

60 point Futura Medium (Foundry)

ABCDEFGHIJKLMNO
PQRSTUVWXYZ&
abcdefghijklmnopqrst
uvwxyz
1234567890$

Gallia

18 point Gallia, Cap font (Foundry)

ABCDEFGHIJKLMNOPQRSTUVWXYZ&
1234567890$

SWASH

A E R S T

---

24 point Gallia, Cap font (Foundry)

ABCDEFGHIJKLMNOPQRST
UVWXYZ&
1234567890$

SWASH

A E R S T

---

36 point Gallia, Cap font (Foundry)

ABCDEFGHIJKLMN
OPQRSTUVWXYZ&
1234567890$

SWASH

A E R S T

Garamond

18 point Garamond, Caps only (Foundry)

ABCDEFGHIJKLMNOPQRSTUVWXYZ&

18 point Garamond (Ludlow)

ABCDEFGHIJKLMNOPQRSTUVWXYZ&
abcdefghijklmnopqrstuvwxyz
1234567890$

24 point Garamond (Ludlow)

ABCDEFGHIJKLMNOPQRSTUVWXYZ&
abcdefghijklmnopqrstuvwxyz
1234567890$

30 point Garamond (Foundry)

ABCDEFGHIJKLMNOPQRSTUVWXYZ&
abcdefghijklmnopqrstuvwxyz
1234567890$

36 point Garamond, Caps only (Foundry)

ABCDEFGHIJKLMNOPQRSTUV
WXYZ&

36 point Garamond (Ludlow)

ABCDEFGHIJKLMNOPQRSTUV
WXYZ&
abcdefghijklmnopqrstuvwxyz
1234567890$

(Continued on Page 248)

48 point Garamond (Foundry)

ABCDEFGHIJKLMNOPQRS
TUVWXYZ&
abcdefghijklmnopqrstuvwxyz
1234567890$

60 point Garamond (Foundry)

ABCDEFGHIJKLMNO
PQRSTUVWXYZ&
abcdefghijklmnopqrstuv
wxyz
1234567890$

(Continued on Page 249)

72 point Garamond (Foundry)

ABCDEFGHIJKLM
NOPQRSTUV
WXYZ&
abcdefghijklmnopq
rstuvwxyz
1234567890$

Garamond

Garamond Italic

6 point Garamond (Intertype)

The basic character in a type design is determined by the uniform design char acteristics of all letters in the alphabet. However, this alone does not determine the standard of the type face and the quality of composition set with it. The appearance is something complex which forms itself out of many details, like form, proportion, ductus, rhythm etc. If everything harmonizes, the total result

ABCDEFGHIJKLMNOPQRSTUVWXYZ&
abcdefghijklmnopqrstuvwxyz   1234567890$
ABCDEFGHIJKLMNOPQRSTUVWXYZ

6 point Garamond Italic (Intertype)

The basic character in a type design is determined by the uniform design char acteristics of all letters in the alphabet. However, this alone does not determine the standard of the type face and the quality of composition set with it. The appearance is something complex which forms itself out of many details, like form, proportion, ductus, rhythm etc. If everything harmonizes, the total result will be more than the sum of its components. The only reliable basis for the

ABCDEFGHIJKLMNOPQRSTUVWXYZ&
abcdefghijklmnopqrstuvwxyz   1234567890$

7 point Garamond (Intertype)

The basic character in a type design is determined by the uniform design characteristics of all letters in the alphabet. However, this alone does not determine the standard of the type face and the quality of composition set with it. The appearance is something complex which forms itself out of

ABCDEFGHIJKLMNOPQRSTUVWXYZ&
abcdefghijklmnopqrstuvwxyz   1234567890$
ABCDEFGHIJKLMNOPQRSTUVWXYZ

7 point Garamond Italic (Intertype)

The basic character in a type design is determined by the uniform design characteristics of all letters in the alphabet. However, this alone does not determine the standard of the type face and the quality of composition set with it. The appearance is something complex which forms itself out of many details, like form, proportion, ductus, rhythm etc. If everything har

ABCDEFGHIJKLMNOPQRSTUVWXYZ&
abcdefghijklmnopqrstuvwxyz   1234567890$

8 point Garamond (Intertype)

The basic character in a type design is determined by the uniform de sign characteristics of all letters in the alphabet. However, this alone does not determine the standard of the type face and the quality of

ABCDEFGHIJKLMNOPQRSTUVWXYZ&
abcdefghijklmnopqrstuvwxyz   1234567890$
ABCDEFGHIJKLMNOPQRSTUVWXYZ

8 point Garamond Italic (Intertype)

The basic character in a type design is determined by the uniform de sign characteristics of all letters in the alphabet. However, this alone does not determine the standard of the type face and the quality of composition set with it. The appearance is something complex which

ABCDEFGHIJKLMNOPQRSTUVWXYZ&
abcdefghijklmnopqrstuvwxyz   1234567890$

9 point Garamond (Intertype)

The basic character in a type design is determined by the uniform design characteristics of all letters in the alphabet. However, this

ABCDEFGHIJKLMNOPQRSTUVWXYZ&
abcdefghijklmnopqrstuvwxyz   1234567890$
ABCDEFGHIJKLMNOPQRSTUVWXYZ

9 point Garamond Italic (Intertype)

The basic character in a type design is determined by the uniform design characteristics of all letters in the alphabet. However, this alone does not determine the standard of the type face and the

ABCDEFGHIJKLMNOPQRSTUVWXYZ&
abcdefghijklmnopqrstuvwxyz   1234567890$

10 point Garamond (Intertype)

The basic character in a type design is determined by the uni form design characteristics of all letters in the alphabet. How

ABCDEFGHIJKLMNOPQRSTUVWXYZ&
abcdefghijklmnopqrstuvwxyz   1234567890$
ABCDEFGHIJKLMNOPQRSTUVWXYZ

10 point Garamond Italic (Intertype)

The basic character in a type design is determined by the uni form design characteristics of all letters in the alphabet. How ever, this alone does not determine the standard of the type

ABCDEFGHIJKLMNOPQRSTUVWXYZ&
abcdefghijklmnopqrstuvwxyz   1234567890$

11 point Garamond (Intertype)

The basic character in a type design is determined by the uniform design characteristics of all letters in the alpha bet. However, this alone does not determine the standard

ABCDEFGHIJKLMNOPQRSTUVWXYZ&
abcdefghijklmnopqrstuvwxyz   1234567890$
ABCDEFGHIJKLMNOPQRSTUVWXYZ

11 point Garamond Italic (Intertype)

The basic character in a type design is determined by the uniform design characteristics of all letters in the alpha bet. However, this alone does not determine the standard of the type face and the quality of composition set with it.

ABCDEFGHIJKLMNOPQRSTUVWXYZ&
abcdefghijklmnopqrstuvwxyz   1234567890$

12 point Garamond (Intertype)

The basic character in a type design is determined by the uniform design characteristics of all letters in the alpha bet. However, this alone does not determine the stand

ABCDEFGHIJKLMNOPQRSTUVWXYZ&
abcdefghijklmnopqrstuvwxyz   1234567890$
ABCDEFGHIJKLMNOPQRSTUVWXYZ

12 point Garamond Italic (Intertype)

The basic character in a type design is determined by the uniform design characteristics of all letters in the alpha bet. However, this alone does not determine the stand ard of the type face and the quality of composition set

ABCDEFGHIJKLMNOPQRSTUVWXYZ&
abcdefghijklmnopqrstuvwxyz   1234567890$

14 point Garamond (Intertype)

The basic character in a type design is determined by the uniform design characteristics of all letters

ABCDEFGHIJKLMNOPQRSTUVWXYZ&
abcdefghijklmnopqrstuvwxyz   1234567890$
ABCDEFGHIJKLMNOPQRSTUVWXYZ

14 point Garamond Italic (Intertype)

The basic character in a type design is determined by the uniform design characteristics of all letters in the alphabet. However, this alone does not de

ABCDEFGHIJKLMNOPQRSTUVWXYZ&
abcdefghijklmnopqrstuvwxyz   1234567890$

Garamond Italic

16 point Garamond Italic (Foundry)

ABCDEFGHIJKLMNOPQRSTUVWXYZ&

abcdefghijklmnopqrstuvwxyz

1234567890$

18 point Garamond Italic (Ludlow)

ABCDEFGHIJKLMNOPQRSTUVWXYZ&

abcdefghijklmnopqrstuvwxyz

1234567890$

SWASH AND TERMINALS

A B C D E F G L M N P R Y

a e k m n t v w

24 point Garamond Italic (Ludlow)

ABCDEFGHIJKLMNOPQRSTUVWXYZ&

abcdefghijklmnopqrstuvwxyz

1234567890$

SWASH AND TERMINALS

A B C D E F G L M N P R Y

a e k m n t v w

24 point Garamond Italic (Foundry)

ABCDEFGHIJKLMNOPQRSTUVWXYZ&

abcdefghijklmnopqrstuvwxyz

1234567890$

30 point Garamond Italic (Foundry)

ABCDEFGHIJKLMNOPQRSTUVWXYZ&

abcdefghijklmnopqrstuvwxyz

1234567890$

36 point Garamond Italic (Ludlow)

ABCDEFGHIJKLMNOPQRSTUV
WXYZ&

abcdefghijklmnopqrstuvwxyz

1234567890$

SWASH AND TERMINALS

A B C D E F G L M N P R Y

a e k m n t v w

(Continued on Page 252)

36 point Garamond Italic (Foundry)

ABCDEFGHIJKLMNOPQRSTUVWXYZ
abcdefghijklmnopqrstuvwxyz&
1234567890$

42 point Garamond Italic (Foundry)

ABCDEFGHIJKLMNOPQRSTUV
WXYZ&
abcdefghijklmnopqrstuvwxyz
1234567890$

48 point Garamond Italic (Foundry)

ABCDEFGHIJKLMNOPQRS
TUVWXYZ&
abcdefghijklmnopqrstuvwxyz
1234567890$

Garamond No. 3

Garamond Italic No. 3

Garamond Bold No. 3

Garamond Bold Italic No. 3

6 point Garamond Bold No. 3 (Linotype)

The basic character in a type design is determined by the uniform design characteristics of all letters in the alphabet However, this alone does not determine the standard of the type face and the quality of composition set with it. The appearance is something complex which forms itself out of many details, like form, proportion, ductus, rhythm etc. If everything harmonizes, the total result will be more than the sum of its components. The only reliable basis for the design in a type is a positive feeling for

ABCDEFGHIJKLMNOPQRSTUVWXYZ&
abcdefghijklmnopqrstuvwxyz 1234567890$
ABCDEFGHIJKLMNOPQRSTUVWXYZ

6 point Garamond Bold No. 3 Italic (Linotype)

The basic character in a type design is determined by the uniform design characteristics of all letters in the alphabet However, this alone does not determine the standard of the type face and the quality of composition set with it. The appearance is something complex which forms itself out of many details, like form, proportion, ductus, rhythm etc. If everything harmonizes, the total result will be more than the sum of its components. The only reliable basis for the design in a type is a positive feeling for

ABCDEFGHIJKLMNOPQRSTUVWXYZ&
abcdefghijklmnopqrstuvwxyz 1234567890$

8 point Garamond Bold No. 3 (Linotype)

The basic character in a type design is determined by the uni form design characteristics of all letters in the alphabet. How ever, this alone does not determine the standard of the type face and the quality of composition set with it. The appearance is something complex which forms itself out of many details,

ABCDEFGHIJKLMNOPQRSTUVWXYZ&
abcdefghijklmnopqrstuvwxyz 1234567890$
ABCDEFGHIJKLMNOPQRSTUVWXYZ

8 point Garamond Bold No. 3 Italic (Linotype)

The basic character in a type design is determined by the uni form design characteristics of all letters in the alphabet. How ever, this alone does not determine the standard of the type face and the quality of composition set with it. The appearance is something complex which forms itself out of many details,

ABCDEFGHIJKLMNOPQRSTUVWXYZ&
abcdefghijklmnopqrstuvwxyz 1234567890$

10 point Garamond Bold No. 3 (Linotype)

The basic character in a type design is determined by the uniform design characteristics of all letters in the alpha bet. However, this alone does not determine the standard of the type face and the quality of composition set with

ABCDEFGHIJKLMNOPQRSTUVWXYZ&
abcdefghijklmnopqrstuvwxyz 1234567890$
ABCDEFGHIJKLMNOPQRSTUVWXYZ

10 point Garamond Bold No. 3 Italic (Linotype)

The basic character in a type design is determined by the uniform design characteristics of all letters in the alpha bet. However, this alone does not determine the standard of the type face and the quality of composition set with

ABCDEFGHIJKLMNOPQRSTUVWXYZ&
abcdefghijklmnopqrstuvwxyz 1234567890$

12 point Garamond Bold No. 3 (Linotype)

The basic character in a type design is determined by the uniform design characteristics of all letters in the alphabet. However, this alone does not de

ABCDEFGHIJKLMNOPQRSTUVWXYZ&
abcdefghijklmnopqrstuvwxyz 1234567890$
ABCDEFGHIJKLMNOPQRSTUVWXYZ

12 point Garamond Bold No. 3 Italic (Linotype)

The basic character in a type design is determined by the uniform design characteristics of all letters in the alphabet. However, this alone does not de

ABCDEFGHIJKLMNOPQRSTUVWXYZ&
abcdefghijklmnopqrstuvwxyz 1234567890$

14 point Garamond Bold No. 3 (Linotype)

The basic character in a type design is deter mined by the uniform design characteristics

ABCDEFGHIJKLMNOPQRSTUVWXYZ&
abcdefghijklmnopqrstuvwxyz 1234567890$
ABCDEFGHIJKLMNOPQRSTUVWXYZ

14 point Garamond Bold No. 3 Italic (Linotype)

The basic character in a type design is deter mined by the uniform design characteristics

ABCDEFGHIJKLMNOPQRSTUVWXYZ&
abcdefghijklmnopqrstuvwxyz 1234567890$

Garamond Bold

16 point Garamond Bold (Foundry)

ABCDEFGHIJKLMNOPQRSTUVWXYZ&
abcdefghijklmnopqrstuvwxyz
1234567890$

18 point Garamond Bold (Ludlow)

ABCDEFGHIJKLMNOPQRSTUVWXYZ&
abcdefghijklmnopqrstuvwxyz
1234567890$

24 point Garamond Bold (Ludlow)

ABCDEFGHIJKLMNOPQRSTUVWXYZ&
abcdefghijklmnopqrstuvwxyz   1234567890$

30 point Garamond Bold (Ludlow)

ABCDEFGHIJKLMNOPQRSTUVWXYZ&
abcdefghijklmnopqrstuvwxyz   1234567890$

30 point Garamond Bold, Caps only (Foundry)

ABCDEFGHIJKLMNOPQRSTUVWXYZ&

36 point Garamond Bold, Caps only (Foundry)

ABCDEFGHIJKLMNOPQRSTUV
WXYZ&
1234567890$

36 point Garamond Bold (Ludlow)

ABCDEFGHIJKLMNOPQRSTUV
WXYZ&
abcdefghijklmnopqrstuvwxyz
1234567890$

(Continued on Page 256)

42 point Garamond Bold (Foundry)

ABCDEFGHIJKLMNOPQRST
UVWXYZ& 1234567890$
abcdefghijklmnopqrstuvwxyz

48 point Garamond Bold (Ludlow)

ABCDEFGHIJKLMNOPQ
RSTUVWXYZ&
abcdefghijklmnopqrstuvwxyz
1234567890$

60 point Garamond Bold (Foundry)

ABCDEFGHIJKLMN
OPQRSTUVWXYZ&
abcdefghijklmnopqrstu
vwxyz 1234567890$

Garamond Bold Italic

18 point Garamond Bold Italic (Ludlow)

ABCDEFGHIJKLMNOPQRSTUVWXYZ&
abcdefghijklmnopqrstuvwxyz
1234567890$

SWASH AND TERMINALS

A B C D E F G L M N P R Y
a e k m n t v w

24 point Garamond Bold Italic (Ludlow)

ABCDEFGHIJKLMNOPQRSTUVWXYZ&
abcdefghijklmnopqrstuvwxyz
1234567890$

SWASH AND TERMINALS

A B C E F G L M P R Y
a e k m n t v w

30 point Garamond Bold Italic (Ludlow)

ABCDEFGHIJKLMNOPQRSTUVWXYZ&
abcdefghijklmnopqrstuvwxyz
1234567890$

SWASH AND TERMINALS

A B C D E F G L M N P R Y
a e k m n t v w

36 point Garamond Bold Italic (Ludlow)

ABCDEFGHIJKLMNOPQRSTUV
WXYZ&
abcdefghijklmnopqrstuvwxyz
1234567890$

(Continued on Page 258)

36 Garamond Bold Italic (Ludlow)

SWASH AND TERMINALS

ABCDEFGLMN PRY

a e k m n t v w

48 point Garamond Bold Italic, Caps only (Foundry)

ABCDEFGHIJKLMNOPQRS
TUVWXYZ&

48 point Garamond Bold Italic (Ludlow)

ABCDEFGHIJKLMNOP
QRSTUVWXYZ&
abcdefghijklmnopqrstuvwxyz
1234567890$

SWASH AND TERMINALS

ABCDEFGLMN
PRY a e k m n t v w

(Continued on Page 259)

60 point Garamond Bold Italic (Ludlow)

ABCDEFGHIJKLM
NOPQRSTUVW
XYZ&

abcdefghijklmnopqrst
uvwxyz
1234567890$

SWASH AND TERMINALS

ABCDEFGLM
N PRY
a e k m n t v w

18 point Garamont Roman (Foundry)

ABCDEFGHIJKLMNOPQRSTUVWXYZ&
abcdefghijklmnopqrstuvwxyz
1234567890$

24 point Garamont Roman (Foundry)

ABCDEFGHIJKLMNOPQRSTUVWXYZ&
abcdefghijklmnopqrstuvwxyz
1234567890$

30 point Garamont Roman (Foundry)

ABCDEFGHIJKLMNOPQRSTUVWXYZ
abcdefghijklmnopqrstuvwxyz&
1234567890$

36 point Garamont Roman (Foundry)

ABCDEFGHIJKLMNOPQRSTUV
WXYZ&
abcdefghijklmnopqrstuvwxyz
1234567890$

(Continued on Page 261)

48 point Garamont Roman (Foundry)

ABCDEFGHIJKLMNOP
QRSTUVWXYZ&
abcdefghijklmnopqrstuv
wxyz
1234567890$

60 point Garamont Roman (Foundry)

ABCDEFGHIJKLM
NOPQRSTUV
WXYZ&
abcdefghijklmnopqrs
tuvwxyz
1234567890$

(Continued on Page 262)

72 point Garamont Roman (Foundry)

ABCDEFGHIJKL
MNOPQRSTUV
WXYZ&

abcdefghijklmnopq

rstuvwxyz

1234567890$

Garamont Italic

18 point Garamont Italic (Foundry)

ABCDEFGHIJKLMNOPQRSTUVWXYZ&
abcdefghijklmnopqrstuvwxyz
1234567890$

24 point Garamont Italic (Foundry)

ABCDEFGHIJKLMNOPQRSTUVWXYZ&
abcdefghijklmnopqrstuvwxyz
1234567890$

30 point Garamont Italic (Foundry)

ABCDEFGHIJKLMNOPQRSTUVWXYZ
abcdefghijklmnopqrstuvwxyz&
1234567890$

36 point Garamont Italic (Foundry)

ABCDEFGHIJKLMNOPQRSTUV
WXYZ&
abcdefghijklmnopqrstuvwxyz
1234567890$

(Continued on Page 264)

72 point Garamont Italic (Foundry)

ABCDEFGHIJKL MNOPQRSTU VWXYZ&

abcdefghijklmnopqrs
tuvwxyz
1234567890$

Gillies Gothic Bold

18 point Gillies Gothic Bold (Foundry)

ABCDEFGHIJKLMNOPQRSTUVWXYZ&
abcdefghijklmnopqrstuvwxyz
1234567890$

24 point Gillies Gothic Bold (Foundry)

ABCDEFGHIJKLMNOPQRSTUVWXYZ&
abcdefghijklmnopqrstuvwxyz
1234567890$

30 point Gillies Gothic Bold (Foundry)

ABCDEFGHIJKLMNOPQRSTUVWXYZ&
abcdefghijklmnopqrstuvwxyz
1234567890$

Gold Rush

24 point Gold Rush, Cap font (Foundry)

ABCDEFGHIJKLMNOPQRST
UVWXYZ&
1234567890$

Gothic No. 545

14 point Gothic No. 545 (Foundry)

ABCDEFGHIJKLMNOPQRSTUVWXYZ&
abcdefghijklmnopqrstuvwxyz
1234567890$

18 point Gothic Condensed No. 529 (Foundry)

ABCDEFGHIJKLMNOPQRSTUVWXYZ&
abcdefghijklmnopqrstuvwxyz
1234567890$

36 point Gothic Condensed No. 529 (Foundry)

ABCDEFGHIJKLMNOPQRSTUVWXYZ&
abcdefghijklmnopqrstuvwxyz
1234567890$

42 point Gothic Condensed No. 529 (Foundry)

ABCDEFGHIJKLMNOPQRSTUVWXYZ&
abcdefghijklmnopqrstuvwxyz
1234567890$

60 point Gothic Condensed No. 529 (Foundry)

ABCDEFGHIJKLMNOPQRSTUV
WXYZ&
abcdefghijklmnopqrstuvwxyz
1234567890$

Gothic Outline Title No. 61

24 point Gothic Outline Title No. 61, Cap font (Foundry)

ABCDEFGHIJKLMNNPQRSTUVWXYZ&
1234567890$

36 point Gothic Outline Title No. 61, Cap font (Foundry)

ABCDEFGHIJKLMNOPQRSTUVWXYZ&
1234567890$

42 point Gothic Outline Title No. 61, Cap font (Foundry)

ABCDEFGHIJKLMNOPQRSTUV
WXYZ&
1234567890$

48 point Gothic Outline Title No. 61, Cap font (Foundry)

ABCDEFGHIJKLMNOPQRS
TUVWXYZ&
1234567890$

Gothic Condensed No. 4

5½ point Gothic Condensed No. 4, Caps only (Linotype)

THE BASIC CHARACTER IN A TYPE DESIGN IS DETERMINED BY THE UNIFORM
DESIGN CHARACTERISTICS OF ALL LETTERS IN THE ALPHABET. HOWEVER, THIS
ALONE DOES NOT DETERMINE THE STANDARD OF THE TYPE FACE AND THE QUAL
ITY OF COMPOSITION SET WITH IT. THE APPEARANCE IS SOMETHING COMPLEX
WHICH FORMS ITSELF OUT OF MANY DETAILS, LIKE FORM, PROPORTION, DUCTUS,
RHYTHM ETC. IF EVERYTHING HARMONIZES, THE TOTAL RESULT WILL BE MORE
THAN THE SUM OF ITS COMPONENTS. THE ONLY RELIABLE BASIS FOR THE DE
SIGN IN A TYPE IS A POSITIVE FEELING FOR FORM AND STYLE. THE BASIC
CHARACTER IN A TYPE DESIGN IS DETERMINED BY THE UNIFORM DESIGN CHAR

ABCDEFGHIJKLMNOPQRSTUVWXYZ&

Gothic No. Three

THE BASIC CHARACTER IN A TYPE DESIGN IS DETERMINED BY
THE UNIFORM DESIGN CHARACTERISTICS OF ALL LETTERS IN
THE ALPHABET. HOWEVER, THIS ALONE DOES NOT DETERMINE
THE STANDARD OF THE TYPE FACE AND THE QUALITY OF COM
POSITION SET WITH IT. THE APPEARANCE IS SOMETHING COM
PLEX WHICH FORMS ITSELF OUT OF MANY DETAILS, LIKE FORM,
PROPORTION DUCTUS, RHYTHM ETC. IF EVERYTHING HARMO
NIZES, THE TOTAL RESULT WILL BE MORE THAN THE SUM OF
ITS COMPONENTS. THE ONLY RELIABLE BASIS FOR THE DESIGN

ABCDEFGHIJKLMNOPQRSTUVWXYZ&

Gothic No. 16

**The basic character in a type design is determined by the uniform
design characteristics of all letters in the alphabet. However, this
alone does not determine the standard of the type face and the
quality of composition set with it. The appearance is something
complex which forms itself out of many details, like form, propor
tion, ductus, rhythm etc. If everything harmonizes, the total result
will be more than the sum of its components. The only reliable
basis for the design in a type is a positive feeling for form and**

**ABCDEFGHIJKLMNOPQRSTUVWXYZ&
abcdefghijklmnopqrstuvwxyz** **1234567890$**

Goudy Bold

**ABCDEFGHIJKLMNOPQRSTUVWXYZ&
abcdefghijklmnopqrstuvwxyz
1234567890$**

**ABCDEFGHIJKLMNOPQRSTUVWXYZ&
abcdefghijklmnopqrstuvwxyz
1234567890$**

**ABCDEFGHIJKLMNOPQRSTUV
WXYZ&
abcdefghijklmnopqrstuvwxyz
1234567890$**

(Continued on Page 269)

(Continued from Page 268)

36 point Goudy Bold (Foundry)

ABCDEFGHIJKLMNOPQRST
UVWXYZ&
abcdefghijklmnopqrstuvwxyz
1234567890$

42 point Goudy Bold (Foundry)

ABCDEFGHIJKLMNOPQ
RSTUVWXYZ&
abcdefghijklmnopqrstuvwxyz
1234567890$

48 point Goudy Bold (Foundry)

ABCDEFGHIJKLMNO
PQRSTUVWXYZ&
abcdefghijklmnopqrstuv
wxyz
1234567890$

(Continued on Page 270)

48 point Goudy Bold (Ludlow)

ABCDEFGHIJKLMNO PQRSTUVWXYZ&

abcdefghijklmnopqrstu vwxyz 1234567890$

Goudy Bold Italic

14 point Goudy Bold Italic (Foundry)

ABCDEFGHIJKLMNOPQRSTUVWXYZ&
abcdefghijklmnopqrstuvwxyz *1234567890$*

18 point Goudy Bold Italic (Foundry)

ABCDEFGHIJKLMNOPQRSTUVWXYZ&
abcdefghijklmnopqrstuvwxyz *1234567890$*

30 point Goudy Bold Italic (Foundry)

ABCDEFGHIJKLMNOPQRSTUV
WXYZ& *1234567890$*
abcdefghijklmnopqrstuvwxyz

36 point Goudy Bold Italic (Foundry)

ABCDEFGHIJKLMNOPQRSTU
VWXYZ& *1234567890$*
abcdefghijklmnopqrstuvwxyz

12 point Goudy Handtool (Foundry)

ABCDEFGHIJKLMNOPQRSTUVWXYZ&
abcdefghijklmnopqrstuvwxyz
1234567890$

14 point Goudy Handtool (Foundry)

ABCDEFGHIJKLMNOPQRSTUVWXYZ&
abcdefghijklmnopqrstuvwxyz
1234567890$

18 point Goudy Handtool (Foundry)

ABCDEFGHIJKLMNOPQRSTUVWXYZ&
abcdefghijklmnopqrstuvwxyz
1234567890$

24 point Goudy Handtool (Foundry)

ABCDEFGHIJKLMNOPQRSTUVWXYZ&
abcdefghijklmnopqrstuvwxyz
1234567890$

30 point Goudy Handtool (Foundry)

ABCDEFGHIJKLMNOPQRSTUV
WXYZ&
abcdefghijklmnopqrstuvwxyz
1234567890$

36 point Goudy Handtool (Foundry)

ABCDEFGHIJKLMNOPQRST
UVWXYZ&
abcdefghijklmnopqrstuvwxyz
1234567890$

(Continued on Page 272)

Goudy Handtool

(Continued from Page 271)

48 point Goudy Handtool (Foundry)

ABCDEFGHIJKLMNO PQRSTUVWXYZ& abcdefghijklmnopqrst uvwxyz 1234567890$

Goudy Handtool Italic

14 point Goudy Handtool Italic (Foundry)

ABCDEFGHIJKLMNOPQRSTUVWXYZ&
abcdefghijklmnopqrstuvwxyz
1234567890$

18 point Goudy Handtool Italic (Foundry)

ABCDEFGHIJKLMNOPQRSTUVWXYZ&
abcdefghijklmnopqrstuvwxyz
1234567890$

24 point Goudy Handtool Italic (Foundry)

ABCDEFGHIJKLMNOPQRSTUVWXYZ&
abcdefghijklmnopqrstuvwxyz
1234567890$

(Continued on Page 273)

(Continued from Page 272)

30 point Goudy Handtool Italic (Foundry)

ABCDEFGHIJKLMNOPQRSTUV
WXYZ&
abcdefghijklmnopqrstuvwxyz
1234567890$

36 point Goudy Handtool Italic (Foundry)

ABCDEFGHIJKLMNOPQRST
UVWXYZ&
abcdefghijklmnopqrstuvwxyz
1234567890$

Goudy Light

6 point Goudy Light (Ludlow)
ABCDEFGHIJKLMNOPQRSTUVWXYZ&
abcdefghijklmnopqrstuvwxyz
1234567890$

8 point Goudy Light (Ludlow)
ABCDEFGHIJKLMNOPQRSTUVWXYZ&
abcdefghijklmnopqrstuvwxyz
1234567890$

10 point Goudy Light (Ludlow)
ABCDEFGHIJKLMNOPQRSTUVWXYZ&
abcdefghijklmnopqrstuvwxyz
1234567890$

12 point Goudy Light (Ludlow)
ABCDEFGHIJKLMNOPQRSTUVWXYZ&
abcdefghijklmnopqrstuvwxyz
1234567890$

14 point Goudy Light (Ludlow)
ABCDEFGHIJKLMNOPQRSTUV
WXYZ&
1234567890$
abcdefghijklmnopqrstuvwxyz

18 point Goudy Light (Ludlow)
ABCDEFGHIJKLMNOPQRSTUVWXYZ&
abcdefghijklmnopqrstuvwxyz
1234567890$

24 point Goudy Light (Ludlow)
ABCDEFGHIJKLMNOPQRSTUVWXYZ&
abcdefghijklmnopqrstuvwxyz
1234567890$

Goudy Italic

14 point Goudy Italic (Foundry)

ABCDEFGHIJKLMNOPQRSTUVWXYZ&
abcdefghijklmnopqrstuvwxyz
1234567890$

18 point Goudy Italic (Foundry)

ABCDEFGHIJKLMNOPQRSTUVWXYZ&
abcdefghijklmnopqrstuvwxyz
1234567890$

24 point Goudy Italic (Foundry)

ABCDEFGHIJKLMNOPQRSTUVWXYZ&
abcdefghijklmnopqrstuvwxyz
1234567890$

30 point Goudy Italic (Foundry)

ABCDEFGHIJKLMNOPQRSTUVWXYZ&
abcdefghijklmnopqrstuvwxyz
1234567890$

36 point Goudy Italic (Foundry)

ABCDEFGHIJKLMNOPQRSTUV
WXYZ&
abcdefghijklmnopqrstuvwxyz
1234567890$

Goudy Oldstyle

ABCDEFGHIJKLMNOPQRSTUVWXYZ&
abcdefghijklmnopqrstuvwxyz
1234567890$

ABCDEFGHIJKLMNOPQRSTUVWXYZ&
abcdefghijklmnopqrstuvwxyz
1234567890$

ABCDEFGHIJKLMNOPQRSTUVWXYZ&
abcdefghijklmnopqrstuvwxyz
1234567890$

ABCDEFGHIJKLMNOPQRSTUVWXYZ
abcdefghijklmnopqrstuvwxyz&
1234567890$

ABCDEFGHIJKLMNOPQRSTUV
WXYZ&
abcdefghijklmnopqrstuvwxyz
1234567890$

Goudy Oldstyle Italic

ABCDEFGHIJKLMNOPQRSTUVWXYZ&
abcdefghijklmnopqrstuvwxyz
1234567890$

14 point Goudy Open (Foundry)

ABCDEFGHIJKLMNOPQRSTUVWXYZ&
abcdefghijklmnopqrstuvwxyz
1234567890$

18 point Goudy Open (Foundry)

ABCDEFGHIJKLMNOPQRSTUVWXYZ&
abcdefghijklmnopqrstuvwxyz
1234567890$

24 point Goudy Open (Foundry)

ABCDEFGHIJKLMNOPQRSTUVWXYZ&
abcdefghijklmnopqrstuvwxyz
1234567890$

30 point Goudy Open (Foundry)

ABCDEFGHIJKLMNOPQRSTUVWXYZ&
abcdefghijklmnopqrstuvwxyz
1234567890$

36 point Goudy Open (Foundry)

ABCDEFGHIJKLMNOPQRSTUV
WXYZ&
abcdefghijklmnopqrstuvwxyz
1234567890$

Goudy Open Italic

18 point Goudy Open Italic (Foundry)

ABCDEFGHIJKLMNOPQRSTUVWXYZ&
abcdefghijklmnopqrstuvwxyz
1234567890$

24 point Goudy Open Italic (Foundry)

ABCDEFGHIJKLMNOPQRSTUVWXYZ&
abcdefghijklmnopqrstuvwxyz
1234567890$

30 point Goudy Open Italic (Foundry)

ABCDEFGHIJKLMNOPQRSTUVWXYZ
abcdefghijklmnopqrstuvwxyz&
1234567890$

36 point Goudy Open Italic (Foundry)

ABCDEFGHIJKLMNOPQRSTUV
WXYZ&
abcdefghijklmnopqrstuvwxyz
1234567890$

18 point Goudy Text (Foundry)

ABCDEFGHIJKLMNOPQRSTUVWXYZ&
abcdefghijklmnopqrstuvwxyz
1234567890$

36 point Goudy Text (Foundry)

ABCDEFGHIJKLMNOPQRS
TUVWXYZ&
abcdefghijklmnopqrstuvwxyz
1234567890$

60 point Goudy Text (Foundry)

ABCDEFGHIJKL
MNOPQRSTUV
WXYZ&
abcdefghijklmnopqrstuv
wxyz
1234567890$

(Continued on Page 279)

72 point Goudy Text (Foundry)

ABCDEFGHI
JKLMNOP
QRSTUV
WXYZ&
abcdefghijklmnopqrstu
vwxyz
1234567890$

Graphic Bold *(Also known as Lucian Bold)*

14 point Graphic Bold (Foundry)

ABCDEFGHIJKLMNOPQRSTUVWXYZ&
abcdefghijklmnopqrstuvwxyz
1234567890$

18 point Graphic Bold (Foundry)

ABCDEFGHIJKLMNOPQRSTUVWXYZ&
abcdefghijklmnopqrstuvwxyz
1234567890$

30 point Graphic Bold (Foundry)

ABCDEFGHIJKLMNOPQRSTUV
WXYZ&
abcdefghijklmnopqrstuvwxyz
1234567890$

48 point Graphic Bold (Foundry)

ABCDEFGHIJKLMNOP
QRSTUVWXYZ&
abcdefghijklmnopqrstuv
wxyz
1234567890$

Granjon

Granjon Italic

8 point Granjon (Linotype)

The basic character in a type design is determined by the uniform design characteristics of all letters in the alphabet. However, this alone does not determine the standard of the type face and the quality of composition set with it. The appearance is something complex which forms itself out of many details, like form, proportion, ductus, rhythm etc. If everything

ABCDEFGHIJKLMNOPQRSTUVWXYZ&
abcdefghijklmnopqrstuvwxyz 1234567890$
ABCDEFGHIJKLMNOPQRSTUVWXYZ

8 point Granjon Italic (Linotype)

The basic character in a type design is determined by the uniform design characteristics of all letters in the alphabet. However, this alone does not determine the standard of the type face and the quality of composition set with it. The appearance is something complex which forms itself out of many details, like form, proportion, ductus, rhythm etc. If everything

ABCDEFGHIJKLMNOPQRSTUVWXYZ&
abcdefghijklmnopqrstuvwxyz 1234567890$

9 point Granjon (Linotype)

The basic character in a type design is determined by the uniform design characteristics of all letters in the alphabet. However, this alone does not determine the standard of the type face and the quality of composition set with it. The appearance is something

ABCDEFGHIJKLMNOPQRSTUVWXYZ&
abcdefghijklmnopqrstuvwxyz 1234567890$
ABCDEFGHIJKLMNOPQRSTUVWXYZ

9 point Granjon Italic (Linotype)

The basic character in a type design is determined by the uniform design characteristics of all letters in the alphabet. However, this alone does not determine the standard of the type face and the quality of composition set with it. The appearance is something

ABCDEFGHIJKLMNOPQRSTUVWXYZ&
abcdefghijklmnopqrstuvwxyz 1234567890$

10 point Granjon (Linotype)

The basic character in a type design is determined by the uniform design characteristics of all letters in the alphabet. However, this alone does not determine the standard of the type face and the quality of composition set with it. The appear

ABCDEFGHIJKLMNOPQRSTUVWXYZ&
abcdefghijklmnopqrstuvwxyz 1234567890$
ABCDEFGHIJKLMNOPQRSTUVWXYZ

10 point Granjon Italic (Linotype)

The basic character in a type design is determined by the uniform design characteristics of all letters in the alphabet. However, this alone does not determine the standard of the type face and the quality of composition set with it. The appear

ABCDEFGHIJKLMNOPQRSTUVWXYZ&
abcdefghijklmnopqrstuvwxyz 1234567890$

11 point Granjon (Linotype)

The basic character in a type design is determined by the uniform design characteristics of all letters in the alphabet. However, this alone does not determine the standard of the

ABCDEFGHIJKLMNOPQRSTUVWXYZ&
abcdefghijklmnopqrstuvwxyz 1234567890$
ABCDEFGHIJKLMNOPQRSTUVWXYZ

11 point Granjon Italic (Linotype)

The basic character in a type design is determined by the uniform design characteristics of all letters in the alphabet. However, this alone does not determine the standard of the

ABCDEFGHIJKLMNOPQRSTUVWXYZ&
abcdefghijklmnopqrstuvwxyz 1234567890$

12 point Granjon (Linotype)

The basic character in a type design is determined by the uniform design characteristics of all letters in the alphabet. However, this alone does not determine the

ABCDEFGHIJKLMNOPQRSTUVWXYZ&
abcdefghijklmnopqrstuvwxyz 1234567890$
ABCDEFGHIJKLMNOPQRSTUVWXYZ

12 point Granjon Italic (Linotype)

The basic character in a type design is determined by the uniform design characteristics of all letters in the alphabet. However, this alone does not determine the

ABCDEFGHIJKLMNOPQRSTUVWXYZ&
abcdefghijklmnopqrstuvwxyz 1234567890$

Granjon Bold

The basic character in a type design is determined by the uniform design characteristics of all letters in the alphabet. However, this alone does not determine the standard of the type face and the quality of composition set with it. The appearance is something complex which forms itself out of many details, like form, proportion, ductus, rhythm etc. If everything harmonizes, the total result will be more than the sum of its components.

ABCDEFGHIJKLMNOPQRSTUVWXYZ&
abcdefghijklmnopqrstuvwxyz   1234567890$

The basic character in a type design is determined by the uni form design characteristics of all letters in the alphabet. How ever, this alone does not determine the standard of the type face and the quality of composition set with it. The appear ance is something complex which forms itself out of many

ABCDEFGHIJKLMNOPQRSTUVWXYZ&
abcdefghijklmnopqrstuvwxyz   1234567890$

The basic character in a type design is determined by the uniform design characteristics of all letters in the alphabet. However, this alone does not determine the standard of the type face and the quality of composi

ABCDEFGHIJKLMNOPQRSTUVWXYZ&
abcdefghijklmnopqrstuvwxyz   1234567890$

Grotesque No. 6

ABCDEFGHIJKLMNOPQRSTUVWXYZ&
abcdefghijklmnopqrstuvwxyz
1234567890$

ABCDEFGHIJKLMNOPQRSTUVWXYZ&
abcdefghijklmnopqrstuvwxyz
1234567890$

Grotesque No. 8

ABCDEFGHIJKLMNOPQRSTUVWXYZ&
abcdefghijklmnopqrstuvwxyz
1234567890$

(Continued on Page 283)

(Continued from Page 282)

36 point Grotesque No. 8 (Foundry)

ABCDEFGHIJKLMNOPQ
RSTUVWXYZ&
abcdefghijklmnopqrst
uvwxyz
1234567890$

60 point Grotesque No. 8 (Foundry)

ABCDEFGHIJK
LMNOPQRST
UVWXYZ&
abcdefghijklmn
opqrstuvwxyz
1234567890$

(Continued on Page 284)

72 point Grotesque No. 8 (Foundry)

ABCDEFGHI
JKLMNOPQ
RSTUV
WXYZ&
abcdefghijkl
mnopqrstuv
wxyz 12345
67890$

Grotesque No. 9

ABCDEFGHIJKLMNOPQRSTUVWXYZ&
abcdefghijklmnopqrstuvwxyz
1234567890$

ABCDEFGHIJKLMNOPQRSTUVWXYZ&
abcdefghijklmnopqrstuvwxyz
1234567890$

ABCDEFGHIJKLMNOPQRSTUVWXYZ&
abcdefghijklmnopqrstuvwxyz
1234567890$

ABCDEFGHIJKLMNOPQRSTUVWXYZ&
abcdefghijklmnopqrstuvwxyz
1234567890$

ABCDEFGHIJKLMNOPQRSTUVWXYZ&
abcdefghijklmnopqrstuvwxyz
1234567890$

ABCDEFGHIJKLMNOPQRSTUVWXYZ&
abcdefghijklmnopqrstuvwxyz
1234567890$

ABCDEFGHIJKLMNOPQRSTUVWXYZ&
abcdefghijklmnopqrstuvwxyz
1234567890$

Hauser Script

ABCDEFGHIJKLMNOPQRSTUVWXYZ&
abcdefghijklmnopqrstuvwxyz
1234567890$

Headline Gothic

48 point Headline Gothic, Cap font (Foundry)

ABCDEFGHIJKLMNOPQRSTU VWXYZ& 1234567890$

Hellenic Wide

10 point Hellenic Wide (Foundry)

ABCDEFGHIJKLMNOPQRSTUVWXYZ&
abcdefghijklmnopqrstuvwxyz
1234567890$

12 point Hellenic Wide (Foundry)

ABCDEFGHIJKLMNOPQRSTUVWXYZ&
abcdefghijklmnopqrstuvwxyz
1234567890$

14 point Hellenic Wide (Foundry)

ABCDEFGHIJKLMNOPQRSTUVWXYZ&
abcdefghijklmnopqrstuvwxyz
1234567890$

18 point Hellenic Wide (Foundry)

ABCDEFGHIJKLMNOPQRSTUVWXYZ
abcdefghijklmnopqrstuvwxyz&
1234567890$

24 point Hellenic Wide (Foundry)

ABCDEFGHIJKLMNOPQR
STUVWXYZ&
abcdefghijklmnopqrstuv
wxyz
1234567890$

(Continued on Page 287)

30 point Hellenic Wide (Foundry)

ABCDEFGHIJKL
MNOPQRSTUV
WXYZ&
abcdefghijklmnopq
rstuvwxyz
1234567890$

42 point Hellenic Wide (Foundry)

ABCDEFGHI
JKLMNOPQ
RSTUV
WXYZ&
abcdefghijkl
mnopqrstuv
wxyz
12345
67890$

Helvetica

6 point Helvetica (Linotype)

The basic character in a type design is determined by the uniform design characteristics of all letters in the alphabet. However, this alone does not determine the standard of the type face and the quality of composition set with it. The appearance is something complex which forms itself out of many details, like form, proportion, ductus, rhythm etc. If everything harmonizes, the total result will be more than the sum of its components. The only reliable basis for the design in a type is a positive feeling for form and style. The basic character in a type design is determined by the uniform

ABCDEFGHIJKLMNOPQRSTUVWXYZ&
abcdefghijklmnopqrstuvwxyz   1234567890$

---

7 point Helvetica (Linotype)

The basic character in a type design is determined by the uniform design characteristics of all letters in the alphabet. However, this alone does not determine the standard of the type face and the quality of composition set with it. The appearance is something complex which forms itself out of many details, like form, proportion, ductus, rhythm etc. If everything harmonizes, the total result will be more than the sum of its components. The only reliable basis for the design in a

ABCDEFGHIJKLMNOPQRSTUVWXYZ&
abcdefghijklmnopqrstuvwxyz   1234567890$

---

8 point Helvetica (Linotype)

The basic character in a type design is determined by the uniform design characteristics of all letters in the alphabet. However, this alone does not determine the standard of the type face and the quality of composition set with it. The appearance is something complex which forms itself out of many details, like form, proportion, ductus, rhythm etc. If everything harmo

ABCDEFGHIJKLMNOPQRSTUVWXYZ&
abcdefghijklmnopqrstuvwxyz   1234567890$

---

9 point Helvetica (Linotype)

The basic character in a type design is determined by the uniform design characteristics of all letters in the alphabet. However, this alone does not determine the standard of the type face and the quality of composition set with it. The appearance is something complex which forms itself

ABCDEFGHIJKLMNOPQRSTUVWXYZ&
abcdefghijklmnopqrstuvwxyz   1234567890$

---

10 point Helvetica (Linotype)

The basic character in a type design is determined by the uniform design characteristics of all letters in the alphabet. However, this alone does not determine the standard of the type face and the quality of com position set with it. The appearance is something

ABCDEFGHIJKLMNOPQRSTUVWXYZ&
abcdefghijklmnopqrstuvwxyz   1234567890$

---

11 point Helvetica (Linotype)

The basic character in a type design is deter mined by the uniform design characteristics of all letters in the alphabet. However, this alone does not determine the standard of the type face

ABCDEFGHIJKLMNOPQRSTUVWXYZ&
abcdefghijklmnopqrstuvwxyz   1234567890$

---

12 point Helvetica (Linotype)

The basic character in a type design is deter mined by the uniform design characteristics of all letters in the alphabet. However, this alone does not determine the standard of the

ABCDEFGHIJKLMNOPQRSTUVWXYZ&
abcdefghijklmnopqrstuvwxyz   1234567890$

---

14 point Helvetica (Linotype)

The basic character in a type design is determined by the uniform design char acteristics of all letters in the alphabet.

ABCDEFGHIJKLMNOPQRSTUV
WXYZ&   1234567890$
abcdefghijklmnopqrstuvwxyz

---

16 point Helvetica (Foundry)

ABCDEFGHIJKLMNOPQRSTUVWXYZ&
abcdefghijklmnopqrstuvwxyz
1234567890$

---

18 point Helvetica (Foundry)

ABCDEFGHIJKLMNOPQRSTUVWXYZ&
abcdefghijklmnopqrstuvwxyz
1234567890$

---

24 point Helvetica Small (Foundry)

ABCDEFGHIJKLMNOPQRSTUVWXYZ&
abcdefghijklmnopqrstuvwxyz
1234567890$

(Continued on Page 289)

24 point Helvetica Large (Foundry)

ABCDEFGHIJKLMNOPQRSTUVWXYZ&
abcdefghijklmnopqrstuvwxyz
1234567890$

30 point Helvetica (Foundry)

ABCDEFGHIJKLMNOPQRSTUVWXYZ
abcdefghijklmnopqrstuvwxyz&
1234567890$

42 point Helvetica (Foundry)

ABCDEFGHIJKLMNOPQRST
UVWXYZ&
abcdefghijklmnopqrstuvwxyz
1234567890$

48 point Helvetica (Foundry)

ABCDEFGHIJKLMNOP
QRSTUVWXYZ&
abcdefghijklmnopqrst
uvwxyz
1234567890$

(Continued on Page 290)

(Continued from Page 289)

60 point Helvetica (Foundry)

ABCDEFGHIJKLM
NOPQRSTUV
WXYZ&
abcdefghijklmnopq
rstuvwxyz
1234567890$

Helvetica Bold

10 point Helvetica Bold (Foundry)
**ABCDEFGHIJKLMNOPQRSTUVWXYZ&
abcdefghijklmnopqrstuvwxyz
1234567890$**

12 point Helvetica Bold (Foundry)
**ABCDEFGHIJKLMNOPQRSTUVWXYZ&
abcdefghijklmnopqrstuvwxyz
1234567890$**

14 point Helvetica Bold (Foundry)
**ABCDEFGHIJKLMNOPQRSTUVWXYZ&
abcdefghijklmnopqrstuvwxyz
1234567890$**

16 point Helvetica Bold (Foundry)
**ABCDEFGHIJKLMNOPQRSTUVWXYZ&
abcdefghijklmnopqrstuvwxyz
1234567890$**

(Continued on Page 291)

(Continued from Page 290)

18 point Helvetica Bold (Foundry)

**ABCDEFGHIJKLMNOPQRSTUVWXYZ&
abcdefghijklmnopqrstuvwxyz
1234567890$**

24 point Helvetica Bold Small (Foundry)

**ABCDEFGHIJKLMNOPQRSTUVWXYZ&
abcdefghijklmnopqrstuvwxyz
1234567890$**

24 point Helvetica Bold Large (Foundry)

**ABCDEFGHIJKLMNOPQRSTUVWXYZ&
abcdefghijklmnopqrstuvwxyz
1234567890$**

30 point Helvetica Bold (Foundry)

**ABCDEFGHIJKLMNOPQRSTUV
WXYZ&
abcdefghijklmnopqrstuvwxyz
1234567890$**

42 point Helvetica Bold (Foundry)

**ABCDEFGHIJKLMNOPQR
STUVWXYZ&
abcdefghijklmnopqrstuv
wxyz
1234567890$**

(Continued on Page 292)

(Continued from Page 291)

48 point Helvetica Bold (Foundry)

ABCDEFGHIJKLMN
OPQRSTUVWXYZ&
abcdefghijklmnopq
rstuvwxyz
1234567890$

60 point Helvetica Bold (Foundry)

ABCDEFGHIJKL
MNOPQRSTUV
WXYZ&
abcdefghijklmn
opqrstuvwxyz
1234567890$

Helvetica Bold Condensed

12 point Helvetica Bold Condensed (Foundry)

ABCDEFGHIJKLMNOPQRSTUVWXYZ&
abcdefghijklmnopqrstuvwxyz
1234567890$

14 point Helvetica Bold Condensed (Foundry)

ABCDEFGHIJKLMNOPQRSTUVWXYZ&
abcdefghijklmnopqrstuvwxyz
1234567890$

18 point Helvetica Bold Condensed (Foundry)

ABCDEFGHIJKLMNOPQRSTUVWXYZ&
abcdefghijklmnopqrstuvwxyz
1234567890$

24 point Small Helvetica Bold Condensed (Foundry)

ABCDEFGHIJKLMNOPQRSTUVWXYZ&
abcdefghijklmnopqrstuvwxyz
1234567890$

30 point Helvetica Bold Condensed (Foundry)

ABCDEFGHIJKLMNOPQRSTUVWXYZ&
abcdefghijklmnopqrstuvwxyz
1234567890$

54 point Helvetica Bold Condensed (Foundry)

ABCDEFGHIJKLMNOPQRSTUV
WXYZ&
abcdefghijklmnopqrstuvwxyz
1234567890$

Helvetica Bold Compact Italic

14 point Helvetica Bold Compact Italic (Foundry)

ABCDEFGHIJKLMNOPQRSTUVWXYZ&
abcdefghijklmnopqrstuvwxyz
1234567890$

18 point Helvetica Bold Compact Italic (Foundry)

ABCDEFGHIJKLMNOPQRSTUVWXYZ&
abcdefghijklmnopqrstuvwxyz
1234567890$

24 point Helvetica Bold Compact Italic (Foundry)

ABCDEFGHIJKLMNOPQRSTUVWXYZ&
abcdefghijklmnopqrstuvwxyz
1234567890$

30 point Helvetica Bold Compact Italic (Foundry)

ABCDEFGHIJKLMNOPQRSTUV
WXYZ&
abcdefghijklmnopqrstuvwxyz
1234567890$

Helvetica Bold Extended

10 point Helvetica Bold Extended Large (Foundry)
ABCDEFGHIJKLMNOPQRSTUVWXYZ&
abcdefghijklmnopqrstuvwxyz
1234567890$

12 point Helvetica Bold Extended (Foundry)
ABCDEFGHIJKLMNOPQRSTUVWXYZ&
abcdefghijklmnopqrstuvwxyz
1234567890$

14 point Helvetica Bold Extended (Foundry)
ABCDEFGHIJKLMNOPQRSTUVWXYZ&
abcdefghijklmnopqrstuvwxyz
1234567890$

16 point Helvetica Bold Extended (Foundry)
ABCDEFGHIJKLMNOPQRSTUVWXYZ&
abcdefghijklmnopqrstuvwxyz
1234567890$

18 point Helvetica Bold Extended (Foundry)
ABCDEFGHIJKLMNOPQRSTUVWXYZ&
abcdefghijklmnopqrstuvwxyz **1234567890$**

24 point Helvetica Bold Extended Large (Foundry)
ABCDEFGHIJKLMNOPQRSTUV
WXYZ&
abcdefghijklmnopqrstuvwxyz
1234567890$

48 point Helvetica Bold Extended (Foundry)
ABCDEFGHIJKLM
NOPQRSTUV
WXYZ&
abcdefghijklmnop
qrstuvwxyz
1234567890$

Helvetica Regular Condensed

18 point Helvetica Regular Condensed (Foundry)

ABCDEFGHIJKLMNOPQRSTUVWXYZ&
abcdefghijklmnopqrstuvwxyz
1234567890$

Helvetica Regular Extended

14 point Helvetica Regular Extended (Foundry)

ABCDEFGHIJKLMNOPQRSTUVWXYZ&
abcdefghijklmnopqrstuvwxyz
1234567890$

16 point Helvetica Regular Extended (Foundry)

ABCDEFGHIJKLMNOPQRSTUVWXYZ&
abcdefghijklmnopqrstuvwxyz
1234567890$

18 point Helvetica Regular Extended (Foundry)

ABCDEFGHIJKLMNOPQRSTUVWXYZ&
abcdefghijklmnopqrstuvwxyz
1234567890$

48 point Helvetica Regular Extended (Foundry)

ABCDEFGHIJKLMN
OPQRSTUVWXYZ&
abcdefghijklmnopq
rstuvwxyz
1234567890$

Helvetica Extra Bold Condensed

18 point Helvetica Extra Bold Condensed (Foundry)

ABCDEFGHIJKLMNOPQRSTUVWXYZ&
abcdefghijklmnopqrstuvwxyz
1234567890$

24 point Helvetica Extra Bold Condensed (Foundry)

ABCDEFGHIJKLMNOPQRSTUVWXYZ&
abcdefghijklmnopqrstuvwxyz
1234567890$

30 point Helvetica Extra Bold Condensed (Foundry)

ABCDEFGHIJKLMNOPQRSTUVWXYZ&
abcdefghijklmnopqrstuvwxyz
1234567890$

42 point Helvetica Extra Bold Condensed (Foundry)

ABCDEFGHIJKLMNOPQRSTUVWXYZ
abcdefghijklmnopqrstuvwxyz&
1234567890$

54 point Helvetica Extra Bold Condensed (Foundry)

ABCDEFGHIJKLMNOPQRS
TUVWXYZ&
abcdefghijklmnopqrstuv
wxyz 1234567890$

(Continued on Page 298)

(Continued from Page 297)

84 point Helvetica Extra Bold Condensed (Foundry)

ABCDEFGHIJKL
MNOPQRSTUV
WXYZ&
abcdefghijklmno
pqrstuvwxyz
1234567890$

Helvetica Extra Bold Extended

ABCDEFGHIJKLMNOPQRSTUVWXYZ&
abcdefghijklmnopqrstuvwxyz
1234567890$

ABCDEFGHIJKLMNOPQRSTUVWXYZ&
abcdefghijklmnopqrstuvwxyz
1234567890$

ABCDEFGHIJKLMNOPQRSTUVWXYZ&
abcdefghijklmnopqrstuvwxyz
1234567890$

ABCDEFGHIJKLMNOPQRSTUVWXYZ&
abcdefghijklmnopqrstuvwxyz
1234567890$

ABCDEFGHIJKLMNOPQRSTUVWXYZ&
abcdefghijklmnopqrstuvwxyz
1234567890$

ABCDEFGHIJKLMNOPQRSTUV
WXYZ&
abcdefghijklmnopqrstuvwxyz
1234567890$

Helvetica Italic

6 point Helvetica Italic (Linotype)
The basic character in a type design is determined by the uniform design characteristics of all letters in the alphabet. However, this alone does not determine the standard of the type face and the quality of composition set with it. The appearance is something complex which forms itself out of many details, like form, proportion, ductus, rhythm etc. If everything harmonizes, the total result .will be more than the sum of its components. The only reliable basis for the design in a type is a positive feeling for form and style. The basic character in a type design is determined by the uniform

ABCDEFGHIJKLMNOPQRSTUVWXYZ&
abcdefghijklmnopqrstuvwxyz *1234567890$*

7 point Helvetica Italic (Linotype)
The basic character in a type design is determined by the uniform design characteristics of all letters in the alphabet. However, this alone does not determine the standard of the type face and the quality of composition set with it. The appearance is something complex which forms itself out of many details, like form, proportion, ductus, rhythm etc. If everything harmonizes, the total result will be more than the sum of its components. The only reliable basis for the design in a

ABCDEFGHIJKLMNOPQRSTUVWXYZ&
abcdefghijklmnopqrstuvwxyz *1234567890$*

8 point Helvetica Italic (Linotype)
The basic character in a type design is determined by the uniform design characteristics of all letters in the alphabet. However, this alone does not determine the standard of the type face and the quality of composition set with it. The appearance is something complex which forms itself out of many details, like form, proportion, ductus, rhythm etc. If everything harmo

ABCDEFGHIJKLMNOPQRSTUVWXYZ&
abcdefghijklmnopqrstuvwxyz *1234567890$*

9 point Helvetica Italic (Linotype)
The basic character in a type design is determined by the uniform design characteristics of all letters in the alphabet. However, this alone does not determine the standard of the type face and the quality of composition set with it. The appearance is something complex which forms itself

ABCDEFGHIJKLMNOPQRSTUVWXYZ&
abcdefghijklmnopqrstuvwxyz *1234567890$*

10 point Helvetica Italic (Linotype)
The basic character in a type design is determined by the uniform design characteristics of all letters in the alphabet. However, this alone does not determine the standard of the type face and the quality of com position set with it. The appearance is something

ABCDEFGHIJKLMNOPQRSTUVWXYZ&
abcdefghijklmnopqrstuvwxyz *1234567890$*

11 point Helvetica Italic (Linotype)
The basic character in a type design is deter mined by the uniform design characteristics of all letters in the alphabet. However, this alone does not determine the standard of the type face

ABCDEFGHIJKLMNOPQRSTUVWXYZ&
abcdefghijklmnopqrstuvwxyz *1234567890$*

12 point Helvetica Italic (Linotype)
The basic character in a type design is deter mined by the uniform design characteristics of all letters in the alphabet. However, this alone does not determine the standard of the

ABCDEFGHIJKLMNOPQRSTUVWXYZ&
abcdefghijklmnopqrstuvwxyz *1234567890$*

14 point Helvetica Italic (Linotype)
The basic character in a type design is determined by the uniform design char acteristics of all letters in the alphabet.

ABCDEFGHIJKLMNOPQRSTUV WXYZ& *1234567890$*
abcdefghijklmnopqrstuvwxyz

16 point Helvetica Italic (Foundry)
ABCDEFGHIJKLMNOPQRSTUVWXYZ&
abcdefghijklmnopqrstuvwxyz *1234567890$*

18 point Helvetica Italic (Foundry)
ABCDEFGHIJKLMNOPQRSTUVWXYZ&
abcdefghijklmnopqrstuvwxyz *1234567890$*

24 point Helvetica Italic Small (Foundry)
ABCDEFGHIJKLMNOPQRSTUVWXYZ&
abcdefghijklmnopqrstuvwxyz *1234567890$*

(Continued on Page 301)

24 point Helvetica Italic Large (Foundry)

ABCDEFGHIJKLMNOPQRSTUVWXYZ&
abcdefghijklmnopqrstuvwxyz   1234567890$

30 point Helvetica Italic (Foundry)

ABCDEFGHIJKLMNOPQRSTUVWXYZ&
abcdefghijklmnopqrstuvwxyz
1234567890$

Helvetica Light

6 point Helvetica Light (Linotype)

The basic character in a type design is determined by the uniform design characteristics of all letters in the alphabet. However, this alone does not determine the standard of the type face and the quality of composition set with it. The appearance is something complex which forms itself out of many details, like form, proportion, ductus, rhythm etc. If everything harmonizes, the total result will be more than the sum of its components. The only reliable basis for the design in a type is a positive feeling for form and style. The basic character in a type design is determined by the uniform design char

ABCDEFGHIJKLMNOPQRSTUVWXYZ&
abcdefghijklmnopqrstuvwxyz   1234567890$

7 point Helvetica Light (Linotype)

The basic character in a type design is determined by the uniform design characteristics of all letters in the alphabet. However, this alone does not determine the standard of the type face and the quality of composition set with it. The appearance is something complex which forms itself out of many details, like form, proportion, ductus, rhythm etc. If everything harmonizes, the total result will be more than the sum of its components. The only reliable basis for the design in a

ABCDEFGHIJKLMNOPQRSTUVWXYZ&
abcdefghijklmnopqrstuvwxyz   1234567890$

8 point Helvetica Light (Linotype)

The basic character in a type design is determined by the uniform design characteristics of all letters in the alphabet. However, this alone does not determine the standard of the type face and the quality of composition set with it. The appearance is something complex which forms itself out of many details, like form, proportion, ductus, rhythm etc. If everything harmonizes, the total result

ABCDEFGHIJKLMNOPQRSTUVWXYZ&
abcdefghijklmnopqrstuvwxyz   1234567890$

9 point Helvetica Light (Linotype)

The basic character in a type design is determined by the uniform design characteristics of all letters in the alphabet. However, this alone does not determine the standard of the type face and the quality of composition set with it. The appearance is something complex which forms itself out of

ABCDEFGHIJKLMNOPQRSTUVWXYZ&
abcdefghijklmnopqrstuvwxyz   1234567890$

10 point Helvetica Light (Linotype)

The basic character in a type design is determined by the uniform design characteristics of all letters in the alphabet. However, this alone does not determine the standard of the type face and the quality of composition set with it. The appearance is something complex which

ABCDEFGHIJKLMNOPQRSTUVWXYZ&
abcdefghijklmnopqrstuvwxyz   1234567890$

11 point Helvetica Light (Linotype)

The basic character in a type design is determined by the uniform design characteristics of all letters in the alphabet. However, this alone does not determine the standard of the type face and the qual

ABCDEFGHIJKLMNOPQRSTUVWXYZ&
abcdefghijklmnopqrstuvwxyz   1234567890$

12 point Helvetica Light (Linotype)

The basic character in a type design is determined by the uniform design characteristics of all letters in the alphabet. However, this alone does not determine the standard of the type

ABCDEFGHIJKLMNOPQRSTUVWXYZ&
abcdefghijklmnopqrstuvwxyz   1234567890$

14 point Helvetica Light (Linotype)

The basic character in a type design is determined by the uniform design characteristics of all letters in the alphabet.

ABCDEFGHIJKLMNOPQRSTUVWXYZ&
abcdefghijklmnopqrstuvwxyz
1234567890$

(Continued on Page 302)

(Continued from Page 301)

16 point Helvetica Light (Foundry)

ABCDEFGHIJKLMNOPQRSTUVWXYZ&
abcdefghijklmnopqrstuvwxyz
1234567890$

18 point Helvetica Light (Foundry)

ABCDEFGHIJKLMNOPQRSTUVWXYZ&
abcdefghijklmnopqrstuvwxyz
1234567890$

24 point Helvetica Light Small (Foundry)

ABCDEFGHIJKLMNOPQRSTUVWXYZ&
abcdefghijklmnopqrstuvwxyz
1234567890$

24 point Helvetica Light Large (Foundry)

ABCDEFGHIJKLMNOPQRSTUVWXYZ&
abcdefghijklmnopqrstuvwxyz
1234567890$

30 point Helvetica Light (Foundry)

ABCDEFGHIJKLMNOPQRSTUVWXYZ&
abcdefghijklmnopqrstuvwxyz
1234567890$

(Continued on Page 303)

42 point Helvetica Light (Foundry)

ABCDEFGHIJKLMNOPQRST UVWXYZ&
abcdefghijklmnopqrstuvwxyz
1234567890$

48 point Helvetica Light (Foundry)

ABCDEFGHIJKLMNOP QRSTUVWXYZ&
abcdefghijklmnopqrstuv wxyz 1234567890$

Helvetica Light Italic

6 point Helvetica Light Italic (Linotype)

The basic character in a type design is determined by the uniform design characteristics of all letters in the alphabet. However, this alone does not determine the standard of the type face and the quality of composition set with it. The appearance is something complex which forms itself out of many details, like form, proportion, ductus, rhythm etc. If everything harmonizes, the total result will be more than the sum of its components. The only reliable basis for the design in a type is a positive feeling for form and style. The basic character in a type design is determined by the uniform design char

ABCDEFGHIJKLMNOPQRSTUVWXYZ&
abcdefghijklmnopqrstuvwxyz   1234567890$

7 point Helvetica Light Italic (Linotype)

The basic character in a type design is determined by the uniform design characteristics of all letters in the alphabet. However, this alone does not determine the standard of the type face and the quality of composition set with it. The appearance is something complex which forms itself out of many details, like form, proportion, ductus, rhythm etc. If everything harmonizes, the total result will be more than the sum of its components. The only reliable basis for the design in a

ABCDEFGHIJKLMNOPQRSTUVWXYZ&
abcdefghijklmnopqrstuvwxyz   1234567890$

8 point Helvetica Light Italic (Linotype)

The basic character in a type design is determined by the uniform design characteristics of all letters in the alphabet. However, this alone does not determine the standard of the type face and the quality of composition set with it. The appearance is something complex which forms itself out of many details, like form, proportion, ductus, rhythm etc. If everything harmonizes, the total result

ABCDEFGHIJKLMNOPQRSTUVWXYZ&
abcdefghijklmnopqrstuvwxyz   1234567890$

9 point Helvetica Light Italic (Linotype)

The basic character in a type design is determined by the uniform design characteristics of all letters in the alphabet. However, this alone does not determine the standard of the type face and the quality of composition set with it. The appearance is something complex which forms itself out of

ABCDEFGHIJKLMNOPQRSTUVWXYZ&
abcdefghijklmnopqrstuvwxyz   1234567890$

10 point Helvetica Light Italic (Linotype)

The basic character in a type design is determined by the uniform design characteristics of all letters in the alphabet. However, this alone does not determine the standard of the type face and the quality of composition set with it. The appearance is something complex which

ABCDEFGHIJKLMNOPQRSTUVWXYZ&
abcdefghijklmnopqrstuvwxyz   1234567890$

11 point Helvetica Light Italic (Linotype)

The basic character in a type design is determined by the uniform design characteristics of all letters in the alphabet. However, this alone does not determine the standard of the type face and the qual

ABCDEFGHIJKLMNOPQRSTUVWXYZ&
abcdefghijklmnopqrstuvwxyz   1234567890$

12 point Helvetica Light Italic (Linotype)

The basic character in a type design is deter mined by the uniform design characteristics of all letters in the alphabet. However, this alone does not determine the standard of the type

ABCDEFGHIJKLMNOPQRSTUVWXYZ&
abcdefghijklmnopqrstuvwxyz   1234567890$

14 point Helvetica Light Italic (Linotype)

The basic character in a type design is determined by the uniform design char acteristics of all letters in the alphabet.

ABCDEFGHIJKLMNOPQRSTUVWXYZ&
abcdefghijklmnopqrstuvwxyz
1234567890$

24 point Helvetica Light Italic Small (Foundry)

ABCDEFGHIJKLMNOPQRSTUVWXYZ&
abcdefghjiklmnopqrstuvwxyz
1234567890$

6 point Helvetica Medium (Linotype)

The basic character in a type design is determined by the uniform design characteristics of all letters in the alphabet. However, this alone does not determine the standard of the type face and the quality of composition set with it. The appearance is something complex which forms itself out of many details, like form, proportion, ductus, rhythm etc. If everything har monizes, the total result will be more than the sum of its components. The only reliable basis for the design in a type is a positive feeling for form and style. The basic character in a type design is determined by the

ABCDEFGHIJKLMNOPQRSTUVWXYZ&
abcdefghijklmnopqrstuvwxyz   1234567890$

7 point Helvetica Medium (Linotype)

The basic character in a type design is determined by the uniform design characteristics of all letters in the alphabet. However, this alone does not determine the standard of the type face and the quality of composition set with it. The appearance is something com plex which forms itself out of many details, like form, proportion, ductus, rhythm etc. If everything harmonizes, the total result will be more than the sum of its components. The only reliable basis for

ABCDEFGHIJKLMNOPQRSTUVWXYZ&
abcdefghijklmnopqrstuvwxyz   1234567890$

8 point Helvetica Medium (Linotype)

The basic character in a type design is determined by the uni form design characteristics of all letters in the alphabet. How ever, this alone does not determine the standard of the type face and the quality of composition set with it. The appearance is something complex which forms itself out of many details, like form, proportion, ductus, rhythm etc. If everything harmon

ABCDEFGHIJKLMNOPQRSTUVWXYZ&
abcdefghijklmnopqrstuvwxyz   1234567890$

9 point Helvetica Medium (Linotype)

The basic character in a type design is determined by the uniform design characteristics of all letters in the alphabet. However, this alone does not determine the standard of the type face and the quality of composition set with it. The appearance is something complex which

ABCDEFGHIJKLMNOPQRSTUVWXYZ&
abcdefghijklmnopqrstuvwxyz   1234567890$

10 point Helvetica Medium (Linotype)

The basic character in a type design is determined by the uniform design characteristics of all letters in the alphabet. However, this alone does not determine the standard of the type face and the quality of com position set with it. The appearance is something

ABCDEFGHIJKLMNOPQRSTUVWXYZ&
abcdefghijklmnopqrstuvwxyz   1234567890$

11 point Helvetica Medium (Linotype)

The basic character in a type design is deter mined by the uniform design characteristics of all letters in the alphabet. However, this alone does not determine the standard of the type face

ABCDEFGHIJKLMNOPQRSTUVWXYZ&
abcdefghijklmnopqrstuvwxyz   1234567890$

12 point Helvetica Medium (Linotype)

The basic character in a type design is deter mined by the uniform design characteristics of all letters in the alphabet. However, this alone does not determine the standard of the

ABCDEFGHIJKLMNOPQRSTUVWXYZ&
abcdefghijklmnopqrstuvwxyz   1234567890$

14 point Helvetica Medium (Linotype)

The basic character in a type design is determined by the uniform design char acteristics of all letters in the alphabet.

ABCDEFGHIJKLMNOPQRSTUV
WXYZ&   1234567890$
abcdefghijklmnopqrstuvwxyz

12 point Helvetica Medium (Foundry)

ABCDEFGHIJKLMNOPQRSTUVWXYZ&
abcdefghijklmnopqrstuvwxyz
1234567890$

14 point Helvetica Medium (Foundry)

ABCDEFGHIJKLMNOPQRSTUVWXYZ&
abcdefghijklmnopqrstuvwxyz
1234567890$

16 point Helvetica Medium (Foundry)

ABCDEFGHIJKLMNOPQRSTUVWXYZ&
abcdefghijklmnopqrstuvwxyz
1234567890$

(Continued on Page 306)

(Continued from Page 305)

18 point Helvetica Medium (Foundry)

ABCDEFGHIJKLMNOPQRSTUVWXYZ&
abcdefghijklmnopqrstuvwxyz
1234567890$

24 Helvetica Medium Small (Foundry)

ABCDEFGHIJKLMNOPQRSTUVWXYZ&
abcdefghijklmnopqrstuvwxyz
1234567890$

24 point Helvetica Medium Large (Foundry)

ABCDEFGHIJKLMNOPQRSTUVWXYZ&
abcdefghijklmnopqrstuvwxyz
1234567890$

30 point Helvetica Medium (Foundry)

ABCDEFGHIJKLMNOPQRSTUV
WXYZ&
abcdefghijklmnopqrstuvwxyz
1234567890$

42 point Helvetica Medium (Foundry)

ABCDEFGHIJKLMNOPQRST
UVWXYZ&
abcdefghijklmnopqrstuv
wxyz
1234567890$

(Continued on Page 307)

48 point Helvetica Medium (Foundry)

ABCDEFGHIJKLMNOP
QRSTUVWXYZ&
abcdefghijklmnopqrst
uvwxyz
1234567890O$

60 point Helvetica Medium (Foundry)

ABCDEFGHIJKL
MNOPQRSTUV
WXYZ&
abcdefghijklmn
opqrstuvwxyz
1234567890O$

(Continued on Page 308)

(Continued from Page 307)

72 point Helvetica Medium (Foundry)

ABCDEFGHIJK
LMNOPQRSTU
VWXYZ&
abcdefghijkl
mnopqrstuv
wxyz
1234567890$

Helvetica Medium Italic

6 point Helvetica Medium Italic (Linotype)

The basic character in a type design is determined by the uniform design characteristics of all letters in the alphabet. However, this alone does not determine the standard of the type face and the quality of composition set with it. The appearance is something complex which forms itself out of many details, like form, proportion, ductus, rhythm etc. If everything har monizes, the total result will be more than the sum of its components. The only reliable basis for the design in a type is a positive feeling for form and style. The basic character in a type design is determined by the

ABCDEFGHIJKLMNOPQRSTUVWXYZ&
abcdefghijklmnopqrstuvwxyz 1234567890$

7 point Helvetica Medium Italic (Linotype)

The basic character in a type design is determined by the uniform design characteristics of all letters in the alphabet. However, this alone does not determine the standard of the type face and the quality of composition set with it. The appearance is something com plex which forms itself out of many details, like form, proportion, ductus, rhythm etc. If everything harmonizes, the total result will be more than the sum of its components. The only reliable basis for

ABCDEFGHIJKLMNOPQRSTUVWXYZ&
abcdefghijklmnopqrstuvwxyz 1234567890$

8 point Helvetica Medium Italic (Linotype)

The basic character in a type design is determined by the uni form design characteristics of all letters in the alphabet. How ever, this alone does not determine the standard of the type type face and the quality of composition set with it. The appear ance is something complex which forms itself out of many details, like form, proportion, ductus, rhythm etc. If everything

ABCDEFGHIJKLMNOPQRSTUVWXYZ&
abcdefghijklmnopqrstuvwxyz 1234567890$

9 point Helvetica Medium Italic (Linotype)

The basic character in a type design is determined by the uniform design characteristics of all letters in the alphabet. However, this alone does not determine the standard of the type face and the quality of composition set with it. The appearance is something complex which

ABCDEFGHIJKLMNOPQRSTUVWXYZ&
abcdefghijklmnopqrstuvwxyz 1234567890$

10 point Helvetica Medium Italic (Linotype)

The basic character in a type design is determined by the uniform design characteristics of all letters in the alphabet. However, this alone does not determine the standard of the type face and the quality of com position set with it. The appearance is something

ABCDEFGHIJKLMNOPQRSTUVWXYZ&
abcdefghijklmnopqrstuvwxyz 1234567890$

11 point Helvetica Medium Italic (Linotype)

The basic character in a type design is deter mined by the uniform design characteristics of all letters in the alphabet. However, this alone does not determine the standard of the type face

ABCDEFGHIJKLMNOPQRSTUVWXYZ&
abcdefghijklmnopqrstuvwxyz 1234567890$

12 point Helvetica Medium Italic (Linotype)

The basic character in a type design is deter mined by the uniform design characteristics of all letters in the alphabet. However, this alone does not determine the standard of the

ABCDEFGHIJKLMNOPQRSTUVWXYZ&
abcdefghijklmnopqrstuvwxyz 1234567890$

14 point Helvetica Medium Italic (Linotype)

The basic character in a type design is determined by the uniform design char acteristics of all letters in the alphabet.

ABCDEFGHIJKLMNOPQRSTUV
WXYZ& 1234567890$
abcdefghijklmnopqrstuvwxyz

18 point Helvetica Medium Italic (Foundry)

ABCDEFGHIJKLMNOPQRSTUVWXYZ&
abcdefghijklmnopqrstuvwxyz
1234567890$

24 point Helvetica Medium Italic Small (Foundry)

ABCDEFGHIJKLMNOPQRSTUVWXYZ&
abcdefghijklmnopqrstuvwxyz
1234567890$

(Continued on Page 310)

24 point Helvetica Medium Italic Large (Foundry)

ABCDEFGHIJKLMNOPQRSTUVWXYZ&
abcdefghijklmnopqrstuvwxyz
1234567890$

30 point Helvetica Medium Italic (Foundry)

ABCDEFGHIJKLMNOPQRSTUVWXYZ
abcdefghijklmnopqrstuvwxyz&
1234567890$

Horizon Light

30 point Horizon Light (Foundry)

ABCDEFGHIJKLMNOPQRSTUVWXYZ&
abcdefghijklmnopqrstuvwxyz
1234567890$

Huxley Vertical

30 point Huxley Vertical, Cap font (Foundry)

ABCDEFGHIJKLMNOPQRSTUVWXYZ&
1234567890$

36 point Huxley Vertical, Cap font (Foundry)

ABCDEFGHIJKLMNOPQRSTUVWXYZ&
1234567890$

48 point Huxley Vertical, Cap font (Foundry)

ABCDEFGHIJKLMNOPQRSTUVWXYZ&
1234567890$

60 point Huxley Vertical, Cap font (Foundry)

ABCDEFGHIJKLMNOPQRSTUVWXYZ&
1234567890$

Imperial

12 point Imperial (Intertype)

The basic character in a type design is deter mined by the uniform design characteristics of all letters in the alphabet. However, this alone does not determine the standard of the type face

ABCDEFGHIJKLMNOPQRSTUVWXYZ&
abcdefghijklmnopqrstuvwxyz   1234567890$

Imperial Bold

12 point Imperial Bold (Intertype)

The basic character in a type design is deter mined by the uniform design characteristics of all letters in the alphabet. However, this alone does not determine the standard of the type face

ABCDEFGHIJKLMNOPQRSTUVWXYZ&
abcdefghijklmnopqrstuvwxyz   1234567890$

Ionic No. 5

7 point Ionic No. 5 (Linotype)

The basic character in a type design is determined by the uniform design characteristics of all letters in the alphabet. However, this alone does not determine the standard of the type face and the quality of composition set with it. The ap pearance is something complex which forms itself out of many details, like form, proportion, ductus, rhythm etc. If everything harmonizes, the total result will be more than the sum of its

ABCDEFGHIJKLMNOPQRSTUVWXYZ&
abcdefghijklmnopqrstuvwxyz   1234567890$

Ionic No. 5 Italic

7 point Ionic No. 5 Italic (Linotype)

The basic character in a type design is determined by the uniform design characteristics of all letters in the alphabet. However, this alone does not determine the standard of the type face and the quality of composition set with it. The ap pearance is something complex which forms itself out of many details, like form, proportion, ductus, rhythm etc. If everything harmonizes, the total result will be more than the sum of its

ABCDEFGHIJKLMNOPQRSTUVWXYZ&
abcdefghijklmnopqrstuvwxyz   1234567890$

Janson *(Long descenders must be set 1 point leaded)*

8 point Janson (Linotype)

The basic character in a type design is determined by the uniform design characteristics of all letters in the alphabet. However, this alone does not determine the standard of the type face and the quality of composition set with it. The appearance is something complex which forms itself out of many details, like form, pro

ABCDEFGHIJKLMNOPQRSTUVWXYZ&
abcdefghijklmnopqrstuvwxyz   1234567890$
ABCDEFGHIJKLMNOPQRSTUVWXYZ

9 point Janson (Linotype)

The basic character in a type design is determined by the uniform design characteristics of all letters in the alphabet. However, this alone does not determine the standard of the type face and the quality of composition set with it. The

ABCDEFGHIJKLMNOPQRSTUVWXYZ&
abcdefghijklmnopqrstuvwxyz   1234567890$
ABCDEFGHIJKLMNOPQRSTUVWXYZ

10 point Janson (Linotype)

The basic character in a type design is determined by the uniform design characteristics of all letters in the alpha bet. However, this alone does not determine the standard of the type face and the quality of composition set with

ABCDEFGHIJKLMNOPQRSTUVWXYZ&
abcdefghijklmnopqrstuvwxyz   1234567890$
ABCDEFGHIJKLMNOPQRSTUVWXYZ

11 point Janson (Linotype)

The basic character in a type design is determined by the uniform design characteristics of all letters in the alphabet. However, this alone does not determine the

ABCDEFGHIJKLMNOPQRSTUVWXYZ&
abcdefghijklmnopqrstuvwxyz   1234567890$
ABCDEFGHIJKLMNOPQRSTUVWXYZ

12 point Janson (Linotype)

The basic character in a type design is determined by the uniform design characteristics of all letters in the alphabet. However, this alone does not de

ABCDEFGHIJKLMNOPQRSTUVWXYZ&
abcdefghijklmnopqrstuvwxyz   1234567890$
ABCDEFGHIJKLMNOPQRSTUVWXYZ

14 point Janson (Linotype)

The basic character in a type design is deter mined by the uniform design characteristics

ABCDEFGHIJKLMNOPQRSTUV
WXYZ&   1234567890$
abcdefghijklmnopqrstuvwxyz
ABCDEFGHIJKLMNOPQRSTUVWXYZ

(Continued on Page 313)

14 point Janson (Foundry)

ABCDEFGHIJKLMNOPQRSTUVWXYZ&
abcdefghijklmnopqrstuvwxyz
1234567890$

18 point Janson (Foundry)

ABCDEFGHIJKLMNOPQRSTUVWXYZ&
abcdefghijklmnopqrstuvwxyz
1234567890$

24 point Janson (Foundry)

ABCDEFGHIJKLMNOPQRSTUVWXYZ&
abcdefghijklmnopqrstuvwxyz
1234567890$

30 point Janson (Foundry)

ABCDEFGHIJKLMNOPQRSTUVWXYZ&
abcdefghijklmnopqrstuvwxyz
1234567890$

36 point Janson (Foundry)

ABCDEFGHIJKLMNOPQRSTUV
WXYZ&
abcdefghijklmnopqrstuvwxyz
1234567890$

Janson Italic *(Long descenders must be set 1 point leaded)*

8 point Janson Italic (Linotype)

The basic character in a type design is determined by the uniform design characteristics of all letters in the alphabet. However, this alone does not determine the standard of the type face and the quality of composition set with it. The appearance is something complex which forms itself out of many details, like form, pro

ABCDEFGHIJKLMNOPQRSTUVWXYZ&
abcdefghijklmnopqrstuvwxyz   *1234567890$*

9 point Janson Italic (Linotype)

The basic character in a type design is determined by the uniform design characteristics of all letters in the alphabet. However, this alone does not determine the standard of the type face and the quality of composition set with it. The

ABCDEFGHIJKLMNOPQRSTUVWXYZ&
abcdefghijklmnopqrstuvwxyz   *1234567890$*

10 point Janson Italic (Linotype)

The basic character in a type design is determined by the uniform design characteristics of all letters in the alphabet. However, this alone does not determine the standard of the type face and the quality of composition set with

ABCDEFGHIJKLMNOPQRSTUVWXYZ&
abcdefghijklmnopqrstuvwxyz   *1234567890$*

11 point Janson Italic (Linotype)

The basic character in a type design is determined by the uniform design characteristics of all letters in the alphabet. However, this alone does not determine the

ABCDEFGHIJKLMNOPQRSTUVWXYZ&
abcdefghijklmnopqrstuvwxyz   *1234567890$*

12 Janson Italic (Linotype)

The basic character in a type design is determined by the uniform design characteristics of all letters in the alphabet. However, this alone does not de

ABCDEFGHIJKLMNOPQRSTUVWXYZ&
abcdefghijklmnopqrstuvwxyz   *1234567890$*

14 point Janson Italic (Linotype)

The basic character in a type design is deter mined by the uniform design characteristics

ABCDEFGHIJKLMNOPQRSTUV WXYZ&   *1234567890$*
abcdefghijklmnopqrstuvwxyz

18 point Janson Italic (Foundry)

ABCDEFGHIJKLMNOPQRSTUVWXYZ&
abcdefghijklmnopqrstuvwxyz
1234567890$

24 point Janson Italic (Foundry)

ABCDEFGHIJKLMNOPQRSTUVWXYZ&
abcdefghijklmnopqrstuvwxyz
1234567890$

30 point Janson Italic (Foundry)

ABCDEFGHIJKLMNOPQRSTUVWXYZ&
abcdefghijklmnopqrstuvwxyz
1234567890$

SWASH

ABDJPRY

(Continued on Page 315)

36 point Janson Italic (Foundry)

ABCDEFGHIJKLMNOPQRSTUV
WXYZ&
abcdefghijklmnopqrstuvwxyz
1234567890$

Jim Crow

24 point Jim Crow, Cap font (Foundry)

ABCDEFGHIJKLMNOPQRSTUVWXYZ&
1234567890$

Karnak Black

10 point Karnak Black (Ludlow)

ABCDEFGHIJKLMNOPQRSTUVWXYZ&
abcdefghijklmnopqrstuvwxyz
1234567890$

12 point Karnak Black (Ludlow)

ABCDEFGHIJKLMNOPQRSTUVWXYZ&
abcdefghijklmnopqrstuvwxyz
1234567890$

14 point Karnak Black (Ludlow)

ABCDEFGHIJKLMNOPQRSTUVWXYZ&
abcdefghijklmnopqrstuvwxyz
1234567890$

18 point Karnak Black (Ludlow)

ABCDEFGHIJKLMNOPQRSTUVWXYZ&
abcdefghijklmnopqrstuvwxyz
1234567890$

24 point Karnak Black (Ludlow)

ABCDEFGHIJKLMNOPQRSTUVWXYZ&
abcdefghijklmnopqrstuvwxyz
1234567890$

Karnak Black Condensed

18 point Karnak Black Condensed (Ludlow)

ABCDEFGHIJKLMNOPQRSTUVWXYZ&
abcdefghijklmnopqrstuvwxyz
1234567890$

Karnak Medium

6 point Karnak Medium (Ludlow)

ABCDEFGHIJKLMNOPQRSTUVWXYZ&
abcdefghijklmnopqrstuvwxyz
1234567890$

Karnak Light

18 point Karnak Light (Ludlow)

ABCDEFGHIJKLMNOPQRSTUVWXYZ&
abcdefghijklmnopqrstuvwxyz
1234567890$

Kaufmann Bold

18 point Kaufmann Bold (Foundry)

ABCDEFGHIJKLMNOP2RSTUVWXYZ&
abcdefghijklmnopqrstuvwxyz
1234567890$

36 point Kaufmann Bold (Foundry)

ABCDEFGHIJKLMNOP2RSTUV
WXYZ&
abcdefghijklmnopqrstuvwxyz
1234567890$

Kennerly

10 point Kennerly (Foundry)

ABCDEFGHIJKLMNOPQRSTUVWXYZ&
abcdefghijklmnopqrstuvwxyz
1234567890$

12 point Kennerly (Foundry)

ABCDEFGHIJKLMNOPQRSTUVWXYZ&
abcdefghijklmnopqrstuvwxyz
1234567890$

14 point Kennerly (Foundry)

ABCDEFGHIJKLMNOPQRSTUVWXYZ&
abcdefghijklmnopqrstuvwxyz
1234567890$

18 point Kennerly (Foundry)

ABCDEFGHIJKLMNOPQRSTUVWXYZ&
abcdefghijklmnopqrstuvwxyz
1234567890$

24 point Kennerly (Foundry)

ABCDEFGHIJKLMNOPQRSTUVWXYZ&
abcdefghijklmnopqrstuvwxyz
1234567890$

36 point Kennerly (Foundry)

ABCDEFGHIJKLMNOPQRSTU
VWXYZ&
abcdefghijklmnopqrstuvwxyz
1234567890$

Kennerly Italic

10 point Kennerly Italic (Foundry)

ABCDEFGHIJKLMNOPQRSTUVWXYZ&
abcdefghijklmnopqrstuvwxyz
1234567890$

14 point Kennerly Italic (Foundry)

ABCDEFGHIJKLMNOPQRSTUVWXYZ&
abcdefghijklmnopqrstuvwxyz
1234567890$

18 point Kennerly Italic (Foundry)

ABCDEFGHIJKLMNOPQRSTUVWXYZ&
abcdefghijklmnopqrstuvwxyz
1234567890$

24 point Kennerly Italic (Foundry)

ABCDEFGHIJKLMNOPQRSTUVWXYZ&
abcdefghijklmnopqrstuvwxyz
1234567890$

30 point Kennerly Italic (Foundry)

ABCDEFGHIJKLMNOPQRSTUV
WXYZ&
abcdefghijklmnopqrstuvwxyz
1234567890$

Keynote

18 point Keynote (Foundry)

ABCDEFGHIJKLMNOPQRSTUVWXYZ&
abcdefghijklmnopqrstuvwxyz   1234567890$

24 point Keynote (Foundry)

ABCDEFGHIJKLMNOPQRSTUVWXYZ&
abcdefghijklmnopqrstuvwxyz   1234567890$

Latin Bold

18 point Latin Bold (Foundry)

ABCDEFGHIJKLMNOPQRSTUVWXYZ&
abcdefghijklmnopqrstuvwxyz
1234567890$

24 point Latin Bold (Foundry)

ABCDEFGHIJKLMNOPQRSTUVWXYZ&
abcdefghijklmnopqrstuvwxyz
1234567890$

30 point Latin Bold (Foundry)

ABCDEFGHIJKLMNOPQRSTU
VWXYZ&
abcdefghijklmnopqrstuvwxyz
1234567890$

36 point Latin Bold (Foundry)

ABCDEFGHIJKLMNOP
QRSTUVWXYZ&
abcdefghijklmnopqrst
uvwxyz
1234567890$

(Continued on Page 320)

(Continued from Page 319)

48 point Latin Bold (Foundry)

ABCDEFGHIJKL MNOPQRSTUV WXYZ& abcdefghijklmnop qrstuvwxyz 1234567890$

Latin Bold Condensed

10 point Latin Bold Condensed (Foundry)

ABCDEFGHIJKLMNOPQRSTUVWXYZ&
abcdefghijklmnopqrstuvwxyz
1234567890$

12 point Latin Bold Condensed (Foundry)

ABCDEFGHIJKLMNOPQRSTUVWXYZ&
abcdefghijklmnopqrstuvwxyz
1234567890$

24 point Latin Bold Condensed (Foundry)

ABCDEFGHIJKLMNOPQRSTUVWXYZ&
abcdefghijklmnopqrstuvwxyz
1234567890$

30 point Latin Bold Condensed (Foundry)

ABCDEFGHIJKLMNOPQRSTUVWXYZ&
abcdefghijklmnopqrstuvwxyz
1234567890$

(Continued on Page 321)

36 point Latin Bold Condensed (Foundry)

ABCDEFGHIJKLMNOPQRSTU VWXYZ&
abcdefghijklmnopqrstuvwxyz 1234567890$

72 point Latin Bold Condensed (Foundry)

ABCDEFGHIJK LMNOPQRSTU VWXYZ&
abcdefghijklmn opqrstuvwxyz 1234567890$

Latin Elongated

12 point Latin Elongated (Foundry)
ABCDEFGHIJKLMNOPQRSTUVWXYZ&
abcdefghijklmnopqrstuvwxyz
1234567890$

18 point Latin Elongated (Foundry)
ABCDEFGHIJKLMNOPQRSTUVWXYZ&
abcdefghijklmnopqrstuvwxyz
1234567890$

36 point Latin Elongated (Foundry)
ABCDEFGHIJKLMNOPQRSTUVWXYZ&
abcdefghijklmnopqrstuvwxyz
1234567890$

Latin Wide

12 point Latin Wide (Foundry)
ABCDEFGHIJKLMNOPQRSTUVWXYZ&
abcdefghijklmnopqrstuvwxyz
1234567890$

18 Latin Wide (Foundry)
ABCDEFGHIJKLMNO
PQRSTUVWXYZ&
abcdefghijklmnopqrst
uvwxyz
1234567890$

Legend

30 point Legend (Foundry)

ABCDEFGHIJK LMNOPQR STUVWXYZ

abcdefghijklmnopqrstuvwxyz&

1234567890$

48 point Legend (Foundry)

ABCDEFGHIJK LMNOP QR STUVWXYZ&

abcdefghijklmnopqrstuvwxyz

1234567890$

Libra

12 point Libra, Cap font (Foundry)

ABCDEFGHIJKLMNOPQRSTUVWXYZ&
1234567890$

18 point Libra Small, Cap font (Foundry)

ABCDEFGHIJKLMNOPQRSTUVWXYZ&
1234567890$

18 point Libra Large, Cap font (Foundry)

ABCDEFGHIJKLMNOPQRSTUVWXYZ&
1234567890$

24 point Libra, Cap font (Foundry)

ABCDEFGHIJKLMNOPQRSTUVWXYZ&
1234567890$

30 point Libra Small, Cap font (Foundry)

ABCDEFGHIJKLMNOPQRSTUVWXYZ&
1234567890$

30 point Libra Large, Cap font (Foundry)

ABCDEFGHIJKLMNOPQRSTUVWXYZ&
1234567890$

36 point Libra (Foundry)

ABCDEFGHIJKLMNOPQRSTUV
WXYZ&
1234567890$

48 point Libra, Cap font (Foundry)

ABCDEFGHIJKLMNOPQR
STUVWXYZ&
1234567890$

Lightline Gothic

14 point Lightline Gothic (Foundry)

ABCDEFGHIJKLMNOPQRSTUVWXYZ&
abcdefghijklmnopqrstuvwxyz
1234567890$

Lining Plate Gothic Heavy

6 point Lining Plate Gothic Heavy No. 1, Cap font (Ludlow)

ABCDEFGHIJKLMNOPQRSTUVWXYZ&   1234567890$

6 point Lining Plate Gothic Heavy No. 3, Cap font (Ludlow)

ABCDEFGHIJKLMNOPQRSTUVWXYZ   1234567890$

6 point Lining Plate Gothic Heavy No. 2, Cap font (Ludlow)

ABCDEFGHIJKLMNOPQRSTUVWXYZ&   1234567890$

6 point Lining Plate Gothic Heavy No. 4, Cap font (Ludlow)

ABCDEFGHIJKLMNOPQRSTUVWXYZ   1234567890$

12 point Lining Plate Gothic Heavy No. 1, Cap font (Ludlow)

ABCDEFGHIJKLMNOPQRSTUVWXYZ&
1234567890$

12 point Lining Plate Gothic Heavy No. 2, Cap font (Ludlow)

ABCDEFGHIJKLMNOPQRSTUVWXYZ&
1234567890$

12 point Lining Plate Gothic Heavy No. 3, Cap font (Ludlow)

ABCDEFGHIJKLMNOPQRSTUVWXYZ&
1234567890$

12 point Lining Plate Gothic Heavy No. 4, Cap font (Ludlow)

ABCDEFGHIJKLMNOPQRSTUVWXYZ&
1234567890$

Lining Plate Gothic Heavy Condensed

6 point Lining Plate Gothic Heavy Cond. No. 1, Cap font (Ludlow)

ABCDEFGHIJKLMNOPQRSTUVWXYZ&   1234567890$

6 point Lining Plate Gothic Heavy Cond. No. 3, Cap font (Ludlow)

ABCDEFGHIJKLMNOPQRSTUVWXYZ&   1234567890$

6 point Lining Plate Gothic Heavy Cond. No. 2, Cap font (Ludlow)

ABCDEFGHIJKLMNOPQRSTUVWXYZ&   1234567890$

6 point Lining Plate Gothic Heavy Cond. No. 4, Cap font (Ludlow)

ABCDEFGHIJKLMNOPQRSTUVWXYZ&   1234567890$

24 point Lining Plate Gothic Heavy Cond. No.1, Cap font (Foundry)

ABCDEFGHIJKLMNOPQRSTUVWXYZ&
1234567890$

24 point Lombardic Initials, Cap font (Foundry)

ABCDEFGHIJKLMNOPQRSTUV
WXYZ&

48 point Lombardic Initials, Cap font (Foundry)

ABCDEFGHIJKL
MNOPQRSTUV
WXYZ&

60 point Lombardic Initials, Cap font (Foundry)

ABCDEFGHIJ
KLMNOPQRST
UVWXYZ&

(Continued on Page 327)

72 point Lombardic Initials, Cap font (Foundry)

ABCDEFGH
IJKLMNO
PQRSTUV
WXYZ&

Lucian

ABCDEFGHIJKLMNOPQRSTUVWXYZ&
abcdefghijklmnopqrstuvwxyz
1234567890$

ABCDEFGHIJKLMNOPQRSTUVWXYZ&
abcdefghijklmnopqrstuvwxyz
1234567890$

Lucian Italic

ABCDEFGHIJKLMNOPQRSTUVWXYZ&
abcdefghijklmnopqrstuvwxyz
1234567890$

ABCDEFGHIJKLMNOPQRSTUVWXYZ&
abcdefghijklmnopqrstuvwxyz
1234567890$

ABCDEFGHIJKLMNOPQRSTUVWXYZ&
abcdefghijklmnopqrstuvwxyz
1234567890$

ABCDEFGHIJKLMNOPQRSTUVWXYZ&
abcdefghijklmnopqrstuvwxyz
1234567890$

ABCDEFGHIJKLMNOPQRSTUVWXYZ&
abcdefghijklmnopqrstuvwxyz
1234567890$

Lucian Bold (Also known as Graphic Bold)

14 point Lucian Bold (Foundry)

ABCDEFGHIJKLMNOPQRSTUVWXYZ&
abcdefghijklmnopqrstuvwxyz
1234567890$

18 point Lucian Bold (Foundry)

ABCDEFGHIJKLMNOPQRSTUVWXYZ&
abcdefghijklmnopqrstuvwxyz
1234567890$

24 point Lucian Bold (Foundry)

ABCDEFGHIJKLMNOPQRSTUVWXYZ&
abcdefghijklmnopqrstuvwxyz
1234567890$

30 point Lucian Bold (Foundry)

ABCDEFGHIJKLMNOPQRSTUV
WXYZ&
abcdefghijklmnopqrstuvwxyz
1234567890$

48 point Lucian Bold (Foundry)

ABCDEFGHIJKLMNOP
QRSTUVWXYZ&
abcdefghijklmnopqrstuv
wxyz
1234567890$

Lydian

10 point Lydian (Foundry)
ABCDEFGHIJKLMNOPQRSTUVWXYZ&
abcdefghijklmnopqrstuvwxyz
1234567890$

12 point Lydian (Foundry)
ABCDEFGHIJKLMNOPQRSTUVWXYZ&
abcdefghijklmnopqrstuvwxyz
1234567890$

14 point Lydian (Foundry)
ABCDEFGHIJKLMNOPQRSTUVWXYZ&
abcdefghijklmnopqrstuvwxyz
1234567890$

18 point Lydian (Foundry)
ABCDEFGHIJKLMNOPQRSTUVWXYZ&
abcdefghijklmnopqrstuvwxyz
1234567890$

24 point Lydian (Foundry)
ABCDEFGHIJKLMNOPQRSTUVWXYZ&
abcdefghijklmnopqrstuvwxyz
1234567890$

30 point Lydian (Foundry)
ABCDEFGHIJKLMNOPQRSTUVWXYZ&
abcdefghijklmnopqrstuvwxyz
1234567890$

36 point Lydian (Foundry)
ABCDEFGHIJKLMNOPQRSTUV
WXYZ&
abcdefghijklmnopqrstuvwxyz
1234567890$

(Continued on Page 331)

48 point Lydian (Foundry)

ABCDEFGHIJKLMNOPQRS
TUVWXYZ&
abcdefghijklmnopqrstuv
wxyz
1234567890$

60 point Lydian (Foundry)

ABCDEFGHIJKLMNO
PQRSTUVWXYZ&
abcdefghijklmnopqrst
uvwxyz
1234567890$

Lydian Italic

10 point Lydian Italic (Foundry)
ABCDEFGHIJKLMNOPQRSTUVWXYZ&
abcdefghijklmnopqrstuvwxyz
1234567890$

12 point Lydian Italic (Foundry)
ABCDEFGHIJKLMNOPQRSTUVWXYZ&
abcdefghijklmnopqrstuvwxyz
1234567890$

14 point Lydian Italic (Foundry)
ABCDEFGHIJKLMNOPQRSTUVWXYZ&
abcdefghijklmnopqrstuvwxyz
1234567890$

18 point Lydian Italic (Foundry)
ABCDEFGHIJKLMNOPQRSTUVWXYZ&
abcdefghijklmnopqrstuvwxyz
1234567890$

24 point Lydian Italic (Foundry)
ABCDEFGHIJKLMNOPQRSTUVWXYZ&
abcdefghijklmnopqrstuvwxyz
1234567890$

30 point Lydian Italic (Foundry)
ABCDEFGHIJKLMNOPQRSTUVWXYZ&
abcdefghijklmnopqrstuvwxyz
1234567890$

36 point Lydian Italic (Foundry)
ABCDEFGHIJKLMNOPQRSTUV
WXYZ&
abcdefghijklmnopqrstuvwxyz
1234567890$

(Continued on Page 333)

48 point Lydian Italic (Foundry)

ABCDEFGHIJKLMNOPQRST UVWXYZ&

abcdefghijklmnopqrstuvwxyz 1234567890$

Lydian Bold

10 point Lydian Bold (Foundry)
ABCDEFGHIJKLMNOPQRSTUVWXYZ&
abcdefghijklmnopqrstuvwxyz
1234567890$

12 point Lydian Bold (Foundry)
ABCDEFGHIJKLMNOPQRSTUVWXYZ&
abcdefghijklmnopqrstuvwxyz
1234567890$

14 point Lydian Bold (Foundry)
ABCDEFGHIJKLMNOPQRSTUVWXYZ&
abcdefghijklmnopqrstuvwxyz
1234567890$

18 point Lydian Bold (Foundry)
ABCDEFGHIJKLMNOPQRSTUVWXYZ&
abcdefghijklmnopqrstuvwxyz
1234567890$

24 point Lydian Bold (Foundry)
ABCDEFGHIJKLMNOPQRSTUVWXYZ&
abcdefghijklmnopqrstuvwxyz
1234567890$

30 point Lydian Bold (Foundry)
ABCDEFGHIJKLMNOPQRSTUVWXYZ&
abcdefghijklmnopqrstuvwxyz
1234567890$

36 point Lydian Bold (Foundry)
ABCDEFGHIJKLMNOPQRSTUV
WXYZ&
abcdefghijklmnopqrstuvwxyz
1234567890$

Lydian Bold Italic

18 point Lydian Bold Italic (Foundry)

ABCDEFGHIJKLMNOPQRSTUVWXYZ&
abcdefghijklmnopqrstuvwxyz
1234567890$

24 point Lydian Bold Italic (Foundry)

ABCDEFGHIJKLMNOPQRSTUVWXYZ&
abcdefghijklmnopqrstuvwxyz
1234567890$

30 point Lydian Bold Italic (Foundry)

ABCDEFGHIJKLMNOPQRSTUVWXYZ&
abcdefghijklmnopqrstuvwxyz
1234567890$

36 point Lydian Bold Italic (Foundry)

ABCDEFGHIJKLMNOPQRSTUV
WXYZ&
abcdefghijklmnopqrstuvwxyz
1234567890$

18 point Lydian Cursive (Foundry)

ABCDEFGHIJKLMNOPQRSTUVWXYZ&
abcdefghijklmnopqrstuvwxyz
1234567890$

24 point Lydian Cursive (Foundry)

ABCDEFGHIJKLMNOPQRSTUVWXYZ&
abcdefghijklmnopqrstuvwxyz
1234567890$

30 point Lydian Cursive (Foundry)

ABCDEFGHIJKLMNOPQRSTUVWXYZ&
abcdefghijklmnopqrstuvwxyz
1234567890$

36 point Lydian Cursive (Foundry)

ABCDEFGHIJKLMNOPQRSTUVW
XYZ& 1234567890$
abcdefghijklmnopqrstuvwxyz

48 point Lydian Cursive (Foundry)

ABCDEFGHIJKLMNOPQ
RSTUVWXYZ&
abcdefghijklmnopqrstuvwxyz
1234567890$

Marble Heart

42 point Marble Heart, Cap font (Foundry)

ABCDEFGHIJKLMNOPQRSTUV
WXYZ&
1234567890$

Medium Condensed Gothic

42 point Medium Condensed Gothic (Ludlow)

18 point Medium Condensed Gothic (Ludlow)

ABCDEFGHIJKLMNOPQRSTUVWXYZ&
abcdefghijklmnopqrstuvwxyz 1234567890$

24 point Medium Condensed Gothic (Ludlow)

ABCDEFGHIJKLMNOPQRSTUVWXYZ&
abcdefghijklmnopqrstuvwxyz 1234567890$

30 point Medium Condensed Gothic (Ludlow)

ABCDEFGHIJKLMNOPQRSTUVWXYZ&
abcdefghijklmnopqrstuvwxyz 1234567890$

42 point Medium Condensed Gothic (Ludlow)

ABCDEFGHIJKLMNOPQRSTUV
WXYZ&
abcdefghijklmnopqrstuvwxyz
1234567890$

6 point Melior (Linotype)

The basic character in a type design is determined by the uniform design characterstics of all letters in the alphabet. However, this alone does not determine the standard of the type face and the quality of composition set with it. The appearance is something complex which forms itself out of many details, like form, proportion, ductus, rhythm etc. If everything harmonizes, the total result will be more than the sum of its components. The only reliable basis for the design in a type is a positive feeling for form and style. The basic character in a type design is determined by the

ABCDEFGHIJKLMNOPQRSTUVWXYZ&
abcdefghijklmnopqrstuvwxyz   1234567890$

7 point Melior (Linotype)

The basic character in a type design is determined by the uniform design characteristics of all letters in the alphabet. However, this alone does not determine the standard of the type face and the quality of composition set with it. The appearance is something complex which forms itself out of many details, like form, proportion, ductus, rhythm etc. If everything harmonizes, the total result will be more than the sum of its components. The only

ABCDEFGHIJKLMNOPQRSTUVWXYZ&
abcdefghijklmnopqrstuvwxyz   1234567890$

8 point Melior (Linotype)

The basic character in a type design is determined by the uniform design characteristics of all letters in the alphabet. However, this alone does not determine the standard of the type face and the quality of composition set with it. The appearance is something complex which forms itself out of many details, like form, proportion, ductus, rhythm etc. If

ABCDEFGHIJKLMNOPQRSTUVWXYZ&
abcdefghijklmnopqrstuvwxyz   1234567890$

9 point Melior (Linotype)

The basic character in a type design is determined by the uniform design characteristics of all letters in the alphabet. However, this alone does not determine the standard of the type face and the quality of composition set with it. The appearance is something complex which forms itself out of many details, like form, proportion, ductus,

ABCDEFGHIJKLMNOPQRSTUVWXYZ&
abcdefghijklmnopqrstuvwxyz   1234567890$

10 point Melior (Linotype)

The basic character in a type design is determined by the uniform design characteristics of all letters in the alphabet. However, this alone does not determine the standard of the type face and the quality of com position set with it. The appearance is something

ABCDEFGHIJKLMNOPQRSTUVWXYZ&
abcdefghijklmnopqrstuvwxyz   1234567890$

12 point Melior (Linotype)

The basic character in a type design is deter mined by the uniform design characteristics of all letters in the alphabet. However, this alone does not determine the standard of the

ABCDEFGHIJKLMNOPQRSTUVWXYZ&
abcdefghijklmnopqrstuvwxyz   1234567890$

10 point Melior (Foundry)

ABCDEFGHIJKLMNOPQRSTUVWXYZ&
abcdefghijklmnopqrstuvwxyz
1234567890$

12 point Melior Small (Foundry)

ABCDEFGHIJKLMNOPQRSTUVWXYZ&
abcdefghijklmnopqrstuvwxyz
1234567890$

12 point Melior Large (Foundry)

ABCDEFGHIJKLMNOPQRSTUVWXYZ&
abcdefghijklmnopqrstuvwxyz
1234567890$

14 point Melior (Foundry)

ABCDEFGHIJKLMNOPQRSTUVWXYZ&
abcdefghijklmnopqrstuvwxyz
1234567890$

18 point Melior (Foundry)

ABCDEFGHIJKLMNOPQRSTUVWXYZ&
abcdefghijklmnopqrstuvwxyz
1234567890$

24 point Melior Small (Foundry)

ABCDEFGHIJKLMNOPQRSTUVWXYZ&
abcdefghijklmnopqrstuvwxyz
1234567890$

(Continued on Page 339)

(Continued from Page 338)

24 point Melior Large (Foundry)

ABCDEFGHIJKLMNOPQRSTUVWXYZ&
abcdefghijklmnopqrstuvwxyz
1234567890$

30 point Melior (Foundry)

ABCDEFGHIJKLMNOPQRSTUVWXYZ
abcdefghijklmnopqrstuvwxyz&
1234567890$

36 point Melior (Foundry)

ABCDEFGHIJKLMNOPQRST
UVWXYZ&
abcdefghijklmnopqrstuvwxyz
1234567890$

48 point Melior (Foundry)

ABCDEFGHIJKLMNOP
QRSTUVWXYZ&
abcdefghijklmnopqrstuv
wxyz
1234567890$

(Continued on Page 340)

60 point Melior (Foundry)

ABCDEFGHIJKLM
NOPQRSTUV
WXYZ&
abcdefghijklmnopq
rstuvwxyz
1234567890$

Melior Italic *(Must be leaded 1 point)*

6 point Melior Italic (Linotype)
The basic character in a type design is determined by the uniform design characterstics of all letters in the alphabet. However, this alone does not determine the standard of the type face and the quality of composition set with it. The appearance is something complex which forms itself out of many details, like form, proportion, ductus, rhythm etc. If everything harmonizes, the total result will be more than the sum of its components. The only reliable basis for the design in a type is a positive feeling for form and style. The basic character in a type design is determined by the

ABCDEFGHIJKLMNOPQRSTUVWXYZ&
abcdefghijklmnopqrstuvwxyz   *1234567890$*

7 point Melior Italic (Linotype)
The basic character in a type design is determined by the uniform design characteristics of all letters in the alphabet. However, this alone does not determine the standard of the type face and the quality of composition set with it. The appearance is something complex which forms itself out of many details, like form, pro portion, ductus, rhythm etc. If everything harmonizes, the total result will be more than the sum of its components. The only

ABCDEFGHIJKLMNOPQRSTUVWXYZ&
abcdefghijklmnopqrstuvwxyz   *1234567890$*

8 point Melior Italic (Linotype)
The basic character in a type design is determined by the uniform design characteristics of all letters in the alphabet. However, this alone does not determine the standard of the type face and the quality of composition set with it. The appearance is something complex which forms itself out of many details, like form, proportion, ductus, rhythm etc. If

ABCDEFGHIJKLMNOPQRSTUVWXYZ&
abcdefghijklmnopqrstuvwxyz   *1234567890$*

9 point Melior Italic (Linotype)
The basic character in a type design is determined by the uniform design characteristics of all letters in the alpha bet. However, this alone does not determine the standard of the type face and the quality of composition set with it. The appearance is something complex which forms itself out of many details, like form, proportion, ductus,

ABCDEFGHIJKLMNOPQRSTUVWXYZ&
abcdefghijklmnopqrstuvwxyz   *1234567890$*

10 point Melior Italic (Linotype)
The basic character in a type design is determined by the uniform design characteristics of all letters in the alphabet. However, this alone does not determine the standard of the type face and the quality of com position set with it. The appearance is something

ABCDEFGHIJKLMNOPQRSTUVWXYZ&
abcdefghijklmnopqrstuvwxyz   *1234567890$*

14 point Melior Italic (Foundry)
ABCDEFGHIJKLMNOPQRSTUV WXYZ&
abcdefghijklmnopqrstuvwxyz
1234567890$

18 point Melior Italic (Foundry)
ABCDEFGHIJKLMNOPQRSTUVWXYZ&
abcdefghijklmnopqrstuvwxyz
1234567890$

24 point Melior Italic Small (Foundry)
ABCDEFGHIJKLMNOPQRSTUVWXYZ&
abcdefghijklmnopqrstuvwxyz
1234567890$

24 point Melior Italic Large (Foundry)
ABCDEFGHIJKLMNOPQRSTUVWXYZ&
abcdefghijklmnopqrstuvwxyz
1234567890$

(Continued on Page 342)

(Continued from Page 341)

48 point Melior Italic (Foundry)

ABCDEFGHIJKLMNOPQ RSTUVWXYZ& abcdefghijklmnopqrstuv wxyz 1234567890$

Melior Bold Condensed

12 point Melior Bold Condensed (Foundry)
ABCDEFGHIJKLMNOPQRSTUVWXYZ&
abcdefghijklmnopqrstuvwxyz
1234567890$

14 point Melior Bold Condensed (Foundry)
ABCDEFGHIJKLMNOPQRSTUVWXYZ&
abcdefghijklmnopqrstuvwxyz
1234567890$

24 point Melior Bold Condensed (Foundry)
ABCDEFGHIJKLMNOPQRSTUVWXYZ&
abcdefghijklmnopqrstuvwxyz
1234567890$

36 point Melior Bold Condensed (Foundry)
ABCDEFGHIJKLMNOPQRSTUVWXYZ&
abcdefghijklmnopqrstuvwxyz
1234567890$

6 point Melior Semi-Bold (Linotype)

The basic character in a type design is determined by the uniform design characteristics of all letters in the alphabet. However, this alone does not determine the standard of the type face and the quality of composition set with it. The appearance is something complex which forms itself out of many details, like form, proportion, ductus, rhythm etc. If everything harmonizes, the total result will be more than the sum of its components. The only reliable basis for the design in a type is a positive feeling for form and style. The basic character in a type design is determined by the

ABCDEFGHIJKLMNOPQRSTUVWXYZ&
abcdefghijklmnopqrstuvwxyz   1234567890$

7 point Melior Semi-Bold (Linotype)

The basic character in a type design is determined by the uniform design characteristics of all letters in the alphabet. However, this alone does not determine the standard of the type face and the quality of composition set with it. The appearance is something complex which forms itself out of many details, like form, proportion, ductus, rhythm etc. If everything harmonizes the total result will be more than the sum of its components. The only reliable

ABCDEFGHIJKLMNOPQRSTUVWXYZ&
abcdefghijklmnopqrstuvwxyz   1234567890$

8 point Melior Semi-Bold (Linotype)

The basic character in a type design is determined by the uniform design characteristics of all letters in the alphabet. However, this alone does not determine the standard of the type face and the quality of composition set with it. The appearance is something complex which forms itself out of many details, like form, proportion, ductus, rhythm etc. If

ABCDEFGHIJKLMNOPQRSTUVWXYZ&
abcdefghijklmnopqrstuvwxyz   1234567890$

9 point Melior Semi-Bold (Linotype)

The basic character in a type design is determined by the uniform design characteristics of all letters in the alphabet. However, this alone does not determine the standard of the type face and the quality of composition set with it. The appearance is something complex which forms itself out of many details, like form, proportion, ductus,

ABCDEFGHIJKLMNOPQRSTUVWXYZ&
abcdefghijklmnopqrstuvwxyz   1234567890$

10 point Melior Semi-Bold (Linotype)

The basic character in a type design is determined by the uniform design characteristics of all letters in the adphabet. However, this alone does not deter mine the standard of the type face and the quality of composition set with it. The appearance is something

ABCDEFGHIJKLMNOPQRSTUVWXYZ&
abcdefghijklmnopqrstuvwxyz   1234567890$

12 point Melior Semi-Bold (Linotype)

The basic character in a type design is deter mined by the uniform design characteristics of all letters in the alphabet. However, this alone does not determine the standard of the

ABCDEFGHIJKLMNOPQRSTUVWXYZ&
abcdefghijklmnopqrstuvwxyz   1234567890$

10 point Melior Semi-Bold (Foundry)

ABCDEFGHIJKLMNOPQRSTUVWXYZ&
abcdefghijklmnopqrstuvwxyz
1234567890$

12 point Melior Semi-Bold Small (Foundry)

ABCDEFGHIJKLMNOPQRSTUVWXYZ&
abcdefghijklmnopqrstuvwxyz
1234567890$

12 point Melior Semi-Bold Large (Foundry)

ABCDEFGHIJKLMNOPQRSTUVWXYZ&
abcdefghijklmnopqrstuvwxyz
1234567890$

18 point Melior Semi-Bold (Foundry)

ABCDEFGHIJKLMNOPQRSTUVWXYZ&
abcdefghijklmnopqrstuvwxyz
1234567890$

24 point Melior Semi-Bold Small (Foundry)

ABCDEFGHIJKLMNOPQRSTUVWXYZ&
abcdefghijklmnopqrstuvwxyz
1234567890$

(Continued on Page 344)

(Continued from Page 343)

24 point Melior Semi-Bold Large (Foundry)

ABCDEFGHIJKLMNOPQRSTUVWXYZ&
abcdefghijklmnopqrstuvwxyz
1234567890$

36 point Melior Semi-Bold (Foundry)

ABCDEFGHIJKLMNOPQRSTU
VWXYZ&
abcdefghijklmnopqrstuvwxyz
1234567890$

60 point Melior Semi-Bold (Foundry)

ABCDEFGHIJKLM
NOPQRSTUV
WXYZ&
abcdefghijklmnop
qrstuvwxyz
1234567890$

Metropol 416

24 point Metropol 416 (Ludlow)

ABCDEFGHIJKLMNOPQRSTUVWXYZ&
abcdefghijklmnopqrstuvwxyz
1234567890$

Michelangelo Titling

16 point Michelangelo Titling, Cap font (Foundry)

ABCDEFGHIJKLMNOPQRSTUVWXYZ&
1234567890$

30 point Michelangelo Titling, Cap font (Foundry)

ABCDEFGHIJKLMNOPQRSTUV
WXYZ&
1234567890$

Microgramma

12 point Microgramma, Cap font (Foundry)

ABCDEFGHIJKLMNOPQRSTUVWXYZ&
1234567890$

14 point Microgramma, Cap font (Foundry)

ABCDEFGHIJKLMNOPQRSTUVWXYZ&
1234567890$

Microgramma Condensed

10 point Microgramma Condensed, Cap font (Foundry)

ABCDEFGHIJKLMNOPQRSTUVWXYZ&
1234567890$

Microgramma Bold

8 point Microgramma Bold, Cap font (Foundry)
ABCDEFGHIJKLMNOPQRSTUVWXYZ&
1234567890$

12 point Microgramma Bold, Cap font (Foundry)
ABCDEFGHIJKLMNOPQRSTUV
WXYZ&   1234567890$

10 point Microgramma Bold, Cap font (Foundry)
ABCDEFGHIJKLMNOPQRSTUVWXYZ&
1234567890$

14 point Microgramma Bold, Cap font (Foundry)
ABCDEFGHIJKLMNOPQRST
UVWXYZ&   1234567890$

18 point Microgramma Bold, Cap font (Foundry)
ABCDEFGHIJKLMNOPQRSTUVWXYZ&
1234567890$

24 point Microgramma Bold, Cap font (Foundry)
ABCDEFGHIJKLMNOPQRSTUV
WXYZ&
1234567890$

30B point Microgramma Bold, Cap font (Foundry)
ABCDEFGHIJKLMNOPQR
STUVWXYZ&
1234567890$

36 point Microgramma Bold, Cap font (Foundry)
ABCDEFGHIJKLMNO
PQRSTUVWXYZ&
1234567890$

Microgramma Bold Extended

6 point Microgramma Bold Extended, Cap font (Foundry)
ABCDEFGHIJKLMNOPQRSTUVWXYZ&
1234567890$

12 point Microgramma Bold Extended, Cap font (Foundry)
ABCDEFGHIJKLMNOPQR
STUVWXYZ&
1234567890$

8 point Microgramma Bold Extended, Cap font (Foundry)
ABCDEFGHIJKLMNOPQRSTUVWXYZ&
1234567890$

14 point Microgramma Bold Extended, Cap font (Foundry)
ABCDEFGHIJKLMNOPQRSTUVWXYZ&
1234567890$

18 point Microgramma Bold Extended, Cap font (Foundry)
ABCDEFGHIJKLMNOPQRSTUV
WXYZ&
1234567890$

24 point Microgramma Bold Extended, Cap font (Foundry)
ABCDEFGHIJKLMNOPQR
STUVWXYZ&
1234567890$

30A point Microgramma Bold Extended, Cap font (Foundry)
ABCDEFGHIJKLMNO
PQRSTUVWXYZ&
1234567890$

Microgramma Extended

6B point Microgramma Extended, Cap font (Foundry)
ABCDEFGHIJKLMNOPQRSTUVWXYZ&
1234567890$

8 point Microgramma Extended, Cap font (Foundry)
ABCDEFGHIJKLMNOPQRSTUVWXYZ&
1234567890$

10 point Microgramma Extended, Cap font (Foundry)
ABCDEFGHIJKLMNOPQRSTUVWXYZ&
1234567890$

12 point Microgramma Extended, Cap font (Foundry)
ABCDEFGHIJKLMNOPQRSTUVWXYZ&
1234567890$

Mistral

18 point Mistral (Foundry)

ABCDEFGHIJKLMNOPQRSTUVWXYZ&
abcdefghijklmnopqrstuvwxyz
1234567890$

24 point Mistral Large (Foundry)

ABCDEFGHIJKLMNOPQRSTUVWXYZ&
abcdefghijklmnopqrstuvwxyz
1234567890$

30 point Mistral (Foundry)

ABCDEFGHIJKLMNOPQRSTUVWXYZ&
abcdefghijklmnopqrstuvwxyz
1234567890$

36 point Mistral, Caps only (Foundry)

ABCDEFGHIJKLMNOPQRSTUVWXYZ&
1234567890$

48 point Mistral (Foundry)

ABCDEFGHIJKLMNOPQRSTUV
WXYZ&
abcdefghijklmnopqrstuvwxyz
1234567890$

Modern No. 20

14 point Modern No. 20 (Foundry)

ABCDEFGHIJKLMNOPQRSTUVWXYZ&
abcdefghijklmnopqrstuvwxyz
1234567890$

18 point Modern No. 20 (Foundry)

ABCDEFGHIJKLMNOPQRSTUVWXYZ&
abcdefghijklmnopqrstuvwxyz
1234567890$

24 point Modern No. 20 (Foundry)

ABCDEFGHIJKLMNOPQRSTUVWXYZ&
abcdefghijklmnopqrstuvwxyz
1234567890$

30 point Modern No. 20 (Foundry)

ABCDEFGHIJKLMNOPQRSTUV
WXYZ&
abcdefghijklmnopqrstuvwxyz
1234567890$

36 point Modern No. 20 (Foundry)

ABCDEFGHIJKLMNOPQRST
UVWXYZ&
abcdefghijklmnopqrstuvwxyz
1234567890$

(Continued on Page 350)

48 point Modern No. 20 (Foundry)

ABCDEFGHIJKLM NOPQRSTUVWXYZ abcdefghijklmnopqrstu vwxyz& 1234567890$

Modern No. 20 Italic

18 point Modern No. 20 Italic (Foundry)

ABCDEFGHIJKLMNOPQRSTUVWXYZ&
abcdefghijklmnopqrstuvwxyz
1234567890$

24 point Modern No. 20 Italic (Foundry)

ABCDEFGHIJKLMNOPQRSTUVWXYZ&
abcdefghijklmnopqrstuvwxyz
1234567890$

30 point Modern No. 20 Italic (Foundry)

ABCDEFGHIJKLMNOPQRSTUV
WXYZ&
abcdefghijklmnopqrstuvwxyz
1234567890$

Monticello

The basic character in a type design is determined by the uniform design characteristics of all letters in the alphabet. However, this alone does not determine the standard of the type face and the quality of composition set with it. The appearance is something complex which forms itself out of many details, like form, propor

ABCDEFGHIJKLMNOPQRSTUVWXYZ&
abcdefghijklmnopqrstuvwxyz   1234567890$
ABCDEFGHIJKLMNOPQRSTUVWXYZ

The basic character in a type design is determined by the uni form design characteristics of all letters in the alphabet. How ever, this alone does not determine the standard of the type face and the quality of composition set with it. The appearance

ABCDEFGHIJKLMNOPQRSTUVWXYZ&
abcdefghijklmnopqrstuvwxyz   1234567890$
ABCDEFGHIJKLMNOPQRSTUVWXYZ

The basic character in a type design is determined by the uniform design characteristics of all letters in the alphabet. However, this alone does not determine the standard of the type face and the quality of composition set with it. The

ABCDEFGHIJKLMNOPQRSTUVWXYZ&
abcdefghijklmnopqrstuvwxyz   1234567890$
ABCDEFGHIJKLMNOPQRSTUVWXYZ

The basic character in a type design is determined by the uniform design characteristics of all letters in the alphabet. However, this alone does not determine the standard of the type face and the quality of composition

ABCDEFGHIJKLMNOPQRSTUVWXYZ&
abcdefghijklmnopqrstuvwxyz   1234567890$
ABCDEFGHIJKLMNOPQRSTUVWXYZ

The basic character in a type design is determined by the uniform design characteristics of all letters in the alphabet. However, this alone does not deter

ABCDEFGHIJKLMNOPQRSTUVWXYZ&
abcdefghijklmnopqrstuvwxyz   1234567890$
ABCDEFGHIJKLMNOPQRSTUVWXYZ

The basic character in a type design is determined by the uniform design characteristics of all letters in the alphabet. However, this alone does not de

ABCDEFGHIJKLMNOPQRSTUVWXYZ&
abcdefghijklmnopqrstuvwxyz   1234567890$
ABCDEFGHIJKLMNOPQRSTUVWXYZ

The basic character in a type design is deter mined by the uniform design characteristics

ABCDEFGHIJKLMNOPQRSTUV
WXYZ&   1234567890$
abcdefghijklmnopqrstuvwxyz
ABCDEFGHIJKLMNOPQRSTUVWXYZ

Monticello Italic

The basic character in a type design is determined by the uniform design characteristics of all letters in the alphabet. However, this alone does not determine the standard of the type face and the quality of composition set with it. The appearance is something complex which forms itself out of many details, like form, propor

ABCDEFGHIJKLMNOPQRSTUVWXYZ&
abcdefghijklmnopqrstuvwxyz   1234567890$

The basic character in a type design is determined by the uni form design characteristics of all letters in the alphabet. How ever, this alone does not determine the standard of the type face and the quality of composition set with it. The appearance

ABCDEFGHIJKLMNOPQRSTUVWXYZ&
abcdefghijklmnopqrstuvwxyz   1234567890$

The basic character in a type design is determined by the uniform design characteristics of all letters in the alphabet. However, this alone does not determine the standard of the type face and the quality of composition set with it. The

ABCDEFGHIJKLMNOPQRSTUVWXYZ&
abcdefghijklmnopqrstuvwxyz   1234567890$

The basic character in a type design is determined by the uniform design characteristics of all letters in the alphabet. However, this alone does not determine the standard of the type face and the quality of composition

ABCDEFGHIJKLMNOPQRSTUVWXYZ&
abcdefghijklmnopqrstuvwxyz   1234567890$

The basic character in a type design is determined by the uniform design characteristics of all letters in the alphabet. However, this alone does not deter

ABCDEFGHIJKLMNOPQRSTUVWXYZ&
abcdefghijklmnopqrstuvwxyz   1234567890$

The basic character in a type design is determined by the uniform design characteristics of all letters in the alphabet. However, this alone does not de

ABCDEFGHIJKLMNOPQRSTUVWXYZ&
abcdefghijklmnopqrstuvwxyz   1234567890$

The basic character in a type design is deter mined by the uniform design characteristics

ABCDEFGHIJKLMNOPQRSTUV
WXYZ&   1234567890$
abcdefghijklmnopqrstuvwxyz

Murray Hill Bold

ABCDEFGHIJKLMNOPQRS
TUVWXYZ&
abcdefghijklmnopqrstuvwxyz
1234567890$

Neuland

ABCDEFGHIJKLMNOPQRSTUVWXYZ&
1234567890O$

ABCDEFGHIJKLMNOPQRSTUVWXYZ&
1234567890O$

ABCDEFGHIJKLMNOPQRSTUVWXYZ&
1234567890O$

ABCDEFGHIJKLMNOPQRST
UVWXYZ&
1234567890O$

14 point New Caslon (Foundry)

ABCDEFGHIJKLMNOPQRSTUVWXYZ&
abcdefghijklmnopqrstuvwxyz
1234567890$

18 point New Caslon (Foundry)

ABCDEFGHIJKLMNOPQRSTUVWXYZ&
abcdefghijklmnopqrstuvwxyz
1234567890$

24 point New Caslon (Foundry)

ABCDEFGHIJKLMNOPQRSTUVWXYZ
abcdefghijklmnopqrstuvwxyz&
1234567890$

30 point New Caslon (Foundry)

ABCDEFGHIJKLMNOPQRSTUV
WXYZ&
abcdefghijklmnopqrstuvwxyz
1234567890$

48 point New Caslon (Foundry)

ABCDEFGHIJKLM
NOPQRSTUVWXYZ
abcdefghijklmnopqrstuv
wxyz&
1234567890$

14 point New Caslon Italic (Foundry)

ABCDEFGHIJKLMNOPQRSTUVWXYZ&
abcdefghijklmnopqrstuvwxyz 1234567890$

18 point New Caslon Italic (Foundry)

ABCDEFGHIJKLMNOPQRSTUVWXYZ&
abcdefghijklmnopqrstuvwxyz 1234567890$

24 point New Caslon Italic (Foundry)

ABCDEFGHIJKLMNOPQRSTUVWXYZ&
abcdefghijklmnopqrstuvwxyz 1234567890$

30 point New Caslon Italic (Foundry)

ABCDEFGHIJKLMNOPQRSTUV
WXYZ&
abcdefghijklmnopqrstuvwxyz
1234567890$

36 point New Caslon Italic (Foundry)

ABCDEFGHIJKLMNOPQRS
TUVWXYZ&
abcdefghijklmnopqrstuvwxyz
1234567890$

42 point New Caslon Italic (Foundry)

ABCDEFGHIJKLMNOP
QRSTUVWXYZ&
abcdefghijklmnopqrstuvwxyz
1234567890$

6 point News Gothic (Intertype)

The basic character in a type design is determined by the uniform de sign characteristics of all letters in the alphabet. However, this alone does not determine the standard of the type face and the quality of composition set with it. The appearance is something complex which forms itself out of many details, like form, proportion, ductus, rhythm etc. If everything harmonizes, the total result will be more than the sum of its components. The only reliable basis for the design in a type is a positive feeling for form and style. The basic character in a type design

ABCDEFGHIJKLMNOPQRSTUVWXYZ&
abcdefghijklmnopqrstuvwxyz   1234567890$

8 point News Gothic (Linotype)

The basic character in a type design is determined by the uni form design characteristics of all letters in the alphabet. How ever, this alone does not determine the standard of the type face and the quality of composition set with it. The appearance is something complex which forms itself out of many details, like form, proportion, ductus, rhythm etc. If everything har

ABCDEFGHIJKLMNOPQRSTUVWXYZ&
abcdefghijklmnopqrstuvwxyz   1234567890$

10 point News Gothic (Foundry)

ABCDEFGHIJKLMNOPQRSTUVWXYZ&
abcdefghijklmnopqrstuvwxyz
1234567890$

9 point News Gothic (Linotype)

The basic character in a type design is determined by the uniform design characteristics of all letters in the alpha bet. However, this alone does not determine the standard of the type face and the quality of composition set with it. The appearance is something complex which forms itself

ABCDEFGHIJKLMNOPQRSTUVWXYZ&
abcdefghijklmnopqrstuvwxyz   1234567890$

6 point News Gothic (Foundry)

ABCDEFGHIJKLMNOPQRSTUVWXYZ&
abcdefghijklmnopqrstuvwxyz
1234567890$

8 point News Gothic (Foundry)

ABCDEFGHIJKLMNOPQRSTUVWXYZ&
abcdefghijklmnopqrstuvwxyz
1234567890$

12 point News Gothic (Foundry)

ABCDEFGHIJKLMNOPQRSTUVWXYZ&
abcdefghijklmnopqrstuvwxyz
1234567890$

14 point News Gothic (Foundry)

ABCDEFGHIJKLMNOPQRSTUVWXYZ&
abcdefghijklmnopqrstuvwxyz
1234567890$

18 point News Gothic (Foundry)

ABCDEFGHIJKLMNOPQRSTUVWXYZ&
abcdefghijklmnopqrstuvwxyz
1234567890$

24 point News Gothic (Foundry)

ABCDEFGHIJKLMNOPQRSTUVWXYZ&
abcdefghijklmnopqrstuvwxyz
1234567890$

30 point News Gothic (Foundry)

ABCDEFGHIJKLMNOPQRSTUVWXYZ&
abcdefghijklmnopqrstuvwxyz
1234567890$

(Continued on Page 356)

36 point News Gothic (Foundry)

ABCDEFGHIJKLMNOPQRSTUV
WXYZ&
abcdefghijklmnopqrstuvwxyz
1234567890$

42 point News Gothic (Foundry)

ABCDEFGHIJKLMNOPQRSTU
VWXYZ&
abcdefghijklmnopqrstuvwxyz
1234567890$

48 point News Gothic (Foundry)

ABCDEFGHIJKLMNOPQR
STUVWXYZ&
abcdefghijklmnopqrstuv
wxyz
1234567890$

(Continued on Page 357)

72 point News Gothic (Foundry)

ABCDEFGHIJKLM
NOPQRSTUV
WXYZ&
abcdefghijklmnop
qrstuvwxyz
1234567890$

News Gothic Bold

6 point News Gothic Bold (Intertype)

The basic character in a type design is determined by the uniform de sign characteristics of all letters in the alphabet. However, this alone does not determine the standard of the type face and the quality of composition set with it. The appearance is something complex which forms itself out of many details, like form, proportion, ductus, rhythm etc. If everything harmonizes, the total result will be more than the sum of its components. The only reliable basis for the design in a type is a positive feeling for form and style. The basic character in a type design

ABCDEFGHIJKLMNOPQRSTUVWXYZ&
abcdefghijklmnopqrstuvwxyz   1234567890$

9 point News Gothic Bold (Linotype)

uniform design characteristics of all letters in the alpha The basic character in a type design is determined by the bet. However, this alone does not determine the standard of the type face and the quality of composition set with it. The appearance is something complex which forms itself

ABCDEFGHIJKLMNOPQRSTUVWXYZ&
abcdefghijklmnopqrstuvwxyz   1234567890$

8 point News Gothic Bold (Linotype)

The basic character in a type design is determined by the uni form design characteristics of all letters in the alphabet. How ever, this alone does not determine the standard of the type face and the quality of composition set with it. The appearance is something complex which forms itself out of many details, like form, proportion, ductus, rhythm etc. If everything har

ABCDEFGHIJKLMNOPQRSTUVWXYZ&
abcdefghijklmnopqrstuvwxyz   1234567890$

6 point News Gothic Bold (Foundry)

ABCDEFGHIJKLMNOPQRSTUVWXYZ&
abcdefghijklmnopqrstuvwxyz
1234567890$

10 point News Gothic Bold (Foundry)

ABCDEFGHIJKLMNOPQRSTUVWXYZ&
abcdefghijklmnopqrstuvwxyz
1234567890$

12 point News Gothic Bold (Foundry)

ABCDEFGHIJKLMNOPQRSTUVWXYZ&
abcdefghijklmnopqrstuvwxyz
1234567890$

14 point News Gothic Bold (Foundry)

ABCDEFGHIJKLMNOPQRSTUVWXYZ
abcdefghijklmnopqrstuvwxyz&
1234567890$

18 point News Gothic Bold (Foundry)

ABCDEFGHIJKLMNOPQRSTUVWXYZ&
abcdefghijklmnopqrstuvwxyz
1234567890$

24 point News Gothic Bold (Foundry)

ABCDEFGHIJKLMNOPQRSTUVWXYZ&
abcdefghijklmnopqrstuvwxyz
1234567890$

30 point News Gothic Bold (Foundry)

ABCDEFGHIJKLMNOPQRSTUVWXYZ&
abcdefghijklmnopqrstuvwxyz
1234567890$

(Continued on Page 359)

36 point News Gothic Bold (Foundry)

ABCDEFGHIJKLMNOPQRSTUV
WXYZ&
abcdefghijklmnopqrstuvwxyz
1234567890$

42 point News Gothic Bold (Foundry)

ABCDEFGHIJKLMNOPQRS
TUVWXYZ&
abcdefghijklmnopqrstuv
wxyz
1234567890$

48 point News Gothic Bold (Foundry)

ABCDEFGHIJKLMNOPQ
RSTUVWXYZ&
abcdefghijklmnopqrstu
vwxyz
1234567890$

News Gothic Bold Condensed

6 point News Gothic Bold Condensed (Linotype)

The basic character in a type design is determined by the uniform design char acteristics of all letters in the alphabet. However, this alone does not determine the standard of the type face and the quality of composition set with it. The appearance is something complex which forms itself out of many details, like form, proportion, ductus, rhythm etc. If everything harmonizes, the total result will be more than the sum of its components. The only reliable basis for the design in a type ·is a positive feeling for form and style. The basic character in a type design is determined by the uniform design characteristics of all

ABCDEFGHIJKLMNOPQRSTUVWXYZ&
abcdefghijklmnopqrstuvwxyz   1234567890$

10 point News Gothic Bold Condensed (Linotype)

The basic character in a type design is determined by the uni form design characteristics of all letters in the alphabet. However, this alone does not determine the standard of the type face and the quality of composition set with it. The appearance is some thing complex which forms itself out of many details, like form,

ABCDEFGHIJKLMNOPQRSTUVWXYZ&
abcdefghijklmnopqrstuvwxyz   1234567890$

7 point News Gothic Bold Condensed (Linotype)

The basic character in a type design is determined by the uniform design characteristics of all letters in the alphabet. However, this alone does not determine the standard of the type face and the quality of composition set with it. The appearance is something complex which forms itself out of many details, like form, proportion, ductus, rhythm etc. If everything har monizes, the total result will be more than the sum of its components. The only reliable basis for the design in a type is a positive feeling for form

ABCDEFGHIJKLMNOPQRSTUVWXYZ&
abcdefghijklmnopqrstuvwxyz   1234567890$

11 point News Gothic Bold Condensed (Linotype)

The basic character in a type design is determined by the uniform design characteristics of all letters in the alphabet. However, this alone does not determine the standard of the type face and the quality of composition set with it. The ap

ABCDEFGHIJKLMNOPQRSTUVWXYZ&
abcdefghijklmnopqrstuvwxyz   1234567890$

8 point News Gothic Bold Condensed (Linotype)

The basic character in a type design is determined by the uniform de sign characteristics of all letters in the alphabet. However, this alone does not determine the standard of the type face and the quality of composition set with it. The appearance is something complex which forms itself out of many details, like form, proportion, ductus, rhythm etc. If everything harmonizes, the total result will be more than the sum of

ABCDEFGHIJKLMNOPQRSTUVWXYZ&
abcdefghijklmnopqrstuvwxyz   1234567890$

12 point News Gothic Bold Condensed (Linotype)

The basic character in a type design is determined by the uniform design characteristics of all letters in the alphabet. However, this alone does not determine the standard of the type face and the quality of composition set with it. The

ABCDEFGHIJKLMNOPQRSTUVWXYZ&
abcdefghijklmnopqrstuvwxyz   1234567890$

9 point News Gothic Bold Condensed (Linotype)

The basic character in a type design is determined by the uniform design characteristics of all letters in the alphabet. However, this alone does not determine the standard of the type face and the quality of composition set with it. The appearance is something complex which forms itself out of many details, like form, propor

ABCDEFGHIJKLMNOPQRSTUVWXYZ&
abcdefghijklmnopqrstuvwxyz   1234567890$

14 point News Gothic Bold Condensed (Linotype)

The basic character in a type design is determined by the uniform design characteristics of all letters in the alphabet. However, this alone does not deter

ABCDEFGHIJKLMNOPQRSTUVWXYZ&
abcdefghijklmnopqrstuvwxyz   1234567890$

News Gothic Condensed

6 point News Gothic Condensed (Linotype)
The basic character in a type design is determined by the uniform design char acteristics of all letters in the alphabet. However, this alone does not determine the standard of the type face and the quality of composition set with it. The appearance is something complex which forms itself out of many details, like form, proportion, ductus, rhythm etc. If everything harmonizes, the total result will be more than the sum of its components. The only reliable basis for the design in a type is a positive feeling for form and style. The basic character in a type design is determined by the uniform design characteristics of all

ABCDEFGHIJKLMNOPQRSTUVWXYZ&
abcdefghijklmnopqrstuvwxyz 1234567890$

7 point News Gothic Condensed (Linotype)
The basic character in a type design is determined by the uniform design characteristics of all letters in the alphabet. However, this alone does not determine the standard of the type face and the quality of composition set with it. The appearance is something complex which forms itself out of many details, like form, proportion, ductus, rhythm etc. If everything har monizes, the total result will be more than the sum of its components. The only reliable basis for the design in a type is a positive feeling for form

ABCDEFGHIJKLMNOPQRSTUVWXYZ&
abcdefghijklmnopqrstuvwxyz 1234567890$

8 point News Gothic Condensed (Linotype)
The basic character in a type design is determined by the uniform de sign characteristics of all letters in the alphabet. However, this alone does not determine the standard of the type face and the quality of composition set with it. The appearance is something complex which forms itself out of many details, like form, proportion, ductus, rhythm etc. If everything harmonizes, the total result will be more than the sum of

ABCDEFGHIJKLMNOPQRSTUVWXYZ&
abcdefghijklmnopqrstuvwxyz 1234567890$

9 point News Gothic Condensed (Linotype)
The basic character in a type design is determined by the uniform design characteristics of all letters in the alphabet. However, this alone does not determine the standard of the type face and the quality of composition set with it. The appearance is something complex which forms itself out of many details, like form, propor

ABCDEFGHIJKLMNOPQRSTUVWXYZ&
abcdefghijklmnopqrstuvwxyz 1234567890$

10 point News Gothic Condensed (Linotype)
The basic character in a type design is determined by the uni form design characteristics of all letters in the alphabet. However, this alone does not determine the standard of the type face and the quality of composition set with it. The appearance is some thing complex which forms itself out of many details, like form,

ABCDEFGHIJKLMNOPQRSTUVWXYZ&
abcdefghijklmnopqrstuvwxyz 1234567890$

11 point News Gothic Condensed (Linotype)
The basic character in a type design is determined by the uniform design characteristics of all letters in the alphabet. However, this alone does not determine the standard of the type face and the quality of composition set with it. The

ABCDEFGHIJKLMNOPQRSTUVWXYZ&
abcdefghijklmnopqrstuvwxyz 1234567890$

12 point News Gothic Condensed (Linotype)
The basic character in a type design is determined by the uniform design characteristics of all letters in the alphabet. However, this alone does not determine the standard of the type face and the quality of composition set with it. The

ABCDEFGHIJKLMNOPQRSTUVWXYZ&
abcdefghijklmnopqrstuvwxyz 1234567890$

14 point News Gothic Condensed (Linotype)
The basic character in a type design is determined by the uniform design characteristics of all letters in the alphabet. However, this alone does not deter

ABCDEFGHIJKLMNOPQRSTUVWXYZ&
abcdefghijklmnopqrstuvwxyz 1234567890$

6 point News Gothic Condensed (Foundry)
ABCDEFGHIJKLMNOPQRSTUVWXYZ&
abcdefghijklmnopqrstuvwxyz
1234567890$

8 point News Gothic Condensed (Foundry)
ABCDEFGHIJKLMNOPQRSTUVWXYZ&
abcdefghijklmnopqrstuvwxyz
1234567890$

10 point News Gothic Condensed (Foundry)
ABCDEFGHIJKLMNOPQRSTUVWXYZ&
abcdefghijklmnopqrstuvwxyz
1234567890$

12 point News Gothic Condensed (Foundry)
ABCDEFGHIJKLMNOPQRSTUVWXYZ&
abcdefghijklmnopqrstuvwxyz
1234567890$

14 point News Gothic Condensed (Foundry)
ABCDEFGHIJKLMNOPQRSTUVWXYZ&
abcdefghijklmnopqrstuvwxyz
1234567890$

18 point News Gothic Condensed (Foundry)
ABCDEFGHIJKLMNOPQRSTUVWXYZ&
abcdefghijklmnopqrstuvwxyz
1234567890$

(Continued on Page 362)

(Continued from Page 361)

24 point News Gothic Condensed (Foundry)

ABCDEFGHIJKLMNOPQRSTUVWXYZ&
abcdefghijklmnopqrstuvwxyz
1234567890$

30 point News Gothic Condensed (Foundry)

ABCDEFGHIJKLMNOPQRSTUVWXYZ&
abcdefghijklmnopqrstuvwxyz
1234567890$

36 point News Gothic Condensed (Foundry)

ABCDEFGHIJKLMNOPQRSTUVWXYZ&
abcdefghijklmnopqrstuvwxyz 1234567890$

42 point News Gothic Condensed (Foundry)

ABCDEFGHIJKLMNOPQRSTUVWXYZ&
abcdefghijklmnopqrstuvwxyz
1234567890$

48 point News Gothic Condensed (Foundry)

ABCDEFGHIJKLMNOPQRSTUV
WXYZ&
abcdefghijklmnopqrstuvwxyz
1234567890$

(Continued on Page 363)

60 point News Gothic Condensed (Foundry)

ABCDEFGHIJKLMNOPQRST
UVWXYZ&
abcdefghijklmnopqrstuv
wxyz
1234567890$

72 point News Gothic Condensed (Foundry)

ABCDEFGHIJKLMNOPQ
RSTUVWXYZ&
abcdefghijklmnopqrstuv
wxyz 1234567890$

News Gothic Extra Condensed

6 point News Gothic Extra Condensed (Foundry)
ABCDEFGHIJKLMNOPQRSTUVWXYZ&
abcdefghijklmnopqrstuvwxyz
1234567890$

8 point News Gothic Extra Condensed (Foundry)
ABCDEFGHIJKLMNOPQRSTUVWXYZ&
abcdefghijklmnopqrstuvwxyz
1234567890$

10 point News Gothic Extra Condensed (Foundry)
ABCDEFGHIJKLMNOPQRSTUVWXYZ&
abcdefghijklmnopqrstuvwxyz
1234567890$

12 point News Gothic Extra Condensed (Foundry)
ABCDEFGHIJKLMNOPQRSTUVWXYZ&
abcdefghijklmnopqrstuvwxyz
1234567890$

14 point News Gothic Extra Condensed (Foundry)
ABCDEFGHIJKLMNOPQRSTUVWXYZ&
abcdefghijklmnopqrstuvwxyz
1234567890$

18 point News Gothic Extra Condensed (Foundry)
ABCDEFGHIJKLMNOPQRSTUVWXYZ&
abcdefghijklmnopqrstuvwxyz
1234567890$

24 point News Gothic Extra Condensed (Foundry)
ABCDEFGHIJKLMNOPQRSTUVWXYZ&
abcdefghijklmnopqrstuvwxyz
1234567890$

30 point News Gothic Extra Condensed (Foundry)
ABCDEFGHIJKLMNOPQRSTUVWXYZ&
abcdefghijklmnopqrstuvwxyz
1234567890$

36 point News Gothic Extra Condensed (Foundry)
ABCDEFGHIJKLMNOPQRSTUVWXYZ
abcdefghijklmnopqrstuvwxyz&
1234567890$

42 point News Gothic Extra Condensed (Foundry)
ABCDEFGHIJKLMNOPQRSTUVWXYZ&
abcdefghijklmnopqrstuvwxyz
1234567890$

(Continued on Page 365)

48 point News Gothic Extra Condensed (Foundry)

ABCDEFGHIJKLMNOPQRSTUVWXYZ&
abcdefghijklmnopqrstuvwxyz
1234567890$

60 point News Gothic Extra Condensed (Foundry)

ABCDEFGHIJKLMNOPQRSTUVWXYZ&
abcdefghijklmnopqrstuvwxyz
1234567890$

72 point News Gothic Extra Condensed (Foundry)

ABCDEFGHIJKLMNOPQRSTUVWXYZ&
abcdefghijklmnopqrstuvwxyz
1234567890$

News Gothic Light

8 point News Gothic Light (Linotype)
The basic character in a type design is determined by the uni
form design characteristics of all letters in the alphabet. How
ever, this alone does not determine the standard of the type
face and the quality of composition set with it. The appearance
is something complex which forms itself out of many details,
like form, proportion, ductus, rhythm etc. If everything harmo

ABCDEFGHIJKLMNOPQRSTUVWXYZ&
abcdefghijklmnopqrstuvwxyz   1234567890$

---

9 point News Gothic Light (Linotype)
The basic character in a type design is determined by the
uniform design characteristics of all letters in the alpha
bet. However, this alone does not determine the standard
of the type face and the quality of composition set with it.
The appearance is something complex which forms itself

ABCDEFGHIJKLMNOPQRSTUVWXYZ&
abcdefghijklmnopqrstuvwxyz   1234567890$

---

10 point News Gothic Light (Linotype)
The basic character in a type design is determined by
the uniform design characteristics of all letters in the
alphabet. However, this alone does not determine the
standard of the type face and the quality of composition
set with it. The appearance is something complex which

ABCDEFGHIJKLMNOPQRSTUVWXYZ&
abcdefghijklmnopqrstuvwxyz   1234567890$

News Gothic Light Italic

8 point News Gothic Light Italic (Linotype)
*The basic character in a type design is determined by the uni
form design characteristics of all letters in the alphabet. How
ever, this alone does not determine the standard of the type
face and the quality of composition set with it. The appearance
is something complex which forms itself out of many details,
like form, proportion, ductus, rhythm etc. If everything harmo*

*ABCDEFGHIJKLMNOPQRSTUVWXYZ&
abcdefghijklmnopqrstuvwxyz   1234567890$*

---

9 point News Gothic Light Italic (Linotype)
*The basic character in a type design is determined by the
uniform design characteristics of all letters in the alpha
bet. However, this alone does not determine the standard
of the type face and the quality of composition set with it.
The appearance is something complex which forms itself*

*ABCDEFGHIJKLMNOPQRSTUVWXYZ&
abcdefghijklmnopqrstuvwxyz   1234567890$*

---

10 point News Gothic Light Italic (Linotype)
*The basic character in a type design is determined by
the uniform design characteristics of all letters in the
alphabet. However, this alone does not determine the
standard of the type face and the quality of composition
set with it. The appearance is something complex which*

*ABCDEFGHIJKLMNOPQRSTUVWXYZ&
abcdefghijklmnopqrstuvwxyz   1234567890$*

Nicholas Cochin

ABCDEFGHIJKLMNOPQRSTUVWXYZ&
abcdefghijklmnopqrstuvwxyz
1234567890$

ABCDEFGHIJKLMNOPQRSTUVWXYZ&
abcdefghijklmnopqrstuvwxyz
1234567890$

ABCDEFGHIJKLMNOPQRSTUVWXYZ&
abcdefghijklmnopqrstuvwxyz
1234567890$

ABCDEFGHIJKLMNOPQRST
UVWXYZ&
abcdefghijklmnopqrstuvwxyz
1234567890$

12 point Nova Augustea (Foundry)

ABCDEFGHIJKLMNOPQRSTUVWXYZ&
abcdefghijklmnopqrstuvwxyz
1234567890$

18 point Nova Augustea (Foundry)

ABCDEFGHIJKLMNOPQRSTUVWXYZ&
abcdefghijklmnopqrstuvwxyz
1234567890$

24 point Nova Augustea Small (Foundry)

ABCDEFGHIJKLMNOPQRSTUVWXYZ&
abcdefghijklmnopqrstuvwxyz
1234567890$

36 point Nova Augustea (Foundry)

ABCDEFGHIJKLMNOPQRST
UVWXYZ&
abcdefghijklmnopqrstuvwxyz
1234567890$

Number Eighteen

6 point Number Eighteen (Linotype)

The basic character in a type design is determined by the uniform design char acteristics of all letters in the alphabet. However, this alone does not determine the standard of the type face and the quality of composition set with it. The appearance is something complex which forms itself out of many details, like form, proportion, ductus, rhythm etc. If everything harmonizes, the total result will be more than the sum of its components. The only reliable basis for the

ABCDEFGHIJKLMNOPQRSTUVWXYZ&
abcdefghijklmnopqrstuvwxyz 1234567890$

7 point Number Eighteen (Linotype)

The basic character in a type design is determined by the uniform design characteristics of all letters in the alphabet. However, this alone does not determine the standard of the type face and the quality of composition set with it. The appearance is something complex which forms itself out of many details, like form, proportion, ductus, rhythm etc. If everything har monizes, the total result will be more than the sum of its components. The

ABCDEFGHIJKLMNOPQRSTUVWXYZ&
abcdefghijklmnopqrstuvwxyz 1234567890$

8 point Number Eighteen (Linotype)

The basic character in a type design is determined by the uniform de sign characteristics of all letters in the alphabet. However, this alone does not determine the standard of the type face and the quality of composition set with it. The appearance is something complex which forms itself out of many details, like form, proportion, ductus, rhythm etc.

ABCDEFGHIJKLMNOPQRSTUVWXYZ&
abcdefghijklmnopqrstuvwxyz 1234567890$

9 point Number Eighteen (Linotype)

The basic character in a type design is determined by the uniform design characteristics of all letters in the alphabet. However, this alone does not determine the standard of the type face and the quality of composition set with it. The appearance is something

ABCDEFGHIJKLMNOPQRSTUVWXYZ&
abcdefghijklmnopqrstuvwxyz 1234567890$

10 point Number Eighteen (Linotype)

The basic character in a type design is determined by the uni form design characteristics of all letters in the alphabet. However, this alone does not determine the standard of the type face and the quality of composition set with it. The appearance is some

ABCDEFGHIJKLMNOPQRSTUVWXYZ&
abcdefghijklmnopqrstuvwxyz 1234567890$

11 point Number Eighteen (Linotype)

The basic character in a type design is determined by the uniform design characteristics of all letters in the alphabet. However, this alone does not determine the standard of the

ABCDEFGHIJKLMNOPQRSTUVWXYZ&
abcdefghijklmnopqrstuvwxyz 1234567890$

12 point Number Eighteen (Linotype)

The basic character in a type design is determined by the uniform design characteristics of all letters in the alphabet. However, this alone does not determine the standard of the

ABCDEFGHIJKLMNOPQRSTUVWXYZ&
abcdefghijklmnopqrstuvwxyz 1234567890$

14 point Number Eighteen (Linotype)

The basic character in a type design is determined by the uniform design characteristics of all letters

ABCDEFGHIJKLMNOPQRSTUVWXYZ&
abcdefghijklmnopqrstuvwxyz 1234567890$

Number Twenty

6 point Number Twenty (Linotype)

The basic character in a type design is determined by the uniform design char acteristics of all letters in the alphabet. However, this alone does not determine the standard of the type face and the quality of composition set with it. The appearance is something complex which forms itself out of many details, like form, proportion, ductus, rhythm etc. If everything harmonizes, the total result will be more than the sum of its components. The only reliable basis for the

ABCDEFGHIJKLMNOPQRSTUVWXYZ&
abcdefghijklmnopqrstuvwxyz 1234567890$

7 point Number Twenty (Linotype)

The basic character in a type design is determined by the uniform design characteristics of all letters in the alphabet. However, this alone does not determine the standard of the type face and the quality of composition set with it. The appearance is something complex which forms itself out of many details, like form, proportion, ductus, rhythm etc. If everything har monizes, the total result will be more than the sum of its components. The

ABCDEFGHIJKLMNOPQRSTUVWXYZ&
abcdefghijklmnopqrstuvwxyz 1234567890$

8 point Number Twenty (Linotype)

The basic character in a type design is determined by the uniform de sign characteristics of all letters in the alphabet. However, this alone does not determine the standard of the type face and the quality of composition set with it. The appearance is something complex which forms itself out of many details, like form, proportion, ductus, rhythm etc.

ABCDEFGHIJKLMNOPQRSTUVWXYZ&
abcdefghijklmnopqrstuvwxyz 1234567890$

9 point Number Twenty (Linotype)

The basic character in a type design is determined by the uniform design characteristics of all letters in the alphabet. However, this alone does not determine the standard of the type face and the quality of composition set with it. The appearance is something

ABCDEFGHIJKLMNOPQRSTUVWXYZ&
abcdefghijklmnopqrstuvwxyz 1234567890$

10 point Number Twenty (Linotype)

The basic character in a type design is determined by the uni form design characteristics of all letters in the alphabet. However, this alone does not determine the standard of the type face and the quality of composition set with it. The appearance is some

ABCDEFGHIJKLMNOPQRSTUVWXYZ&
abcdefghijklmnopqrstuvwxyz 1234567890$

11 point Number Twenty (Linotype)

The basic character in a type design is determined by the uniform design characteristics of all letters in the alphabet. However, this alone does not determine the standard of the

ABCDEFGHIJKLMNOPQRSTUVWXYZ&
abcdefghijklmnopqrstuvwxyz 1234567890$

12 point Number Twenty (Linotype)

The basic character in a type design is determined by the uniform design characteristics of all letters in the alphabet. However, this alone does not determine the standard of the

ABCDEFGHIJKLMNOPQRSTUVWXYZ&
abcdefghijklmnopqrstuvwxyz 1234567890$

14 point Number Twenty (Linotype)

The basic character in a type design is determined by the uniform design characteristics of all letters

ABCDEFGHIJKLMNOPQRSTUVWXYZ&
abcdefghijklmnopqrstuvwxyz 1234567890$

V & M TYPOGRAPHICAL, INCORPORATED

Number Twenty-one

8 point Number Twenty-one (Linotype)

The basic character in a type design is determined by the uniform design characteristics of all letters in the alphabet. However this alone does not determine the standard of the type face and the quality of composition set with it. The appearance is something complex which forms itself out of many details, like form, propor

ABCDEFGHIJKLMNOPQRSTUVWXYZ&
abcdefghijklmnopqrstuvwxyz 1234567890$
ABCDEFGHIJ KLM N OPQRSTUVWXYZ

9 point Number Twenty-one (Linotype)

The basic character in a type design is determined by the uni form design characteristics of all letters in the alphabet. How ever, this alone does not determine the standard of the type face and the quality of composition set with it. The appear

ABCDEFGHIJKLMNOPQRSTUVWXYZ&
abcdefghijklmnopqrstuvwxyz 1234567890$
ABCDEFGHIJ KLM NOPQRSTUVWXYZ

11 point Number Twenty-one (Linotype)

The basic character in a type design is determined by the uniform design charcteristics of all letters in the alphabet. However, this alone does not deter

ABCDEFGHIJKLMNOPQRSTUVWXYZ&
abcdefghijklmnopqrstuvwxyz 1234567890$
ABCDEFGHIJ KLM NOPQRSTUVWXYZ

Number Twenty-one Italic

8 point Number Twenty-one Italic (Linotype)

The basic character in a type design is determined by the uniform design characteristics of all letters in the alphabet. However this alone does not determine the standard of the type face and the quality of composition set with it. The appearance is something complex which forms itself out of many details, like form, propor

ABCDEFGHIJKLMNOPQRSTUVWXYZ&
abcdefghijklmnopqrstuvwxyz 1234567890$

9 point Number Twenty-one Italic (Linotype)

The basic character in a type design is determined by the uni form design characteristics of all letters in the alphabet. How ever, this alone does not determine the standard of the type face and the quality of composition set with it. The appear

ABCDEFGHIJKLMNOPQRSTUVWXYZ&
abcdefghijklmnopqrstuvwxyz 1234567890$

11 point Number Twenty-one Italic (Linotype)

The basic character in a type design is determined by the uniform design charcteristics of all letters in the alphabet. However, this alone does not deter

ABCDEFGHIJKLMNOPQRSTUVWXYZ&
abcdefghijklmnopqrstuvwxyz 1234567890$

Nubian

12 point Nubian (Foundry)

ABCDEFGHIJKLMNOP
QRSTUVWXYZ&
abcdefghijklmnopqrstuv
wxyz
1234567890$

Number Eleven

5½ point Number Eleven, Caps only (Linotype)

THE BASIC CHARACTER IN A TYPE DESIGN IS DETERMINED BY THE UNIFORM DESIGN CHARACTERISTICS OF ALL LETTERS IN THE ALPHABET. HOWEVER, THIS ALONE DOES NOT DETERMINE THE STANDARD OF THE TYPE FACE AND THE QUAL ITY OF COMPOSITION SET WITH IT. THE APPEARANCE IS SOMETHING COMPLEX WHICH FORMS ITSELF OUT OF MANY DETAILS, LIKE FORM, PROPORTION, DUCTUS, RHYTHM ETC. IF EVERYTHING HARMONIZES, THE TOTAL RESULT WILL BE MORE THAN THE SUM OF ITS COMPONENTS. THE ONLY RELIABLE BASIS FOR THE DE SIGN IN A TYPE IS A POSITIVE FEELING FOR FORM AND STYLE. THE BASIC CHARACTER IN A TYPE DESIGN IS DETERMINED BY THE UNIFORM DESIGN CHAR

ABCDEFGHIJKLMNOPQRSTUVWXYZ&

Old Bowery

30 point Old Bowery, Cap font (Foundry)

ABCDEFGHIJKLMNOPQRSTUVWXYZ&

Old English

8 point Old English (Ludlow)

ABCDEFGHIJKLMNOPQRSTUVWXYZ&
abcdefghijklmnopqrstuvwxyz
1234567890$

10 point Old English (Ludlow)

ABCDEFGHIJKLMNOPQRSTUVWXYZ&
abcdefghijklmnopqrstuvwxyz
1234567890$

12 point Old English (Ludlow)

ABCDEFGHIJKLMNOPQRSTUVWXYZ&
abcdefghijklmnopqrstuvwxyz
1234567890$

14 point Old English (Ludlow)

ABCDEFGHIJKLMNOPQRSTUVWXYZ&
abcdefghijklmnopqrstuvwxyz
1234567890$

18 point Old English (Ludlow)

ABCDEFGHIJKLMNOPQRSTUVWXYZ&
abcdefghijklmnopqrstuvwxyz
1234567890$

24 point Old English (Ludlow)

ABCDEFGHIJKLMNOPQRSTUVWXYZ&
abcdefghijklmnopqrstuvwxyz
1234567890$

30 point Old English (Ludlow)

ABCDEFGHIJKLMNOPQRSTUVWXYZ&
abcdefghijklmnopqrstuvwxyz
1234567890$

Old Face Open

ABCDEFGHIJKLMNOPQRSTUVWXYZ&
1234567890$

ABCDEFGHIJKLMNOPQRSTUVWXYZ&
1234567890$

ABCDEFGHIJKLMNOPQRSTUV
WXYZ&
1234567890$

ABCDEFGHIJKLMNOPQRS
TUVWXYZ&
1234567890$

ABCDEFGHIJKLMN
OPQRSTUVWXYZ&

ABCDEFGHIJKL
MNOPQRSTUV
WXYZ&

Old Gothic Bold Italic

10 point Old Gothic Bold Italic (Foundry)

ABCDEFGHIJKLMNOPQRSTUVWXYZ&
abcdefghijklmnopqrstuvwxyz
1234567890$

14 point Old Gothic Bold Italic (Foundry)

ABCDEFGHIJKLMNOPQRSTUVWXYZ&
abcdefghijklmnopqrstuvwxyz
1234567890$

60 point Old Gothic Bold Italic (Foundry)

ABCDEFGHIJKL
MNOPQRSTU
VWXYZ&
abcdefghijklmno
pqrstuvwxyz
1234567890$

Oldstyle No. 1

7 point Oldstyle No. 1 (Linotype)

The basic character in a type design is determined by the uniform de sign characteristics of all letters in the alphabet. However, this alone does not determine the standard of the type face and the quality of com

ABCDEFGHIJKLMNOPQRSTUVWXYZ&
abcdefghijklmnopqrstuvwxyz   1234567890$
ABCDEFGHIJKLMNOPQRSTUVWXYZ

8 point Oldstyle No. 1 (Linotype)

The basic character in a type design is determined by the uniform design characteristics of all letters in the alphabet. However, this alone does not determine the standard of the type face and the quality of composition set with it. The appearance is something

ABCDEFGHIJKLMNOPQRSTUVWXYZ&
abcdefghijklmnopqrstuvwxyz   1234567890$
ABCDEFGHIJKLMNOPQRSTUVWXYZ

9 point Oldstyle No. 1 (Linotype)

The basic character in a type design is determined by the uni form design characteristics of all letters in the alphabet. How ever, this alone does not determine the standard of the type

ABCDEFGHIJKLMNOPQRSTUVWXYZ&
abcdefghijklmnopqrstuvwxyz   1234567890$
ABCDEFGHIJKLMNOPQRSTUVWXYZ

10 point Oldstyle No. 1 (Linotype)

The basic character in a type design is determined by the uniform design characteristics of all letters in the alpha bet. However, this alone does not determine the standard

ABCDEFGHIJKLMNOPQRSTUVWXYZ&
abcdefghijklmnopqrstuvwxyz   1234567890$
ABCDEFGHIJKLMNOPQRSTUVWXYZ

11 point Oldstyle No. 1 (Linotype)

The basic character in a type design is determined by the uniform design characteristics of all letters in the

ABCDEFGHIJKLMNOPQRSTUVWXYZ&
abcdefghijklmnopqrstuvwxyz   1234567890$
ABCDEFGHIJKLMNOPQRSTUVWXYZ

12 point Oldstyle No. 1 (Linotype)

The basic character in a type design is determined by the uniform design characteristics of all letters

ABCDEFGHIJKLMNOPQRSTUVWXYZ&
abcdefghijklmnopqrstuvwxyz   1234567890$
ABCDEFGHIJKLMNOPQRSTUVWXYZ

14 point Oldstyle No. 1 (Linotype)

The basic character in a type design is determined by the uniform design char
ABCDEFGHIJKLMNOPQRSTUV
WXYZ&   1234567890$
abcdefghijklmnopqrstuvwxyz

Oldstyle No. 1 Italic

6 point Oldstyle No. 1 Italic (Linotype)

The basic character in a type design is determined by the uniform design characteristics of all letters in the alphabet. However, this alone does not determine the standard of the type face and the quality of composition set with it. The appearance is something complex which forms itself out of many details, like form, proportion, ductus, rhythm etc. If everything harmonizes, the total result will be more than the sum of its components. The only reliable basis for the design in a type is a positive feeling for form and

ABCDEFGHIJKLMNOPQRSTUVWXYZ&
abcdefghijklmnopqrstuvwxyz   1234567890$

7 point Oldstyle No. 1 Italic (Linotype)

The basic character in a type design is determined by the uniform de sign characteristics of all letters in the alphabet. However, this alone does not determine the standard of the type face and the quality of com position set with it. The appearance is something complex which forms itself out of many details, like form, ductus, rhythm etc. If everything harmonizes, the total result will be more than the sum of its components.

ABCDEFGHIJKLMNOPQRSTUVWXYZ&
abcdefghijklmnopqrstuvwxyz   1234567890$

8 point Oldstyle No. 1 Italic (Linotype)

The basic character in a type design is determined by the uniform design characteristics of all letters in the alphabet. However, this alone does not determine the standard of the type face and the quality of composition set with it. The appearance is something complex which forms itself out of many details, like form, pro

ABCDEFGHIJKLMNOPQRSTUVWXYZ&
abcdefghijklmnopqrstuvwxyz   1234567890$

9 point Oldstyle No. 1 Italic (Linotype)

The basic character in a type design is determined by the uni form design characteristics of all letters in the alphabet. How ever, this alone does not determine the standard of the type face and the quality of composition set with it. The appearance

ABCDEFGHIJKLMNOPQRSTUVWXYZ&
abcdefghijklmnopqrstuvwxyz   1234567890$

10 point Oldstyle No. 1 Italic (Linotype)

The basic character in a type design is determined by the uniform design characteristics of all letters in the alpha bet. However, this alone does not determine the standard of the type face and the quality of composition set with

ABCDEFGHIJKLMNOPQRSTUVWXYZ&
abcdefghijklmnopqrstuvwxyz   1234567890$

11 point Oldstyle No. 1 Italic (Linotype)

The basic character in a type design is determined by the uniform design characteristics of all letters in the alphabet. However, this alone does not determine the

ABCDEFGHIJKLMNOPQRSTUVWXYZ&
abcdefghijklmnopqrstuvwxyz   1234567890$

12 point Oldstyle No. 1 Italic (Linotype)

The basic character in a type design is determined by the uniform design characteristics of all letters in the alphabet. However, this alone does not de

ABCDEFGHIJKLMNOPQRSTUVWXYZ&
abcdefghijklmnopqrstuvwxyz   1234567890$

Onyx

18 point Onyx (Foundry)

ABCDEFGHIJKLMNOPQRSTUVWXYZ&
abcdefghijklmnopqrstuvwxyz
1234567890$

24 point Onyx (Foundry)

ABCDEFGHIJKLMNOPQRSTUVWXYZ&
abcdefghijklmnopqrstuvwxyz
1234567890$

30 point Onyx (Foundry)

ABCDEFGHIJKLMNOPQRSTUVWXYZ&
abcdefghijklmnopqrstuvwxyz
1234567890$

42 point Onyx (Foundry)

ABCDEFGHIJKLMNOPQRSTUVWXYZ&
abcdefghijklmnopqrstuvwxyz
1234567890$

48 point Onyx (Foundry)

ABCDEFGHIJKLMNOPQRSTUVWXYZ&
abcdefghijklmnopqrstuvwxyz
1234567890$

(Continued on Page 376)

60 point Onyx (Foundry)

ABCDEFGHIJKLMNOPQRSTUVWXYZ

abcdefghijklmnopqrstuvwxyz&

1234567890$

72 point Onyx (Foundry)

ABCDEFGHIJKLMNOPQRSTUV

WXYZ&

abcdefghijklmnopqrstuvwxyz

1234567890$

Onyx Italic

48 point Onyx Italic (Foundry)

ABCDEFGHIJKLMNOPQRSTUVWXYZ&

abcdefghijklmnopqrstuvwxyz

1234567890$

Opticon

6 point Opticon (Linotype)
The basic character in a type design is determined by the uniform design characteristics of all letters in the alphabet. However, this alone does not determine the standard of the type face and the quality of composition set with it. The appearance is something complex which forms itself out of many details, like form, proportion, ductus, rhythm etc. If everything harmonizes, the total result will be more than the sum of its components. The only reliable basis for the design in a type is a positive feeling for form and

ABCDEFGHIJKLMNOPQRSTUVWXYZ&
abcdefghijklmnopqrstuvwxyz   1234567890$

Optima *(Must be leaded 1 point)*

6 point Optima (Linotype)
The basic character in a type design is determined by the uniform design characteristics of all letters in the alphabet. However, this alone does not determine the standard of the type face and the quality of composition set with it. The appearance is something complex which forms itself out of many details, like form, proportion, ductus, rhythm etc. If everything harmonizes, the total result will be more than the sum of its components. The only reliable basis for the design in a type is a positive feeling for form and style. The basic character in a type design is determined by the uniform
ABCDEFGHIJKLMNOPQRSTUVWXYZ&
abcdefghijklmnopqrstuvwxyz   1234567890$

7 point Optima (Linotype)
The basic character in a type design is determined by the uniform design characteristics of all letters in the alphabet. However, this alone does not determine the standard of the type face and the quality of composition set with it. The appearance is something complex which forms itself out of many details, like form, proportion, ductus, rhythm etc. If everything harmonizes, the total result will be more than the sum of its components. The only reliable basis for
ABCDEFGHIJKLMNOPQRSTUVWXYZ&
abcdefghijklmnopqrstuvwxyz   1234567890$

8 point Optima (Linotype)
The basic character in a type design is determined by the uniform design characteristics of all letters in the alphabet. However, this alone does not determine the standard of the type face and the quality of composition set with it. The appearance is something complex which forms itself out of many details, like form, proportion, ductus, rhythm etc. If everything harmonizes, the total result
ABCDEFGHIJKLMNOPQRSTUVWXYZ&
abcdefghijklmnopqrstuvwxyz   1234567890$

9 point Optima (Linotype)
The basic character in a type design is determined by the uniform design characteristics of all letters in the alphabet. However, this alone does not determine the standard of the type face and the quality of composition set with it. The appearance is something complex which forms itself
ABCDEFGHIJKLMNOPQRSTUVWXYZ&
abcdefghijklmnopqrstuvwxyz   1234567890$

10 point Optima (Linotype)
The basic character in a type design is determined by the uniform design characteristics of all letters in the alphabet. However, this alone does not determine the standard of the type face and the quality of composi
ABCDEFGHIJKLMNOPQRSTUVWXYZ&
abcdefghijklmnopqrstuvwxyz   1234567890$

12 point Optima (Linotype)
The basic character in a type design is determined by the uniform design characteristics of all letters in the alphabet. However, this alone does not determine the standard of the
ABCDEFGHIJKLMNOPQRSTUVWXYZ&
abcdefghijklmnopqrstuvwxyz   1234567890$

(Continued on Page 378)

V & M TYPOGRAPHICAL, INCORPORATED |

377

(Continued from Page 377)

8 point Optima Large (Foundry)
ABCDEFGHIJKLMNOPQRSTUVWXYZ&
abcdefghijklmnopqrstuvwxyz
1234567890$

10 point Optima (Foundry)
ABCDEFGHIJKLMNOPQRSTUVWXYZ&
abcdefghijklmnopqrstuvwxyz
1234567890$

12 point Optima Large (Foundry)
ABCDEFGHIJKLMNOPQRSTUVWXYZ&
abcdefghijklmnopqrstuvwxyz
1234567890$

14 point Optima (Foundry)
ABCDEFGHIJKLMNOPQRSTUVWXYZ&
abcdefghijklmnopqrstuvwxyz
1234567890$

18 point Optima (Foundry)
ABCDEFGHIJKLMNOPQRSTUVWXYZ&
abcdefghijklmnopqrstuvwxyz
1234567890$

24 point Optima Small (Foundry)
ABCDEFGHIJKLMNOPQRSTUVWXYZ&
abcdefghijklmnopqrstuvwxyz
1234567890$

24 point Optima Large (Foundry)
ABCDEFGHIJKLMNOPQRSTUVWXYZ&
abcdefghijklmnopqrstuvwxyz
1234567890$

30 point Optima (Foundry)
ABCDEFGHIJKLMNOPQRSTUVWXYZ&
abcdefghijklmnopqrstuvwxyz
1234567890$

(Continued on Page 379)

36 point Optima (Foundry)

ABCDEFGHIJKLMNOPQRSTUV
WXYZ&
abcdefghijklmnopqrstuvwxyz
1234567890$

48 point Optima (Foundry)

ABCDEFGHIJKLMNOPQRS
TUVWXYZ&
abcdefghijklmnopqrstuv
wxyz
1234567890$

Optima Black *(Must be leaded 1 point)*

6 point Optima Black (Linotype)
The basic character in a type design is determined by the uniform design characteristics of all letters in the alphabet. However, this alone does not determine the standard of the type face and the quality of composition set with it. The appearance is something complex which forms itself out of many details, like form, proportion, ductus, rhythm etc. If everything harmonizes, the total result will be more than the sum of its components. The only reliable basis for the design in a type is a positive feeling for form and style. The basic character in a type design is determined by the uniform de

ABCDEFGHIJKLMNOPQRSTUVWXYZ&
abcdefghijklmnopqrstuvwxyz 1234567890$

7 point Optima Black (Linotype)
The basic character in a type design is determined by the uniform design characteristics of all letters in the alphabet. However, this alone does not determine the standard of the type face and the quality of composition set with it. The appearance is something complex which forms itself out of many details, like form, proportion, ductus, rhythm etc. If everything harmonizes, the total result will be more than the sum of its components. The only reliable

ABCDEFGHIJKLMNOPQRSTUVWXYZ&
abcdefghijklmnopqrstuvwxyz 1234567890$

8 point Optima Black (Linotype)
The basic character in a type design is determined by the uniform design characteristics of all letters in the alphabet. However, this alone does not determine the standard of the type face and the quality of composition set with it. The appearance is something complex which forms itself out of many details, like form, proportion, ductus, rhythm etc. If everything har

ABCDEFGHIJKLMNOPQRSTUVWXYZ&
abcdefghijklmnopqrstuvwxyz 1234567890$

9 point Optima Black (Linotype)
The basic character in a type design is determined by the uniform design characteristics of all letters in the alphabet. However, this alone does not determine the standard of the type face and the quality of composition set with it. The appearance is something complex which forms itself

ABCDEFGHIJKLMNOPQRSTUVWXYZ&
abcdefghijklmnopqrstuvwxyz 1234567890$

10 point Optima Black (Linotype)
The basic character in a type design is determined by the uniform design characteristics of all letters in the alphabet. However, this alone does not determine the standard of the type face and the quality of composition set with it. The appearance is something

ABCDEFGHIJKLMNOPQRSTUVWXYZ&
abcdefghijklmnopqrstuvwxyz 1234567890$

12 point Optima Black (Linotype)
The basic character in a type design is determined by the uniform design characteristics of all letters in the alphabet. However, this alone does not determine the standard of the

ABCDEFGHIJKLMNOPQRSTUVWXYZ&
abcdefghijklmnopqrstuvwxyz 1234567890$

Optima Italic *(Must be leaded 1 point)*

6 point Optima Italic (Linotype)
The basic character in a type design is determined by the uniform design characteristics of all letters in the alphabet. However, this alone does not determine the standard of the type face and the quality of composition set with it. The appearance is something complex which forms itself out of many details, like form, proportion, ductus, rhythm etc. If everything harmonizes, the total result will be more than the sum of its components. The only reliable basis for the design in a type is a positive feeling for form and style. The basic character in a type design is determined by the uniform

ABCDEFGHIJKLMNOPQRSTUVWXYZ&
abcdefghijklmnopqrstuvwxyz 1234567890$

7 point Optima Italic (Linotype)
The basic character in a type design is determined by the uniform design characteristics of all letters in the alphabet. However, this alone does not determine the standard of the type face and the quality of composition set with it. The appearance is something com plex which forms itself out of many details, like form, proportion, ductus, rhythm etc. If everything harmonizes, the total result will be more than the sum of its components. The only reliable basis for

ABCDEFGHIJKLMNOPQRSTUVWXYZ&
abcdefghijklmnopqrstuvwxyz 1234567890$

8 point Optima Italic (Linotype)
The basic character in a type design is determined by the uniform design characteristics of all letters in the alphabet. However, this alone does not determine the standard of the type face and the quality of composition set with it. The appearance is something complex which forms itself out of many details, like form, propor tion, ductus, rhythm etc. If everything harmonizes, the total result

ABCDEFGHIJKLMNOPQRSTUVWXYZ&
abcdefghijklmnopqrstuvwxyz 1234567890$

9 point Optima Italic (Linotype)
The basic character in a type design is determined by the uniform design characteristics of all letters in the alphabet. However, this alone does not determine the standard of the type face and the quality of composition set with it. The appearance is something complex which forms itself

ABCDEFGHIJKLMNOPQRSTUVWXYZ&
abcdefghijklmnopqrstuvwxyz 1234567890$

10 point Optima Italic (Linotype)
The basic character in a type design is determined by the uniform design characteristics of all letters in the alphabet. However, this alone does not determine the standard of the type face and the quality of composi tion set with it. The appearance is something complex

ABCDEFGHIJKLMNOPQRSTUVWXYZ&
abcdefghijklmnopqrstuvwxyz 1234567890$

12 point Optima Italic Large (Foundry)
ABCDEFGHIJKLMNOPQRSTUVWXYZ&
abcdefghijklmnopqrstuvwxyz
1234567890$

14 point Optima Italic (Foundry)
ABCDEFGHIJKLMNOPQRSTUVWXYZ&
abcdefghijklmnopqrstuvwxyz
1234567890$

(Continued on Page 381)

18 point Optima Italic (Foundry)

ABCDEFGHIJKLMNOPQRSTUVWXYZ&
abcdefghijklmnopqrstuvwxyz
1234567890$

24 point Optima Italic Small (Foundry)

ABCDEFGHIJKLMNOPQRSTUVWXYZ&
abcdefghijklmnopqrstuvwxyz
1234567890$

24 point Optima Italic Large (Foundry)

ABCDEFGHIJKLMNOPQRSTUVWXYZ&
abcdefghijklmnopqrstuvwxyz
1234567890$

30 point Optima Italic (Foundry)

ABCDEFGHIJKLMNOPQRSTUVWXYZ&
abcdefghijklmnopqrstuvwxyz
1234567890$

36 point Optima Italic (Foundry)

ABCDEFGHIJKLMNOPQRSTUV
WXYZ&
abcdefghijklmnopqrstuvwxyz
1234567890$

(Continued on Page 382)

48 point Optima Italic (Linotype)

ABCDEFGHIJKLMNOPQRS TUVWXYZ& abcdefghijklmnopqrstuv wxyz 1234567890$

Optima Medium *(Must be leaded 1 point)*

6 point Optima Medium (Linotype)

The basic character in a type design is determined by the uniform design characteristics of all letters in the alphabet. However, this alone does not determine the standard of the type face and the quality of composition set with it. The appearance is something complex which forms itself out of many details, like form, proportion, ductus, rhythm etc. If everything harmonizes, the total result will be more than the sum of its components. The only reliable basis for the design in a type is a positive feeling for form and style. The basic character in a type design is determined by the uniform de

ABCDEFGHIJKLMNOPQRSTUVWXYZ&
abcdefghijklmnopqrstuvwxyz   1234567890$

7 point Optima Medium (Linotype)

The basic character in a type design is determined by the uniform design characteristics of all letters in the alphabet. However, this alone does not determine the standard of the type face and the quality of composition set with it. The appearance is something complex which forms itself out of many details, like form, propor tion, ductus, rhythm etc. If everything harmonizes, the total result will be more than the sum of its components. The only reliable

ABCDEFGHIJKLMNOPQRSTUVWXYZ&
abcdefghijklmnopqrstuvwxyz   1234567890$

8 point Optima Medium (Linotype)

The basic character in a type design is determined by the uni form design characteristics of all letters in the alphabet. How ever, this alone does not determine the standard of the type face and the quality of composition set with it. The appearance is something complex which forms itself out of many details, like form, proportion, ductus, rhythm etc. If everything har

ABCDEFGHIJKLMNOPQRSTUVWXYZ&
abcdefghijklmnopqrstuvwxyz   1234567890$

9 point Optima Medium (Linotype)

The basic character in a type design is determined by the uniform design characteristics of all letters in the alphabet. However, this alone does not determine the standard of the type face and the quality of composition set with it. The appearance is something complex which forms itself

ABCDEFGHIJKLMNOPQRSTUVWXYZ&
abcdefghijklmnopqrstuvwxyz   1234567890$

10 point Optima Medium (Linotype)

The basic character in a type design is determined by the uniform design characteristics of all letters in the alphabet. However, this alone does not determine the standard of the type face and the quality of com position set with it. The appearance is something

ABCDEFGHIJKLMNOPQRSTUVWXYZ&
abcdefghijklmnopqrstuvwxyz   1234567890$

12 point Optima Medium (Linotype)

The basic character in a type design is deter mined by the uniform design characteristics of all letters in the alphabet. However, this alone does not determine the standard of the

ABCDEFGHIJKLMNOPQRSTUVWXYZ&
abcdefghijklmnopqrstuvwxyz   1234567890$

Optima Semi-Bold *(Must be leaded 1 point)*

6 point Optima Semi-Bold (Linotype)

The basic character in a type design is determined by the uniform design characteristics of all letters in the alphabet. However, this alone does not determine the standard of the type face and the quality of composition set with it. The appearance is something complex which forms itself out of many details, like form, proportion, ductus, rhythm etc. If everything harmonizes, the total result will be more than the sum of its components. The only reliable basis for the design in a type is a positive feeling for form and style. The basic character in a type design is determined by the uniform

ABCDEFGHIJKLMNOPQRSTUVWXYZ&
abcdefghijklmnopqrstuvwxyz 1234567890$

7 point Optima Semi-Bold (Linotype)

The basic character in a type design is determined by the uniform design characteristics of all letters in the alphabet. However, this alone does not determine the standard of the type face and the quality of composition set with it. The appearance is something complex which forms itself out of many details, like form, proportion, ductus, rhythm etc. If everything harmonizes, the total result will be more than the sum of its components. The only reliable basis for the

ABCDEFGHIJKLMNOPQRSTUVWXYZ&
abcdefghijklmnopqrstuvwxyz 1234567890$

8 point Optima Semi-Bold (Linotype)

The basic character in a type design is determined by the uniform design characteristics of all letters in the alphabet. However, this alone does not determine the standard of the type face and the quality of composition set with it. The appearance is something complex which forms itself out of many details, like form, proportion, ductus, rhythm etc. If everything harmonizes, the total result

ABCDEFGHIJKLMNOPQRSTUVWXYZ&
abcdefghijklmnopqrstuvwxyz 1234567890$

9 point Optima Semi-Bold (Linotype)

The basic character in a type design is determined by the uniform design characteristics of all letters in the alphabet. However, this alone does not determine the standard of the type face and the quality of composition set with it. The appearance is something complex which forms itself out of

ABCDEFGHIJKLMNOPQRSTUVWXYZ&
abcdefghijklmnopqrstuvwxyz 1234567890$

10 point Optima Semi-Bold (Linotype)

The basic character in a type design is determined by the uniform design characteristics of all letters in the alphabet. However, this alone does not determine the standard of the type face and the quality of composition set with it. The appearance is something complex

ABCDEFGHIJKLMNOPQRSTUVWXYZ&
abcdefghijklmnopqrstuvwxyz 1234567890$

12 point Optima Semi-Bold (Linotype)

The basic character in a type design is determined by the uniform design characteristics of all letters in the alphabet. However, this alone does not determine the standard of the

ABCDEFGHIJKLMNOPQRSTUVWXYZ&
abcdefghijklmnopqrstuvwxyz 1234567890$

10 point Optima Semi-Bold (Foundry)

ABCDEFGHIJKLMNOPQRSTUVWXYZ&
abcdefghijklmnopqrstuvwxyz
1234567890$

12 point Optima Semi-Bold Large (Foundry)

ABCDEFGHIJKLMNOPQRSTUVWXYZ&
abcdefghijklmnopqrstuvwxyz
1234567890$

14 point Optima Semi-Bold (Foundry)

ABCDEFGHIJKLMNOPQRSTUVWXYZ&
abcdefghijklmnopqrstuvwxyz
1234567890$

18 point Optima Semi-Bold (Foundry)

ABCDEFGHIJKLMNOPQRSTUVWXYZ&
abcdefghijklmnopqrstuvwxyz
1234567890$

24 point Optima Semi-Bold Small (Foundry)

ABCDEFGHIJKLMNOPQRSTUVWXYZ&
abcdefghijklmnopqrstuvwxyz
1234567890$

(Continued on Page 384)

(Continued from Page 383)

24 point Optima Semi-Bold Large (Foundry)

ABCDEFGHIJKLMNOPQRSTUVWXYZ&
abcdefghijklmnopqrstuvwxyz
1234567890$

30 point Optima Semi-Bold (Foundry)

ABCDEFGHIJKLMNOPQRSTUVWXYZ&
abcdefghijklmnopqrstuvwxyz
1234567890$

36 point Optima Semi-Bold (Foundry)

ABCDEFGHIJKLMNOPQRSTUV
WXYZ&
abcdefghijklmnopqrstuvwxyz
1234567890$

48 point Optima Semi-Bold (Foundry)

ABCDEFGHIJKLMNOPQR
STUVWXYZ&
abcdefghijklmnopqrstuv
wxyz
1234567890$

Orplid

24 point Orplid, Cap font (Foundry)

ABCDEFGHIJKLMNOPQRSTUVWXYZ&
1234567890$

Pabst

10 point Pabst (Foundry)

ABCDEFGHIJKLMNOPQRSTUVWXYZ&
abcdefghijklmnopqrstuvwxyz
1234567890$

12 point Pabst (Foundry)

ABCDEFGHIJKLMNOPQRSTUVWXYZ&
abcdefghijklmnopqrstuvwxyz
1234567890$

14 point Pabst (Foundry)

ABCDEFGHIJKLMNOPQRSTUVWXYZ&
abcdefghijklmnopqrstuvwxyz
1234567890$

Pabst Extra Bold

10 point Pabst Extra Bold (Linotype)

The basic character in a type design is deter mined by the uniform design characteristics of all letters in the alphabet. However, this alone does not determine the standard of the type face and the quality of composition set

**ABCDEFGHIJKLMNOPQRSTUVWXYZ&
abcdefghijklmnopqrstuvwxyz 1234567890$**

14 point Pabst Extra Bold (Linotype)

The basic character in a type de sign is determined by the uni form design characteristics of all

**ABCDEFGHIJKLMNOPQRSTU
VWXYZ& 1234567890$
abcdefghijklmnopqrstuvwxyz**

Pabst Extra Bold Italic

10 point Pabst Extra Bold Italic (Linotype)

The basic character in a type design is deter mined by the uniform design characteristics of all letters in the alphabet. However, this alone does not determine the standard of the type face and the quality of composition set

***ABCDEFGHIJKLMNOPQRSTUVWXYZ&
abcdefghijklmnopqrstuvwxyz 1234567890$***

14 point Pabst Extra Bold Italic (Linotype)

The basic character in a type de sign is determined by the uni form design characteristics of all

***ABCDEFGHIJKLMNOPQRSTU
VWXYZ& 1234567890$
abcdefghijklmnopqrstuvwxyz***

Palatino *(Must be leaded 1 point)*

6 point Palatino (Linotype)

The basic character in a type design is determined by the uniform design characteristics of all letters in the alphabet. However, this alone does not determine the standard of the type face and the quality of composition set with it. The appearance is something complex which forms itself out of many details, like form, proportion, ductus, rhythm etc. If everything har monizes, the total result will be more than the sum of its components. The only reliable basis for the design in a type is a positive feeling for form

ABCDEFGHIJKLMNOPQRSTUVWXYZ&
abcdefghijklmnopqrstuvwxyz   1234567890$
ABCDEFGHIJKLMNOPQRSTUVWXYZ

7 point Palatino (Linotype)

The basic character in a type design is determined by the uniform de sign characteristics of all letters in the alphabet. However, this alone does not determine the standard of the type face and the quality of composition set with it. The appearance is something complex which forms itself out of many details, like form, proportion, ductus, rhythm etc. If everything harmonizes, the total result will be more than the

ABCDEFGHIJKLMNOPQRSTUVWXYZ&
abcdefghijklmnopqrstuvwxyz   1234567890$
ABCDEFGHIJKLMNOPQRSTUVWXYZ

8 point Palatino (Linotype)

The basic character in a type design is determined by the uni form design characteristics of all letters in the alphabet. How ever, this alone does not determine the standard of the type face and the quality of composition set with it. The appearance is something complex which forms itself out of many details, like

ABCDEFGHIJKLMNOPQRSTUVWXYZ&
abcdefghijklmnopqrstuvwxyz   1234567890$
ABCDEFGHIJKLMNOPQRSTUVWXYZ

9 point Palatino (Linotype)

The basic character in a type design is determined by the uniform design characteristics of all letters in the alphabet. However, this alone does not determine the standard of the type face and the quality of composition set with it. The

ABCDEFGHIJKLMNOPQRSTUVWXYZ&
abcdefghijklmnopqrstuvwxyz   1234567890$
ABCDEFGHIJKLMNOPQRSTUVWXYZ

10 point Palatino (Linotype)

The basic character in a type design is determined by the uniform design characteristics of all letters in the alphabet. However, this alone does not determine the standard of the type face and the quality of composition

ABCDEFGHIJKLMNOPQRSTUVWXYZ&
abcdefghijklmnopqrstuvwxyz   1234567890$
ABCDEFGHIJKLMNOPQRSTUVWXYZ

12 point Palatino (Linotype)

The basic character in a type design is deter mined by the uniform design characteristics of all letters in the alphabet. However, this alone

ABCDEFGHIJKLMNOPQRSTUVWXYZ&
abcdefghijklmnopqrstuvwxyz   1234567890$
ABCDEFGHIJKLMNOPQRSTUVWXYZ

10 point Palatino (Foundry)

ABCDEFGHIJKLMNOPQRSTUVWXYZ&
abcdefghijklmnopqrstuvwxyz
1234567890$

12 point Palatino (Foundry)

ABCDEFGHIJKLMNOPQRSTUVWXYZ&
abcdefghijklmnopqrstuvwxyz
1234567890$

14 point Palatino (Foundry)

ABCDEFGHIJKLMNOPQRSTUVWXYZ&
abcdefghijklmnopqrstuvwxyz
1234567890$

18 point Palatino (Foundry)

ABCDEFGHIJKLMNOPQRSTUVWXYZ&
abcdefghijklmnopqrstuvwxyz
1234567890$

20 point Palatino (Foundry)

ABCDEFGHIJKLMNOPQRSTUVWXYZ&
abcdefghijklmnopqrstuvwxyz
1234567890$

24 point Palatino (Foundry)

ABCDEFGHIJKLMNOPQRSTUVWXYZ&
abcdefghijklmnopqrstuvwxyz
1234567890$

(Continued on Page 387)

(Continued from Page 386)

30 point Palatino (Foundry)

ABCDEFGHIJKLMNOPQRSTUVWXYZ&
abcdefghijklmnopqrstuvwxyz
1234567890$

42 point Palatino (Foundry)

ABCDEFGHIJKLMNOPQRSTU
VWXYZ&
abcdefghijklmnopqrstuvwxyz
1234567890$

54 point Palatino (Foundry)

ABCDEFGHIJKLMNOP
QRSTUVWXYZ&
abcdefghijklmnopqrstuv
wxyz
1234567890$

Palatino Italic *(Must be leaded 1 point)*

6 point Palatino Italic (Linotype)
The basic character in a type design is determined by the uniform design characteristics of all letters in the alphabet. However, this alone does not determine the standard of the type face and the quality of composition set with it. The appearance is something complex which forms itself out of many details, like form, proportion, ductus, rhythm etc. If everything harmonizes, the total result will be more than the sum of its components. The only reliable basis for the design in a type is a positive feeling for form

ABCDEFGHIJKLMNOPQRSTUVWXYZ&
abcdefghijklmnopqrstuvwxyz　　　*1234567890$*

7 point Palatino Italic (Linotype)
The basic character in a type design is determined by the uniform design characteristics of all letters in the alphabet. However, this alone does not determine the standard of the type face and the quality of composition set with it. The appearance is something complex which forms itself out of many details, like form, proportion, ductus, rhythm etc. If everything harmonizes, the total result will be more than the

ABCDEFGHIJKLMNOPQRSTUVWXYZ&
abcdefghijklmnopqrstuvwxyz　　　*1234567890$*

8 point Palatino Italic (Linotype)
The basic character in a type design is determined by the uniform design characteristics of all letters in the alphabet. However, this alone does not determine the standard of the type face and the quality of composition set with it. The appearance is something complex which forms itself out of many details, like

ABCDEFGHIJKLMNOPQRSTUVWXYZ&
abcdefghijklmnopqrstuvwxyz　　　*1234567890$*

9 point Palatino Italic (Linotype)
The basic character in a type design is determined by the uniform design characteristics of all letters in the alphabet. However, this alone does not determine the standard of the type face and the quality of composition set with it. The

ABCDEFGHIJKLMNOPQRSTUVWXYZ&
abcdefghijklmnopqrstuvwxyz　　　*1234567890$*

10 point Palatino Italic (Linotype)
The basic character in a type design is determined by the uniform design characteristics of all letters in the alphabet. However, this alone does not determine the standard of the type face and the quality of composition

ABCDEFGHIJKLMNOPQRSTUVWXYZ&
abcdefghijklmnopqrstuvwxyz　　　*1234567890$*

12 point Palatino Italic (Linotype)
The basic character in a type design is deter mined by the uniform design characteristics of all letters in the alphabet. However, this alone

ABCDEFGHIJKLMNOPQRSTUVWXYZ&
abcdefghijklmnopqrstuvwxyz　　*1234567890$*

10 point Palatino Italic (Foundry)
ABCDEFGHIJKLMNOPQRSTUVWXYZ&
abcdefghijklmnopqrstuvwxyz
1234567890$

12 point Palatino Italic (Foundry)
ABCDEFGHIJKLMNOPQRSTUVWXYZ&
abcdefghijklmnopqrstuvwxyz
1234567890$

14 point Palatino Italic (Foundry)
ABCDEFGHIJKLMNOPQRSTUVWXYZ&
abcdefghijklmnopqrstuvwxyz
1234567890$

18 point Palatino Italic (Foundry)
ABCDEFGHIJKLMNOPQRSTUVWXYZ&
abcdefghijklmnopqrstuvwxyz
1234567890$

SWASH
A B D E F G H J K L M N P R S T U W Z e k z &

20 point Palatino Italic (Foundry)
ABCDEFGHIJKLMNOPQRSTUVWXYZ&
abcdefghijklmnopqrstuvwxyz
1234567890$

SWASH
A B D E F G H J K L M N P R S T U W Z e k z &

(Continued on Page 389)

24 point Palatino Italic (Foundry)

ABCDEFGHIJKLMNOPQRSTUVWXYZ&
adcdefghijklmnopqrstuvwxyz
1234567890$

SWASH

A B D E F G H J K L M N P R S T U W Z
e k z &

30 point Palatino Italic (Foundry)

ABCDEFGHIJKLMNOPQRSTUVWXYZ
abcdefghijklmnopqrstuvwxyz&
1234567890$

SWASH

A B D E F G H J K L M N P R S T U
W Z e k z &

42 point Palatino Italic (Foundry)

ABCDEFGHIJKLMNOPQRSTU
VWXYZ&
abcdefghijklmnopqrstuvwxyz
1234567890$

SWASH

A B D E F G H J K L M N P R
R S T U W Z e k z &

(Continued on Page 390)

(Continued from Page 389)

54 point Palatino Italic (Foundry)

ABCDEFGHIJKLMNOP
QRSTUVWXYZ&
abcdefghijklmnopqrstuvwxyz
1234567890$

SWASH

ABCDEFGHJKLMN
PRSTUWZekz&

Palatino Semi-Bold (Must be leaded 1 point)

6 point Palatino Semi-Bold (Linotype)

The basic character in a type design is determined by the uniform design characterstics of all letters in the alphabet. However, this alone does not determine the standard of the type face and the quality of composition set with it. The appearance is something complex which forms itself out of many details, like form, proportion, ductus, rhythm etc. If everything har monizes, the total result will be more than the sum of its components. The only reliable basis for the design in a type is a positive feeling for form and style. The basic character in a type design is determined by the uniform

ABCDEFGHIJKLMNOPQRSTUVWXYZ&
abcdefghijklmnopqrstuvwxyz   1234567890$

7 point Palatino Semi-Bold (Linotype)

The basic character in a type design is determined by the uniform design characteristics of all letters in the alphabet. However, this alone does not determine the standard of the type face and the quality of composition set with it. The appearance is something complex which forms itself out of many details, like form, proportion, ductus, rhythm etc. If everything harmonizes, the total result will be more than the sum of its components. The only reliable basis for the design in a

ABCDEFGHIJKLMNOPQRSTUVWXYZ&
abcdefghijklmnopqrstuvwxyz   1234567890$

8 point Palatino Semi-Bold (Linotype)

The basic character in a type design is determined by the uni form design characteristics of all letters in the alphabet. How ever, this alone does not determine the standard of the type face and the quality of composition set with it. The appearance is something complex which forms itself out of many details, like form, proportion, ductus, rhythm etc. If everything harmonizes,

ABCDEFGHIJKLMNOPQRSTUVWXYZ&
abcdefghijklmnopqrstuvwxyz   1234567890$

9 point Palatino Semi-Bold (Linotype)

The basic character in a type design is determined by the uniform design characteristics of all letters in the alphabet. However, this alone does not determine the standard of the type face and the quality of composition set with it. The appearance is something complex which forms itself out of

ABCDEFGHIJKLMNOPQRSTUVWXYZ&
abcdefghijklmnopqrstuvwxyz   1234567890$

(Continued on Page 391)

10 point Palatino Semi-Bold (Linotype)

The basic character in a type design is determined by the uniform design characteristics of all letters in the alphabet. However, this alone does not determine the standard of the type face and the quality of composition set with it. The appearance is something complex which

ABCDEFGHIJKLMNOPQRSTUVWXYZ&
abcdefghijklmnopqrstuvwxyz   1234567890$

12 point Palatino Semi-Bold (Linotype)

The basic character in a type design is deter mined by the uniform design characteristics of all letters in the alphabet. However, this alone does not determine the standard of the type face

ABCDEFGHIJKLMNOPQRSTUVWXYZ&
abcdefghijklmnopqrstuvwxyz   1234567890$

14 point Palatino Semi-Bold (Foundry)

ABCDEFGHIJKLMNOPQRSTUVWXYZ&
abcdefghijklmnopqrstuvwxyz
1234567890$

18 point Palatino Semi-Bold (Foundry)

ABCDEFGHIJKLMNOPQRSTUVWXYZ&
abcdefghijklmnopqrstuvwxyz
1234567890$

20 point Palatino Semi-Bold (Foundry)

ABCDEFGHIJKLMNOPQRSTUVWXYZ&
abcdefghijklmnopqrstuvwxyz
1234567890$

24 point Palatino Semi-Bold (Foundry)

ABCDEFGHIJKLMNOPQRSTUVWXYZ&
abcdefghijklmnopqrstuvwxyz
1234567890$

30 point Palatino Semi-Bold (Foundry)

ABCDEFGHIJKLMNOPQRSTUV
WXYZ&
abcdefghijklmnopqrstuvwxyz
1234567890$

(Continued on Page 392)

(Continued from Page 391)

42 point Palatino Semi-Bold (Foundry)

ABCDEFGHIJKLMNOPQRST
UVWXYZ&
abcdefghijklmnopqrstuvwxyz
1234567890$

54 point Palatino Semi-Bold (Foundry)

ABCDEFGHIJKLMNOP
QRSTUVWXYZ&
abcdefghijklmnopqrstuv
wxyz
1234567890$

Park Avenue

36 point Park Avenue (Foundry)

ABCDEFGHIJKLMNOPQ
RSTUVWXYZ&
abcdefghijklmnopqrstuvwxyz
1234567890$

Peignot Medium

14 point Peignot Medium (Foundry)

ABCDEFGHIJKLMNOPQRSTUVWXYZ&
abcdefghijklmnopqrstuvwxyz
1234567890$

24 point Peignot Medium (Foundry)

ABCDEFGHIJKLMNOPQRSTUVWXYZ&
abcdefghijklmnopqrstuvwxyz
1234567890$

Perpetua

10 point Perpetua (Foundry)

ABCDEFGHIJKLMNOPQRSTUVWXYZ&
abcdefghijklmnopqrstuvwxyz
1234567890$

12 point Perpetua (Foundry)

ABCDEFGHIJKLMNOPQRSTUVWXYZ&
abcdefghijklmnopqrstuvwxyz
1234567890$

14 point Perpetua (Foundry)

ABCDEFGHIJKLMNOPQRSTUVWXYZ&
abcdefghijklmnopqrstuvwxyz
1234567890$

18 point Perpetua (Foundry)

ABCDEFGHIJKLMNOPQRSTUVWXYZ&
abcdefghijklmnopqrstuvwxyz
1234567890$

(Continued on Page 394)

(Continued from Page 393)

24 point Perpetua (Foundry)

ABCDEFGHIJKLMNOPQRSTUVWXYZ&
abcdefghijklmnopqrstuvwxyz
1234567890$

30 point Perpetua (Foundry)

ABCDEFGHIJKLMNOPQRSTUVWXYZ&
abcdefghijklmnopqrstuvwxyz
1234567890$

36 point Perpetua (Foundry)

ABCDEFGHIJKLMNOPQRSTUV
WXYZ&
abcdefghijklmnopqrstuvwxyz
1234567890$

42 point Perpetua (Foundry)

ABCDEFGHIJKLMNOPQRST
UVWXYZ&
abcdefghijklmnopqrstuvwxyz
1234567890$

(Continued on Page 395)

(Continued from Page 394)

48 point Perpetua (Foundry)

ABCDEFGHIJKLMNOPQ
RSTUVWXYZ&
abcdefghijklmnopqrstuvwxyz
1234567890$

60 point Perpetua (Foundry)

ABCDEFGHIJKLMN
OPQRSTUVWXYZ&
abcdefghijklmnopqrst
uvwxyz
1234567890$

(Continued on Page 396)

(Continued from Page 395)

72 point Perpetua (Foundry)

ABCDEFGHIJKL MNOPQRSTUV WXYZ&

abcdefghijklmnopq rstuvwxyz 1234567890$

Perpetua Bold

ABCDEFGHIJKLMNOPQRSTUVWXYZ&
abcdefghijklmnopqrstuvwxyz
1234567890$

ABCDEFGHIJKLMNOPQRSTUVWXYZ&
abcdefghijklmnopqrstuvwxyz
1234567890$

ABCDEFGHIJKLMNOPQRSTUVWXYZ&
abcdefghijklmnopqrstuvxwyz
1234567890$

ABCDEFGHIJKLMNOPQRSTUVWXYZ&
abcdefghijklmnopqrstuvwxyz
1234567890$

ABCDEFGHIJKLMNOPQRSTUV
WXYZ&
abcdefghijklmnopqrstuvwxyz
1234567890$

Perpetua Italic

10 point Perpetua Italic (Foundry)
ABCDEFGHIJKLMNOPQRSTUVWXYZ&
abcdefghijklmnopqrstuvwxyz
1234567890$

12 point Perpetua Italic (Foundry)
ABCDEFGHIJKLMNOPQRSTUVWXYZ&
abcdefghijklmnopqrstuvwxyz
1234567890$

14 point Perpetua Italic (Foundry)
ABCDEFGHIJKLMNOPQRSTUVWXYZ&
abcdefghijklmnopqrstuvwxyz
1234567890$

18 point Perpetua Italic (Foundry)
ABCDEFGHIJKLMNOPQRSTUVWXYZ&
abcdefghijklmnopqrstuvwxyz
1234567890$

24 point Perpetua Italic (Foundry)
ABCDEFGHIJKLMNOPQRSTUVWXYZ&
abcdefghijklmnopqrstuvwxyz
1234567890$

30 point Perpetua Italic (Foundry)
ABCDEFGHIJKLMNOPQRSTUVWXYZ&
abcdefghijklmnopqrstuvwxyz
1234567890$

36 point Perpetua Italic (Foundry)
ABCDEFGHIJKLMNOPQRSTUV
WXYZ&
abcdefghijklmnopqrstuvwxyz
1234567890$

(Continued on Page 399)

42 point Perpetua Italic (Foundry)

ABCDEFGHIJKLMNOPQRSTUV
WXYZ&
abcdefghijklmnopqrstuvwxyz
1234567890$

48 point Perpetua Italic (Foundry)

ABCDEFGHIJKLMNOPQRS
TUVWXYZ&
abcdefghijklmnopqrstuvwxyz
1234567890$

Perpetua Titling

18 point Perpetua Titling, Cap font (Foundry)

ABCDEFGHIJKLMNOPQRSTUVWXYZ&
1234567890$

24 point Perpetua Titling, Cap font (Foundry)

ABCDEFGHIJKLMNOPQRSTUVWXYZ&
1234567890$

30 point Perpetua Titling, Cap font (Foundry)

ABCDEFGHIJKLMNOPQRSTUV
WXYZ&
1234567890$

36 point Perpetua Titling, Cap font (Foundry)

ABCDEFGHIJKLMNOPQRS
TUVWXYZ&
1234567890$

48 point Perpetua Titling, Cap font (Foundry)

ABCDEFGHIJKLMN
OPQRSTUVWXYZ&
1234567890$

(Continued on Page 401)

60 point Perpetua Titling, Cap font (Foundry)

ABCDEFGHIJKL
MNOPQRSTUV
WXYZ&
1234567890$

72 point Perpetua Titling, Cap font (Foundry)

ABCDEFGHIJ
KLMNOPQRS
TUVWXYZ&
1234567890$

Post Italic

ABCDEFGHIJKLMNOPQRSTUVWXYZ&
abcdefghijklmnopqrstuvwxyz
1234567890$

Post Roman Bold

ABCDEFGHIJKLMNOPQRSTUVWXYZ&
abcdefghijklmnopqrstuvwxyz
1234567890$

ABCDEFGHIJKLMNOPQRSTUVWXYZ&
abcdefghijklmnopqrstuvwxyz
1234567890$

ABCDEFGHIJKLMNOPQRSTUVWXYZ&
abcdefghijklmnopqrstuvwxyz
1234567890$

ABCDEFGHIJKLMNOPQRSTUVWXYZ&
abcdefghijklmnopqrstuvwxyz
1234567890$

ABCDEFGHIJKLMNOPQRSTUV
WXYZ&
abcdefghijklmnopqrstuvwxyz
1234567890$

(Continued on Page 403)

42 point Post Roman Bold (Foundry)

ABCDEFGHIJKLMNOPQRST
UVWXYZ&
abcdefghijklmnopqrstuvwxyz
1234567890$

60 point Post Roman Bold (Foundry)

ABCDEFGHIJKL
MNOPQRSTU
VWXYZ&
abcdefghijklmnopq
rstuvwxyz
1234567890$

Post Roman Light

14 point Post Roman Light Small (Foundry)
ABCDEFGHIJKLMNOPQRSTUVWXYZ&
abcdefghijklmnopqrstuvwxyz
1234567890$

14 point Post Roman Light Large (Foundry)
ABCDEFGHIJKLMNOPQRSTUVWXYZ&
abcdefghijklmnopqrstuvwxyz
1234567890$

18 point Post Roman Light (Foundry)
ABCDEFGHIJKLMNOPQRSTUVWXYZ&
abcdefghijklmnopqrstuvwxyz
1234567890$

24 point Post Roman Light Small (Foundry)
ABCDEFGHIJKLMNOPQRSTUVWXYZ&
abcdefghijklmnopqrstuvwxyz
1234567890$

24 point Post Roman Light Large (Foundry)
ABCDEFGHIJKLMNOPQRSTUVWXYZ&
abcdefghijklmnopqrstuvwxyz
1234567890$

Post Roman Medium

12 point Post Roman Medium (Foundry)

ABCDEFGHIJKLMNOPQRSTUVWXYZ&
abcdefghijklmnopqrstuvwxyz
1234567890$

14 point Post Roman Medium Small (Foundry)

ABCDEFGHIJKLMNOPQRSTUV
WXYZ&
abcdefghijklmnopqrstuvwxyz
1234567890$

14 point Post Roman Medium Large (Foundry)

ABCDEFGHIJKLMNOPQRSTUV
WXYZ&
abcdefghijklmnopqrstuvwxyz
1234567890$

18 point Post Roman Medium (Foundry)

ABCDEFGHIJKLMNOPQRSTUVWXYZ&
abcdefghijklmnopqrstuvwxyz
1234567890$

24 point Post Roman Medium Small (Foundry)

ABCDEFGHIJKLMNOPQRSTUVWXYZ&
abcdefghijklmnopqrstuvwxyz
1234567890$

24 point Post Roman Medium Large (Foundry)

ABCDEFGHIJKLMNOPQRSTUVWXYZ&
abcdefghijklmnopqrstuvwxyz
1234567890$

(Continued on Page 406)

(Continued from Page 405)

30 point Post Roman Medium (Foundry)

ABCDEFGHIJKLMNOPQRSTUV
WXYZ&
abcdefghijklmnopqrstuvwxyz
1234567890$

42 point Post Roman Medium (Foundry)

ABCDEFGHIJKLMNOPQRST
UVWXYZ&
abcdefghijklmnopqrstuvwxyz
1234567890$

48 point Post Roman Medium (Foundry)

ABCDEFGHIJKLMNOP
QRSTUVWXYZ&
abcdefghijklmnopqrstuv
wxyz
1234567890$

Primer

6 point Primer (Linotype)

The basic character in a type design is determined by the uniform design characteristics of all letters in the alphabet. However, this alone does not determine the standard of the type face and the quality of composition set with it. The appearance is something

ABCDEFGHIJKLMNOPQRSTUVWXYZ&
abcdefghijklmnopqrstuvwxyz 1234567890$
ABCDEFGHIJKLMNOPQRSTUVWXYZ

7 point Primer (Linotype)

The basic character in a type face is determined by the uniform design characteristics of all letters in the alphabet. However, this alone does not determine the standard of the type face and the quality of composition set with it. The appearance is some

ABCDEFGHIJKLMNOPQRSTUVWXYZ&
abcdefghijklmnopqrstuvwxyz 1234567890$
ABCDEFGHIJKLMNOPQRSTUVWXYZ

8 point Primer (Linotype)

The basic character in a type design is determined by the uniform design characteristics of all letters in the alphabet. However, this alone does not determine the standard of the

ABCDEFGHIJKLMNOPQRSTUVWXYZ&
abcdefghijklmnopqrstuvwxyz 1234567890$
ABCDEFGHIJKLMNOPQRSTUVWXYZ

9 point Primer (Linotype)

The basic character in a type design is determined by the uniform design characteristics of all letters in the alphabet. However, this alone does not determine the

ABCDEFGHIJKLMNOPQRSTUVWXYZ&
abcdefghijklmnopqrstuvwxyz 1234567890$
ABCDEFGHIJKLMNOPQRSTUVWXYZ

10 point Primer (Linotype)

The basic character in a type design is determined by the uniform design characteristics of all letters in the alphabet. However, this alone does not deter

ABCDEFGHIJKLMNOPQRSTUVWXYZ&
abcdefghijklmnopqrstuvwxyz 1234567890$
ABCDEFGHIJKLMNOPQRSTUVWXYZ

11 point Primer (Linotype)

The basic character in a type design is determined by the uniform design characteristics of all letters

ABCDEFGHIJKLMNOPQRSTUVWXYZ&
abcdefghijklmnopqrstuvwxyz 1234567890$
ABCDEFGHIJKLMNOPQRSTUVWXYZ

12 point Primer (Linotype)

The basic character in a type design is deter mined by the uniform design characteristics of

ABCDEFGHIJKLMNOPQRSTUVWXYZ&
abcdefghijklmnopqrstuvwxyz 1234567890$
ABCDEFGHIJKLMNOPQRSTUVWXYZ

14 point Primer (Linotype)

The basic character in a type design is determined by the uniform design char

ABCDEFGHIJKLMNOPQRSTUV
WXYZ& 1234567890$
abcdefghijklmnopqrstuvwxyz
ABCDEFGHIJKLMNOPQRSTUVWXYZ

Primer Italic

6 point Primer Italic (Linotype)

The basic character in a type design is determined by the uniform design characteristics of all letters in the alphabet. However, this alone does not determine the standard of the type face and the quality of composition set with it. The appearance is something

ABCDEFGHIJKLMNOPQRSTUVWXYZ&
abcdefghijklmnopqrstuvwxyz 1234567890$

7 point Primer Italic (Linotype)

The basic character in a type face is determined by the uniform design characteristics of all letters in the alphabet. However, this alone does not determine the standard of the type face and the quality of composition set with it. The appearance is some

ABCDEFGHIJKLMNOPQRSTUVWXYZ&
abcdefghijklmnopqrstuvwxyz 1234567890$

8 point Primer Italic (Linotype)

The basic character in a type design is determined by the uniform design characteristics of all letters in the alphabet. However, this alone does not determine the standard of the

ABCDEFGHIJKLMNOPQRSTUVWXYZ&
abcdefghijklmnopqrstuvwxyz 1234567890$

9 point Primer Italic (Linotype)

The basic character in a type design is determined by the uniform design characteristics of all letters in the alphabet. However, this alone does not determine the

ABCDEFGHIJKLMNOPQRSTUVWXYZ&
abcdefghijklmnopqrstuvwxyz 1234567890$

10 point Primer Italic (Linotype)

The basic character in a type design is determined by the uniform design characteristics of all letters in the alphabet. However, this alone does not deter

ABCDEFGHIJKLMNOPQRSTUVWXYZ&
abcdefghijklmnopqrstuvwxyz 1234567890$

11 point Primer Italic (Linotype)

The basic character in a type design is determined by the uniform design characteristics of all letters

ABCDEFGHIJKLMNOPQRSTUVWXYZ&
abcdefghijklmnopqrstuvwxyz 1234567890$

12 point Primer Italic (Linotype)

The basic character in a type design is deter mined by the uniform design characteristics of

ABCDEFGHIJKLMNOPQRSTUVWXYZ&
abcdefghijklmnopqrstuvwxyz 1234567890$

14 point Primer Italic (Linotype)

The basic character in a type design is determined by the uniform design char

ABCDEFGHIJKLMNOPQRSTUV
WXYZ& 1234567890$
abcdefghijklmnopqrstuvwxyz

Poster Bodoni

The basic character in a type design is de termined by the uniform design character istics of all letters in the alphabet. However, this alone does not determine the standard of the type face and the quality of composi

ABCDEFGHIJKLMNOPQRSTUVWXYZ& abcdefghijklmnopqrstuvwxyz 1234567890$

Poster Bodoni Italic

The basic character in a type design is de termined by the uniform design character istics of all letters in the alphabet. However, this alone does not determine the standard of the type face and the quality of composi

ABCDEFGHIJKLMNOPQRSTUVWXYZ& abcdefghijklmnopqrstuvwxyz 1234567890$

Prisma

24 point Prisma, Cap font (Foundry)

ABCDEFGHIJKLMNOPQRSTUVWXYZ&
1234567890$

30 point Prisma, Cap font (Foundry)

ABCDEFGHIJKLMNOPQRSTUV
WXYZ&
1234567890$

36 point Prisma, Cap font (Foundry)

ABCDEFGHIJKLMNOPQR
STUVWXYZ&
1234567890$

P. T. Barnum

ABCDEFGHIJKLMNOPQRSTUVWXYZ&
abcdefghijklmnopqrstuvwxyz
1234567890$

ABCDEFGHIJKLMNOPQRSTUVWXYZ&
abcdefghijklmnopqrstuvwxyz
1234567890$

ABCDEFGHIJKLMNOPQRSTUVWXYZ&
abcdefghijklmnopqrstuvwxyz
1234567890$

ABCDEFGHIJKLMNOPQRSTUVWXYZ&
abcdefghijklmnopqrstuvwxyz
1234567890$

ABCDEFGHIJKLMNOPQRSTUV
WXYY&
abcdefghijklmnopqrstuvwxyz
1234567890$

Radiant Bold

14 point Radiant Bold Foundry)

ABCDEFGHIJKLMNOPQRSTUVWXYZ&
abcdefghijklmnopqrstuvwxyz
1234567890$

18 point Radiant Bold (Foundry)

ABCDEFGHIJKLMNOPQRSTUVWXYZ&
abcdefghijklmnopqrstuvwxyz
1234567890$

36 point Radiant Bold (Foundry)

ABCDEFGHIJKLMNOPQRSTUV
WXYZ&
abcdefghijklmnopqrstuvwxyz
1234567890$

Radiant Bold Condensed

14 point Radiant Bold Condensed (Foundry)

ABCDEFGHIJKLMNOPQRSTUVWXYZ&
abcdefghijklmnopqrstuvwxyz
1234567890$

Record Gothic

10 point Record Gothic (Ludlow)

ABCDEFGHIJKLMNOPQRSTUVWXYZ&
abcdefghijklmnopqrstuvwxyz
1234567890$

410

Reiner Script

30 point Reiner Script Large (Foundry)

ABCDEFGHIJKLMNOPQRSTUVWXYZ

abcdefghijklmnopqrstuvwxyz

1234567890$

60 point Reiner Script (Foundry)

ABCDEFGHIJKLMNOPQRS
TUVWXYZ

abcdefghijklmnopqrstuvwxyz

1234567890$

Repro Script

18 point Repro Script (Foundry)

ABCDEFGHIJKLMNOPQRSTUVWXYZ&
abcdefghijklmnopqrstuvwxyz
1234567890$

36 point Repro Script (Foundry)

ABCDEFGHIJKLMNOPQRSTUVWXYZ&

abcdefghijklmnopqrstuvwxyz

1234567890$

Reverse Gothic

24 point Reverse Gothic, Cap font (Ludlow)

ABCDEFGHIJKLMNOPQRSTUVWXYZ&
1234567890$

Roman Compressed No. 3

30 point Roman Compressed No. 3 (Foundry)

ABCDEFGHIJKLMNOPQRSTUVWXYZ&
abcdefghijklmnopqrstuvwxyz
1234567890$

48 point Roman Compressed No. 3 (Foundry)

ABCDEFGHIJKLMNOPQRSTUV
WXYZ&
abcdefghijklmnopqrstuvwxyz
1234567890$

Romantique No. 5

ABCDEFGHIJKLMNOPQRSTUV
WXYZ&
1234567890

ABCDEFGHIJKLMNO
PQRSTUVWXYZ&
1234567890

Sans Serif Bold

ABCDEFGHIJKLMNOPQRSTUVWXYZ&
abcdefghijklmnopqrstuvwxyz
1234567890$

ABCDEFGHIJKLMNOPQRSTUVWXYZ&
abcdefghijklmnopqrstuvwxyz
1234567890$

ABCDEFGHIJKLMNOPQRSTUVWXYZ&
abcdefghijklmnopqrstuvwxyz 1234567890$

ABCDEFGHIJKLMNOPQRSTUV
WXYZ&
abcdefghijklmnopqrstuvwxyz
1234567890$

Sans Serif Light

8 point Sans Serif Light (Foundry)
ABCDEFGHIJKLMNOPQRSTUVWXYZ&
abcdefghijklmnopqrstuvwxyz
1234567890$

10 point Sans Serif Light (Foundry)
ABCDEFGHIJKLMNOPQRSTUVWXYZ&
abcdefghijklmnopqrstuvwxyz
1234567890$

14 point Sans Serif Light (Foundry)
ABCDEFGHIJKLMNOPQRSTUVWXYZ&
abcdefghijklmnopqrstuvwxyz
1234567890$

18 point Sans Serif Light (Foundry)
ABCDEFGHIJKLMNOPQRSTUVWXYZ&
abcdefghijklmnopqrstuvwxyz
1234567890$

24 point Sans Serif Light (Foundry)
ABCDEFGHIJKLMNOPQRSTUVWXYZ&
abcdefghijklmnopqrstuvwxyz
1234567890$

30 point Sans Serif Light (Foundry)
ABCDEFGHIJKLMNOPQRSTUVWXYZ&
abcdefghijklmnopqrstuvwxyz
1234567890$

36 point Sans Serif Light Foundry)
ABCDEFGHIJKLMNOPQRSTUV
WXYZ&
abcdefghijklmnopqrstuvwxyz
1234567890$

(Continued on Page 415)

(Continued from Page 414)

48 point Sans Serif Light (Foundry)

ABCDEFGHIJKLMNOPQRS
TUVWXYZ&
abcdefghijklmnopqrstuvwxyz
1234567890$

Sans Serif Light Italic

18 point Sans Serif Light Italic (Foundry)

ABCDEFGHIJKLMNOPQRSTUVWXYZ&
abcdefghijklmnopqrstuvwxyz
1234567890$

Sans Serif Extra Bold

24 point Sans Serif Extra Bold (Foundry)

ABCDEFGHIJKLMNOPQRSTUVWXYZ&
abcdefghijklmnopqrstuvwxyz
1234567890$

Sans Serif Medium

ABCDEFGHIJKLMNOPQRSTUV
WXYZ&
abcdefghijklmnopqrstuvwxyz
1234567890$

Scotch Italic

ABCDEFGHIJKLMNOPQRSTUVWXYZ&
abcdefghijklmnopqrstuvwxyz
1234567890$

ABCDEFGHIJKLMNOPQRSTUVWXYZ&
abcdefghijklmnopqrstuvwxyz
1234567890$

ABCDEFGHIJKLMNOPQRSTUV
WXYZ&
abcdefghijklmnopqrstuvwxyz
1234567890$

Scotch Roman

ABCDEFGHIJKLMNOPQRSTUVWXYZ&
abcdefghijklmnopqrstuvwxyz
1234567890$

ABCDEFGHIJKLMNOPQRSTUVWXYZ&
abcdefghijklmnopqrstuvwxyz
1234567890$

ABCDEFGHIJKLMNOPQRSTUVWXYZ&
abcdefghijklmnopqrstuvwxyz
1234567890$

ABCDEFGHIJKLMNOPQRSTUV
WXYZ&
abcdefghijklmnopqrstuvwxyz
1234567890$

ABCDEFGHIJKLMNOPQR
STUVWXYZ&
abcdefghijklmnopqrstuvwxyz
1234567890$

Sistina Titling

16 point Sistina Titling, Cap font (Foundry)

ABCDEFGHIJKLMNOPQRSTUVWXYZ&
1234567890O$

20 point Sistina Titling, Cap font (Foundry)

ABCDEFGHIJKLMNOPQRSTUVWXYZ&
1234567890O$

24 point Sistina Titling, Cap font (Foundry)

ABCDEFGHIJKLMNOPQRSTUVWXYZ&
1234567890O$

30 point Sistina Titling, Cap font (Foundry)

ABCDEFGHIJKLMNOPQRSTUV
WXYZ&
1234567890O$

36 point Sistina Titling, Cap font (Foundry)

ABCDEFGHIJKLMNOPQRST
UVWXYZ&
1234567890O$

Solemnis

18 point Solemnis, Cap font (Foundry)

ABCDEFGHIJKLMNOPQRSTUVWXYZ&
1234567890$

24 point Solemnis, Cap font (Foundry)

ABCDEFGHIJKLMNOPQRSTUVWXYZ&
1234567890$

(Continued on Page 419)

30 point Solemnis, Cap font (Foundry)

ABCDEFGHiJKLMNOpqRSTUVWXYZ&
1234567890$

36 point Solemnis, Cap font (Foundry)

ABCDEFGHiJKLMNOpqRSTUV
WXYZ&
1234567890$

48 point Solemnis, Cap font (Foundry)

ABCDEFGHiJKLMNOpqR
STUVWXYZ&
1234567890$

60 point Solemnis, Cap font (Foundry)

ABCDEFGHiJKLMNO
pqRSTUVWXYZ&
1234567890$

6 point Spartan Black (Linotype)

The basic character in a type design is determined by the uniform design characteristics of all letters in the alphabet. However, this alone does not determine the standard of the type face and the quality of composition set with it. The appearance is something complex which forms itself out of many details, like form, proportion, ductus, rhythm etc. If everything harmonizes, the total result will be more than the sum of its components. The only reliable basis for the design in a type is a positive feeling for form and style. The basic

ABCDEFGHIJKLMNOPQRSTUVWXYZ&
abcdefghijklmnopqrstuvwxyz 1234567890$

8 point Spartan Black (Linotype)

The basic character in a type design is determined by the uniform design characteristics of all letters in the alphabet. However, this alone does not determine the standard of the type face and the quality of composition set with it. The appearance is something complex which forms itself out of many details, like form, proportion, ductus, rhythm etc. If everything harmo

ABCDEFGHIJKLMNOPQRSTUVWXYZ&
abcdefghijklmnopqrstuvwxyz 1234567890$

10 point Spartan Black (Linotype)

The basic character in a type design is determined by the uniform design characteristics of all letters in the alphabet. However, this alone does not determine the standard of the type face and the quality of composition set with it. The appearance is

ABCDEFGHIJKLMNOPQRSTUVWXYZ&
abcdefghijklmnopqrstuvwxyz 1234567890$

12 point Spartan Black (Linotype)

The basic character in a type design is deter mined by the uniform design characteristics of all letters in the alphabet. However, this alone does not determine the standard of

ABCDEFGHIJKLMNOPQRSTUVWXYZ&
abcdefghijklmnopqrstuvwxyz 1234567890$

14 point Spartan Black (Linotype)

The basic character in a type design is determined by the uniform design char acteristics of all letters in the alphabet.

ABCDEFGHIJKLMNOPQRSTUVWXYZ&
abcdefghijklmnopqrstuvwxyz
1234567890$

18 point Spartan Black (Foundry)

ABCDEFGHIJKLMNOPQRSTU
VWXYZ&
abcdefghijklmnopqrstuvwxyz
1234567890$

24 point Spartan Black (Foundry)

ABCDEFGHIJKLMNOPQRSTUVWXYZ&
abcdefghijklmnopqrstuvwxyz
1234567890$

30 point Spartan Black (Foundry)

ABCDEFGHIJKLMNOPQRSTUVWXYZ
abcdefghijklmnopqrstuvwxyz&
1234567890$

420

(Continued on Page 421)

(Continued from Page 420)

36 point Spartan Black (Foundry)

ABCDEFGHIJKLMNOPQRSTU
VWXYZ&
abcdefghijklmnopqrstuv
wxyz
1234567890$

42 point Spartan Black (Foundry)

ABCDEFGHIJKLMNOPQR
STUVWXYZ&
abcdefghijklmnopqrstuv
wxyz
1234567890$

48 point Spartan Black (Foundry)

ABCDEFGHIJKLMNOP
QRSTUVWXYZ&
abcdefghijklmnopqrst
uvwxyz 1234567890$

(Continued on Page 422)

(Continued from Page 421)

60 point Spartan Black (Foundry)

ABCDEFGHIJKLM
NOPQRSTUV
WXYZ&
abcdefghijklmno
pqrstuvwxyz
1234567890$

(Continued on Page 423)

72 point Spartan Black (Foundry)

ABCDEFGHIJKL
MNOPQRSTU
VWXYZ&
abcdefghijklm
nopqrstuv
wxyz
1234567890$

(Continued on Page 424)

84 point Spartan Black (Foundry)

ABCDEFGHIJ
KLMNOPQR
STUVWXYZ
abcdefghijkl
mnopqrstuv
wxyz&$
1234567890

Spartan Black Condensed

14 point Spartan Black Condensed (Foundry)
ABCDEFGHIJKLMNOPQRSTUVWXYZ&
abcdefghijklmnopqrstuvwxyz
1234567890$

18 point Spartan Black Condensed (Foundry)
ABCDEFGHIJKLMNOPQRSTUVWXYZ&
abcdefghijklmnopqrstuvwxyz
1234567890$

24 point Spartan Black Condensed (Foundry)
ABCDEFGHIJKLMNOPQRSTUVWXYZ&
abcdefghijklmnopqrstuvwxyz
1234567890$

30 point Spartan Black Condensed (Foundry)
ABCDEFGHIJKLMNOPQRSTUVWXYZ&
abcdefghijklmnopqrstuvwxyz
1234567890$

36 point Spartan Black Condensed (Foundry)
ABCDEFGHIJKLMNOPQRSTUVWXYZ&
abcdefghijklmnopqrstuvwxyz
1234567890$

42 point Spartan Black Condensed (Foundry)
ABCDEFGHIJKLMNOPQRSTUVWXYZ&
abcdefghijklmnopqrstuvwxyz
1234567890$

(Continued on Page 426)

(Continued from Page 425)

48 point Spartan Black Condensed (Foundry)

ABCDEFGHIJKLMNOPQRSTUV WXYZ&
abcdefghijklmnopqrstuvwxyz
1234567890$

60 point Spartan Black Condensed (Foundry)

ABCDEFGHIJKLMNOPQR STUVWXYZ&
abcdefghijklmnopqrstuv wxyz
1234567890$

(Continued on Page 427)

72 point Spartan Black Condensed (Foundry)

ABCDEFGHIJKLMNOP
QRSTUVWXYZ&
abcdefghijklmnopqrst
uvwxyz
1234567890$

Spartan Black Condensed Italic

ABCDEFGHIJKLMNOPQRSTUVWXYZ&
abcdefghijklmnopqrstuvwxyz
1234567890$

ABCDEFGHIJKLMNOPQRSTUVWXYZ&
abcdefghijklmnopqrstuvwxyz
1234567890$

ABCDEFGHIJKLMNOPQRSTUVWXYZ&
abcdefghijklmnopqrstuvwxyz
1234567890$

ABCDEFGHIJKLMNOPQRSTUVWXYZ&
abcdefghijklmnopqrstuvwxyz
1234567890$

ABCDEFGHIJKLMNOPQRSTUV
WXYZ&
abcdefghijklmnopqrstuvwxyz
1234567890$

(Continued on Page 429)

60 point Spartan Black Condensed Italic (Foundry)

ABCDEFGHIJKLMNOPQRST UVWXYZ& abcdefghijklmnopqrstuv wxyz 1234567890$

Spartan Black Italic

6 point Spartan Black Italic (Linotype)

The basic character in a type design is determined by the uniform design characteristics of all letters in the alphabet. However, this alone does not determine the standard of the type face and the quality of composition set with it. The appearance is something complex which forms itself out of many details, like form, proportion, ductus, rhythm etc. If everything harmonizes, the total result will be more than the sum of its components. The only reliable basis for the design in a type is a positive feeling for form and style. The basic

ABCDEFGHIJKLMNOPQRSTUVWXYZ&
abcdefghijklmnopqrstuvwxyz   *1234567890$*

8 point Spartan Black Italic (Linotype)

The basic character in a type design is determined by the uniform design characteristics of all letters in the alphabet. However, this alone does not determine the standard of the type face and the quality of composition set with it. The appearance is something complex which forms itself out of many details, like form, proportion, ductus, rhythm etc. If everything harmo

ABCDEFGHIJKLMNOPQRSTUVWXYZ&
abcdefghijklmnopqrstuvwxyz   *1234567890$*

10 point Spartan Black Italic (Linotype)

The basic character in a type design is determined by the uniform design characteristics of all letters in the alphabet. However, this alone does not determine the standard of the type face and the quality of composition set with it. The appearance is

ABCDEFGHIJKLMNOPQRSTUVWXYZ&
abcdefghijklmnopqrstuvwxyz   *1234567890$*

12 point Spartan Black Italic (Linotype)

The basic character in a type design is determined by the uniform design characteristics of all letters in the alphabet. However, this alone does not determine the standard of

ABCDEFGHIJKLMNOPQRSTUVWXYZ&
abcdefghijklmnopqrstuvwxyz 1234567890$

14 point Spartan Black Italic (Linotype)

The basic character in a type design is determined by the uniform design characteristics of all letters in the alphabet.

ABCDEFGHIJKLMNOPQRSTUVWXYZ&
abcdefghijklmnopqrstuvwxyz
1234567890$

24 point Spartan Black Italic (Foundry)

ABCDEFGHIJKLMNOPQRSTUVWXYZ&
abcdefghijklmnopqrstuvwxyz
1234567890$

Spartan Book

The basic character in a type design is determined by the uniform design characteristics of all letters in the alphabet. However, this alone does not determine the standard of the type face and the quality of composition set with it. The appearance is something complex which forms itself out of many details, like form, proportion, ductus, rhythm etc. If everything harmonizes, the total result will be more than the sum of its components. The only reliable basis for the design in a type is a positive feeling for form and style. The basic character in a type design is determined by the uniform design charac

ABCDEFGHIJKLMNOPQRSTUVWXYZ&
abcdefghijklmnopqrstuvwxyz   1234567890$

The basic character in a type design is determined by the uniform design characteristics of all letters in the alphabet. However, this alone does not determine the standard of the type face and the quality of composition set with it. The appearance is something complex which forms itself out of many details, like form, proportion, ductus, rhythm etc. If everything harmonizes, the total result will be more than the sum of its

ABCDEFGHIJKLMNOPQRSTUVWXYZ&
abcdefghijklmnopqrstuvwxyz   1234567890$

The basic character in a type design is determined by the uniform design characteristics of all letters in the alpha bet. However, this alone does not determine the standard of the type face and the quality of composition set with it. The appearance is something complex which forms

ABCDEFGHIJKLMNOPQRSTUVWXYZ&
abcdefghijklmnopqrstuvwxyz   1234567890$

The basic character in a type design is determined by the uniform design characteristics of all letters in the alphabet. However, this alone does not de termine the standard of the type face and the

ABCDEFGHIJKLMNOPQRSTUVWXYZ&
abcdefghijklmnopqrstuvwxyz   1234567890$

The basic character in a type design is deter mined by the uniform design characteristics of all letters in the alphabet. However, this

ABCDEFGHIJKLMNOPQRSTUVWXYZ&
abcdefghijklmnopqrstuvwxyz   1234567890$

ABCDEFGHIJKLMNOPQRSTUV WXYZ&
abcdefghijklmnopqrstuvwxyz
1234567890$

ABCDEFGHIJKLMNOPQRSTUVWXYZ&
abcdefghijklmnopqrstuvwxyz
1234567890$

Spartan Book Condensed

6 point Spartan Book Condensed (Linotype)

The basic character in a type design is determined by the uniform design characteristics ot all letters in the alphabet. However, this alone does not determine the standard of the type face and the quality of composition set with it. The appearance is something complex which forms itself out of many details, like form, proportion, ductus, rhythm etc. If everything harmonizes, the total result will be more than the sum of its components. The only reliable basis for the design in a type is a positive feeling for form and style. The basic character in a type design is determined by the uniform design character

ABCDEFGHIJKLMNOPQRSTUVWXYZ&
abcdefghijklmnopqrstuvwxyz   1234567890$

8 point Spartan Book Condensed (Linotype)

The basic character in a type design is determined by the uniform design characteristics of all letters in the alphabet. However, this alone does not determine the standard of the type face and the quality of composition set with it. The appearance is something complex which forms itself out of many details, like form, propor tion, ductus, rhythm etc. If everything harmonizes, the total result

ABCDEFGHIJKLMNOPQRSTUVWXYZ&
abcdefghijklmnopqrstuvwxyz   1234567890$

10 point Spartan Book Condensed (Linotype)

The basic character in a type design is determined by the uni form design characteristics of all letters in the alphabet. However, this alone does not determine the standard of the type face and the quality of composition set with it. The ap pearance is something complex which forms itself out of

ABCDEFGHIJKLMNOPQRSTUVWXYZ&
abcdefghijklmnopqrstuvwxyz   1234567890$

12 point Spartan Book Condensed (Linotype)

The basic character in a type design is determined by the uniform design characteristics of all letters in the alphabet. However, this alone does not determine the standard of the type face and the quality of composition

ABCDEFGHIJKLMNOPQRSTUVWXYZ&
abcdefghijklmnopqrstuvwxyz   1234567890$

14 point Spartan Book Condensed (Linotype)

The basic character in a type design is determined by the uniform design characteristics of all letters in the alphabet. However, this alone does not deter

ABCDEFGHIJKLMNOPQRSTUVWXYZ&
abcdefghijklmnopqrstuvwxyz   1234567890$

Spartan Extra Black

18 point Spartan Extra Black (Foundry)

ABCDEFGHIJKLMNOPQRSTUVWXYZ&
abcdefghijklmnopqrstuvwxyz
1234567890$

24 point Spartan Extra Black (Foundry)

ABCDEFGHIJKLMNOPQRSTUVWXYZ&
abcdefghijklmnopqrstuvwxyz
1234567890$

30 point Spartan Extra Black (Foundry)

ABCDEFGHIJKLMNOPQRSTUV
WXYZ&
abcdefghijklmnopqrstuvwxyz
1234567890$

36 point Spartan Extra Black (Foundry)

ABCDEFGHIJKLMNOPQRST
UVWXYZ&
abcdefghijklmnopqrstuv
wxyz
1234567890$

(Continued on Page 434)

(Continued from Page 433)

42 point Spartan Extra Black (Foundry)

ABCDEFGHIJKLMNOPQ
RSTUVWXYZ&
abcdefghijklmnopqrstu
vwxyz
1234567890$

48 point Spartan Extra Black (Foundry)

ABCDEFGHIJKLMNO
PQRSTUVWXYZ&
abcdefghijklmnopqrs
tuvwxyz
1234567890$

Spartan Heavy

6 point Spartan Heavy (Linotype)
The basic character in a type design is determined by the uniform design characteristics of all letters in the alphabet. However, this alone does not determine the standard of the type face and the quality of composition set with it. The appearance is something complex which forms itself out of many details, like form, proportion, ductus, rhythm etc. If everything harmonizes, the total result will be more than the sum of its components. The only reliable basis for the design in a type is a positive feeling for form and style. The basic character in a type design is determined by the uniform design charac

ABCDEFGHIJKLMNOPQRSTUVWXYZ&
abcdefghijklmnopqrstuvwxyz   1234567890$

8 point Spartan Heavy (Linotype)
The basic character in a type design is determined by the uniform design characteristics of all letters in the alphabet. However, this alone does not determine the standard of the type face and the quality of composition set with it. The appearance is something complex which forms itself out of many details, like form, proportion, ductus, rhythm etc. If everything harmonizes, the total result will be more than the sum of its

ABCDEFGHIJKLMNOPQRSTUVWXYZ&
abcdefghijklmnopqrstuvwxyz   1234567890$

10 point Spartan Heavy (Linotype)
The basic character in a type design is determined by the uniform design characteristics of all letters in the alpha bet. However, this alone does not determine the standard of the type face and the quality of composition set with it. The appearance is something complex which forms

ABCDEFGHIJKLMNOPQRSTUVWXYZ&
abcdefghijklmnopqrstuvwxyz   1234567890$

12 point Spartan Heavy (Linotype)
The basic character in a type design is determined by the uniform design characteristics of all letters in the alphabet. However, this alone does not de termine the standard of the type face and the

ABCDEFGHIJKLMNOPQRSTUVWXYZ&
abcdefghijklmnopqrstuvwxyz   1234567890$

14 point Spartan Heavy (Linotype)
The basic character in a type design is deter mined by the uniform design characteristics of all letters in the alphabet. However, this

ABCDEFGHIJKLMNOPQRSTUVWXYZ&
abcdefghijklmnopqrstuvwxyz   1234567890$

18 point Spartan Heavy (Foundry)
ABCDEFGHIJKLMNOPQRSTUV
WXYZ&
abcdefghijklmnopqrstuvwxyz
1234567890$

24 point Spartan Heavy (Foundry)
ABCDEFGHIJKLMNOPQRSTUVWXYZ&
abcdefghijklmnopqrstuvwxyz
1234567890$

30 point Spartan Heavy (Foundry)
ABCDEFGHIJKLMNOPQRSTUVWXYZ&
abcdefghijklmnopqrstuvwxyz
1234567890$

(Continued on Page 436)

(Continued from Page 435)

36 point Spartan Heavy (Foundry)

ABCDEFGHIJKLMNOPQRSTUV
WXYZ&
abcdefghijklmnopqrstuvwxyz
1234567890$

60 point Spartan Heavy (Foundry)

ABCDEFGHIJKLM
NOPQRSTUV
WXYZ&
abcdefghijklmnopq
rstuvwxyz
1234567890$

(Continued on Page 437)

72 point Spartan Heavy (Foundry)

ABCDEFGHIJKL
MNOPQRSTUV
WXYZ&
abcdefghijklmno
pqrstuvwxyz
1234567890$

Spartan Heavy Condensed

6 point Spartan Heavy Condensed (Linotype)

The basic character in a type design is determined by the uniform design characteristics of all letters in the alphabet. However, this alone does not determine the standard of the type face and the quality of composition set with it. The appearance is something complex which forms itself out of many details, like form, proportion, ductus, rhythm etc. If everything harmonizes, the total result will be more than the sum of its components. The only reliable basis for the design in a type is a positive feeling for form and style. The basic character in a type design is determined by the uniform design character

ABCDEFGHIJKLMNOPQRSTUVWXYZ &
abcdefghijklmnopqrstuvwxyz   1234567890$

8 point Spartan Heavy Condensed (Linotype)

The basic character in a type design is determined by the uniform design characteristics of all letters in the alphabet. However, this alone does not determine the standard of the type face and the quality of composition set with it. The appearance is something complex which forms itself out of many details, like form, proportion, ductus, rhythm etc. If everything harmonizes, the total result

ABCDEFGHIJKLMNOPQRSTUVWXYZ&
abcdefghijklmnopqrstuvwxyz   1234567890$

10 point Spartan Heavy Condensed (Linotype)

The basic character in a type design is determined by the uniform design characteristics of all letters in the alphabet. However, this alone does not determine the standard of the type face and the quality of composition set with it. The appearance is something complex which forms itself out of

ABCDEFGHIJKLMNOPQRSTUVWXYZ&
abcdefghijklmnopqrstuvwxyz   1234567890$

12 point Spartan Heavy Condensed (Linotype)

The basic character in a type design is determined by the uniform design characteristics of all letters in the alphabet. However, this alone does not determine the standard of the type face and the quality of composition

ABCDEFGHIJKLMNOPQRSTUVWXYZ&
abcdefghijklmnopqrstuvwxyz   1234567890$

14 point Spartan Heavy Condensed (Linotype)

The basic character in a type design is determined by the uniform design characteristics of all letters in the alphabet. However, this alone does not deter

ABCDEFGHIJKLMNOPQRSTUVWXYZ&
abcdefghijklmnopqrstuvwxyz   1234567890$

Spartan Heavy Italic

8 point Spartan Heavy Italic (Linotype)

The basic character in a type design is determined by the uniform design characteristics of all letters in the alphabet. However, this alone does not determine the standard of the type face and the quality of composition set with it. The appearance is something complex which forms itself out of many details, like form, proportion, ductus, rhythm etc. If everything harmonizes, the total result will be more than the

ABCDEFGHIJKLMNOPQRSTUVWXYZ&
abcdefghijklmnopqrstuvwxyz   *1234567890$*

10 point Spartan Heavy Italic (Linotype)

The basic character in a type design is determined by the uniform design characteristics of all letters in the alphabet. However, this alone does not determine the standard of the type face and the quality of composition set with it. The appearance is something complex which

ABCDEFGHIJKLMNOPQRSTUVWXYZ&
abcdefghijklmnopqrstuvwxyz   *1234567890$*

12 point Spartan Heavy Italic (Linotype)

The basic character in a type design is determined by the uniform design characteristics of all letters in the alphabet. However, this alone does not determine the standard of the type face and the

ABCDEFGHIJKLMNOPQRSTUVWXYZ&
abcdefghijklmnopqrstuvwxyz   *1234567890$*

14 point Spartan Heavy Italic (Linotype)

The basic character in a type design is determined by the uniform design characteristics of all letters in the alphabet. However, this

ABCDEFGHIJKLMNOPQRSTUVWXYZ&
abcdefghijklmnopqrstuvwxyz 1234567890$

14 point Spartan Heavy Italic (Foundry)

ABCDEFGHIJKLMNOPQRSTUVWXYZ&
abcdefghijklmnopqrstuvwxyz
1234567890$

(Continued on Page 439)

(Continued from Page 438)

18 point Spartan Heavy Italic (Foundry)

ABCDEFGHIJKLMNOPQRSTUVWXYZ&
abcdefghijklmnopqrstuvwxyz
1234567890$

24 point Spartan Heavy Italic (Foundry)

ABCDEFGHIJKLMNOPQRSTUVWXYZ&
abcdefghijklmnopqrstuvwxyz
1234567890$

36 point Spartan Heavy Italic (Foundry)

ABCDEFGHIJKLMNOPQRSTUV
WXYZ&
abcdefghijklmnopqrstuvwxyz
1234567890$

60 point Spartan Heavy Italic (Foundry)

ABCDEFGHIJKLMN
OPQRSTUVWXYZ&
abcdefghijklmnopqr
stuvwxyz
1234567890$

Spartan Medium

6 point Spartan Medium (Linotype)
The basic character in a type design is determined by the uniform design characteristics of all letters in the alphabet. However, this alone does not determine the type face and the quality of composition set with it. The appearance is something complex which forms itself out of many details, like form, proportion, ductus, rhythm etc. If everything harmonizes, the total result will be more than the sum of its components. The only reliable basis for the design in a type is a positive feeling for form and style. The basic character in a type design is determined by the uniform design charac

ABCDEFGHIJKLMNOPQRSTUVWXYZ&
abcdefghijklmnopqrstuvwxyz 1234567890$

---

8 point Spartan Medium (Linotype)
The basic character in a type design is determined by the uniform design characteristics of all letters in the alphabet. However, this alone does not determine the standard of the type face and the quality of composition set with it. The appearance is something complex which forms itself out of many details, like form, proportion, ductus, rhythm etc. If everything harmonizes, the total result will be more than the sum of its components.

ABCDEFGHIJKLMNOPQRSTUVWXYZ&
abcdefghijklmnopqrstuvwxyz 1234567890$

---

9 point Spartan Medium (Linotype)
The basic character in a type design is determined by the uniform design characteristics of all letters in the alphabet. However, this alone does not determine the standard of the type face and the quality of composition set with it. The appearance is something complex which forms itself out of many details, like form, proportion,

ABCDEFGHIJKLMNOPQRSTUVWXYZ&
abcdefghijklmnopqrstuvwxyz 1234567890$

---

10 point Spartan Medium (Linotype)
The basic character in a type design is determined by the uniform design characteristics of all letters in the alphabet. However, this alone does not determine the standard of the type face and the quality of composition set with it. The appearance is something complex which forms itself out of

ABCDEFGHIJKLMNOPQRSTUVWXYZ&
abcdefghijklmnopqrstuvwxyz 1234567890$

---

11 point Spartan Medium (Linotype)
The basic character in a type design is determined by the uniform design characteristics of all letters in the alphabet. However, this alone does not determine the standard of the type face and the quality of composition

ABCDEFGHIJKLMNOPQRSTUVWXYZ&
abcdefghijklmnopqrstuvwxyz 1234567890$

---

12 point Spartan Medium (Linotype)
The basic character in a type design is determined by the uniform design characteristics of all letters in the alphabet. However, this alone does not determine the standard of the type face and the quality of

ABCDEFGHIJKLMNOPQRSTUVWXYZ&
abcdefghijklmnopqrstuvwxyz 1234567890$

---

14 point Spartan Medium (Linotype)
The basic character in a type design is deter mined by the uniform design characterstics of all letters in the alphabet. However, this alone

ABCDEFGHIJKLMNOPQRSTUVWXYZ&
abcdefghijklmnopqrstuvwxyz 1234567890$

---

18 point Spartan Medium (Foundry)
ABCDEFGHIJKLMNOPQRSTUV
WXYZ&
abcdefghijklmnopqrstuvwxyz
1234567890$

---

24 point Spartan Medium (Foundry)
ABCDEFGHIJKLMNOPQRSTUVWXYZ&
abcdefghijklmnopqrstuvwxyz
1234567890$

---

30 point Spartan Medium (Foundry)
ABCDEFGHIJKLMNOPQRSTUVWXYZ&
abcdefghijklmnopqrstuvwxyz
1234567890$

(Continued on Page 441)

36 point Spartan Medium (Foundry)

ABCDEFGHIJKLMNOPQRSTUV
WXYZ&
abcdefghijklmnopqrstuvwxyz
1234567890$

48 point Spartan Medium (Foundry)

ABCDEFGHIJKLMNOPQRS
TUVWXYZ&
abcdefghijklmnopqrstuv
wxyz
1234567890$

(Continued on Page 442)

(Continued from Page 441)

72 point Spartan Medium (Foundry)

ABCDEFGHIJKLM
NOPQRSTUV
WXYZ&
abcdefghijklmnop
qrstuvwxyz
1234567890$

(Continued on Page 443)

84 point Spartan Medium (Foundry)

ABCDEFGHIJK
LMNOPQRST
UVWXYZ&
abcdefghijklmn
opqrstuvwxyz
1234567890$

Spartan Medium Condensed

24 point Spartan Medium Condensed (Foundry)

ABCDEFGHIJKLMNOPQRSTUVWXYZ&

abcdefghijklmnopqrstuvwxyz

1234567890$

Spartan Medium Italic

6 point Spartan Medium Italic (Linotype)

The basic character in a type design is determined by the uniform design characteristics of all letters in the alphabet. However, this alone does not determine the standard of the type face and the quality of composition set with it. The appearance is something complex which forms itself out of many details, like form, proportion, ductus, rhythm etc. If everything harmonizes, the total result will be more than the sum of its components. The only reliable basis for the design in a type is a positive feeling for form and style. The basic character in a type design is determined by the uniform design charac

ABCDEFGHIJKLMNOPQRSTUVWXYZ&
abcdefghijklmnopqrstuvwxyz   1234567890$

8 point Spartan Medium Italic (Linotype)

The basic character in a type design is determined by the uniform design characteristics of all letters in the alphabet. However, this alone does not determine the standard of the type face and the quality of composition set with it. The appearance is something complex which forms itself out of many details, like form, proportion, ductus, rhythm etc. If everything harmonizes, the total result will be more than the sum of its components.

ABCDEFGHIJKLMNOPQRSTUVWXYZ&
abcdefghijklmnopqrstuvwxyz   1234567890$

9 point Spartan Medium Italic (Linotype)

The basic character in a type design is determined by the uniform design characteristics of all letters in the alphabet. However, this alone does not determine the standard of the type face and the quality of composition set with it. The appearance is something complex which forms itself out of many details, like form, proportion,

ABCDEFGHIJKLMNOPQRSTUVWXYZ&
abcdefghijklmnopqrstuvwxyz   1234567890$

10 point Spartan Medium Italic (Linotype)

The basic character in a type design is determined by the uniform design characteristics of all letters in the alphabet. However, this alone does not determine the standard of the type face and the quality of composition set with it. The appearance is something complex which forms itself out of

ABCDEFGHIJKLMNOPQRSTUVWXYZ&
abcdefghijklmnopqrstuvwxyz   1234567890$

11 point Spartan Medium Italic (Linotype)

The basic character in a type design is determined by the uniform design characteristics of all letters in the alphabet. However, this alone does not determine the standard of the type face and the quality of composition

ABCDEFGHIJKLMNOPQRSTUVWXYZ&
abcdefghijklmnopqrstuvwxyz   1234567890$

12 point Spartan Medium Italic (Linotype)

The basic character in a type design is determined by the uniform design characteristics of all letters in the alphabet. However, this alone does not determine the standard of the type face and the quality of

ABCDEFGHIJKLMNOPQRSTUVWXYZ&
abcdefghijklmnopqrstuvwxyz   1234567890$

14 point Spartan Medium Italic (Linotype)

The basic character in a type design is deter mined by the uniform design characterstics of all letters in the alphabet. However, this alone

ABCDEFGHIJKLMNOPQRSTUVWXYZ&
abcdefghijklmnopqrstuvwxyz   1234567890$

18 point Spartan Medium Italic (Foundry)

ABCDEFGHIJKLMNOPQRSTUV
WXYZ&
abcdefghijklmnopqrstuvwxyz
1234567890$

24 point Spartan Medium Italic (Foundry)

ABCDEFGHIJKLMNOPQRSTUVWXYZ&
abcdefghijklmnopqrstuvwxyz
1234567890$

30 point Spartan Medium Italic (Foundry)

ABCDEFGHIJKLMNOPQRSTUVWXYZ&
abcdefghijklmnopqrstuvwxyz
1234567890$

444

Spire

24 point Spire, Cap font (Foundry)

ABCDEFGHIJKLMNOPQRSTUVWXYZ&
1234567890$

48 point Spire, Cap font (Foundry)

ABCDEFGHIJKLMNOPQRSTUVWXYZ&
1234567890$

72 point Spire, Cap font (Foundry)

ABCDEFGHIJKLMNOPQRSTUV
WXYZ&
1234567890$

Standard

(Continued on Page 447)

6 point Standard (Foundry)
ABCDEFGHIJKLMNOPQRSTUVWXYZ&
abcdefghijklmnopqrstuvwxyz
1234567890$

8 point Standard (Foundry)
ABCDEFGHIJKLMNOPQRSTUVWXYZ&
abcdefghijklmnopqrstuvwxyz
1234567890$

10 point Standard (Foundry)
ABCDEFGHIJKLMNOPQRSTUVWXYZ&
abcdefghijklmnopqrstuvwxyz
1234567890$

12 point Standard (Foundry)
ABCDEFGHIJKLMNOPQRSTUVWXYZ&
abcdefghijklmnopqrstuvwxyz
1234567890$

14 point Standard (Foundry)
ABCDEFGHIJKLMNOPQRSTUVWXYZ&
abcdefghijklmnopqrstuvwxyz
1234567890$

18 point Standard (Foundry)
ABCDEFGHIJKLMNOPQRSTUVWXYZ&
abcdefghijklmnopqrstuvwxyz
1234567890$

24 point Standard Small (Foundry)
ABCDEFGHIJKLMNOPQRSTUVWXYZ&
abcdefghijklmnopqrstuvwxyz
1234567890$

24 point Standard Large (Foundry)
ABCDEFGHIJKLMNOPQRSTUVWXYZ&
abcdefghijklmnopqrstuvwxyz
1234567890$

30 point Standard (Foundry)
ABCDEFGHIJKLMNOPQRSTUVWXYZ&
abcdefghijklmnopqrstuvwxyz
1234567890$

36 point Standard (Foundry)

ABCDEFGHIJKLMNOPQRST
UVWXYZ&
abcdefghijklmnopqrstuvwxyz
1234567890$

48 point Standard (Foundry)

ABCDEFGHIJKLMNOP
QRSTUVWXYZ&
abcdefghijklmnopqrstuv
wxyz
1234567890$

Standard Italic

14 point Standard Italic (Foundry)

ABCDEFGHIJKLMNOPQRSTUVWXYZ&
abcdefghijklmnopqrstuvwxyz
_1234567890$_

Standard Bold

12 point Standard Bold (Foundry)
ABCDEFGHIJKLMNOPQRSTUVWXYZ&
abcdefghijklmnopqrstuvwxyz
1234567890$

14 point Standard Bold (Foundry)
ABCDEFGHIJKLMNOPQRSTUV
WXYZ&
abcdefghijklmnopqrstuvwxyz
1234567890$

18 point Standard Bold (Foundry)
ABCDEFGHIJKLMNOPQRSTUVWXYZ&
abcdefghijklmnopqrstuvwxyz
1234567890$

24 point Standard Bold Small (Foundry)
ABCDEFGHIJKLMNOPQRSTUVWXYZ&
abcdefghijklmnopqrstuvwxyz
1234567890$

24 point Standard Bold Large (Foundry)
ABCDEFGHIJKLMNOPQRSTUVWXYZ&
abcdefghijklmnopqrstuvwxyz
1234567890$

30 point Standard Bold (Foundry)
ABCDEFGHIJKLMNOPQRSTUV
WXYZ&
abcdefghijklmnopqrstuvwxyz
1234567890$

Standard Bold Condensed

12 point Standard Bold Condensed (Foundry)
ABCDEFGHIJKLMNOPQRSTUVWXYZ&
abcdefghijklmnopqrstuvwxyz
1234567890$

14 point Standard Bold Condensed (Foundry)
ABCDEFGHIJKLMNOPQRSTUVWXYZ&
abcdefghijklmnopqrstuvwxyz
1234567890$

18 point Standard Bold Condensed (Foundry)
ABCDEFGHIJKLMNOPQRSTUVWXYZ&
abcdefghijklmnopqrstuvwxyz
1234567890$

24 point Standard Bold Condensed Small (Foundry)
ABCDEFGHIJKLMNOPQRSTUVWXYZ&
abcdefghijklmnopqrstuvwxyz
1234567890$

24 point Standard Bold Condensed Large (Foundry)
ABCDEFGHIJKLMNOPQRSTUVWXYZ&
abcdefghijklmnopqrstuvwxyz
1234567890$

30 point Standard Bold Condensed (Foundry)
ABCDEFGHIJKLMNOPQRSTUVWXYZ&
abcdefghijklmnopqrstuvwxyz
1234567890$

42 point Standard Bold Condensed (Foundry)
ABCDEFGHIJKLMNOPQRSTUVWXYZ&
abcdefghijklmnopqrstuvwxyz
1234567890$

(Continued on Page 450)

(Continued from Page 449)

60 point Standard Bold Condensed (Foundry)

ABCDEFGHIJKLMNOPQRSTUV
WXYZ&
abcdefghijklmnopqrstuvwxyz
1234567890$

72 point Standard Bold Condensed (Foundry)

ABCDEFGHIJKLMNOPQ
RSTUVWXYZ&
abcdefghijklmnopqrstuv
wxyz
1234567890$

Standard Condensed

14 point Standard Condensed (Foundry)
ABCDEFGHIJKLMNOPQRSTUVWXYZ&
abcdefghijklmnopqrstuvwxyz
1234567890$

18 point Standard Condensed (Foundry)
ABCDEFGHIJKLMNOPQRSTUVWXYZ&
abcdefghijklmnopqrstuvwxyz
1234567890$

24 point Standard Condensed Small (Foundry)
ABCDEFGHIJKLMNOPQRSTUVWXYZ&
abcdefghijklmnopqrstuvwxyz
1234567890$

24 point Standard Condensed Large (Foundry)
ABCDEFGHIJKLMNOPQRSTUVWXYZ&
abcdefghijklmnopqrstuvwxyz
1234567890$

60 point Standard Condensed (Foundry)
ABCDEFGHIJKLMNOPQRSTUV
WXYZ&
abcdefghijklmnopqrstuvwxyz
1234567890$

Standard Extra-Bold Condensed

18 point Standard Extra-Bold Condensed (Foundry)

ABCDEFGHIJKLMNOPQRSTUVWXYZ&
abcdefghijklmnopqrstuvwxyz
1234567890$

24 point Standard Extra-Bold Condensed Small (Foundry)

ABCDEFGHIJKLMNOPQRSTUVWXYZ&
abcdefghijklmnopqrstuvwxyz
1234567890$

24 point Standard Extra-Bold Condensed Large (Foundry)

ABCDEFGHIJKLMNOPQRSTUVWXYZ&
abcdefghijklmnopqrstuvwxyz
1234567890$

30 point Standard Extra-Bold Condensed (Foundry)

ABCDEFGHIJKLMNOPQRSTUVWXYZ&
abcdefghijklmnopqrstuvwxyz
1234567890$

42 point Standard Extra-Bold Condensed (Foundry)

ABCDEFGHIJKLMNOPQRSTUVWXYZ&
abcdefghijklmnopqrstuvwxyz
1234567890$

(Continued on Page 453)

48 point Standard Extra-Bold Condensed (Foundry)

ABCDEFGHIJKLMNOPQRSTUV
WXYZ&
abcdefghijklmnopqrstuv
wxyz
1234567890$

60 point Standard Extra-Bold Condensed (Foundry)

ABCDEFGHIJKLMNOPQ
RSTUVWXYZ&
abcdefghijklmnopqrst
uvwxyz
1234567890$

Standard Extra Bold Extended

24 point Standard Extra Bold Extended Small (Foundry)

ABCDEFGHIJKLMNOPQRSTUVWXYZ&
abcdefghijklmnopqrstuvwxyz
1234567890$

Standard Light Condensed

10 point Standard Light Condensed (Foundry)

ABCDEFGHIJKLMNOPQRSTUVWXYZ&
abcdefghijklmnopqrstuvwxyz
1234567890$

18 point Standard Light Condensed (Foundry)

ABCDEFGHIJKLMNOPQRSTUVWXYZ&
abcdefghijklmnopqrstuvwxyz
1234567890$

Standard Light Extended

10 point Standard Light Extended (Foundry)

ABCDEFGHIJKLMNOPQRSTUVWXYZ&
abcdefghijklmnopqrstuvwxyz
1234567890$

42 point Standard Light Extended (Foundry)

ABCDEFGHIJKLMNOP
QRSTUVWXYZ&
abcdefghijklmnopqrstuv
wxyz
1234567890$

Standard Medium

6 point Standard Medium (Foundry)
ABCDEFGHIJKLMNOPQRSTUVWXYZ&
abcdefghijklmnopqrstuvwxyz
1234567890$

8 point Standard Medium (Foundry)
ABCDEFGHIJKLMNOPQRSTUVWXYZ&
abcdefghijklmnopqrstuvwxyz
1234567890$

10 point Standard Medium (Foundry)
ABCDEFGHIJKLMNOPQRSTUVWXYZ&
abcdefghijklmnopqrstuvwxyz
1234567890$

12 point Standard Medium (Foundry)
ABCDEFGHIJKLMNOPQRSTUVWXYZ&
abcdefghijklmnopqrstuvwxyz
1234567890$

14 point Standard Medium (Foundry)
ABCDEFGHIJKLMNOPQRSTUVWXYZ&
abcdefghijklmnopqrstuvwxyz
1234567890$

18 point Standard Medium (Foundry)
ABCDEFGHIJKLMNOPQRSTUVWXYZ&
abcdefghijklmnopqrstuvwxyz
1234567890$

24 Standard Medium Small (Foundry)
ABCDEFGHIJKLMNOPQRSTUVWXYZ&
abcdefghijklmnopqrstuvwxyz
1234567890$

24 point Standard Medium Large (Foundry)
ABCDEFGHIJKLMNOPQRSTUVWXYZ&
abcdefghijklmnopqrstuvwxyz
1234567890$

30 point Standard Medium (Foundry)
ABCDEFGHIJKLMNOPQRSTUV
WXYZ&
abcdefghijklmnopqrstuvwxyz
1234567890$

(Continued on Page 456)

(Continued from Page 455)

42 point Standard Medium (Foundry)

ABCDEFGHIJKLMNOPQRST
UVWXYZ&
abcdefghijklmnopqrstuv
wxyz
1234567890$

60 point Standard Medium (Foundry)

ABCDEFGHIJKLMNO
PQRSTUVWXYZ&
abcdefghijklmnopqr
stuvwxyz
1234567890$

(Continued on Page 457)

72 point Standard Medium (Foundry)

ABCDEFGHIJKL
MNOPQRSTUV
WXYZ&
abcdefghijklmno
pqrstuvwxyz
1234567890$

Standard Medium Condensed

18 point Standard Medium Condensed (Foundry)

ABCDEFGHIJKLMNOPQRSTUVWXYZ&
abcdefghijklmnopqrstuvwxyz
1234567890$

24 point Standard Medium Condensed Small (Foundry)

ABCDEFGHIJKLMNOPQRSTUVWXYZ&
abcdefghijklmnopqrstuvwxyz
1234567890$

42 point Standard Medium Condensed (Foundry)

ABCDEFGHIJKLMNOPQRSTUVWXYZ&
abcdefghijklmnopqrstuvwxyz
1234567890$

60 point Standard Medium Condensed (Foundry)

ABCDEFGHIJKLMNOPQRSTUVWXYZ&
abcdefghijklmnopqrstuvwxyz
1234567890$

(Continued on Page 459)

72 point Standard Medium Condensed (Foundry)

ABCDEFGHIJKLMNOPQRSTUV
WXYZ&
abcdefghijklmnopqrstuvwxyz
1234567890$

Standard Medium Extended

42 point Standard Medium Extended (Foundry)

ABCDEFGHIJKLMNOP
QRSTUVWXYZ&
abcdefghijklmnopqrs
tuvwxyz
1234567890$

Standard Medium Italic

12 point Standard Medium Italic (Foundry)
ABCDEFGHIJKLMNOPQRSTUVWXYZ&
abcdefghijklmnopqrstuvwxyz
1234567890$

14 point Standard Medium Italic (Foundry)
ABCDEFGHIJKLMNOPQRSTUV
WXYZ&
abcdefghijklmnopqrstuvwxyz
1234567890$

Stencil

18 point Stencil, Cap font (Foundry)
ABCDEFGHIJKLMNOPQRSTUVWXYZ&
1234567890$

24 point Stencil, Cap font (Foundry)
ABCDEFGHIJKLMNOPQRSTUV
WXYZ&
1234567890$

30 point Stencil, Cap font (Foundry)
ABCDEFGHIJKLMNOPQRST
UVWXYZ&
1234567890$

36 point Stencil, Cap font (Foundry)
ABCDEFGHIJKLMN
OPQRSTUVWXYZ&
1234567890$

Stradivarius

18 point Stradivarius (Foundry)

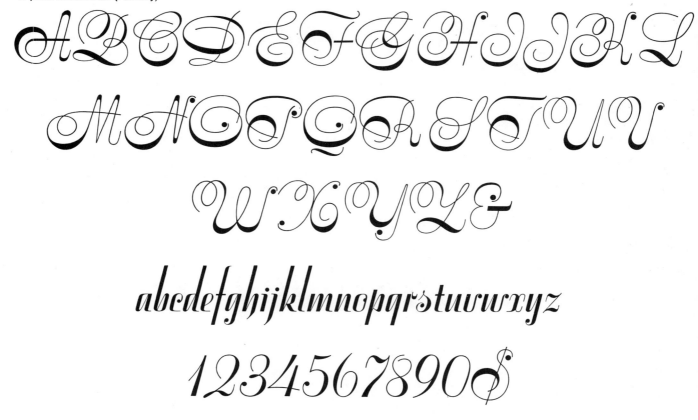

ABCDEFGHIJKLMNOPQRSTUVWXYZ&

abcdefghijklmnopqrstuvwxyz

1234567890$

48 point Stradivarius (Foundry)

ABCDEFGHIJKL
MNOPQRSTUV
WXYZ&

abcdefghijklmnopqrstuvwxyz

1234567890$

(Continued on Page 462)

(Continued from Page 461)

84 point Stradivarius (Foundry)

Studio

ABCDEFGHIJKLMNOPQRSTUVWXYZ&
abcdefghijklmnopqrstuvwxyz
1234567890$

ABCDEFGHIJKLMNOPQRSTUVWXYZ&
abcdefghijklmnopqrstuvwxyz
1234567890$

ABCDEFGHIJKLMNOPQRSTUVWXYZ&
abcdefghijklmnopqrstuvwxyz
1234567890$

ABCDEFGHIJKLMNOPQRSTUVWXYZ&
abcdefghijklmnopqrstuvwxyz
1234567890$

ABCDEFGHIJKLMNOPQRSTUVWXYZ&
abcdefghijklmnopqrstuvwxyz
1234567890$

ABCDEFGHIJKLMNOPQRSTUVWXYZ&
abcdefghijklmnopqrstuvwxyz
1234567890$

ABCDEFGHIJKLMNOPQRSTUVWXYZ&
abcdefghijklmnopqrstuvwxyz
1234567890$

ABCDEFGHIJKLMNOPQRSTUV
WXYZ&
abcdefghijklmnopqrstuvwxyz
1234567890$

(Continued on Page 464)

48 point Studio (Foundry)

ABCDEFGHIJKLMNOPQ
RSTUVWXYZ&
abcdefghijklmnopqrstuv
wxyz
1234567890$

Studio Bold

18 point Studio Bold (Foundry)

ABCDEFGHIJKLMNOPQRSTUVWXYZ&
abcdefghijklmnopqrstuvwxyz
1234567890$

30 point Studio Bold (Foundry)

ABCDEFGHIJKLMNOPQRSTUVWXYZ&
abcdefghijklmnopqrstuvwxyz
1234567890$

Stymie Black

24 point Stymie Black (Foundry)

ABCDEFGHIJKLMNOPQRSTUVWXYZ&
abcdefghijklmnopqrstuvwxyz
1234567890$

36 point Stymie Black (Foundry)

ABCDEFGHIJKLMNOPQRST
UVWXYZ&
abcdefghijklmnopqrstuvwxyz
1234567890$

Stymie Bold

14 point Stymie Bold, Caps only (Foundry)

ABCDEFGHIJKLMNOPQRSTUVWXYZ&

18 point Stymie Bold (Foundry)

ABCDEFGHIJKLMNOPQRSTUVWXYZ&
abcdefghijklmnopqrstuvwxyz
1234567890$

24 point Stymie Bold (Foundry)

ABCDEFGHIJKLMNOPQRSTUVWXYZ&
abcdefghijklmnopqrstuvwxyz
1234567890$

(Continued on Page 466)

(Continued from Page 465)

30 point Stymie Bold (Foundry)

ABCDEFGHIJKLMNOPQRSTUV
WXYZ&
abcdefghijklmnopqrstuvwxyz
1234567890$

36 point Stymie Bold (Foundry)

ABCDEFGHIJKLMNOPQRST
UVWXYZ&
abcdefghijklmnopqrstuvwxyz
1234567890$

48 point Stymie Bold (Foundry)

ABCDEFGHIJKLMN
OPQRSTUVWXYZ
abcdefghijklmnopqrst
uvwxyz&
1234567890$

(Continued on Page 467)

60 point Stymie Bold (Foundry)

ABCDEFGHIJK
LMNOPQRSTU
VWXYZ&
abcdefghijklmno
pqrstuvwxyz
1234567890$

Stymie Bold Condensed

Stymie Bold Extra Condensed

18 point Stymie Bold Extra Condensed (Foundry)
ABCDEFGHIJKLMNOPQRSTUVWXYZ&
abcdefghijklmnopqrstuvwxyz
1234567890$

Stymie Bold Italic

18 point Stymie Bold Italic (Foundry)
ABCDEFGHIJKLMNOPQRSTUVWXYZ&
abcdefghijklmnopqrstuvwxyz
1234567890$

Stymie Extra Bold

18 point Stymie Extra Bold (Foundry)
ABCDEFGHIJKLMNOPQRSTUVWXYZ&
abcdefghijklmnopqrstuvwxyz
1234567890$

24 point Stymie Extra Bold (Foundry)
ABCDEFGHIJKLMNOPQRSTUVWXYZ&
abcdefghijklmnopqrstuvwxyz
1234567890$

Stymie Extra Bold Italic

24 point Stymie Extra Bold Italic (Foundry)
ABCDEFGHIJKLMNOPQRSTUVWXYZ&
abcdefghijklmnopqrstuvwxyz
1234567890$

V & M TYPOGRAPHICAL, INCORPORATED

Stymie Light

14 point Stymie Light (Foundry)

ABCDEFGHIJKLMNOPQRSTUVWXYZ&
abcdefghijklmnopqrstuvwxyz 1234567890$

18 point Stymie Light (Foundry)

ABCDEFGHIJKLMNOPQRSTUVWXYZ&
abcdefghijklmnopqrstuvwxyz 1234567890$

24 point Stymie Light (Foundry)

ABCDEFGHIJKLMNOPQRSTUVWXYZ&
abcdefghijklmnopqrstuvwxyz 1234567890$

48 point Stymie Light (Foundry)

ABCDEFGHIJKLMNOP
QRSTUVWXYZ&
abcdefghijklmnopqrstuv
wxyz 1234567890$

Stymie Light Italic

14 point Stymie Light Italic (Foundry)

ABCDEFGHIJKLMNOPQRSTUVWXYZ&
abcdefghijklmnopqrstuvwxyz
1234567890$

24 point Stymie Light Italic (Foundry)

ABCDEFGHIJKLMNOPQRSTUVWXYZ&
abcdefghijklmnopqrstuvwxyz
1234567890$

Stymie Medium

14 point Stymie Medium (Foundry)

ABCDEFGHIJKLMNOPQRSTUVWXYZ&
abcdefghijklmnopqrstuvwxyz
1234567890$

24 point Stymie Medium (Foundry)

ABCDEFGHIJKLMNOPQRSTUVWXYZ&
abcdefghijklmnopqrstuvwxyz
1234567890$

30 point Stymie Medium (Foundry)

ABCDEFGHIJKLMNOPQRSTUVWXYZ
abcdefghijklmnopqrstuvwxyz&
1234567890$

36 point Stymie Medium (Foundry)

ABCDEFGHIJKLMNOPQRSTUV
WXYZ&
abcdefghijklmnopqrstuvwxyz
1234567890$

Stymie Medium Condensed

30 point Stymie Medium Condensed (Foundry)

ABCDEFGHIJKLMNOPQRSTUVWXYZ&
abcdefghijklmnopqrstuvwxyz
1234567890$

Stymie Open

ABCDEFGHIJKLMNOPQRSTUVWXYZ&
1234567890$

ABCDEFGHIJKLMNOPQRSTUV
WXYZ&
1234567890$

ABCDEFGHIJKLMNOPQRST
UVWXYZ&
1234567890$

ABCDEFGHIJKLMNOP
QRSTUVWXYZ&
1234567890$

ABCDEFGHIJKL
MNOPQRSTUV
WXYZ&
1234567890$

Tempo Bold

18 point Tempo Bold (Ludlow)

ABCDEFGHIJKLMNOPQRSTUVWXYZ&
abcdefghijklmnopqrstuvwxyz
1234567890$

24 point Tempo Bold (Ludlow)

ABCDEFGHIJKLMNOPQRSTUVWXYZ&
abcdefghijklmnopqrstuvwxyz
1234567890$

30 point Tempo Bold (Ludlow)

ABCDEFGHIJKLMNOPQRSTUVWXYZ&
abcdefghijklmnopqrstuvwxyz
1234567890$

36 point Tempo Bold (Ludlow)

ABCDEFGHIJKLMNOPQRST
UVWXYZ&
abcdefghijklmnopqrstuvwxyz
1234567890$

48 point Tempo Bold (Ludlow)

ABCDEFGHIJKLMNOPQ
RSTUVWXYZ&
abcdefghijklmnopqrstuv
wxyz 1234567890$

18 point Tempo Bold Italic (Ludlow)

ABCDEFGHIJKLMNOPQRSTUVWXYZ&
abcdefghijklmnopqrstuvwxyz
1234567890$

24 point Tempo Bold Italic (Ludlow)

ABCDEFGHIJKLMNOPQRSTUVWXYZ&
abcdefghijklmnopqrstuvwxyz
1234567890$

30 point Tempo Bold Italic (Ludlow)

ABCDEFGHIJKLMNOPQRSTUVWXYZ&
abcdefghijklmnopqrstuvwxyz
1234567890$

36 point Tempo Bold Italic (Ludlow)

ABCDEFGHIJKLMNOPQRSTUV
WXYZ&
abcdefghijklmnopqrstuvwxyz
1234567890$

48 point Tempo Bold Italic (Ludlow)

ABCDEFGHIJKLMNOPQ
RSTUVWXYZ&
abcdefghijklmnopqrstuv
wxyz 1234567890$

Tempo Medium

8 point Tempo Medium (Ludlow)
ABCDEFGHIJKLMNOPQRSTUVWXYZ&
abcdefghijklmnopqrstuvwxyz 1234567890$

14 point Tempo Medium (Ludlow)
ABCDEFGHIJKLMNOPQRSTUVWXYZ&
abcdefghijklmnopqrstuvwxyz 1234567890$

10 point Tempo Medium (Ludlow)
ABCDEFGHIJKLMNOPQRSTUVWXYZ&
abcdefghijklmnopqrstuvwxyz 1234567890$

18 point Tempo Medium (Ludlow)
ABCDEFGHIJKLMNOPQRSTUVWXYZ
abcdefghijklmnopqrstuvwxyz&
1234567890$

12 point Tempo Medium (Ludlow)
ABCDEFGHIJKLMNOPQRSTUVWXYZ&
abcdefghijklmnopqrstuvwxyz 1234567890$

24 point Tempo Medium (Ludlow)
ABCDEFGHIJKLMNOPQRSTUVWXYZ&
abcdefghijklmnopqrstuvwxyz
1234567890$

Tempo Medium Italic

10 point Tempo Medium Italic (Ludlow)
ABCDEFGHIJKLMNOPQRSTUVWXYZ&
abcdefghijklmnopqrstuvwxyz
1234567890$

Tempo Heavy Condensed

48 point Tempo Heavy Condensed (Ludlow)
ABCDEFGHIJKLMNOPQRSTUV
WXYZ&
abcdefghijklmnopqrstuvwxyz
1234567890$

Tempo Heavy

8 point Tempo Heavy (Ludlow)

ABCDEFGHIJKLMNOPQRSTUVWXYZ&
abcdefghijklmnopqrstuvwxyz
1234567890$

10 point Tempo Heavy (Ludlow)

ABCDEFGHIJKLMNOPQRSTUVWXYZ&
abcdefghijklmnopqrstuvwxyz
1234567890$

12 point Tempo Heavy (Ludlow)

ABCDEFGHIJKLMNOPQRSTUVWXYZ&
abcdefghijklmnopqrstuvwxyz
1234567890$

18 point Tempo Heavy (Ludlow)

ABCDEFGHIJKLMNOPQRSTUVWXYZ&
abcdefghijklmnopqrstuvwxyz
1234567890$

24 point Tempo Heavy (Ludlow)

ABCDEFGHIJKLMNOPQRSTUVWXYZ&
abcdefghijklmnopqrstuvwxyz
1234567890$

36 point Tempo Heavy (Ludlow)

ABCDEFGHIJKLMNOPQRST
UVWXYZ&
abcdefghijklmnopqrstuvwxyz
1234567890$

Thorne Shaded

ABCDEFGHIJKLMNOPQRSTUV
WXYZ&
1234567890$

ABCDEFGHIJKLMNOPQRS
TUVWXYZ&
1234567890$

ABCDEFGHIJKLMN
OPQRSTUVWXYZ&
1234567890$

ABCDEFGHIJ
KLMNOPQRST
UVWXYZ&
1234567890$

Times Extended Titling

14 point Times Extended Titling, Cap font (Foundry)
ABCDEFGHIJKLMNOPQRSTUVWXYZ&
1234567890$

18 point Times Extended Titling, Cap font (Foundry)
ABCDEFGHIJKLMNOPQRSTUVWXYZ&
1234567890$

24 point Times Extended Titling, Cap font (Foundry)
ABCDEFGHIJKLMNOPQRSTUVWXYZ&
1234567890$

30 point Times Extended Titling, Cap font (Foundry)
ABCDEFGHIJKLMNOPQRSTUV
WXYZ&
1234567890$

36 point Times Extended Titling, Cap font (Foundry)
ABCDEFGHIJKLMNOPQRS
TUVWXYZ&
1234567890$

48 point Times Extended Titling, Cap font (Foundry)
ABCDEFGHIJKLMN
OPQRSTUVWXYZ&
1234567890$

(Continued on Page 479)

(Continued from Page 478)

60 point Times Extended Titling, Cap font (Foundry)

ABCDEFGHIJK
LMNOPQRSTUV
WXYZ&
1234567890$

72 point Times Extended Titling, Cap font (Foundry)

ABCDEFGHIJ
KLMNOPQRS
TUVWXYZ&
1234567890$

14 point Times Heavy Titling, Cap font (Foundry)

ABCDEFGHIJKLMNOPQRSTUVWXYZ&
1234567890$

18 point Times Heavy Titling, Cap font (Foundry)

ABCDEFGHIJKLMNOPQRSTUVWXYZ&
1234567890$

24 point Times Heavy Titling, Cap font (Foundry)

ABCDEFGHIJKLMNOPQRSTUVWXYZ&
1234567890$

30 point Times Heavy Titling, Cap font (Foundry)

ABCDEFGHIJKLMNOPQRSTUVWXYZ&
1234567890$

36 point Times Heavy Titling, Cap font (Foundry)

ABCDEFGHIJKLMNOPQRSTUV
WXYZ&
1234567890$

48 point Times Heavy Titling, Cap font (Foundry)

ABCDEFGHIJKLMNOPQ
RSTUVWXYZ&
1234567890$

(Continued on Page 481)

(Continued from Page 480)

60 point Times Heavy Titling, Cap font (Foundry)

ABCDEFGHIJKLM
NOPQRSTUV
WXYZ&
1234567890$

72 point Times Heavy Titling, Cap font (Foundry)

ABCDEFGHIJK
LMNOPQRSTU
VWXYZ&
1234567890$

Times Roman

6 point Times Roman (Linotype)
The basic character in a type design is determined by the uniform design characteristics of all letters in the alphabet. However, this alone does not determine the standard of the type face and the quality of composition set with it. The appearance is something complex which forms itself out of many details, like form, proportion, ductus, rhythm etc. If everything har monizes, the total result will be more than the sum of its components. The only reliable basis for the design in a type is a positive feeling for form

ABCDEFGHIJKLMNOPQRSTUVWXYZ&
abcdefghijklmnopqrstuvwxyz 1234567890$
ABCDEFGHIJKLMNOPQRSTUVWXYZ

7 point Times Roman (Linotype)
The basic character in a type design is determined by the uniform de sign characteristics of all letters in the alphabet. However, this alone does not determine the standard of the type face and the quality of composition set with it. The appearance is something complex which forms itself out of many details, like form, proportion, ductus, rhythm etc. If everything harmonizes, the total result will be more than the

ABCDEFGHIJKLMNOPQRSTUVWXYZ&
abcdefghijklmnopqrstuvwxyz 1234567890$
ABCDEFGHIJKLMNOPQRSTUVWXYZ

8 point Times Roman (Linotype)
The basic character in a type design is determined by the uniform design characteristics of all letters in the alphabet. However, this alone does not determine the standard of the type face and the quality of composition set with it. The appearance is something complex which forms itself out of many details, like form, propor

ABCDEFGHIJKLMNOPQRSTUVWXYZ&
abcdefghijklmnopqrstuvwxyz 1234567890$
ABCDEFGHIJKLMNOPQRSTUVWXYZ

9 point Times Roman (Linotype)
The basic character in a type design is determined by the uni form design characteristics of all letters in the alphabet. How ever, this alone does not determine the standard of the type face and the quality of composition set with it. The appear

ABCDEFGHIJKLMNOPQRSTUVWXYZ&
abcdefghijklmnopqrstuvwxyz 1234567890$
ABCDEFGHIJKLMNOPQRSTUVWXYZ

10 point Times Roman (Linotype)
The basic character in a type design is determined by the uniform design characteristics of all letters in the alpha bet. However, this alone does not determine the standard of the type face and the quality of composition set with

ABCDEFGHIJKLMNOPQRSTUVWXYZ&
abcdefghijklmnopqrstuvwxyz 1234567890$
ABCDEFGHIJKLMNOPQRSTUVWXYZ

11 point Times Roman (Linotype)
The basic character in a type design is determined by the uniform design characteristics of all letters in the alphabet. However, this alone does not determine the

ABCDEFGHIJKLMNOPQRSTUVWXYZ&
abcdefghijklmnopqrstuvwxyz 1234567890$
ABCDEFGHIJKLMNOPQRSTUVWXYZ

12 point Times Roman (Linotype)
The basic character in a type design is determined by the uniform design characteristics of all letters in the alphabet. However, this alone does not de

ABCDEFGHIJKLMNOPQRSTUVWXYZ&
abcdefghijklmnopqrstuvwxyz 1234567890$
ABCDEFGHIJKLMNOPQRSTUVWXYZ

14 point Times Roman (Linotype)
The basic character in a type design is deter mined by the uniform design characteristics

ABCDEFGHIJKLMNOPQRSTUV
WXYZ& 1234567890$
abcdefghijklmnopqrstuvwxyz
ABCDEFGHIJKLMNOPQRSTUVWXYZ

Times New Roman

14 point Times New Roman (Foundry)
ABCDEFGHIJKLMNOPQRSTUVWXYZ&
abcdefghijklmnopqrstuvwxyz
1234567890$

18 point Times New Roman (Foundry)
ABCDEFGHIJKLMNOPQRSTUVWXYZ&
abcdefghijklmnopqrstuvwxyz
1234567890$

(Continued on Page 483)

24 point Times New Roman (Foundry)

ABCDEFGHIJKLMNOPQRSTUVWXYZ&
abcdefghijklmnopqrstuvwxyz
1234567890$

30 point Times New Roman (Foundry)

ABCDEFGHIJKLMNOPQRSTUV
WXYZ&
abcdefghijklmnopqrstuvwxyz
1234567890$

36 point Times New Roman (Foundry)

ABCDEFGHIJKLMNOPQRST
UVWXYZ&
abcdefghijklmnopqrstuvwxyz
1234567890$

48 point Times New Roman (Foundry)

ABCDEFGHIJKLMN
OPQRSTUVWXYZ&
abcdefghijklmnopqrstuv
wxyz
1234567890$

(Continued on page 484)

60 point Times New Roman (Foundry)

ABCDEFGHIJKL MNOPQRSTUV WXYZ&

abcdefghijklmnopq rstuvwxyz 1234567890$

72 point Times New Roman (Foundry)

ABCDEFGHIJ
KLMNOPQRS
TUVWXYZ&
abcdefghijklmn
opqrstuvwxyz
1234567890$

Times Roman Italic

The basic character in a type design is determined by the uniform design characteristics of all letters in the alphabet. However, this alone does not determine the standard of the type face and the quality of composition set with it. The appearance is something complex which forms itself out of many details, like form, proportion, ductus, rhythm etc. If everything harmonizes, the total result will be more than the sum of its components. The only reliable basis for the design in a type is a positive feeling for form

ABCDEFGHIJKLMNOPQRSTUVWXYZ&
abcdefghijklmnopqrstuvwxyz   *1234567890$*

The basic character in a type design is determined by the uniform design characteristics of all letters in the alphabet. However, this alone does not determine the standard of the type face and the quality of composition set with it. The appearance is something complex which forms itself out of many details, like form, proportion, ductus, rhythm etc. If everything harmonizes, the total result will be more than the

ABCDEFGHIJKLMNOPQRSTUVWXYZ&
abcdefghijklmnopqrstuvwxyz   *1234567890$*

The basic character in a type design is determined by the uniform design characteristics of all letters in the alphabet. However, this alone does not determine the standard of the type face and the quality of composition set with it. The appearance is something complex which forms itself out of many details, like form, propor

ABCDEFGHIJKLMNOPQRSTUVWXYZ&
abcdefghijklmnopqrstuvwxyz   *1234567890$*

The basic character in a type design is determined by the uniform design characteristics of all letters in the alphabet. However, this alone does not determine the standard of the type face and the quality of composition set with it. The appear

ABCDEFGHIJKLMNOPQRSTUVWXYZ&
abcdefghijklmnopqrstuvwxyz   *1234567890$*

The basic character in a type design is determined by the uniform design characteristics of all letters in the alpha bet. However, this alone does not determine the standard of the type face and the quality of composition set with

ABCDEFGHIJKLMNOPQRSTUVWXYZ&
abcdefghijklmnopqrstuvwxyz   *1234567890$*

The basic character in a type design is determined by the uniform design characteristics of all letters in the alphabet. However, this alone does not determine the

ABCDEFGHIJKLMNOPQRSTUVWXYZ&
abcdefghijklmnopqrstuvwxyz   *1234567890$*

The basic character in a type design is determined by the uniform design characteristics of all letters in the alphabet. However, this alone does not de

ABCDEFGHIJKLMNOPQRSTUVWXYZ&
abcdefghijklmnopqrstuvwxyz   *1234567890$*

The basic character in a type design is deter mined by the uniform design characteristics

ABCDEFGHIJKLMNOPQRSTUV WXYZ&   *1234567890$*
abcdefghijklmnopqrstuvwxyz

Times New Roman Italic

ABCDEFGHIJKLMNOPQRSTUVWXYZ&
abcdefghijklmnopqrstuvwxyz
1234567890$

ABCDEFGHIJKLMNOPQRSTUVWXYZ&
abcdefghijklmnopqrstuvwxyz
1234567890$

(Continued on Page 487)

24 point Times New Roman Italic (Foundry)

ABCDEFGHIJKLMNOPQRSTUVWXYZ&
abcdefghijklmnopqrstuvwxyz
1234567890$

30 point Times New Roman Italic (Foundry)

ABCDEFGHIJKLMNOPQRSTUV
WXYZ&
abcdefghijklmnopqrstuvwxyz
1234567890$

36 point Times New Roman Italic (Foundry)

ABCDEFGHIJKLMNOPQRST
UVWXYZ&
abcdefghijklmnopqrstuvwxyz
1234567890$

48 point Times New Roman Italic (Foundry)

ABCDEFGHIJKLMNO
PQRSTUVWXYZ&
abcdefghijklmnopqrstuv
wxyz
1234567890$

(Continued on Page 488)

60 point Times New Roman Italic (Foundry)

ABCDEFGHIJKL
MNOPQRSTUV
WXYZ&
abcdefghijklmnopqr
stuvwxyz
1234567890$

(Continued on Page 489)

72 point Times New Roman Italic (Foundry)

ABCDEFGHIJ
KLMNOPQRS
TUVWXYZ&
abcdefghijklmno
pqrstuvwxyz
1234567890$

Times Roman Bold

The basic character in a type design is determined by the uniform design characteristics of all letters in the alphabet. However, this alone does not determine the standard of the type face and the quality of composition set with it. The appearance is something complex which forms itself out of many details, like form, proportion, ductus, rhythm etc. If everything har monizes, the total result will be more than the sum of its components. The only reliable basis for the design in a type is a positive feeling for form and style. The basic character in a type design is determined by the

ABCDEFGHIJKLMNOPQRSTUVWXYZ&
abcdefghijklmnopqrstuvwxyz 1234567890$

The basic character in a type design is determined by the uniform de sign characteristics of all letters in the alphabet. However, this alone does not determine the standard of the type face and the quality of composition set with it. The appearance is something complex which forms itself out of many details, like form, proportion, ductus, rhythm etc. If everything harmonizes, the total result will be more than the sum of its components. The only reliable basis for the design in a

ABCDEFGHIJKLMNOPQRSTUVWXYZ&
abcdefghijklmnopqrstuvwxyz 1234567890$

The basic character in a type design is determined by the uniform design characteristics of all letters in the alphabet. However, this alone does not determine the standard of the type face and the quality of composition set with it. The appearance is something complex which forms itself out of many details, like form, propor tion, ductus, rhythm etc. If everything harmonizes, the total result

ABCDEFGHIJKLMNOPQRSTUVWXYZ&
abcdefghijklmnopqrstuvwxyz 1234567890$

The basic character in a type design is determined by the uniform design characteristics of all letters in the alphabet. However, this alone does not determine the standard of the type face and the quality of composition set with it. The ap pearance is something complex which forms itself out of

ABCDEFGHIJKLMNOPQRSTUVWXYZ&
abcdefghijklmnopqrstuvwxyz 1234567890$

The basic character in a type design is determined by the uniform design characteristics of all letters in the alphabet. However, this alone does not determine the standard of the type face and the quality of composition set with it. The appearance is something complex which forms itself

ABCDEFGHIJKLMNOPQRSTUVWXYZ&
abcdefghijklmnopqrstuvwxyz 1234567890$

The basic character in a type design is determined by the uniform design characteristics of all letters in the alphabet. However, this alone does not determine the standard of the type face and the quality of composi

ABCDEFGHIJKLMNOPQRSTUVWXYZ&
abcdefghijklmnopqrstuvwxyz 1234567890$

The basic character in a type design is determined by the uniform design characteristics of all letters in the alphabet. However, this alone does not de termine the standard of the type face and the qual

ABCDEFGHIJKLMNOPQRSTUVWXYZ&
abcdefghijklmnopqrstuvwxyz 1234567890$

The basic character in a type design is deter mined by the uniform design characteristics of all letters in the alphabet. However, this

ABCDEFGHIJKLMNOPQRSTUV
WXYZ& 1234567890$
abcdefghijklmnopqrstuvwxyz

Times New Roman Bold

ABCDEFGHIJKLMNOPQRSTUVWXYZ&
abcdefghijklmnopqrstuvwxyz
1234567890$

ABCDEFGHIJKLMNOPQRSTUVWXYZ&
abcdefghijklmnopqrstuvwxyz
1234567890$

(Continued on Page 491)

(Continued from Page 490)

24 point Times New Roman Bold (Foundry)

ABCDEFGHIJKLMNOPQRSTUVWXYZ&
abcdefghijklmnopqrstuvwxyz
1234567890$

30 point Times New Roman Bold (Foundry)

ABCDEFGHIJKLMNOPQRSTUV
WXYZ&
abcdefghijklmnopqrstuvwxyz
1234567890$

36 point Times New Roman Bold (Foundry)

ABCDEFGHIJKLMNOPQRST
UVWXYZ&
abcdefghijklmnopqrstuvwxyz
1234567890$

42 point Times New Roman Bold (Foundry)

ABCDEFGHIJKLMNOPQ
RSTUVWXYZ&
abcdefghijklmnopqrstuvwxyz
1234567890$

(Continued on Page 492)

(Continued from Page 491)

48 point Times New Roman Bold (Foundry)

ABCDEFGHIJKLMNO
PQRSTUVWXYZ&
abcdefghijklmnopqrstuv
wxyz
1234567890$

60 point Times New Roman Bold (Foundry)

ABCDEFGHIJKL
MNOPQRSTUV
WXYZ&
abcdefghijklmnopqr
stuvwxyz
1234567890$

(Continued on Page 493)

72 point Times New Roman Bold (Foundry)

ABCDEFGHIJ
KLMNOPQRS
TUVWXYZ&

abcdefghijklmno
pqrstuvwxyz
1234567890$

14 point Times New Roman Bold Italic (Foundry)
ABCDEFGHIJKLMNOPQRSTUVWXYZ&
abcdefghijklmnopqrstuvwxyz
1234567890$

18 point Times New Roman Bold Italic (Foundry)
ABCDEFGHIJKLMNOPQRSTUVWXYZ&
abcdefghijklmnopqrstuvwxyz
1234567890$

24 point Times New Roman Bold Italic (Foundry)
ABCDEFGHIJKLMNOPQRSTUVWXYZ&
abcdefghijklmnopqrstuvwxyz
1234567890$

30 point Times New Roman Bold Italic (Foundry)
ABCDEFGHIJKLMNOPQRSTUV
WXYZ&
abcdefghijklmnopqrstuvwxyz
1234567890$

(Continued on Page 495)

36 point Times New Roman Bold Italic (Foundry)

ABCDEFGHIJKLMNOPQRST
UVWXYZ&
abcdefghijklmnopqrstuvwxyz
1234567890$

42 point Times New Roman Bold Italic (Foundry)

ABCDEFGHIJKLMNOPQ
RSTUVWXYZ&
abcdefghijklmnopqrstuvwxyz
1234567890$

48 point Times New Roman Bold Italic (Foundry)

ABCDEFGHIJKLMNO
PQRSTUVWXYZ&
abcdefghijklmnopqrstuv
wxyz
1234567890$

(Continued on Page 496)

(Continued from Page 495)

60 point Times New Roman Bold Italic (Foundry)

ABCDEFGHIJKL
MNOPQRSTUV
WXYZ&
abcdefghijklmnopqr
stuvwxyz
1234567890$

(Continued on Page 497)

72 point Times New Roman Bold Italic (Foundry)

ABCDEFGHIJ
KLMNOPQRS
TUVWXYZ&
abcdefghijklmn
opqrstuvwxyz
1234567890$

14 point Times Titling, Cap font (Foundry)

ABCDEFGHIJKLMNOPQRSTUVWXYZ&
1234567890$

18 point Times Titling, Cap font (Foundry)

ABCDEFGHIJKLMNOPQRSTUVWXYZ&
1234567890$

24 point Times Titling, Cap font (Foundry)

ABCDEFGHIJKLMNOPQRSTUVWXYZ&
1234567890$

30 point Times Titling, Cap font (Foundry)

ABCDEFGHIJKLMNOPQRSTUVWXYZ&
1234567890$

36 point Times Titling, Cap font (Foundry)

ABCDEFGHIJKLMNOPQRSTUV
WXYZ&
1234567890$

48 point Times Titling, Cap font (Foundry)

ABCDEFGHIJKLMNOPQR
STUVWXYZ&
1234567890$

(Continued from Page 498)

60 point Times Titling, Cap font (Foundry)

ABCDEFGHIJKLMN
OPQRSTUVWXYZ&
1234567890$

72 point Times Titling, Cap font (Foundry)

ABCDEFGHIJKL
MNOPQRSTUV
WXYZ&
1234567890$

Torino Roman

8 point Torino Roman (Foundry)
ABCDEFGHIJKLMNOPQRSTUVWXYZ&
abcdefghijklmnopqrstuvwxyz
1234567890$

12 point Torino Roman (Foundry)
ABCDEFGHIJKLMNOPQRSTUVWXYZ&
abcdefghijklmnopqrstuvwxyz
1234567890$

14 point Torino Roman (Foundry)
ABCDEFGHIJKLMNOPQRSTUVWXYZ&
abcdefghijklmnopqrstuvwxyz
1234567890$

18 point Torino Roman (Foundry)
ABCDEFGHIJKLMNOPQRSTUVWXYZ&
abcdefghijklmnopqrstuvwxyz
1234567890$

24 point Torino Roman Small (Foundry)
ABCDEFGHIJKLMNOPQRSTUVWXYZ&
abcdefghijklmnopqrstuvwxyz
1234567890$

24 point Torino Roman Large (Foundry)
ABCDEFGHIJKLMNOPQRSTUVWXYZ&
abcdefghijklmnopqrstuvwxyz
1234567890$

36 point Torino Roman (Foundry)
ABCDEFGHIJKLMNOPQRSTUV
WXYZ&
abcdefghijklmnopqrstuvwxyz
1234567890$

(Continued on Page 501)

48 point Torino Roman (Foundry)

ABCDEFGHIJKLMNOPQR
STUVWXYZ&
abcdefghijklmnopqrstuv
wxyz
1234567890$

Torino Italic

Tower

Tower

18 point Tower (Foundry)

ABCDEFGHIJKLMNOPQRSTUVWXYZ&
abcdefghijklmnopqrstuvwxyz
1234567890$

48 point Tower (Foundry)

ABCDEFGHIJKLMNOPQRSTUVWXYZ
abcdefghijklmnopqrstuvwxyz&
1234567890$

60 point Tower (Foundry)

ABCDEFGHIJKLMNOPQRSTU
VWXYZ&
abcdefghijklmnopqrstuvwxyz
1234567890$

Trade Gothic

The basic character in a type design is determined by the uni form design characteristics of all letters in the alphabet. How ever, this alone does not determine the standard of the type face and the quality of composition set with it. The appearance is something complex which forms itself out of many details, like form, proportion, ductus, rhythm etc. If everything har

ABCDEFGHIJKLMNOPQRSTUVWXYZ&
abcdefghijklmnopqrstuvwxyz　　　　1234567890$

The basic character in a type design is determined by the uniform design characteristics of all letters in the alpha bet. However, this alone does not determine the standard of the type face and the quality of composition set with it. The appearance is something complex which forms itself

ABCDEFGHIJKLMNOPQRSTUVWXYZ&
abcdefghijklmnopqrstuvwxyz　　　　1234567890$

Trade Gothic Bold

The basic character in a type design is determined by the uni form design characteristics of all letters in the alphabet. How ever, this alone does not determine the standard of the type face and the quality of composition set with it. The appearance is something complex which forms itself out of many details, like form, proportion, ductus, rhythm etc. If everything har

**ABCDEFGHIJKLMNOPQRSTUVWXYZ&
abcdefghijklmnopqrstuvwxyz　　　　1234567890$**

The basic character in a type design is determined by the uniform design characteristics of all letters in the alpha bet. However, this alone does not determine the standard of the type face and the quality of composition set with it. The appearance is something complex which forms itself

**ABCDEFGHIJKLMNOPQRSTUVWXYZ&
abcdefghijklmnopqrstuvwxyz　　　　1234567890$**

Trade Gothic Light

The basic character in a type design is determined by the uni form design characteristics of all letters in the alphabet. How ever, this alone does not determine the standard of the type face and the quality of composition set with it. The appearance is something complex which forms itself out of many details, like form, proportion, ductus, rhythm etc. If everything harmo

ABCDEFGHIJKLMNOPQRSTUVWXYZ&
abcdefghijklmnopqrstuvwxyz　　　　1234567890$

The basic character in a type design is determined by the uniform design characteristics of all letters in the alpha bet. However, this alone does not determine the standard of the type face and the quality of composition set with it. The appearance is something complex which forms itself

ABCDEFGHIJKLMNOPQRSTUVWXYZ&
abcdefghijklmnopqrstuvwxyz　　　　1234567890$

The basic character in a type design is determined by the uniform design characteristics of all letters in the alphabet. However, this alone does not determine the standard of the type face and the quality of composition set with it. The appearance is something complex which

ABCDEFGHIJKLMNOPQRSTUVWXYZ&
abcdefghijklmnopqrstuvwxyz　　　　1234567890$

Trade Gothic Light Italic

The basic character in a type design is determined by the uni form design characteristics of all letters in the alphabet. How ever, this alone does not determine the standard of the type face and the quality of composition set with it. The appearance is something complex which forms itself out of many details, like form, proportion, ductus, rhythm etc. If everything harmo

*ABCDEFGHIJKLMNOPQRSTUVWXYZ&
abcdefghijklmnopqrstuvwxyz　　　　1234567890$*

The basic character in a type design is determined by the uniform design characteristics of all letters in the alpha bet. However, this alone does not determine the standard of the type face and the quality of composition set with it. The appearance is something complex which forms itself

*ABCDEFGHIJKLMNOPQRSTUVWXYZ&
abcdefghijklmnopqrstuvwxyz　　　　1234567890$*

The basic character in a type design is determined by the uniform design characteristics of all letters in the alphabet. However, this alone does not determine the standard of the type face and the quality of composition set with it. The appearance is something complex which

*ABCDEFGHIJKLMNOPQRSTUVWXYZ&
abcdefghijklmnopqrstuvwxyz　　　　1234567890$*

Trade Gothic Condensed

The basic character in a type design is determined by the uniform design char acteristics of all letters in the alphabet. However, this alone does not determine the standard of the type face and the quality of composition set with it. The appearance is something complex which forms itself out of many details, like form, proportion, ductus, rhythm etc. If everything harmonizes, the total result will be more than the sum of its components. The only reliable basis for the design in a type is a positive feeling for form and style. The basic character
ABCDEFGHIJKLMNOPQRSTUVWXYZ&
abcdefghijklmnopqrstuvwxyz 1234567890$

The basic character in a type design is determined by the uniform design characteristics of all letters in the alphabet. However, this alone does not determine the standard of the type face and the quality of composition set with it. The appearance is something complex which forms itself out of many details, like form, proportion, ductus, rhythm etc. If everything har monizes, the total result will be more than the sum of its components. The
ABCDEFGHIJKLMNOPQRSTUVWXYZ&
abcdefghijklmnopqrstuvwxyz 1234567890$

The basic character in a type design is determined by the uniform de sign characteristics of all letters in the alphabet. However, this alone does not determine the standard of the type face and the quality of composition set with it. The appearance is something complex which forms itself out of many details, like form, proportion, ductus, rhythm etc.
ABCDEFGHIJKLMNOPQRSTUVWXYZ&
abcdefghijklmnopqrstuvwxyz 1234567890$

The basic character in a type design is determined by the uniform design characteristics of all letters in the alphabet. However, this alone does not determine the standard of the type face and the quality of composition set with it. The appearance is something
ABCDEFGHIJKLMNOPQRSTUVWXYZ&
abcdefghijklmnopqrstuvwxyz 1234567890$

The basic character in a type design is determined by the uni form design characteristics of all letters in the alphabet. However, this alone does not determine the standard of the type face and the quality of composition set with it. The appearance is some
ABCDEFGHIJKLMNOPQRSTUVWXYZ&
abcdefghijklmnopqrstuvwxyz 1234567890$

The basic character in a type design is determined by the uniform design characteristics of all letters in the alphabet. However, this alone does not determine the standard of the type face and the quality of composition set with it. The
ABCDEFGHIJKLMNOPQRSTUVWXYZ&
abcdefghijklmnopqrstuvwxyz 1234567890$

The basic character in a type design is determined by the uniform design characteristics of all letters in the alphabet. However, this alone does not determine the standard of the
ABCDEFGHIJKLMNOPQRSTUVWXYZ&
abcdefghijklmnopqrstuvwxyz 1234567890$

The basic character in a type design is determined by the uniform design characteristics of all letters
ABCDEFGHIJKLMNOPQRSTUVWXYZ&
abcdefghijklmnopqrstuvwxyz 1234567890$

Trade Gothic Bold Condensed

The basic character in a type design is determined by the uniform design char acteristics of all letters in the alphabet. However, this alone does not determine the standard of the type face and the quality of composition set with it. The appearance is something complex which forms itself out of many details, like form, proportion, ductus, rhythm etc. If everything harmonizes, the total result will be more than the sum of its components. The only reliable basis for the design in a type is a positive feeling for form and style. The basic character
ABCDEFGHIJKLMNOPQRSTUVWXYZ&
abcdefghijklmnopqrstuvwxyz 1234567890$

The basic character in a type design is determined by the uniform design characteristics of all letters in the alphabet. However, this alone does not determine the standard of the type face and the quality of composition set with it. The appearance is something complex which forms itself out of many details, like form, proportion, ductus, rhythm etc. If everything har monizes, the total result will be more than the sum of its components. The
ABCDEFGHIJKLMNOPQRSTUVWXYZ&
abcdefghijklmnopqrstuvwxyz 1234567890$

The basic character in a type design is determined by the uniform de sign characteristics of all letters in the alphabet. However, this alone does not determine the standard of the type face and the quality of composition set with it. The appearance is something complex which forms itself out of many details, like form, proportion, ductus, rhythm etc.
ABCDEFGHIJKLMNOPQRSTUVWXYZ&
abcdefghijklmnopqrstuvwxyz 1234567890$

The basic character in a type design is determined by the uniform design characteristics of all letters in the alphabet. However, this alone does not determine the standard of the type face and the quality of composition set with it. The appearance is something
ABCDEFGHIJKLMNOPQRSTUVWXYZ&
abcdefghijklmnopqrstuvwxyz 1234567890$

The basic character in a type design is determined by the uni form design characteristics of all letters in the alphabet. However, this alone does not determine the standard of the type face and the quality of composition set with it. The appearance is some
ABCDEFGHIJKLMNOPQRSTUVWXYZ&
abcdefghijklmnopqrstuvwxyz 1234567890$

The basic character in a type design is determined by the uniform design characteristics of all letters in the alphabet. However, this alone does not determine the standard of the type face and the quality of composition set with it. The
ABCDEFGHIJKLMNOPQRSTUVWXYZ&
abcdefghijklmnopqrstuvwxyz 1234567890$

The basic character in a type design is determined by the uniform design characteristics of all letters in the alphabet. However, this alone does not determine the standard of the
ABCDEFGHIJKLMNOPQRSTUVWXYZ&
abcdefghijklmnopqrstuvwxyz 1234567890$

The basic character in a type design is determined by the uniform design characteristics of all letters
ABCDEFGHIJKLMNOPQRSTUVWXYZ&
abcdefghijklmnopqrstuvwxyz 1234567890$

Trafton Script

36 point Trafton Script (Foundry)

ABCDEFGHIJKLMNOPQRSTU
VWXYJ&

abcdefghijklmnopqrstuvwxyz   1234567890$

48 point Trafton Script (Foundry)

ABCDEFGHIJKLMNO
PQRSTUVWXYJ&

abcdefghijklmnopqrstuvwxyz   1234567890$

72 point Trafton Script

ABCDEFGHIJ
KLMNOPQRST
UVWXYJ&

abcdefghijklmnopqrstuvwxyz

1234567890$

True Cut Caslon *(Font contains some Alternate Characters)*

22 point True Cut Caslon (Ludlow)

ABCDEFGHIJKLMNOPQRSTUVWXYZ&
abcdefghijklmnopqrstuvwxyz
1234567890$

30 point True Cut Caslon (Ludlow)

ABCDEFGHIJKLMNOPQRSTUVWXYZ&
abcdefghijklmnopqrstuvwxyz
1234567890$

36 point True Cut Caslon (Foundry)

ABCDEFGHIJKLMNOPQRS
TUVWXYZ&
abcdefghijklmnopqrstuvwxyz
1234567890$

48 point True Cut Caslon (Foundry)

ABCDEFGHIJKLM
NOPQRSTUVWXYZ
abcdefghijklmnopqrstuv
wxyz&
1234567890$

36 point Trump Gravur, Cap font (Foundry)

ABCDEFGHIJKLMNOPQ
RSTUVWXYZ&
1234567890$

60 point Trump Gravur, Cap font (Foundry)

ABCDEFGHIJK
LMNOPQRST
UVWXYZ&
1234567890$

Trump Mediaeval *(Must be leaded 1 point)*

(Continued on Page 510)

36 point Trump Mediaeval (Foundry)

ABCDEFGHIJKLMNOPQRST
UVWXYZ&
abcdefghijklmnopqrstuvwxyz
1234567890$

48 point Trump Mediaeval (Foundry)

ABCDEFGHIJKLMNOP
QRSTUVWXYZ&
abcdefghijklmnopqrstuv
wxyz
1234567890$

Trump Mediaeval Italic *(Must be leaded 1 point)*

6 point Trump Mediaeval Italic (Linotype)

The basic character in a type design is determined by the uniform design characteristics of all letters in the alphabet. However, this alone does not determine the standard of the type face and the quality of composition set with it. The appearance is something complex which forms itself out of many details, like form, proportion, ductus, rhythm etc. If everything harmonizes, the total result will be more than the sum of its components. The only reliable basis for the design in a type is a positive feeling for form

ABCDEFGHIJKLMNOPQRSTUVWXYZ&)
abcdefghijklmnopqrstuvwxyz   *1234567890$*

7 point Trump Mediaeval Italic (Linotype)

The basic character in a type design is determined by the uniform design characteristics of all letters in the alphabet. However, this alone does not determine the standard of the type face and the quality of composition set with it. The appearance is something complex which forms itself out of many details like form, proportion, ductus, rhythm etc. If everything harmonizes, the total result will be more than the

ABCDEFGHIJKLMNOPQRSTUVWXYZ&)
abcdefghijklmnopqrstuvwxyz   *1234567890$*

8 point Trump Mediaeval Italic (Linotype)

The basic character in a type design is determined by the uniform design characteristics of all letters in the alphabet. However, this alone does not determine the standard of the type face and the quality of composition set with it. The appearance is something complex which forms itself out of many details,

ABCDEFGHIJKLMNOPQRSTUVWXYZ&)
abcdefghijklmnopqrstuvwxyz   *1234567890$*

9 point Trump Mediaeval Italic (Linotype)

The basic character in a type design is determined by the uniform design characteristics of all letters in the alphabet. However, this alone does not determine the standard of the type face and the quality of composition set with it. The

ABCDEFGHIJKLMNOPQRSTUVWXYZ&)
abcdefghijklmnopqrstuvwxyz   *1234567890$*

10 point Trump Mediaeval Italic (Linotype)

The basic character in a type design is determined by the uniform design characteristics of all letters in the alphabet. However, this alone does not determine the standard of the type face and the quality of composi

ABCDEFGHIJKLMNOPQRSTUVWXYZ&)
abcdefghijklmnopqrstuvwxyz   *1234567890$*

12 point Trump Mediaeval Italic (Foundry)

CAPS ON ORDER
abcdefghijklmnopqrstuvwxyz
1234567890$

14 point Trump Mediaeval Italic (Foundry)

ABCDEFGHIJKLMNOPQRSTUVWXYZ&)
abcdefghijklmnopqrstuvwxyz
1234567890$

16 point Trump Mediaeval Italic (Foundry)

ABCDEFGHIJKLMNOPQRSTUVWXYZ&)
abcdefghijklmnopqrstuvwxyz
1234567890$

20 point Trump Mediaeval Italic (Foundry)

ABCDEFGHIJKLMNOPQRSTUVWXYZ&)
abcdefghijklmnopqrstuvwxyz
1234567890$

SWASH AND TERMINALS

A B C D E G F M N P T V W a e k m n t v w z

24 point Trump Mediaeval Italic (Foundry)

ABCDEFGHIJKLMNOPQRSTUVWXYZ&)
abcdefghijklmnopqrstuvwxyz
1234567890$

(Continued on Page 512)

28 point Trump Mediaeval Italic (Foundry)

ABCDEFGHIJKLMNOPQRSTUVWXYZ
abcdefghijklmnopqrstuvwxyz&
1234567890$

Trump Mediaeval Bold

16 point Trump Mediaeval Bold (Foundry)

ABCDEFGHIJKLMNOPQRSTUVWXYZ&
abcdefghijklmnopqrstuvwxyz
1234567890$

Trump Mediaeval Medium *(Must be leaded 1 point)*

6 point Trump Mediaeval Medium (Linotype)

The basic character in a type design is determined by the uniform design characteristics of all letters in the alphabet. However, this alone does not determine the standard of the type face and the quality of composition set with it. The appearance is something complex which forms itself out of many details, like form, proportion, ductus, rhythm etc. If everything harmonizes, the total result will be more than the sum of its components. The only re liable basis for the design in a type is a positive feeling for form and style. The basic character in a type design is determined by the uniform design

ABCDEFGHIJKLMNOPQRSTUVWXYZ&
abcdefghijklmnopqrstuvwxyz   1234567890$

8 point Trump Mediaeval Medium (Linotype)

The basic character in a type design is determined by the uni form design characteristics of all letters in the alphabet. How ever, this alone does not determine the standard of the type face and the quality of composition set with it. The appearance is something complex which forms itself out of many details, like form, proportion, ductus, rhythm etc. If everything har

ABCDEFGHIJKLMNOPQRSTUVWXYZ&
abcdefghijklmnopqrstuvwxyz   1234567890$

9 point Trump Mediaeval Medium (Linotype)

The basic character in a type design is determined by the uniform design characteristics of all letters in the alphabet. However, this alone does not determine the standard of the type face and the quality of composition set with it. The appearance is something complex which forms itself out

ABCDEFGHIJKLMNOPQRSTUVWXYZ&
abcdefghijklmnopqrstuvwxyz   1234567890$

10 point Trump Mediaeval Medium (Linotype)

The basic character in a type design is determined by the uniform design characteristics of all letters in the alphabet. However, this alone does not determine the standard of the type face and the quality of com position set with it. The appearance is something

ABCDEFGHIJKLMNOPQRSTUVWXYZ&
abcdefghijklmnopqrstuvwxyz   1234567890$

Trylon

18 point Trylon (Foundry)
ABCDEFGHIJKLMNOPQRSTUVWXYZ&
abcdefghijklmnopqrstuvwxyz
1234567890$

24 point Trylon (Foundry)
ABCDEFGHIJKLMNOPQRSTUVWXYZ&
abcdefghijklmnopqrstuvwxyz
1234567890$

36 point Trylon (Foundry)
ABCDEFGHIJKLMNOPQRSTUVWXYZ&
abcdefghijklmnopqrstuvwxyz
1234567890$

Twentieth Century Light

14 point Twentieth Century Light (Foundry)
ABCDEFGHIJKLMNOPQRSTUVWXYZ&
abcdefghijklmnopqrstuvwxyz
1234567890$

18 point Twentieth Century Light (Foundry)
ABCDEFGHIJKLMNOPQRSTUVWXYZ&
abcdefghijklmnopqrstuvwxyz
1234567890$

30 point Twentieth Century Light (Foundry)
ABCDEFGHIJKLMNOPQRSTUVWXYZ&
abcdefghijklmnopqrstuvwxyz
1234567890$

Twentieth Century Light Italic

ABCDEFGHIJKLMNOPQRSTUVWXYZ&
abcdefghijklmnopqrstuvwxyz
1234567890$

ABCDEFGHIJKLMNOPQRSTUVWXYZ&
abcdefghijklmnopqrstuvwxyz
1234567890$

ABCDEFGHIJKLMNOPQRSTUVWXYZ&
abcdefghijklmnopqrstuvwxyz
1234567890$

Typewriter

The basic character in a type design by
the uniform design characteristics of all
letters in the alphabet. However, this
alone does not determine the standard of
the type face and the quality of composi

ABCDEFGHIJKLMNOPQRSTUVWXYZ&
abcdefghijklmnopqrstuvwxyz   1234567890$

The basic character in a type de
sign is determined by the uniform
design characteristics of all let
ters in the alphabet. However, this

ABCDEFGHIJKLMNOPQRSTUVWXYZ&
abcdefghijklmnopqrstuvwxyz
1234567890$

Typewriter with Underscore

The basic character in a type design by
the uniform design characteristics of all
letters in the alphabet. However, this
alone does not determine the standard of
the type face and the quality of composi

ABCDEFGHIJKLMNOPQRSTUVWXYZ&
abcdefghijklmnopqrstuvwxyz   1234567890$

The basic character in a type de
sign is determined by the uniform
design characteristics of all let
ters in the alphabet. However, this

ABCDEFGHIJKLMNOPQRSTUVWXYZ&
abcdefghijklmnopqrstuvwxyz
1234567890$

Typo Script

14 point Typo Script (Foundry)

ABCDEFGHIJKLMNOPQRSTUVWXYZ&
abcdefghijklmnopqrstuvwxyz
1234567890$

18 point Typo Script (Foundry)

ABCDEFGHIJKLMNOPQRSTUVWXYZ&
abcdefghijklmnopqrstuvwxyz
1234567890$

24 point Typo Script (Foundry)

ABCDEFGHIJKLMNOPQRSTUVWXYZ&
abcdefghijklmnopqrstuvwxyz
1234567890$

30 point Typo Script (Foundry)

ABCDEFGHIJKLMNOPQRSTUVWXYZ&
abcdefghijklmnopqrstuvwvyz
1234567890$

Typo Upright

12 point Typo Upright (Foundry)
ABCDEFGHIJKLMNOPQRSTUVWXYZ&
abcdefghijklmnopqrstuvwxyz
1234567890$

14 point Typo Upright (Foundry)
ABCDEFGHIJKLMNOPQRSTUVWXYZ&
abcdefghijklmnopqrstuvwxyz
1234567890$

18 point Typo Upright (Foundry)
ABCDEFGHIJKLMNOPQRSTUVWXYZ&
abcdefghijklmnopqrstuvwxyz
1234567890$

24 point Typo Upright (Foundry)
ABCDEFGHIJKLMNOPQRST UVWXYZ&
abcdefghijklmnopqrstuvwxyz
1234567890$

30 point Typo Upright (Foundry)
ABCDEFGHIJKLMNOPQRST UVWXYZ&
abcdefghijklmnopqrstuvwxyz
1234567890$

Ultra Bodoni

10 point Ultra Bodoni (Linotype)

The basic character in a type design is de termined by the uniform design character istics of all letters in the alphabet. However, this alone does not determine the standard of the type face and the quality of composi

**ABCDEFGHIJKLMNOPQRSTUVWXYZ&
abcdefghijklmnopqrstuvwxyz 1234567890$**

8 point Ultra Bodoni (Foundry)

**ABCDEFGHIJKLMNOPQRSTUVWXYZ&
abcdefghijklmnopqrstuvwxyz
1234567890$**

12 point Ultra Bodoni (Foundry)

**ABCDEFGHIJKLMNOPQRSTUV
WXYZ&
abcdefghijklmnopqrstuvwxyz
1234567890$**

14 point Ultra Bodoni (Foundry)

**ABCDEFGHIJKLMNOPQRSTUVWXYZ&
abcdefghijklmnopqrstuvwxyz
1234567890$**

18 point Ultra Bodoni (Foundry)

**ABCDEFGHIJKLMNOPQRSTUVWXYZ&
abcdefghijklmnopqrstuvwxyz
1234567890$**

24 point Ultra Bodoni (Foundry)

**ABCDEFGHIJKLMNOPQRSTUV
WXYZ&
abcdefghijklmnopqrstuvwxyz
1234567890$**

30 point Ultra Bodoni (Foundry)

**ABCDEFGHIJKLMNOPQRSTU
VWXYZ&
abcdefghijklmnopqrstuvwxyz
1234567890$**

36 point Ultra Bodoni (Foundry)

**ABCDEFGHIJKLMNOPQ
RSTUVWXYZ&
abcdefghijklmnopqrstuv
wxyz 1234567890$**

(Continued on Page 518)

42 point Ultra Bodoni (Foundry)

ABCDEFGHIJKLMNO
PQRSTUVWXYZ&
abcdefghijklmnopqrst
uvwxyz
1234567890$

48 point Ultra Bodoni (Foundry)

ABCDEFGHIJKLM
NOPQRSTUV
WXYZ&
abcdefghijklmnopq
rstuvwxyz
1234567890$

(Continued on Page 519)

(Continued from Page 518)

60 point Ultra Bodoni (Foundry)

ABCDEFGHIJK
LMNOPQRSTU
VWXYZ&
abcdefghijklmn
opqrstuvwxyz
1234568890$

(Continued on Page 520)

(Continued from Page 519)

72 point Ultra Bodoni (Foundry)

ABCDEFGHI
JKLMNOPQ
RSTUV
WXYZ&
abcdefghijkl
mnopqrstuv
wxyz$
1234567890

Ultra Bodoni Italic

10 point Ultra Bodoni Italic (Linotype)

The basic character in a type design is de termined by the uniform design character istics of all letters in the alphabet. However, this alone does not determine the standard of the type face and the quality of composi

*ABCDEFGHIJKLMNOPQRSTUVWXYZ&
abcdefghijklmnopqrstuvwxyz 1234567890$*

8 point Ultra Bodoni Italic (Foundry)

*ABCDEFGHIJKLMNOPQRSTUVWXYZ&
abcdefghijklmnopqrstuvwxyz
1234567890$*

10 point Ultra Bodoni Italic (Foundry)

*ABCDEFGHIJKLMNOPQRSTUVWXYZ&
abcdefghijklmnopqrstuvwxyz
1234567890$*

12 point Ultra Bodoni Italic (Foundry)

*ABCDEFGHIJKLMNOPQRSTUV
WXYZ&
abcdefghijklmnopqrstuvwxyz
1234567890$*

14 point Ultra Bodoni Italic (Foundry)

*ABCDEFGHIJKLMNOPQRST
UVWXYZ&
abcdefghijklmnopqrstuvwxyz
1234567890$*

18 point Ultra Bodoni Italic (Foundry)

*ABCDEFGHIJKLMNOPQRSTUVWXYZ&
abcdefghijklmnopqrstuvwxyz
1234567890$*

24 point Ultra Bodoni Italic (Foundry)

*ABCDEFGHIJKLMNOPQRSTUV
WXYZ&
abcdefghijklmnopqrstuvwxyz
1234567890$*

30 point Ultra Bodoni Italic (Foundry)

*ABCDEFGHIJKLMNOPQRS
TUVWXYZ&
abcdefghijklmnopqrstuvwxyz
1234567890$*

(Continued on Page 522)

36 point Ultra Bodoni Italic (Foundry)

ABCDEFGHIJKLMNOP
QRSTUVWXYZ&
abcdefghijklmnopqrstuv
wxyz
1234567890$

42 point Ultra Bodoni Italic (Foundry)

ABCDEFGHIJKLMN
OPQRSTUVWXYZ&
abcdefghijklmnopqrst
uvwxyz
1234567890$

Ultra Bodoni Extra Condensed

24 point Ultra Bodoni Extra Condensed (Foundry)

ABCDEFGHIJKLMNOPQRSTUVWXYZ&
abcdefghijklmnopqrstuvwxyz
1234567890$

36 point Ultra Bodoni Extra Condensed (Foundry)

ABCDEFGHIJKLMNOPQRSTUVWXYZ&
abcdefghijklmnopqrstuvwxyz
1234567890$

42 point Ultra Bodoni Extra Condensed (Foundry)

ABCDEFGHIJKLMNOPQRSTUV
WXYZ&
abcdefghijklmnopqrstuvwxyz
1234567890$

V & M TYPOGRAPHICAL, INCORPORATED

Umbra

24 point Umbra, Cap font (Ludlow)

ABCDEFGHIJKLMNOPQRSTUVWXYZ&
1234567890$

36 point Umbra, Cap font (Ludlow)

ABCDEFGHIJKLMNOP
QRSTUVWXYZ&
1234567890$

48 point Umbra, Cap font (Ludlow)

ABCDEFGHIJKLMN
OPQRSTUVWXYZ&
1234567890$

24 point Univers No. 45 Large (Foundry)

ABCDEFGHIJKLMNOPQRSTUVWXYZ&
abcdefghijklmnopqrstuvwxyz
1234567890$

30 point Univers No. 45 (Foundry)

ABCDEFGHIJKLMNOPQRSTUV
WXYZ&
abcdefghijklmnopqrstuvwxyz
1234567890$

48 point Univers No. 45 (Foundry)

ABCDEFGHIJKLMNOP
QRSTUVWXYZ&
abcdefghijklmnopqrstu
vwxyz
1234567890$

Univers No. 46

*ABCDEFGHIJKLMNOPQRSTUV
WXYZ&
abcdefghijklmnopqrstuvwxyz
1234567890$*

Glamour Bold

**ABCDEFGHIJKLMNOPQRSTUV
WXYZ&
abcdefghijklmnopqrstuvwxyz
1234567890$**

Glamour Light

ABCDEFGHIJKLMNOPQRSTUV
WXYZ&
abcdefghijklmnopqrstuvwxyz
1234567890$

Univers No. 55

8 point Univers No. 55 (Foundry)
ABCDEFGHIJKLMNOPQRSTUVWXYZ&
abcdefghijklmnopqrstuvwxyz
1234567890$

10 point Univers No. 55 (Foundry)
ABCDEFGHIJKLMNOPQRSTUVWXYZ&
abcdefghijklmnopqrstuvwxyz
1234567890$

14 point Univers No. 55 (Foundry)
ABCDEFGHIJKLMNOPQRSTUVWXYZ&
abcdefghijklmnopqrstuvwxyz
1234567890$

18 point Univers No. 55 (Foundry)
ABCDEFGHIJKLMNOPQRSTUVWXYZ&
abcdefghijklmnopqrstuvwxyz
1234567890$

24 point Univers No. 55 Small (Foundry)
ABCDEFGHIJKLMNOPQRSTUVWXYZ&
abcdefghijklmnopqrstuvwxyz
1234567890$

24 point Univers No. 55 Large (Foundry)
ABCDEFGHIJKLMNOPQRSTUVWXYZ&
abcdefghijklmnopqrstuvwxyz
1234567890$

30 point Univers No. 55 (Foundry)
ABCDEFGHIJKLMNOPQRSTUV
WXYZ&
abcdefghijklmnopqrstuvwxyz
1234567890$

10 point Univers No. 56 (Foundry)
ABCDEFGHIJKLMNOPQRSTUVWXYZ&
abcdefghijklmnopqrstuvwxyz
1234567890$

12 point Univers No. 56 (Foundry)
ABCDEFGHIJKLMNOPQRSTUVWXYZ&
abcdefghijklmnopqrstuvwxyz
1234567890$

14 point Univers No. 56 (Foundry)
ABCDEFGHIJKLMNOPQRSTUVWXYZ&
abcdefghijklmnopqrstuvwxyz
1234567890$

18 point Univers No. 56 (Foundry)
ABCDEFGHIJKLMNOPQRSTUVWXYZ&
abcdefghijklmnopqrstuvwxyz
1234567890$

24 point Univers No. 56 Small (Foundry)
ABCDEFGHIJKLMNOPQRSTUVWXYZ&
abcdefghijklmnopqrstuvwxyz
1234567890$

24 point Univers No. 56 Large (Foundry)
ABCDEFGHIJKLMNOPQRSTUVWXYZ&
abcdefghijklmnopqrstuvwxyz
1234567890$

30 point Univers No. 56 (Foundry)
*ABCDEFGHIJKLMNOPQRSTUV
WXYZ&*
abcdefghijklmnopqrstuvwxyz
1234567890$

(Continued on Page 529)

36 point Univers No. 56 (Foundry)

ABCDEFGHIJKLMNOPQRST UVWXYZ& abcdefghijklmnopqrstuvwxyz 1234567890$

Caslon

Caslon Italic

10 point Caslon (Linotype)

The basic character in a type design is determined by the uni form design characteristics of all letters in the alphabet. How ever, this alone does not determine the standard of the type face and the quality of composition set with it. The appear ance is something complex which forms itself out of many details, like form, ductus, rhythm etc. If everything harmon izes, the total result will be more than the sum of its compo

ABCDEFGHIJKLMNOPQRSTUVWXYZ&
abcdefghijklmnopqrstuvwxyz   1234567890$
ABCDEFGHIJKLMNOPQRSTUVWXYZ

10 point Caslon Italic (Linotype)

The basic character in a type design is determined by the uni form design characteristics of all letters in the alphabet. How ever, this alone does not determine the standard of the type face and the quality of composition set with it. The appear ance is something complex which forms itself out of many details, like form, ductus, rhythm etc. If everything harmon izes, the total result will be more than the sum of its compo nents. The only reliable basis for the design in a type is a posi

*ABCDEFGHIJKLMNOPQRSTUVWXYZ&
abcdefghijklmnopqrstuvwxyz   1234567890$*

12 point Caslon (Linotype)

The basic character in a type design is deter mined by the uniform design characteristics of all letters in the alphabet. However, this alone does not determine the standard of the type face and the quality of composition set with it. The appearance is something complex which forms itself out of many details, like form, proportion, ductus, rhythm etc. If everything harmonizes,

ABCDEFGHIJKLMNOPQRSTUV
WXYZ&   1234567890$
abcdefghijklmnopqrstuvwxyz
ABCDEFGHIJKLMNOPQRSTUVWXYZ

12 point Caslon Italic (Linotype)

The basic character in a type design is deter mined by the uniform design characteristics of all letters in the alphabet. However, this alone does not determine the standard of the type face and the quality of composition set with it. The appearance is something complex which forms itself out of many details, like form, proportion, ductus, rhythm etc. If everything harmonizes, the total result will be more than the sum of its

*ABCDEFGHIJKLMNOPQRSTUV
WXYZ&   1234567890$
abcdefghijklmnopqrstuvwxyz*

14 point Caslon (Liinotype)

ON ORDER

14 point Caslon Italic (Linotype)

ON ORDER

Univers No. 57

12 point Univers No. 57 (Foundry)

ABCDEFGHIJKLMNOPQRSTUVWXYZ&
abcdefghijklmnopqrstuvwxyz
1234567890$

18 point Univers No. 57 (Foundry)

ABCDEFGHIJKLMNOPQRSTUVWXYZ&
abcdefghijklmnopqrstuvwxyz
1234567890$

24 point Univers No. 57 Small (Foundry)

ABCDEFGHIJKLMNOPQRSTUVWXYZ&
abcdefghijklmnopqrstuvwxyz
1234567890$

24 point Univers No. 57 Large (Foundry)

ABCDEFGHIJKLMNOPQRSTUVWXYZ&
abcdefghijklmnopqrstuvwxyz
1234567890$

30 point Univers No. 57 (Foundry)

ABCDEFGHIJKLMNOPQRSTUVWXYZ&
abcdefghijklmnopqrstuvwxyz
1234567890$

Univers No. 58

10 point Univers No. 58 (Foundry)
ABCDEFGHIJKLMNOPQRSTUVWXYZ&
abcdefghijklmnopqrstuvwxyz
1234567890$

12 point Univers No. 58 (Foundry)
ABCDEFGHIJKLMNOPQRSTUVWXYZ&
abcdefghijklmnopqrstuvwxyz
1234567890$

24 point Univers No. 58 Small (Foundry)
ABCDEFGHIJKLMNOPQRSTUVWXYZ&
abcdefghijklmnopqrstuvwxyz
1234567890$

24 point Univers No. 58 Large (Foundry)
ABCDEFGHIJKLMNOPQRSTUVWXYZ&
abcdefghijklmnopqrstuvwxyz
1234567890$

30 point Univers No. 58 (Foundry)
ABCDEFGHIJKLMNOPQRSTUVWXYZ&
abcdefghijklmnopqrstuvwxyz
1234567890$

8 point Univers No. 65 (Foundry)
ABCDEFGHIJKLMNOPQRSTUVWXYZ&
abcdefghijklmnopqrstuvwxyz
1234567890$

10 point Univers No. 65 (Foundry)
ABCDEFGHIJKLMNOPQRSTUVWXYZ&
abcdefghijklmnopqrstuvwxyz
1234567890$

12 point Univers No. 65 (Foundry)
ABCDEFGHIJKLMNOPQRSTUVWXYZ&
abcdefghijklmnopqrstuvwxyz
1234567890$

14 point Univers No. 65 (Foundry)
ABCDEFGHIJKLMNOPQRSTUVWXYZ
abcdefghijklmnopqrstuvwxyz&
1234567890$

18 point Univers No. 65 (Foundry)
ABCDEFGHIJKLMNOPQRSTUVWXYZ&
abcdefghijklmnopqrstuvwxyz
1234567890$

24 point Univers No. 65 Small (Foundry)
ABCDEFGHIJKLMNOPQRSTUVWXYZ&
abcdefghijklmnopqrstuvwxyz
1234567890$

24 point Univers No. 65 Large (Foundry)
ABCDEFGHIJKLMNOPQRSTUVWXYZ&
abcdefghijklmnopqrstuvwxyz
1234567890$

30 point Univers No. 65 (Foundry)
ABCDEFGHIJKLMNOPQRSTUV
WXYZ&
abcdefghijklmnopqrstuvwxyz
1234567890$

(Continued on Page 533)

36 point Univers No. 65 (Foundry)

ABCDEFGHIJKLMNOPQRS TUVWXYZ& abcdefghijklmnopqrstuv wxyz 1234567890$

48 point Univers No. 65 (Foundry)

ABCDEFGHIJKLMN OPQRSTUVWXYZ& abcdefghijklmnopqrs tuvwxyz 1234567890$

10 point Univers No. 66 (Foundry)
ABCDEFGHIJKLMNOPQRSTUVWXYZ&
abcdefghijklmnopqrstuvwxyz
1234567890$

12 point Univers No. 66 (Foundry)
ABCDEFGHIJKLMNOPQRSTUVWXYZ&
abcdefghijklmnopqrstuvwxyz
1234567890$

14 point Univers No. 66 (Foundry)
ABCDEFGHIJKLMNOPQRSTUVWXYZ&
abcdefghijklmnopqrstuvwxyz
1234567890$

18 point Univers No. 66 (Foundry)
ABCDEFGHIJKLMNOPQRSTUVWXYZ&
abcdefghijklmnopqrstuvwxyz
1234567890$

24 point Univers No. 66 Small (Foundry)
ABCDEFGHIJKLMNOPQRSTUVWXYZ&
abcdefghijklmnopqrstuvwxyz
1234567890$

24 point Univers No. 66 Large (Foundry)
ABCDEFGHIJKLMNOPQRSTUVWXYZ&
abcdefghijklmnopqrstuvwxyz
1234567890$

30 point Univers No. 66 (Foundry)
*ABCDEFGHIJKLMNOPQRSTUV
WXYZ&*
abcdefghijklmnopqrstuvwxyz
1234567890$

(Continued on Page 535)

36 point Univers No. 66 (Foundry)

ABCDEFGHIJKLMNOPQRS TUVWXYZ&
abcdefghijklmnopqrstuv wxyz
1234567890$

Bold Face No. 6 *(For limited use only)*

10 point Bold Face No. 6 Caps only (Linotype)

ABCDEFGHIJKLMNOPQRSTUVWXYZ

Cairo Bold Italic *(For limited use only)*

8 point Cairo Bold Italic Caps only (Intertype)

ABCDEFGHIJKLMNOPQRSTUVWXYZ
1234567890

10 point Cairo Bold Italic Caps only (Intertype)

ABCDEFGHIJKLMNOPQRSTUVWXYZ
1234567890

Card Italic *(For limited use only)*

10 point Card Italic Caps only (Linotype)

ABCDEFGHIJKLMNOPQRSTUVWXYZ

De Vinne Outline *(For limited use only)*

10 point De Vinne Outline Caps only (Linotype)

ABCDEFGHIJKLMNOPQRSTUVWXYZ

10 point Univers No. 67 (Foundry)

ABCDEFGHIJKLMNOPQRSTUVWXYZ&
abcdefghijklmnopqrstuvwxyz
1234567890$

18 point Univers No. 67 (Foundry)

ABCDEFGHIJKLMNOPQRSTUVWXYZ&
abcdefghijklmnopqrstuvwxyz
1234567890$

24 point Univers No. 67 Small (Foundry)

ABCDEFGHIJKLMNOPQRSTUVWXYZ&
abcdefghijklmnopqrstuvwxyz
1234567890$

24 point Univers No. 67 Large (Foundry)

ABCDEFGHIJKLMNOPQRSTUVWXYZ&
abcdefghijklmnopqrstuvwxyz
1234567890$

30 point Univers No. 67 (Foundry)

ABCDEFGHIJKLMNOPQRSTUVWXYZ&
abcdefghijklmnopqrstuvwxyz
1234567890$

36 point Univers No. 67 (Foundry)

ABCDEFGHIJKLMNOPQRSTUV
WXYZ&
abcdefghijklmnopqrstuvwxyz
1234567890$

(Continued on Page 537)

(Continued from Page 536)

48 point Univers No. 67 (Foundry)

ABCDEFGHIJKLMNOPQR
STUVWXYZ&
abcdefghijklmnopqrstuv
wxyz
1234567890$

Univers No. 68

6 point Univers No. 68 (Foundry)

ABCDEFGHIJKLMNOPQRSTUVWXYZ&
abcdefghijklmnopqrstuvwxyz
1234567890$

12 point Univers No. 68 (Foundry)

ABCDEFGHIJKLMNOPQRSTUVWXYZ&
abcdefghijklmnopqrstuvwxyz
1234567890$

14 point Univers No. 68 (Foundry)

ABCDEFGHIJKLMNOPQRSTUVWXYZ&
abcdefghijklmnopqrstuvwxyz
1234567890$

18 point Univers No. 68 (Foundry)

ABCDEFGHIJKLMNOPQRSTUVWXYZ&
abcdefghijklmnopqrstuvwxyz
1234567890$

10 point Univers No. 73 (Foundry)
ABCDEFGHIJKLMNOPQRSTUVWXYZ&
abcdefghijklmnopqrstuvwxyz
1234567890$

12 point Univers No. 73 (Foundry)
ABCDEFGHIJKLMNOPQRSTUV
WXYZ&
abcdefghijklmnopqrstuvwxyz
1234567890$

14 point Univers No. 73 (Foundry)
ABCDEFGHIJKLMNOPQRSTUVWXYZ&
abcdefghijklmnopqrstuvwxyz
1234567890$

18 point Univers No. 73 (Foundry)
ABCDEFGHIJKLMNOPQRSTUVWXYZ&
abcdefghijklmnopqrstuvwxyz
1234567890$

24 point Univers No. 73 Large (Foundry)
ABCDEFGHIJKLMNOPQRSTUV
WXYZ&
abcdefghijklmnopqrstuvwxyz
1234567890$

8 point Univers No. 75 (Foundry)
ABCDEFGHIJKLMNOPQRSTUVWXYZ&
abcdefghijklmnopqrstuvwxyz
1234567890$

12 point Univers No. 75 (Foundry)
ABCDEFGHIJKLMNOPQRSTUVWXYZ&
abcdefghijklmnopqrstuvwxyz
1234567890$

18 point Univers No. 75 (Foundry)
ABCDEFGHIJKLMNOPQRSTUVWXYZ&
abcdefghijklmnopqrstuvwxyz
1234567890$

24 point Univers No. 75 Small (Foundry)
ABCDEFGHIJKLMNOPQRSTUVWXYZ&
abcdefghijklmnopqrstuvwxyz
1234567890$

24 point Univers No. 75 Large (Foundry)
ABCDEFGHIJKLMNOPQRSTUVWXYZ&
abcdefghijklmnopqrstuvwxyz
1234567890$

30 point Univers No. 75 (Foundry)
**ABCDEFGHIJKLMNOPQRSTUV
WXYZ&**
abcdefghijklmnopqrstuvwxyz
1234567890$

(Continued on Page 541)

36 point Univers No. 75 (Foundry)

ABCDEFGHIJKLMNOPQR STUVWXYZ& abcdefghijklmnopqrstuv wxyz 1234567890$

Goudy Heavy

30 point Goudy Heavy (Foundry)

ABCDEFGHIJKLMNOPQRSTUV WXYZ& abcdefghijklmnopqrstuvwxyz 1234567890$

24 point Univers No. 76 Large (Foundry)

ABCDEFGHIJKLMNOPQRSTUVWXYZ&
abcdefghijklmnopqrstuvwxyz
1234567890$

30 point Univers No. 76 (Foundry)

ABCDEFGHIJKLMNOPQRST
UVWXYZ&
abcdefghijklmnopqrstuvwxyz
1234567890$

Vendome

10 point Vendome (Foundry)
ABCDEFGHIJKLMNOPQRSTUVWXYZ&
abcdefghijklmnopqrstuvwxyz
1234567890$

Vendome Bold Italic

24 point Vendome Bold Italic (Foundry)
ABCDEFGHIJKLMNOPQRSTUVWXYZ&
abcdefghijklmnopqrstuvwxyz
1234567890$

42 point Vendome Bold Italic (Foundry)
ABCDEFGHIJKLMNOPQR
STUVWXYZ&
abcdefghijklmnopqrstuv
wxyz
1234567890$

Venus Bold

ABCDEFGHIJKLMNOPQRSTUVWXYZ&
abcdefghijklmnopqrstuvwxyz
1234567890$

ABCDEFGHIJKLMNOPQRS
TUVWXYZ&
abcdefghijklmnopqrstuvwxyz
1234567890$

ABCDEFGHIJKLMN
OPQRSTUVWXYZ&
abcdefghijklmnopqrst
uvwxyz
1234567890$

Venus Bold Italic

8 point Venus Bold Italic (Foundry)
ABCDEFGHIJKLMNOPQRSTUVWXYZ&
abcdefghijklmnopqrstuvwxyz
1234567890$

10 point Venus Bold Italic (Foundry)
ABCDEFGHIJKLMNOPQRSTUVWXYZ&
abcdefghijklmnopqrstuvwxyz
1234567890$

12 point Venus Bold Italic (Foundry)
ABCDEFGHIJKLMNOPQRSTUVWXYZ&
abcdefghijklmnopqrstuvwxyz
1234567890$

14 point Venus Bold Italic (Foundry)
ABCDEFGHIJKLMNOPQRSTUVWXYZ&
abcdefghijklmnopqrstuvwxyz
1234567890$

16 point Venus Bold Italic (Foundry)
ABCDEFGHIJKLMNOPQRSTUVWXYZ&
abcdefghijklmnopqrstuvwxyz
1234567890&

18 point Venus Bold Italic (Foundry)
ABCDEFGHIJKLMNOPQRSTUVWXYZ&
abcdefghijklmnopqrstuvwxyz
1234567890$

24 point Venus Bold Italic (Foundry)
ABCDEFGHIJKLMNOPQRSTUVWXYZ&
abcdefghijklmnopqrstuvwxyz
1234567890$

30 point Venus Bold Italic (Foundry)
ABCDEFGHIJKLMNOPQRSTUV
WXYZ&
abcdefghijklmnopqrstuvwxyz
1234567890$

(Continued on Page 546)

(Continued from Page 545)

36 point Venus Bold Italic (Foundry)

ABCDEFGHIJKLMNOPQRSTU VWXYZ&

abcdefghijklmnopqrstuvwxyz 1234567890$

Venus Bold Condensed

12 point Venus Bold Condensed (Foundry)
ABCDEFGHIJKLMNOPQRSTUVWXYZ&
abcdefghijklmnopqrstuvwxyz
1234567890$

14 point Venus Bold Condensed (Foundry)
ABCDEFGHIJKLMNOPQRSTUVWXYZ&
abcdefghijklmnopqrstuvwxyz
1234567890$

18 point Venus Bold Condensed (Foundry)
ABCDEFGHIJKLMNOPQRSTUVWXYZ&
abcdefghijklmnopqrstuvwxyz
1234567890$

24 point Venus Bold Condensed (Foundry)
ABCDEFGHIJKLMNOPQRSTUVWXYZ&
abcdefghijklmnopqrstuvwxyz
1234567890$

36 point Venus Bold Condensed (Foundry)
ABCDEFGHIJKLMNOPQRSTUVWXYZ&
abcdefghijklmnopqrstuvwxyz
1234567890$

Venus Bold Extended

8 point Venus Bold Extended (Foundry)
ABCDEFGHIJKLMNOPQRSTUVWXYZ&
abcdefghijklmnopqrstuvwxyz
1234567890$

10 point Venus Bold Extended (Foundry)
ABCDEFGHIJKLMNOPQRSTUVWXYZ&
abcdefghijklmnopqrstuvwxyz
1234567890$

12 point Venus Bold Extended (Foundry)
ABCDEFGHIJKLMNOPQRSTUVWXYZ&
abcdefghijklmnopqrstuvwxyz
1234567890$

14 point Venus Bold Extended (Foundry)
ABCDEFGHIJKLMNOPQRSTUVWXYZ&
abcdefghijklmnopqrstuvwxyz
1234567890$

16 point Venus Bold Extended (Foundry)
ABCDEFGHIJKLMNOPQRSTUVWXYZ&
abcdefghijklmnopqrstuvwxyz
1234567890$

18 point Venus Bold Extended (Foundry)
ABCDEFGHIJKLMNOPQRSTUVWXYZ&
abcdefghijklmnopqrstuvwxyz
1234567890$

24 point Venus Bold Extended (Foundry)
ABCDEFGHIJKLMNOPQRSTU
WXYZ&
abcdefghijklmnopqrstuvwxyz
1234567890$

30 point Venus Bold Extended (Foundry)
ABCDEFGHIJKLMNOPQRSTU
VWXYZ&
abcdefghijklmnopqrstuvwxyz
1234567890$

(Continued on Page 549)

(Continued from Page 548)

36 point Venus Bold Extended (Foundry)

ABCDEFGHIJKLMNOPQ
RSTUVWXYZ&
abcdefghijklmnopqrstuv
wxyz
1234567890$

42 point Venus Bold Extended (Foundry)

ABCDEFGHIJKLMN
OPQRSTUVWXYZ&
abcdefghijklmnopq
rstuvwxyz
1234567890$

(Continued on Page 550)

54 point Venus Bold Extended (Foundry)

ABCDEFGHIJ
KLMNOPQRS
TUVWXYZ&
abcdefghijklm
nopqrstuvwxyz
1234567890$

Venus Extrabold

8 point Venus Extrabold (Foundry)
ABCDEFGHIJKLMNOPQRSTUVWXYZ&
abcdefghijklmnopqrstuvwxyz
1234567890$

10 point Venus Extrabold (Foundry)
ABCDEFGHIJKLMNOPQRSTUVWXYZ&
abcdefghijklmnopqrstuvwxyz
1234567890$

12 point Venus Extrabold (Foundry)
ABCDEFGHIJKLMNOPQRSTUVWXYZ&
abcdefghijklmnopqrstuvwxyz
1234567890$

Venus Extrabold Condensed

12 point Venus Extrabold Condensed (Foundry)
ABCDEFGHIJKLMNOPQRSTUVWXYZ&
abcdefghijklmnopqrstuvwxyz
1234567890$

14 point Venus Extrabold Condensed (Foundry)
ABCDEFGHIJKLMNOPQRSTUVWXYZ&
abcdefghijklmnopqrstuvwxyz
1234567890$

18 point Venus Extrabold Condensed (Foundry)
ABCDEFGHIJKLMNOPQRSTUVWXYZ&
abcdefghijklmnopqrstuvwxyz
1234567890$

Venus Extrabold Extended

8 point Venus Extrabold Extended (Foundry)
ABCDEFGHIJKLMNOPQRSTUVWXYZ&
abcdefghijklmnopqrstuvwxyz
1234567890$

10 point Venus Extrabold Extended (Foundry)
ABCDEFGHIJKLMNOPQRSTUVWXYZ&
abcdefghijklmnopqrstuvwxyz
1234567890$

12 point Venus Extrabold Extended (Foundry)
ABCDEFGHIJKLMNOPQRSTUVWXYZ&
abcdefghijklmnopqrstuvwxyz
1234567890$

14 point Venus Extrabold Extended (Foundry)
ABCDEFGHIJKLMNOPQRSTUVWXYZ&
abcdefghijklmnopqrstuvwxyz
1234567890$

16 point Venus Extrabold Extended (Foundry)
ABCDEFGHIJKLMNOPQRSTUVWXYZ&
abcdefghijklmnopqrstuvwxyz
1234567890$

18 point Venus Extrabold Extended (Foundry)
ABCDEFGHIJKLMNOPQRSTUVWXYZ&
abcdefghijklmnopqrstuvwxyz
1234567890$

24 point Venus Extrabold Extended (Foundry)
ABCDEFGHIJKLMNOPQRSTUV
WXYZ&
abcdefghijklmnopqrstuvwxyz
1234567890$

30 point Venus Extrabold Extended (Foundry)
ABCDEFGHIJKLMNOPQRS
TUVWXYZ&
abcdefghijklmnopqrstuv
wxyz
1234567890$

(Continued on Page 553)

36 point Venus Extrabold Extended (Foundry)

ABCDEFGHIJKLMNOP
QRSTUVWXYZ&
abcdefghijklmnopqrst
uvwxyz
1234567890$

42 point Venus Extrabold Extended (Foundry)

ABCDEFGHIJKLM
NOPQRSTUV
WXYZ&
abcdefghijklmno
pqrstuvwxyz
1234567890$

(Continued on Page 554)

54 point Venus Extrabold Extended (Foundry)

ABCDEFGHIJ
KLMNOPQRS
TUVWXYZ&
abcdefghijkl
mnopqrstuv
wxyz
12345
67890$

(Continued on Page 555)

66 point Venus Extrabold Extended (Foundry)

ABCDEFG
HIJKLMNO
PQRSTUV
WXYZ&
abcdefghij
klmnopqrs
tuvwxyz
12345
67890$

(Continued on Page 556)

(Continued from Page 555)

84 point Venus Extrabold Extended (Foundry)

ABCDEF
GHIJKLM
NOPQR
STUVW
XYZ&
123456
7890$

(Continued on Page 557)

84 point Venus Extrabold Extended (Foundry)

abcdefg
hijklmno
pqrstuv
wxyz

Venus Light

12 point Venus Light (Foundry)
ABCDEFGHIJKLMNOPQRSTUVWXYZ&
abcdefghijklmnopqrstuvwxyz
1234567890$

14 point Venus Light (Foundry)
ABCDEFGHIJKLMNOPQRSTUVWXYZ&
abcdefghijklmnopqrstuvwxyz
1234567890$

18 point Venus Light (Foundry)
ABCDEFGHIJKLMNOPQRSTUVWXYZ&
abcdefghijklmnopqrstuvwxyz
1234567890$

24 point Venus Light (Foundry)
ABCDEFGHIJKLMNOPQRSTUVWXYZ&
abcdefghijklmnopqrstuvwxyz
1234567890$

Venus Light Italic

Venus Light Extended

(Continued on Page 561)

(Continued from Page 560)

36 point Venus Light Extended (Foundry)

ABCDEFGHIJKLMNOPQRSTU
VWXYZ&
abcdefghijklmnopqrstuvwxyz
1234567890$

Venus Medium

14 point Venus Medium (Foundry)

ABCDEFGHIJKLMNOPQRSTUVWXYZ&
abcdefghijklmnopqrstuvwxyz
1234567890$

16 point Venus Medium (Foundry)

ABCDEFGHIJKLMNOPQRSTUVWXYZ&
abcdefghijklmnopqrstuvwxyz
1234567890$

18 point Venus Medium (Foundry)

ABCDEFGHIJKLMNOPQRSTUVWXYZ&
abcdefghijklmnopqrstuvwxyz
1234567890$

30 point Venus Medium (Foundry)

ABCDEFGHIJKLMNOPQRSTUVWXYZ&
abcdefghijklmnopqrstuvwxyz
1234567890$

Venus Medium Italic

8 point Venus Medium Italic (Foundry)
ABCDEFGHIJKLMNOPQRSTUVWXYZ&
abcdefghijklmnopqrstuvwxyz
1234567890$

10 point Venus Medium Italic (Foundry)
ABCDEFGHIJKLMNOPQRSTUVWXYZ&
abcdefghijklmnopqrstuvwxyz
1234567890$

12 point Venus Medium Italic (Foundry)
ABCDEFGHIJKLMNOPQRSTUVWXYZ&
abcdefghijklmnopqrstuvwxyz
1234567890$

14 point Venus Medium Italic (Foundry)
ABCDEFGHIJKLMNOPQRSTUVWXYZ&
abcdefghijklmnopqrstuvwxyz
1234567890$

16 point Venus Medium Italic (Foundry)
ABCDEFGHIJKLMNOPQRSTUVWXYZ&
abcdefghijklmnopqrstuvwxyz
1234567890$

18 point Venus Medium Italic (Foundry)
ABCDEFGHIJKLMNOPQRSTUVWXYZ&
abcdefghijklmnopqrstuvwxyz
1234567890$

24 point Venus Medium Italic (Foundry)
ABCDEFGHIJKLMNOPQRSTUVWXYZ&
abcdefghijklmnopqrstuvwxyz
1234567890$

Venus Medium Extended

6 point Venus Medium Extended (Foundry)
ABCDEFGHIJKLMNOPQRSTUVWXYZ&
abcdefghijklmnopqrstuvwxyz
1234567890$

8 point Venus Medium Extended (Foundry)
ABCDEFGHIJKLMNOPQRSTUVWXYZ&
abcdefghijklmnopqrstuvwxyz
1234567890$

10 point Venus Medium Extended (Foundry)
ABCDEFGHIJKLMNOPQRSTUVWXYZ&
abcdefghijklmnopqrstuvwxyz
1234567890$

12 point Venus Medium Extended (Foundry)
ABCDEFGHIJKLMNOPQRSTUVWXYZ
abcdefghijklmnopqrstuvwxyz&
1234567890$

14 point Venus Medium Extended (Foundry)
ABCDEFGHIJKLMNOPQRSTUVWXYZ&
abcdefghijklmnopqrstuvwxyz
1234567890$

16 point Venus Medium Extended (Foundry)
ABCDEFGHIJKLMNOPQRSTUVWXYZ&
abcdefghijklmnopqrstuvwxyz
1234567890$

18 point Venus Medium Extended (Foundry)
ABCDEFGHIJKLMNOPQRSTUVWXYZ&
abcdefghijklmnopqrstuvwxyz
1234567890$

24 point Venus Medium Extended (Foundry)
ABCDEFGHIJKLMNOPQRSTUVWXYZ&
abcdefghijklmnopqrstuvwxyz
1234567890$

30 point Venus Medium Extended (Foundry)
ABCDEFGHIJKLMNOPQRSTUV
WXYZ&
abcdefghijklmnopqrstuvwxyz
1234567890$

(Continued on Page 565)

Venus Medium Extended

(Continued from Page 564)

36 point Venus Medium Extended (Foundry)

ABCDEFGHIJKLMNOPQRSTU
VWXYZ&
abcdefghijklmnopqrstuvwxyz
1234567890$

42 point Venus Medium Extended (Foundry)

ABCDEFGHIJKLMNOP
QRSTUVWXYZ&
abcdefghijklmnopqrstuv
wxyz
1234567890$

Verona

18 point Verona (Foundry)

ABCDEFGHIJKLMNOPQRSTUVWXYZ&
abcdefghijklmnopqrstuvwxyz
1234567890$

30 point Verona (Foundry)

ABCDEFGHIJKLMNOPQRSTUVWXYZ&
abcdefghijklmnopqrstuvwxyz
1234567890$

Weiss Initials Series I

ABCDEFGHIJKLMNOPQRSTUVWXYZ&
1234567890O$

ABCDEFGHIJKLMNOPQRSTUVWXYZ&
1234567890O$

ABCDEFGHIJKLMNOPQRSTUVWXYZ
1234567890O$&

ABCDEFGHIJKLMNOPQRSTU
VWXYZ&
1234567890O$

ABCDEFGHIJKLMNOPQRS
TUVWXYZ&
1234567890O$

ABCDEFGHIJKLMN
OPQRSTUVWXYZ
1234567890O$&

14 point Weiss Initials Series II, Cap font (Foundry)

ABCDEFGHIJKLMNOPQRSTUVWXYZ&
1234567890$

18 point Weiss Initials Series II, Cap font (Foundry)

ABCDEFGHIJKLMNOPQRSTUVWXYZ&
1234567890$

24 point Weiss Initials Series II, Cap font (Foundry)

ABCDEFGHIJKLMNOPQRSTUVWXYZ&
1234567890$

30 point Weiss Initials Series II Small, Cap font (Foundry)

ABCDEFGHIJKLMNOPQRSTUVWXYZ&
1234567890$

30 point Weiss Initials Series II Large, Cap font (Foundry)

ABCDEFGHIJKLMNOPQRSTUV
WXYZ&
1234567890$

42 point Weiss Initials Series II, Cap font (Foundry)

ABCDEFGHIJKLMNOPQRST
UVWXYZ&
1234567890$

(Continued on Page 569)

66 point Weiss Initials Series II, Cap font (Foundry)

ABCDEFGHIJKL
MNOPQRSTUV
WXYZ&
1234567890O$

14 point Weiss Initials Series III, Cap font (Foundry)

ABCDEFGHIJKLMNOPQRSTUVWXYZ&
1234567890O$

18 point Weiss Initials Series III, Cap font (Foundry)

ABCDEFGHIJKLMNOPQRSTUVWXYZ&
1234567890O$

30 point Weiss Initials Series III Small, Cap font (Foundry)

ABCDEFGHIJKLMNOPQRSTUV
WXYZ&
1234567890O$

42 point Weiss Initials Series III, Cap font (Foundry)

ABCDEFGHIJKLMNOPQ
RSTUVWXYZ&
1234567890O$

Weiss Roman

8 point Weiss Roman (Intertype)

The basic character in a type design is determined by the uniform design char acteristics of all letters in the alphabet. However, this alone does not determine the standard of the type face and the quality of composition set with it. The appearance is something complex which forms itself out of many details, like form, proportion, ductus, rhythm etc. If everything harmonizes, the total result

ABCDEFGHIJKLMNOPQRSTUVWXYZ&
abcdefghijklmnopqrstuvwxyz   1234567890$
ABCDEFGHIJKLMNOPQRSTUVWXYZ

9 point Weiss Roman (Intertype)

The basic character in a type design is determined by the uniform de sign characteristics of all letters in the alphabet. However, this alone does not determine the standard of the type face and the quality of composition set with it. The appearance is something complex which

ABCDEFGHIJKLMNOPQRSTUVWXYZ&
abcdefghijklmnopqrstuvwxyz   1234567890$
ABCDEFGHIJKLMNOPQRSTUVWXYZ

10 point Weiss Roman (Intertype)

The basic character in a type design is determined by the uniform design characteristics of all letters in the alphabet. However, this alone does not determine the standard of the type face and the quality of composition set with it. The appearance is something

ABCDEFGHIJKLMNOPQRSTUVWXYZ&
abcdefghijklmnopqrstuvwxyz   1234567890$
ABCDEFGHIJKLMNOPQRSTUVWXYZ

11 point Weiss Roman (Intertype)

The basic character in a type design is determined by the uni form design characteristics of all letters in the alphabet. How ever, this alone does not determine the standard of the type

ABCDEFGHIJKLMNOPQRSTUVWXYZ&
abcdefghijklmnopqrstuvwxyz   1234567890$
ABCDEFGHIJKLMNOPQRSTUVWXYZ

12 point Weiss Roman (Intertype)

The basic character in a type design is determined by the uniform design characteristics of all letters in the alpha bet. However, this alone does not determine the standard

ABCDEFGHIJKLMNOPQRSTUVWXYZ&
abcdefghijklmnopqrstuvwxyz   1234567890$
ABCDEFGHIJKLMNOPQRSTUVWXYZ

14 point Weiss Roman (Intertype)

The basic character in a type design is determined by the uniform design characteristics of all letters

ABCDEFGHIJKLMNOPQRSTUVWXYZ&
abcdefghijklmnopqrstuvwxyz   1234567890$
ABCDEFGHIJKLMNOPQRSTUVWXYZ

10 point Weiss Roman (Foundry)

ABCDEFGHIJKLMNOPQRSTUVWXYZ&
abcdefghijklmnopqrstuvwxyz
1234567890$

12 point Weiss Roman (Foundry)

ABCDEFGHIJKLMNOPQRSTUVWXYZ&
abcdefghijklmnopqrstuvwxyz
1234567890$
ABCDEFGHIJKLMNOPQRSTUVWXYZ

14 point Weiss Roman with Small Caps (Foundry)

ABCDEFGHIJKLMNOPQRSTUVWXYZ&
1234567890$
ABCDEFGHIJKLMNOPQRSTUVWXYZ

16 point Weiss Roman (Foundry)

ABCDEFGHIJKLMNOPQRSTUVWXYZ&
abcdefghijklmnopqrstuvwxyz
1234567890$

18 point Weiss Roman (Foundry)

ABCDEFGHIJKLMNOPQRSTUVWXYZ&
abcdefghijklmnopqrstuvwxyz
1234567890$

24 point Weiss Roman (Foundry)

ABCDEFGHIJKLMNOPQRSTUVWXYZ&
abcdefghijklmnopqrstuvwxyz
1234567890$

(Continued on Page 572)

30 point Weiss Roman (Foundry)

ABCDEFGHIJKLMNOPQRSTUVWXYZ
abcdefghijklmnopqrstuvwxyz&
1234567890$

36 point Weiss Roman (Foundry)

ABCDEFGHIJKLMNOPQRSTU
VWXYZ&
abcdefghijklmnopqrstuvwxyz
1234567890$

48 point Weiss Roman (Foundry)

ABCDEFGHIJKLMNOP
QRSTUVWXYZ&
abcdefghijklmnopqrstuv
wxyz
1234567890$

(Continued on Page 573)

60 point Weiss Roman (Foundry)

ABCDEFGHIJKLM
NOPQRSTUV
WXYZ&
abcdefghijklmnopqrs
tuvwxyz
1234567890$

Weiss Italic

8 point Weiss Italic (Intertype)

The basic character in a type design is determined by the uniform design characteristics of all letters in the alphabet. However, this alone does not determine the standard of the type face and the quality of composition set with it. The appearance is something complex which forms itself out of many details, like form, proportion, ductus, rhythm etc. If everything harmonizes, the total result

ABCDEF GHIJKLMNOPQRSTUVWXYZ&
abcdefghijklmnopqrstuvwxyz   1234567890$

9 point Weiss Italic (Intertype)

The basic character in a type design is determined by the uniform design characteristics of all letters in the alphabet. However, this alone does not determine the standard of the type face and the quality of composition set with it. The appearance is something complex which

ABCDEFGHIJKLMNOPQRSTUVWXYZ&
abcdefghijklmnopqrstuvwxyz   1234567890$

10 point Weiss Italic (Intertype)

The basic character in a type design is determined by the uniform design characteristics of all letters in the alphabet. However, this alone does not determine the standard of the type face and the quality of composition set with it. The appearance is something

ABCDEF GHIJKLMNOPQRSTUVWXYZ&
abcdefghijklmnopqrstuvwxyz   1234567890$

11 point Weiss Italic (Intertype)

The basic character in a type design is determined by the uniform design characteristics of all letters in the alphabet. However, this alone does not determine the standard of the type

ABCDEF GHIJKLMNOPQRSTUVWXYZ&
abcdefghijklmnopqrstuvwxyz   1234567890$

12 point Weiss Italic (Intertype)

The basic character in a type design is determined by the uniform design characteristics of all letters in the alphabet. However, this alone does not determine the standard

ABCDEFGHIJKLMNOPQRSTUVWXYZ&
abcdefghijklmnopqrstuvwxyz   1234567890$

14 point Weiss Italic (Intertype)

The basic character in a type design is determined by the uniform design characteristics of all letters

ABCDEFGHIJKLMNOPQRSTUVWXYZ&
abcdefghijklmnopqrstuvwxyz   1234567890$

10 point Weiss Italic (Foundry)

ABCDEFGHIJKLMNOPQRSTUVWXYZ&
abcdefghijklmnopqrstuvwxyz
1234567890$

12 point Weiss Italic (Foundry)

ABCDEFGHIJKLMNOPQRSTUVWXYZ&
abcdefghijklmnopqrstuvwxyz
1234567890$

14 point Weiss Italic (Foundry)

ABCDEFGHIJKLMNOPQRSTUVWXYZ&
abcdefghijklmnopqrstuvwxyz
1234567890$

16 point Weiss Italic (Foundry)

ABCDEFGHIJKLMNOPQRSTUVWXYZ&
abcdefghijklmnopqrstuvwxyz
1234567890$

18 point Weiss Italic (Foundry)

ABCDEFGHIJKLMNOPQRSTUVWXYZ&
abcdefghijklmnopqrstuvwxyz
1234567890$

SWASH AND TERMINALS

A B D E F G H I J K L M N P R T U V W X Y Z

e m n t & & st

(Continued on Page 575)

24 point Weiss Italic (Foundry)

ABCDEFGHIJKLMNOPQRSTUVWX YZ&
abcdefghijklmnopqrstuvwxyz
1234567890$

SWASH AND TERMINALS

A B C D E F G H I J K L M N P R T U V W X Y Z Th Qu

e m n t & et st

30 point Weiss Italic (Foundry)

ABCDEFGHIJKLMNOPQRSTUVWXYZ&
abcdefghijklmnopqrstuvwxyz
1234567890$

SWASH AND TERMINALS

A B C D E F G H I J K L M N P R T U V W

X Y Z Th Qu e m n t & et st

36 point Weiss Italic (Foundry)

ABCDEFGHIJKLMNOPQRSTUV
WXYZ&
abcdefghijklmnopqrstuvwxyz
1234567890$

SWASH AND TERMINALS

A B C D E F G H I J K L M N P R T

U V W X Y Z Th Qu e m n t et

Weiss Roman Bold

14 point Weiss Roman Bold (Foundry)

ABCDEFGHIJKLMNOPQRSTUVWXYZ&
abcdefghijklmnopqrstuvwxyz
1234567890$

18 point Weiss Roman Bold (Foundry)

ABCDEFGHIJKLMNOPQRSTUVWXYZ&
abcdefghijklmnopqrstuvwxyz
1234567890$

24 point Weiss Roman Bold (Foundry)

ABCDEFGHIJKLMNOPQRSTUVWXYZ&
abcdefghijklmnopqrstuvwxyz
1234567890$

30 point Weiss Roman Bold (Foundry)

ABCDEFGHIJKLMNOPQRSTUVWXYZ
abcdefghijklmnopqrstuvwxyz&
1234567890$

24 point Weiss Roman Extra Bold (Foundry)

ABCDEFGHIJKLMNOPQRSTUVWXYZ&
abcdefghijklmnopqrstuvwxyz
1234567890$

30 point Weiss Roman Extra Bold (Foundry)

ABCDEFGHIJKLMNOPQRSTUV
WXYZ&
abcdefghijklmnopqrstuvwxyz
1234567890$

10 point Windsor (Foundry)

ABCDEFGHIJKLMNOPQRSTUVWXYZ&
abcdefghijklmnopqrstuvwxyz
1234567890$

14 point Windsor (Foundry)

ABCDEFGHIJKLMNOPQRSTUVWXYZ&
abcdefghijklmnopqrstuvwxyz
1234567890$

18 point Windsor (Foundry)

ABCDEFGHIJKLMNOPQRSTUVWXYZ&
abcdefghijklmnopqrstuvwxyz
1234567890$

24 point Windsor (Foundry)

ABCDEFGHIJKLMNOPQRSTUVWXYZ
abcdefghijklmnopqrstuvwxyz&
1234567890$

30 point Windsor (Foundry)

ABCDEFGHIJKLMNOPQRST
UVWXYZ&
abcdefghijklmnopqrstuvwxyz
1234567890$

36 point Windsor (Foundry)

ABCDEFGHIJKLMNOP
QRSTUVWXYZ&
abcdefghijklmnopqrstuv
wxyz
1234567890$

(Continued on Page 579)

48 point Windsor (Foundry)

ABCDEFGHIJKLM
NOPQRSTUV
WXYZ&
abcdefghijklmnopqr
stuvwxyz
1234567890$

Windsor Elongated

60 point Windsor Elongated (Foundry)

ABCDEFGHIJKLMNOPQRST
UVWXYZ&
abcdefghijklmnopqrstuvwxyz
1234567890$

Windsor Light

24 point Windsor Light (Foundry)

ABCDEFGHIJKLMNOPQRSTUVWXYZ&
abcdefghijklmnopqrstuvwxyz
1234567890$

STUBBY ARROWHEADS

Outline Left

12 point	◁
18 point	◁
24 point	◁
30 point	◁
36 point	◁
48 point	◁

Outline Right

12 point	▷
18 point	▷
24 point	▷
30 point	▷
36 point	▷
48 point	▷

Solid Left

12 point	◀
18 point	◀
24 point	◀
30 point	◀
36 point	◀
48 point	◀

Solid Right

12 point	▶
18 point	▶
24 point	▶
30 point	▶
36 point	▶
48 point	▶

COMMERCIAL SECTION MARKS

Roman

18 point	§
24 point	§
30 point	§
36 point	§

Italic

18 point	§
24 point	§
30 point	§
42 point	§

Section Marks are made for Tempo Bold
and Tempo Bold Italic

REGISTER MARKS

6 point	®
8 point	®
10 point	®
12 point	®

COPYRIGHT SIGNS

6 point	©
8 point	©
10 point	©
14 point	©
18 point	©
24 point	©

COMMERCIAL @

8 point	@
10 point	@
12 point	@

CORNER MARKS

Top Pieces

Bottom Pieces

ELECTION SQUARES

8 point	□
10 point	□
12 point	□
18 point	□
24 point	□
36 point	□

Ludlow—Miscellaneous Matrices

BRACES

Lefthand		Righthand
{	12 point	}
{	14 point	}
{	18 point	}
{	24 point	}
{	30 point	}
{	36 point	}
{	42 point	}
{	48 point	}

COMMERCIAL ACCOUNT SIGNS

8 point	a/c
10 point	a/c

FISTS—FULL FACE

Righthand
6 point	
12 point	
18 point	

Lefthand
6 point	
12 point	
18 point	

PLAYING CARDS

16 x 12 points

C1418	♣
C1419	♠
C1420	♦
C1421	♥

30 x 24 points

C1422	♣
C1423	♠
C1424	♦
C1425	♥

PRESCRIPTION MARK

18 point	℞
24 point	℞

CENT MARKS— ROMAN

Lightface
8 point	¢
10 point	¢

Boldface
12 point	¢
18 point	¢

ARROWS

6 point	⟶
12 point	⟶

CROSS

Made for Tempo Bold

24 point	†
48 point	†

ASTERISKS— MODERN

6 point	*
8 point	*
10 point	*
12 point	*
14 point	*
18 point	*

NUMBER SIGNS

Lightface
6 point	#
8 point	#
10 point	#
12 point	#

Boldface
12 point	#
14 point	#
18 point	#

MISCELLANEOUS

1971	
2058	
1934	PRINTED IN U.S.A.

SHILLING STROKES

Lightface
6 point	/
8 point	/
10 point	/
12 point	/
18 point	/
24 point	/

Boldface
6 point	/
8 point	/
10 point	/
12 point	/
18 point	/
24 point	/

PER CENT MARKS

Lightface
8 point	%
10 point	%
12 point	%
18 point	%
24 point	%

Boldface
12 point	%
18 point	%
24 point	%

COMMERCIAL CHECK SIGNS

Lightface
6 point	✓
8 point	✓
10 point	✓
12 point	✓

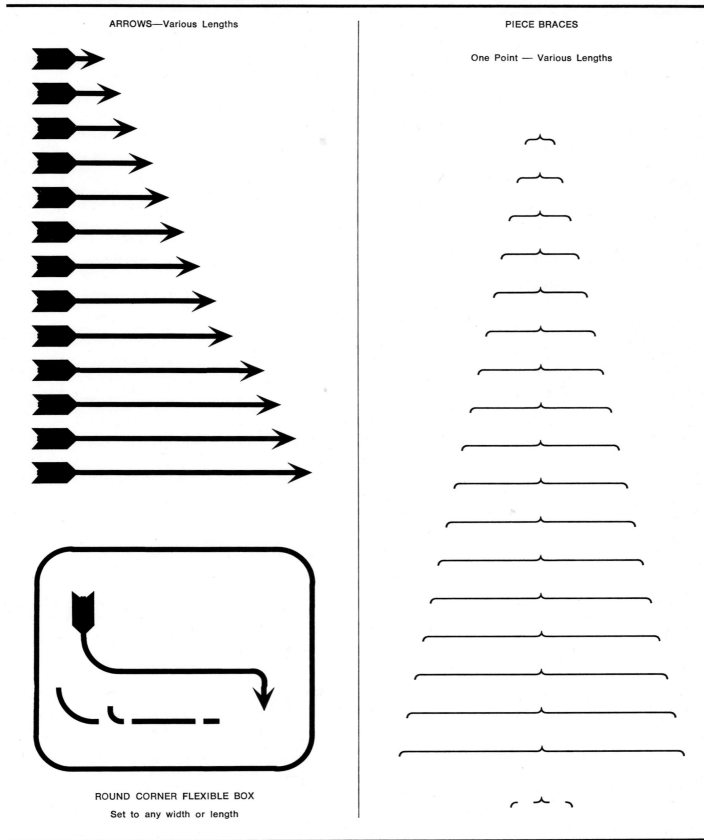

ARROWS—Various Lengths

PIECE BRACES

One Point — Various Lengths

ROUND CORNER FLEXIBLE BOX

Set to any width or length

Ludlow—Gothic Miscellaneous Matrices

FISTS FULLFACE

Righthand

6 point No. 3	
12 point No. 2	
12 point No. 3	
18 point No. 1	

Lefthand

6 point No. 3	
12 point No. 2	
12 point No. 3	
18 point No. 1	

FISTS OUTLINE

Righthand

6 point No. 3	
12 point No. 2	
12 point No. 3	
12 point No. 4	

Lefthand

6 point No. 3	
12 point No. 2	
12 point No. 3	
12 point No. 4	

CHECK SIGNS

6 point No. 4	✓
12 point No. 2	✓
12 point No. 3	✓
12 point No. 4	✓

SOLID DOTS

6 point No. 3	●
12 point No. 1	●

ARROWS

6 point No. 3	
12 point No. 4	

NUMBER SIGNS

12 point No. 2	#
12 point No. 3	#
12 point No. 4	#

COMMERCIAL @

6 point No. 3	@
6 point No. 4	@
12 point No. 1	@
12 point No. 2	@

REGISTER MARKS

6 point No. 3	®
12 point No. 1	®

COPYRIGHT SIGNS

6 point No. 3	©
12 point No. 1	©

ASTERISKS—MODERN

6 point No. 1	*
6 point No. 2	*
6 point No. 3	*
6 point No. 4	*
12 point No. 1	*
12 point No. 2	*
12 point No. 3	*
12 point No. 4	*

ELECTION SQUARES

6 point No. 3	□
12 point No. 1	□
12 point No. 2	□
12 point No. 3	□
12 point No. 4	□

PARENTHESES

Commerce Gothic Light

(	6 point No. 1	)
(	6 point No. 2	)
(	6 point No. 3	)
(	6 point No. 4	)
(	12 point No. 1	)
(	12 point No. 2	)
(	12 point No. 3	)
(	12 point No. 4	)

Lining Plate Gothic

(	6 point No. 2	)
(	6 point No. 3	)
(	6 point No. 4	)
(	12 point No. 1	)
(	12 point No. 2	)
(	12 point No. 3	)
(	12 point No. 4	)

PERCENT MARKS

Lining Plate Gothic

6 point No. 2	
6 point No. 3	%
6 point No. 4	%
12 point No. 1	%
12 point No. 2	%
12 point No. 3	%
12 point No. 4	%

Commerce Gothic Light

6 point No. 1	%
6 point No. 2	%
6 point No. 3	%
6 point No. 4	%
12 point No. 1	%
12 point No. 2	%
12 point No. 3	%
12 point No. 4	%

Ludlow—Em-Set Diagonal Fractions

	BOLD ROMAN DIAGONAL FRACTIONS						LIGHT ROMAN DIAGONAL FRACTIONS			
8 point	10 point	12 point	18 point	24 point		8 point	10 point	12 point	18 point	24 point
¼	¼	¼	¼	¼		¼	¼	¼	¼	¼
½	½	½	½	½		½	½	½	½	½
¾	¾	¾	¾	¾		¾	¾	¾	¾	¾
⅓	⅓	⅓	⅓	⅓		⅓	⅓	⅓	⅓	⅓
⅔	⅔	⅔	⅔	⅔		⅔	⅔	⅔	⅔	
⅛	⅛	⅛	⅛	⅛		⅛	⅛	⅛	⅛	⅛
⅜	⅜	⅜	⅜	⅜		⅜	⅜	⅜	⅜	⅜
⅝	⅝	⅝	⅝	⅝		⅝	⅝	⅝	⅝	⅝
⅞	⅞	⅞	⅞	⅞		⅞	⅞	⅞	⅞	⅞

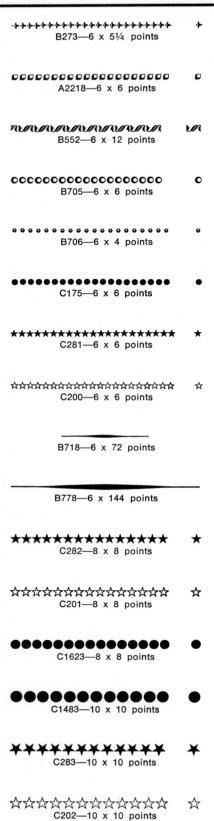

B273—6 x 5¼ points

A2218—6 x 6 points

B552—6 x 12 points

B705—6 x 6 points

B706—6 x 4 points

C175—6 x 6 points

C281—6 x 6 points

C200—6 x 6 points

B718—6 x 72 points

B778—6 x 144 points

C282—8 x 8 points

C201—8 x 8 points

C1623—8 x 8 points

C1483—10 x 10 points

C283—10 x 10 points

C202—10 x 10 points

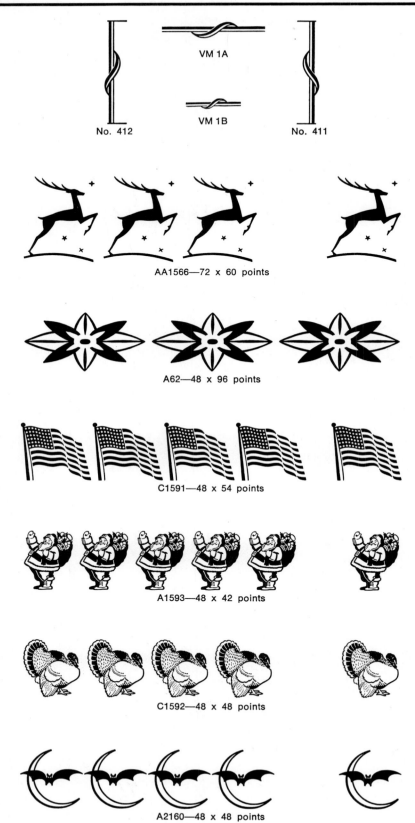

VM 1A

VM 1B

No. 412   No. 411

AA1566—72 x 60 points

A62—48 x 96 points

C1591—48 x 54 points

A1593—48 x 42 points

C1592—48 x 48 points

A2160—48 x 48 points

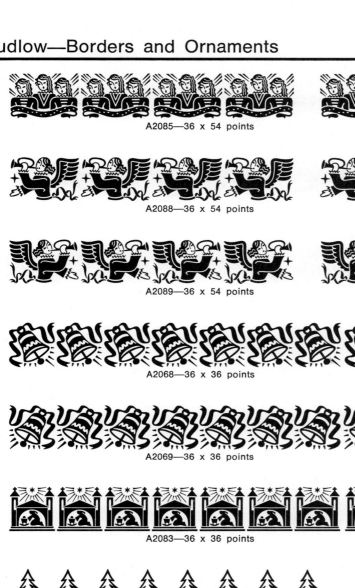

A2085—36 x 54 points

A2088—36 x 54 points

A2089—36 x 54 points

A2068—36 x 36 points

A2069—36 x 36 points

A2083—36 x 36 points

A1563—36 x 30 points

A1564—36 x 30 points

A1580—Wreath—36 x 36 points

A1581—Berries—36 x 36 points

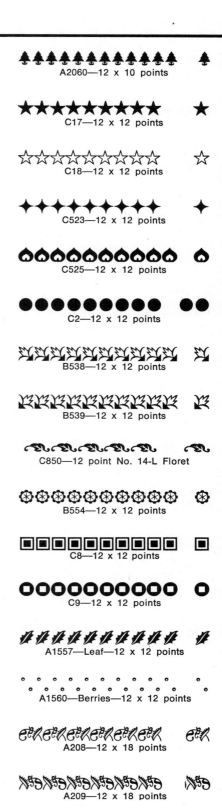

A2060—12 x 10 points

C17—12 x 12 points

C18—12 x 12 points

C523—12 x 12 points

C525—12 x 12 points

C2—12 x 12 points

B538—12 x 12 points

B539—12 x 12 points

C850—12 point No. 14-L Floret

B554—12 x 12 points

C8—12 x 12 points

C9—12 x 12 points

A1557—Leaf—12 x 12 points

A1560—Berries—12 x 12 points

A208—12 x 18 points

A209—12 x 18 points

B21—12 x 12 points

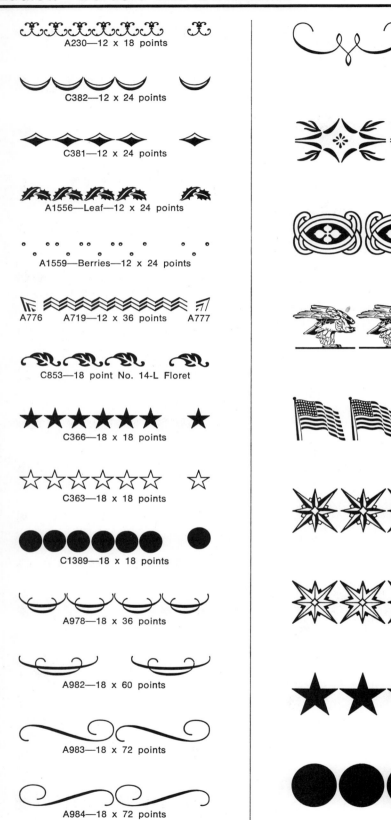

A230—12 x 18 points

C382—12 x 24 points

C381—12 x 24 points

A1556—Leaf—12 x 24 points

A1559—Berries—12 x 24 points

A776   A719—12 x 36 points   A777

C853—18 point No. 14-L Floret

C366—18 x 18 points

C363—18 x 18 points

C1389—18 x 18 points

A978—18 x 36 points

A982—18 x 60 points

A983—18 x 72 points

A984—18 x 72 points

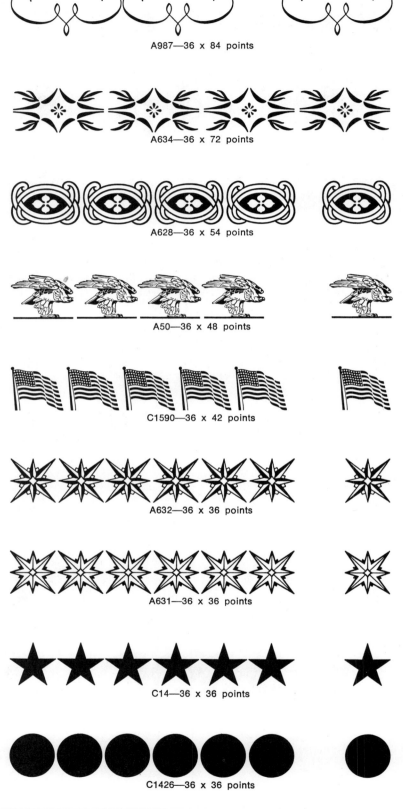

A987—36 x 84 points

A634—36 x 72 points

A628—36 x 54 points

A50—36 x 48 points

C1590—36 x 42 points

A632—36 x 36 points

A631—36 x 36 points

C14—36 x 36 points

C1426—36 x 36 points

A361—36 x 36 points

A2153—36 x 36 points

A2156—36 x 36 points

A2158—36 x 30 points

A2150—36 x 24 points

B842

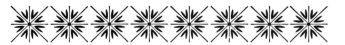

A720—30 x 30 points

C822

A657—24 x 60 points

A2074—24 x 48 points

A985—18 x 72 points

A986—18 x 72 points

C15—24 x 24 points

C16—24 x 24 points

A570—24 x 24 points

A571—24 x 24 points

A572—24 x 24 points

A2062—24 x 24 points

A2064—24 x 24 points

A651—24 x 24 points

A653—24 x 24 points

A655—24 x 24 points

FIVE POINTED STARS FULLFACE

12 point ★

14 point ★

18 point ★

24 point ★

36 point ★

48 point ★

MATHEMATICAL GREEK PI

18 point on
14 point body   Π

18 point   Π

24 point   Π

MATHEMATICAL GREEK SIGMA

12 point   Σ

18 point   Σ

24 point   Σ

36 point   Σ

FIVE POINTED STARS OUTLINE

14 point ☆

18 point ☆

24 point ☆

30 point ☆

36 point ☆

MATHEMATICAL ROOT SIGNS

12 point $\sqrt{}$

12 point Cube Root $\sqrt[3]{}$

18 point $\sqrt{}$

22 point $\sqrt{}$

24 point $\sqrt{}$

36 point $\sqrt{}$

MATHEMATICAL INTEGRAL SIGNS

18 point $\int$

24 point $\int$

SIX POINTED STARS FULLFACE

6 point ✳

8 point ✳

10 point ✳

12 point ✳

14 point ✳

18 point ✳

24 point ✳

COMMERCIAL @ SIGNS

6 point   @

12 point   @

18 point   @

BUSINESS REPLY LOGOTYPES

Postage
Will be Paid
by
Addressee

No
Postage Stamp
Necessary
If Mailed in the
United States

Foundry—Miscellaneous

FISTS

Fullface

12 point	
12 point	
18 point	
18 point	
24 point	
24 point	
48 point	

Shaded

36 point	
36 point	
48 point	

Outline

8 point	
10 point	
12 point	
18 point	
24 point	

SHILLING MARKS

Light

6 point	/
8 point	/
10 point	/
12 point	/
14 point	/
18 point	/
24 point	/
30 point	/
36 point	/

Bold

12 point	/
14 point	/
18 point	/
24 point	/
30 point	/
36 point	/
60 point	/

ASTERISKS

6 point	.
8 point	*
10 point	*
12 point	*
14 point	*
18 point	*
24 point	*
30 point	*
36 point	*
36 point full	*

MODERN ASTERISKS

6 point	*
10 point	*
12 point	*
14 point	*
18 point	*
24 point	*
30 point	*
36 point	*

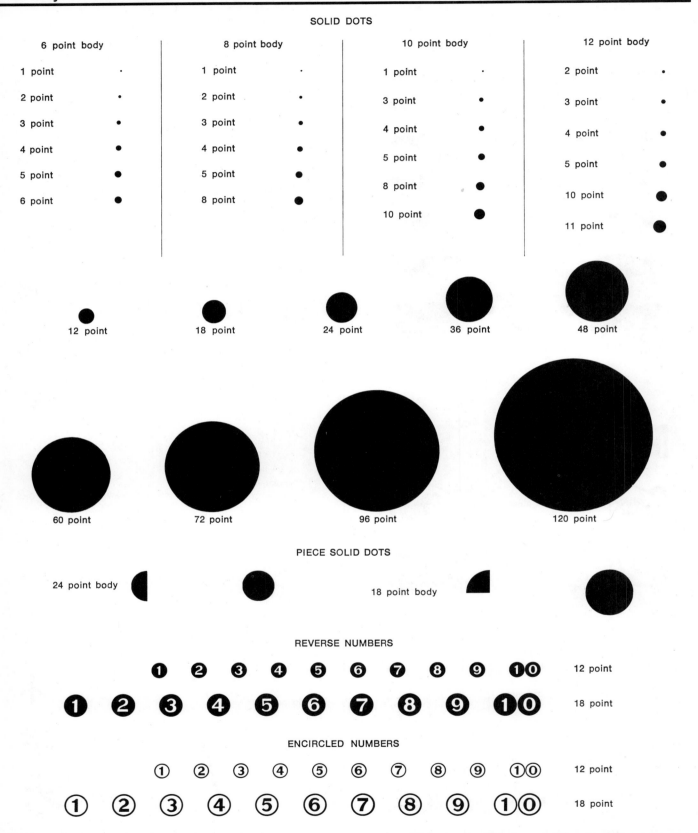

SOLID DOTS

6 point body

1 point
2 point
3 point
4 point
5 point
6 point

8 point body

1 point
2 point
3 point
4 point
5 point
8 point

10 point body

1 point
3 point
4 point
5 point
8 point
10 point

12 point body

2 point
3 point
4 point
5 point
10 point
11 point

12 point
18 point
24 point
36 point
48 point

60 point
72 point
96 point
120 point

PIECE SOLID DOTS

24 point body
18 point body

REVERSE NUMBERS

1 2 3 4 5 6 7 8 9 10   12 point

1 2 3 4 5 6 7 8 9 10   18 point

ENCIRCLED NUMBERS

1 2 3 4 5 6 7 8 9 10   12 point

1 2 3 4 5 6 7 8 9 10   18 point

Foundry—Miscellaneous

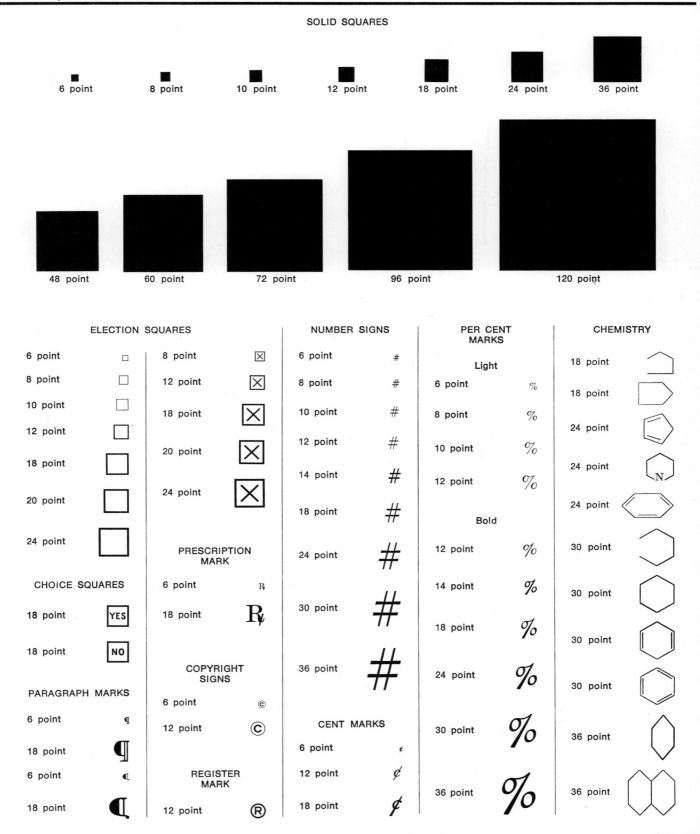

SOLID SQUARES

6 point 8 point 10 point 12 point 18 point 24 point 36 point

48 point 60 point 72 point 96 point 120 point

ELECTION SQUARES		NUMBER SIGNS	PER CENT MARKS	CHEMISTRY
6 point	8 point	6 point #	Light	18 point
8 point	12 point	8 point #	6 point %	18 point
10 point	18 point	10 point #	8 point %	24 point
12 point	20 point	12 point #	10 point %	24 point
18 point	24 point	14 point #	12 point %	24 point
20 point		18 point #	Bold	24 point
24 point	PRESCRIPTION MARK	24 point #	12 point %	30 point
CHOICE SQUARES	6 point	30 point #	14 point %	30 point
18 point YES	18 point ℞	36 point #	18 point %	30 point
18 point NO	COPYRIGHT SIGNS		24 point %	30 point
PARAGRAPH MARKS	6 point ©	CENT MARKS	30 point %	30 point
6 point	12 point ©	6 point ¢	36 point %	36 point
18 point	REGISTER MARK	12 point ¢		36 point
6 point	12 point ®	18 point ¢		
18 point				

Foundry—Miscellaneous

SQUARE BRACKETS

LIGHT

6 point]

[8 point]

[10 point]

[12 point]

[14 point]

[18 point]

[24 point]

[30 point]

[36 point]

[42 point]

[48 point]

[60 point]

[72 point]

BOLD

[14 point]

[18 point]

[24 point]

[30 point]

[36 point]

FANCY

48 point

60 point

72 point

48 point

60 point

72 point

BRACES

LIGHT

{ 12 point }

{ 14 point }

{ 16 point }

{ 18 point }

{ 20 point }

{ 21 point }

{ 24 point }

{ 27 point }

{ 28 point }

{ 30 point }

{ 32 point }

{ 36 point }

{ 39 point }

{ 42 point }

{ 48 point }

LIGHT

{ 60 point }

{ 72 point }

BOLD

{ 30 point }

{ 36 point }

{ 48 point }

{ 60 point }

{ 72 point }

MEDIUM

{ 24 point }

{ 30 point }

{ 36 point }

594

Foundry—Miscellaneous

PARENTHESES

	LIGHT	MEDIUM	BOLD	BOLD ITALIC
6 point	( )		( )	( )
8 point	( )		( )	( )
10 point	( )		( )	( )
12 point	( )		( )	( )
14 point		( )	( )	
18 point	( )	( )		
24 point	( )	( )		
30 point	( )	( )	( )	( )
36 point	( )	( )	( )	( )
42 point			( )	( )
48 point	( )			
60 point	( )		( )	( )
72 point	( )		( )	( )

CIRCLES

6 point	12 point	18 point	20 point	24 point
○	◯	◯	◯	◯

PIECE CIRCLE

36 point body

MORTISE CIRCLE

96 point

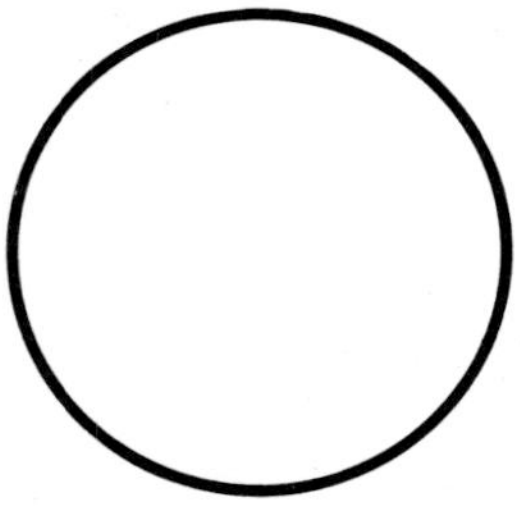

18 point body

BALLOT CIRCLES

12 point	18 point	20 point	24 point
⊗	⊗	⊗	⊗

DIAGONAL FRACTIONS—CHELTENHAM

6 point	8 point	10 point	12 point	14 point	18 point
⅛	⅛	⅛	⅛	⅛	⅛
¼	¼	¼	¼	¼	¼
⅜	⅜	⅜	⅜	⅜	⅜
½	½	½	½	½	½
⅝	⅝	⅝	⅝	⅝	⅝
¾	¾	¾	¾	¾	¾
⅞	⅞	⅞	⅞	⅞	⅞
⅓	⅓	⅓	⅓	⅓	⅓
⅔	⅔	⅔	⅔	⅔	⅔
⅙	⅙	⅙	⅙	⅙	⅙
					⅚

Foundry—Miscellaneous

DIAGONAL FRACTIONS—GOTHIC

6 point	8 point	10 point	12 point	14 point	18 point	24 point
⅛	⅛	⅛	⅛	⅛	⅛	⅛
¼	¼	¼	¼	¼	¼	¼
⅜	⅜	⅜	⅜	⅜	⅜	⅜
½	½	½	½	½	½	½
⅝	⅝	⅝	⅝	⅝	⅝	⅝
¾	¾	¾	¾	¾	¾	¾
⅞	⅞	⅞	⅞	⅞	⅞	⅞
⅓	⅓	⅓	⅓	⅓	⅓	⅓
⅔	⅔	⅔	⅔	⅔	⅔	⅔

DIAGONAL FRACTIONS—STYMIE

6 point	8 point	10 point	12 point	14 point	18 point	24 point
⅛	⅛	⅛	⅛	⅛	⅛	⅛
¼	¼	¼	¼	¼	¼	¼
⅜	⅜	⅜	⅜	⅜	⅜	⅜
½	½	½	½	½	½	½
⅝	⅝	⅝	⅝	⅝	⅝	⅝
¾	¾	¾	¾	¾	¾	¾
⅞	⅞	⅞	⅞	⅞	⅞	⅞
⅓	⅓	⅓	⅓	⅓	⅓	⅓
⅔	⅔	⅔	⅔	⅔	⅔	⅔

DIAGONAL PIECE FRACTIONS

6 point

Superior	1	2	3	4	5	6	7	8	9	0
Inferior	1	2	3	4	5	6	7	8	9	0
Superior	1,	2,	3,	4,	5,	6,	7,	8,	9,	0,
Inferior	1	2	3	4	5	6	7	8	9	0

Example: ⅔ 5⁄9

8 point

Superior	1	2	3	4	5	6	7	8	9	0
Inferior	1	2	3	4	5	6	7	8	9	0
Superior	1,	2,	3,	4,	5,	6,	7,	8,	9,	0,
Inferior	1	2	3	4	5	6	7	8	9	0

Example: 6⁄7 8⁄9

10 point

Superior	1	2	3	4	5	6	7	8	9	0
Inferior	1	2	3	4	5	6	7	8	9	0
Superior	1,	2,	3,	4,	5,	6,	7,	8,	9,	0,
Inferior	1	2	3	4	5	6	7	8	9	0

Example: ⅕ 3⁄5

12 point

Superior	1	2	3	4	5	6	7	8	9	0
Inferior	1	2	3	4	5	6	7	8	9	0
Superior	1,	2,	3,	4,	5,	6,	7,	8,	9,	0,
Inferior	1	2	3	4	5	6	7	8	9	0

Example: 5⁄8 ¼

CIVILITE ORNAMENTS	TELEPHONES	PENLINE FLOURISHES

CIVILITE ORNAMENTS

72 x 144 points VM88

48 x 96 points VM89

36 x 120 points VM90

36 x 120 points VM91

72 x 24 points VM92

72 x 24 points VM93

48 x 54 points VM94

48 x 54 points VM95

TELEPHONES

Solid

60 points

48 points

36 points

24 points

Outline

48 points

36 points

24 points

PENLINE FLOURISHES

39 x 27 points VM96

12 x 42 points VM97

20 x 78 points
VM98

10 x 78 points
VM99

51 x 78 points
VM100

39 x 90 points
VM 101

39 x 90 points
VM102

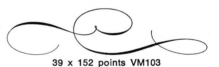

39 x 152 points VM103

39 x 152 points VM104

51 x 51 points
VM105

51 x 51 points
VM106

78 x 78 points
VM107

78 x 78 points
VM108

OMBREE ORNAMENTS

Ombree Ornaments enable the creative printer to turn out a distinctive
piece of printing without extra cost for art work and engravings.

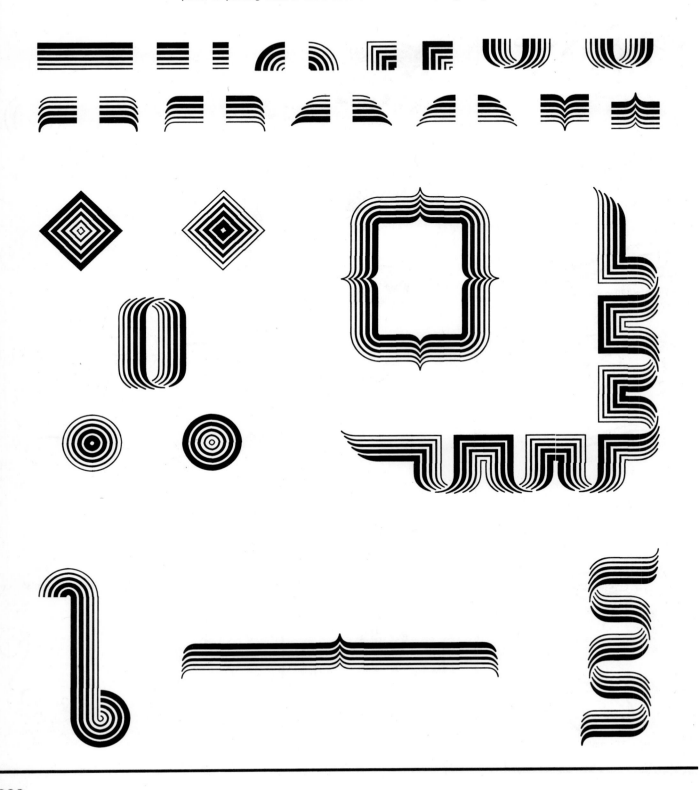

Foundry—Borders and Ornaments

ELECTION SIGNS

18 point VM24   Republican

24 point VM25   Republican

24 point VM26   Republican Elephant

36 point VM27   Republican Elephant

72 point VM28   Republican Elephant

36 point VM29   Democratic Donkey

72 point VM30   Democratic Donkey

24 point VM31   American Labor

24 point VM32   Farmer Labor

24 point VM33   Progressive

24 point VM34   Independent Progressive

24 point VH35   Socialist

CAMEO TYPECUTS

24 point VM36

24 point VM37

24 point VM38

24 point VM39

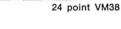
24 point VM40

24 point VM41

24 point VM42

24 point VM43

24 point VM44

24 point VM45

ASTRONOMICAL SIGNS

12 point VM46   New Moon

12 point VM47   First Quarter

12 point VM48   Full Moon

12 point VM49   Last Quarter

12 point VM50   Aries

12 point VM51   Gemini

12 point VM52   Cancer

12 point VM53   Leo

12 point VM54   Virgo

12 point VM55   Libra

12 point VM56   Scorpio

12 point VM57   Sagittarius

12 point VM58   Capricornus

12 point VM59   Aquarius

12 point VM60   Pisces

TROYER ORNAMENTS

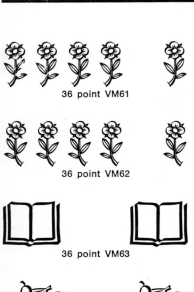

36 point VM61

36 point VM62

36 point VM63

36 point VM64

36 point VM65

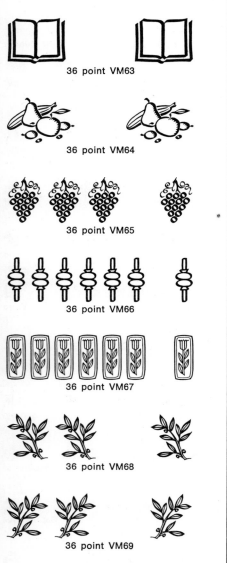

36 point VM66

36 point VM67

36 point VM68

36 point VM69

36 point VM70

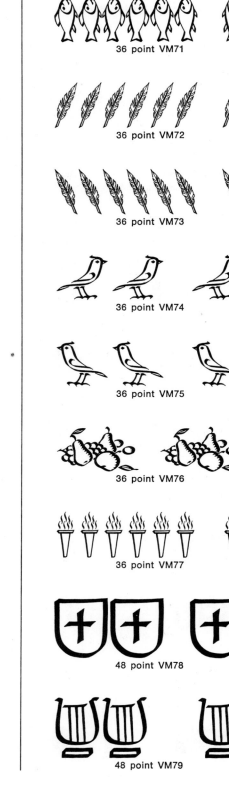

36 point VM71

36 point VM72

36 point VM73

36 point VM74

36 point VM75

36 point VM76

36 point VM77

48 point VM78

48 point VM79

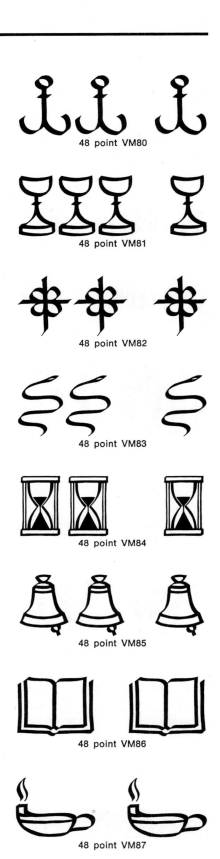

48 point VM80

48 point VM81

48 point VM82

48 point VM83

48 point VM84

48 point VM85

48 point VM86

48 point VM87

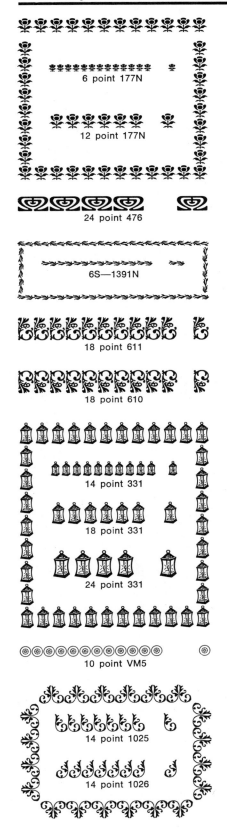

6 point 177N

12 point 177N

24 point 476

6S—1391N

18 point 611

18 point 610

14 point 331

18 point 331

24 point 331

10 point VM5

14 point 1025

14 point 1026

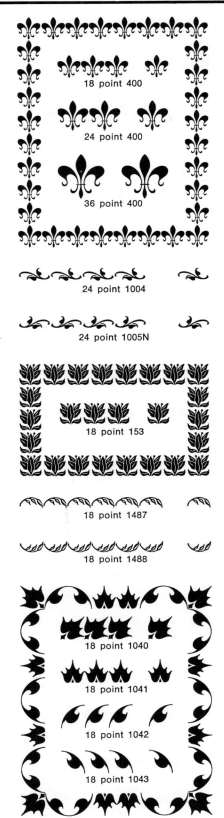

18 point 400

24 point 400

36 point 400

24 point 1004

24 point 1005N

18 point 153

18 point 1487

18 point 1488

18 point 1040

18 point 1041

18 point 1042

18 point 1043

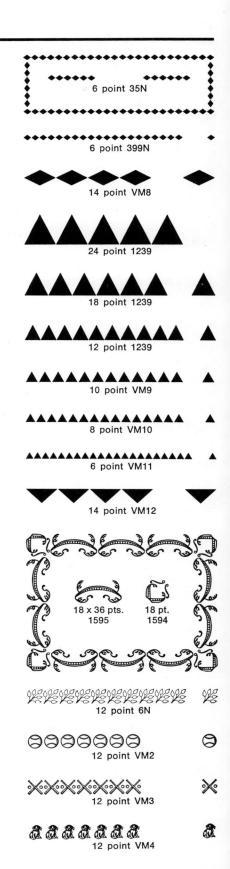

6 point 35N

6 point 399N

14 point VM8

24 point 1239

18 point 1239

12 point 1239

10 point VM9

8 point VM10

6 point VM11

14 point VM12

18 x 36 pts. 1595   18 pt. 1594

12 point 6N

12 point VM2

12 point VM3

12 point VM4

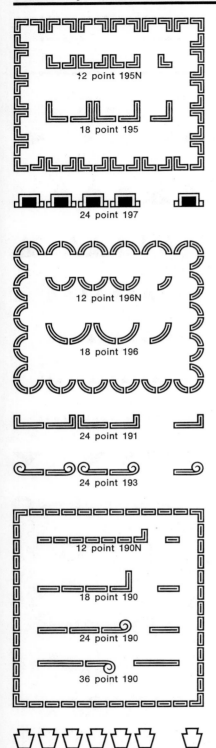

12 point 195N

18 point 195

24 point 197

12 point 196N

18 point 196

24 point 191

24 point 193

12 point 190N

18 point 190

24 point 190

36 point 190

18 point VM6

18 point VM1

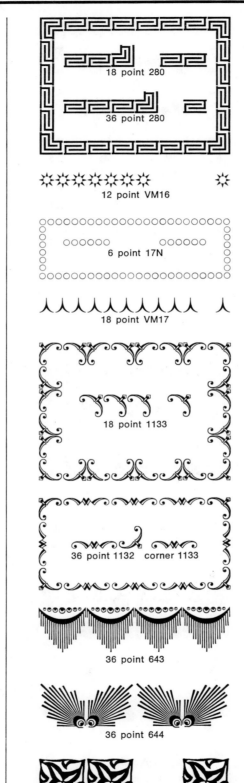

18 point 280

36 point 280

12 point VM16

6 point 17N

18 point VM17

18 point 1133

36 point 1132   corner 1133

36 point 643

36 point 644

36 point 113

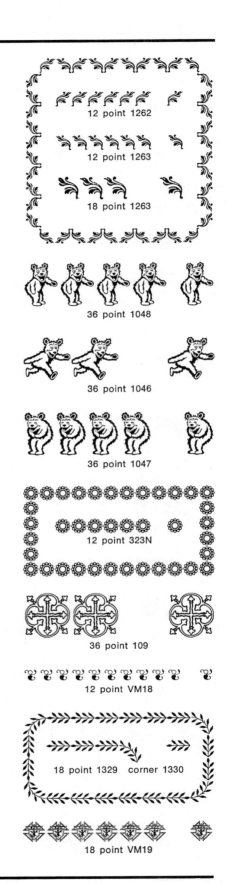

12 point 1262

12 point 1263

18 point 1263

36 point 1048

36 point 1046

36 point 1047

12 point 323N

36 point 109

12 point VM18

18 point 1329   corner 1330

18 point VM19

24 point 550

36 point 552

24 point UM7

24 point 236

18 point 460

12 point 29N

18 point 29

24 point 29

30 point 29

36 point 29

14 point 673

18 point 39

18 point 47

18 point 1427

18 point 1428

24 point 746

24 point 227

24 point 239

12 point VM21

14 point VM22

12 point VM20

12 point 188N

12 point 471N

24 point 1000
corner 1003

24 point 1002

reverse 1001
corner 1003

36 point 30

36 point 28

12 point 609N

36 point 773

36 point 1383

18 point 118

18 point
26A   26B   26C

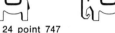

18 point 27

24 point 747

36 point 235

36 point 285

24 point 238

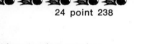

30 point 28

30 point 264

36 point 486

---

14 point 705

14 point 706

24 point 126

30 point 126

30 point 126

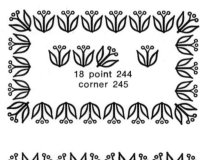

12 point 253N
corner 254N

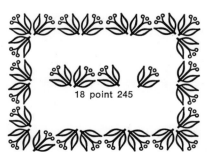

18 point 244
corner 245

18 point 245

---

18 point 720

14 point 1022

12 point 189N

24 point 703

24 point 1574

14 point 187

PATRIOTIC DECORATION

24 point VM13

24 point VM14

12 point 24N

24 point VM23

18 point VM15

Linotype—Borders and Ornaments

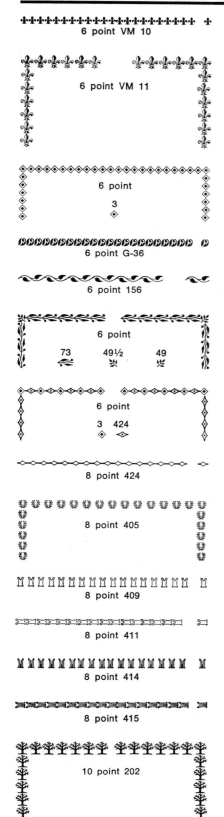

6 point VM 10

6 point VM 11

6 point

3

6 point G-36

6 point 156

6 point

73   49½   49

6 point

3   424

8 point 424

8 point 405

8 point 409

8 point 411

8 point 414

8 point 415

10 point 202

10 point 204

10 point 223

10 point 234

10 point 330

10 point 348

10 point 1606

10 point 1610

10 point 1605

10 point 1612

12 point 525

12 point 1099

12 point 1605

12 point 1606

12 point 1607

12 point 1608

12 point 1609

12 point 1610

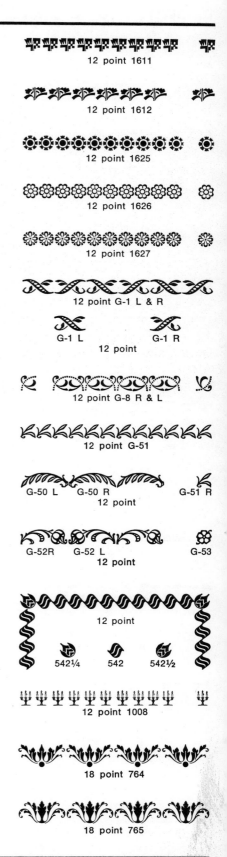

12 point 1611

12 point 1612

12 point 1625

12 point 1626

12 point 1627

12 point G-1 L & R

G-1 L   G-1 R

12 point

12 point G-8 R & L

12 point G-51

G-50 L   G-50 R   G-51 R

12 point

G-52R   G-52 L   G-53

12 point

12 point

542¼   542   542½

12 point 1008

18 point 764

18 point 765

LINOTYPE MATRIX SLIDES

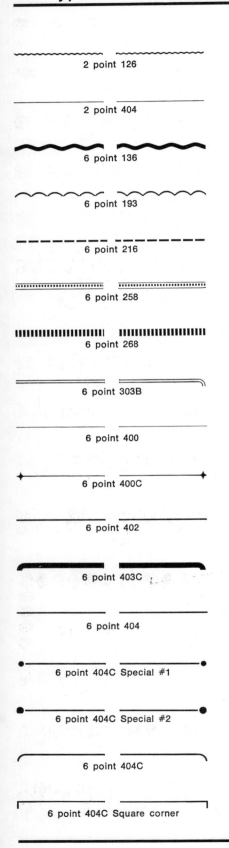

2 point 126

2 point 404

6 point 136

6 point 193

6 point 216

6 point 258

6 point 268

6 point 303B

6 point 400

6 point 400C

6 point 402

6 point 403C

6 point 404

6 point 404C Special #1

6 point 404C Special #2

6 point 404C

6 point 404C Square corner

6 point 404i

6 point 405C

6 point 407

6 point 408

6 point 1255

6 point 1303

6 point 1304

6 point 1317

6 point 1330

6 point 1387

6 point 1401

6 point 1403

6 point 1411

6 point 1426

6 point 1431

6 point 1434

6 point 1436

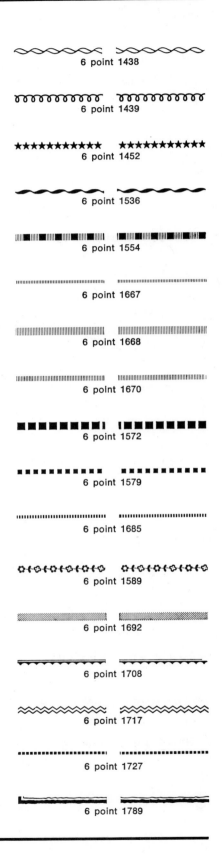

6 point 1438

6 point 1439

6 point 1452

6 point 1536

6 point 1554

6 point 1667

6 point 1668

6 point 1670

6 point 1572

6 point 1579

6 point 1685

6 point 1589

6 point 1692

6 point 1708

6 point 1717

6 point 1727

6 point 1789

LINOTYPE MATRIX SLIDES

6 point 1815A

6 point 1822

6 point 1843

6 point 1852

6 point 1858

6 point 1975A

6 point 1979

6 point 1981

6 point 2000

8 point 1669

8 point 1811

9 point 738

10 point 271

11 point 1486

12 point 140

12 point 267

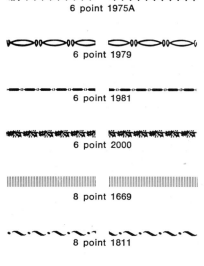
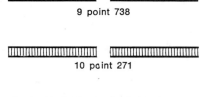

12 point 405C Square corner

12 point 406C

12 point 407½C

12 point 407i

12 point 411C

12 point 417

12 point 417C

12 point 421

12 point 891

12 point 1222C

12 point 1261

12 point 1263

12 point 1267

12 point 1289

12 point 1428

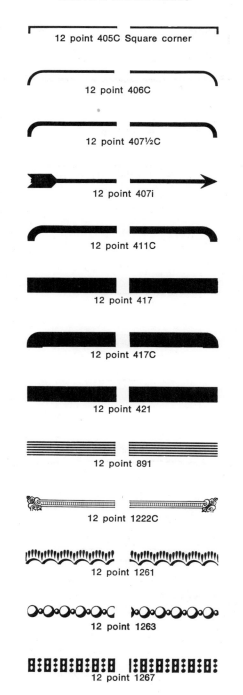

12 point 1433

12 point 1514

12 point 1619

12 point 1673

12 point 1691

12 point 1774

12 point 1788

12 point 1999

18 point 1277

18 point 1289

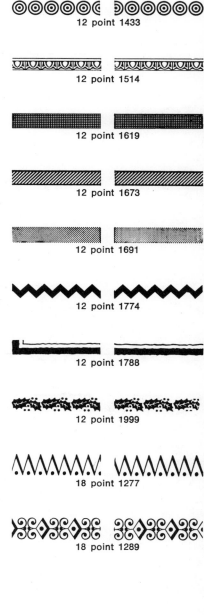

LINOTYPE MATRIX SLIDES

6 poin 2032

6 point 999

6 point 2031

6 point 998

6 point 997

6 point 996

6 point 1015   6 point 954   6 point 2072

6 point 1017   6 point 2070   6 point 956

6 point 983   6 point 917   6 point 945

6 point 1135

6 point 1131

6 point 1128

6 point 1125

6 point 1123

6 point 1119   6 point 1111   6 point 1105

6 point 1115   6 point 1107   6 point 1103

Linotype—Miscellaneous Sorts

ASTRONOMICAL

☉	Sun	8 9 10
⊖	Earth	8 10
⊕	Earth	8 9 10
♁	Earth	8 10
♃	Jupiter	10
☿	Mercury	10
♇	Pluto	10
♇	Pluto	10
♆	Neptune	10
♀	Venus	8 10
♄	Saturn	10
♂	Mars	8 10
☊	Ascending Node	8 10
♏	Scorpio	10
●	Full Moon	8 10 12 14
◑	Half Moon	8 9 10
☾	Last Quarter	9
☋	Descending Node	8 10
△	Trine	6 8 10 12
□	Quadrature	6 8 10 12 14
∝	Variation	8 10
⌓	Runs Highest	10
♎	Libra	10
♉	Taurus	11

METEOROLOGICAL

○	Absolutely no clouds	6 8 10
⦶	Broken Clouds	8 9 10
⊕	Overcast	8 9 10
●	Rain	6 8 10 12 14
═	Light Fog	6 8 9 10 12 14
≡	Fog, sky not discernible	8 10
/	High	6 8 10 12
↯	Lightning	10
↯	Thunderstorm	10
↑	South	6 8 10
↓	North	6 8 10
→	West	6 8 10
←	East	6 8 10
↗	Southwest	6 7 8 9 10
↖	Southeast	6 7 8 9 10
↘	Northwest	6 7 8 9 10
↙	Northeast	6 7 8 9 10
▽	Showers	8 10
∞	Haze	8 10

STARS—BLACK AND OUTLINE

★	Solid Star	6 8 10 12 14
☆	Outline Star	6 8 10 12 14
✪	Circular Star	8

ELECTION

○	Ballot Circle	6 8 10 12
⊗	Ballot Circle	12 14
□	Ballot Square	6 8 10 12 14
☒	Ballot Square	6 8 10 12 14
■	Solid Ballot Square	6 8 9 10 12 14
🦅	Republican	12
★	Democrat	6 8 10 12 14
🕮	Liberal	12
🔔	American	12
💪	American Labor	12
🔥	Socialist	12
⚖	Independent Progressive	14
🫏	Democratic Donkey	10
🐘	Republican Elephant	10
☛	Right Solid	6 8 10 12 14
☚	Left Solid	6 8 10 12 14

PLAYING CARDS

♠	Spade	8 10 11
♥	Heart	8 10 11
♦	Diamond	8 10 11
♣	Club	8 10 11
♤	Spade	8 10
♡	Heart	8 10 11
♢	Diamond	8 10
♧	Club	8 10

ECCLESIASTICAL

†	Latin Cross	6 8 10 12 14
✠	Maltese Cross	6 8 10 11 12 14
✠	Maltese Cross	8 9 10 14
☥	Ansate Cross	12
✡	Star of David	6 8 10 12
℟	Response	7 14
℣	Versicle	7 8 9 10 14

MUSICAL NOTES

♯	Sharp	6 10 11 12
𝄪	Double Sharp	10 12
𝄪	Double Sharp	6 8 10 12
♭	Flat	6 10 11 12
♮	Natural	6 10 11 12
𝅘𝅥𝅯	1⁄16 note	6 10 12
♪	⅛ note	6 10 11 12
♩	¼ note	6 10 12
𝅗𝅥	½ note	6 10 12
𝅝	Full note	6 10 12
♫	Joined ⅛ notes	10 12
♬	Joined ⅛ notes	10 12
𝄞	G clef	6 10 12
𝄢	F clef	6 10 12
𝄐	Hold	6 10 12
𝄋	Repeat	6 10 12
𝄋	Repeat	6 10 12

PARAGRAPH AND REFERENCE MARKS

⁂	Asterism	6 8 10 11 12
⁂	Asterism	6 8 10 12
⟨	Broken Brackets	8 10 11 12
⟩	Broken Brackets	8 10 11 12
†	Reference Sign	6 8 10 12 14
‡	Reference Sign	6 8 10 12 14
*	Serif	6 7 8 9 10 11 12 14
✱	San Serif	6 7 8 9 10 11 12 14
▶	Paragraph Mark	6 10 12 14
◀	Paragraph Mark	6 10 12 14
¶	Paragraph Mark	6 7 8 10 11 12 14
§	Paragraph Mark	6 7 8 10
§	Paragraph Mark	12 14

GERMAN ALPHABET

𝔄	A	8 10
𝔅	B	8 10
ℭ	C	8 10
𝔇	D	8 10
𝔈	E	8 10
𝔉	F	8 10
𝔊	G	8 10
ℌ	H	8 10
ℑ	I	8 10
𝔎	K	8 10
𝔏	L	8 10
𝔐	M	8 10
𝔑	N	8 10
𝔒	O	8 10
𝔓	P	8 10
𝔔	Q	8 10
ℜ	R	8 10
𝔖	S	8 10
𝔗	T	8 10
𝔘	U	8 10
𝔙	V	8 10
𝔚	W	8 10
𝔛	X	8 10
𝔜	Y	8 10
ℨ	Z	8 10

MEDICAL

℞	Recipe, take	6 8 9 10 12 14
℥	Ounce	8 10
ʒ	Dram	8 10
☠	Poison	8 10
♏	Drop	10

BULLETS

·	1 point	8 9 10 11
·	1½ point	10 11
•	2 point	6 7 8 9 10 11 12 14
•	2¼ point	6 10 12 14
•	3 point	8
●	3¾ point	6 8 10 12 14
●	5 point	10
●	6 point	6 10 12 14
●	6½ point	8 12
●	7½ point	14
●	9 point	14

BRACKETS

	10
	10
	7 8 9 10 11 12 14
	7 8 9 10 11 12 14
	8 12
	8 12
	6 7 8 9 10 11 12 14
	6 7 8 9 10 11 12 14
	12
	12
Corner left	6 10
Corner right	6 10

BRACES

	6 7 8 9 10 11 12 14
	6 7 8 9 10 11 12 14
	6 7 8 9 10 11 12 14
	6 7 8 9 10 11 12 14
	6 7 8 9 10 11 12 14
	6 7 8 9 10 11 12 14
	6 7 8 9 10 11 12 14
	6 7 8 9 10 11 12 14
	6 7 8 9 10 11 12 14
	6 7 8 9 10 11 12 14
{	8 10 12
}	8 10 12

TIME TABLE AND TARIFF

©	6 8 9 10 12 14
®	6 8 10 12 14
▲	8 9
◆	8 10 11
●	6 8 10 12
■	6 8 9 10 12 14
★	6 8 10 12
:	6 8 10
◇	8 10 11
□	6 8 10 12 14

Circled		Boxed num		Circled letter		Boxed letter	
①	10	[1]	10	Ⓐ	10	[A]	10
②	10	[2]	10	Ⓑ	10	[B]	10
③	10	[3]	10	Ⓒ	10	[C]	10
④	10	[4]	10	Ⓓ	10	[D]	10
⑤	10	[5]	10	Ⓔ	10	[E]	10
⑥	10	[6]	10	Ⓕ	10	[F]	10
⑦	10	[7]	10	Ⓖ	10	[G]	10
⑧	10	[8]	10	Ⓗ	10	[H]	10
⑨	10	[9]	10	Ⓘ	10	[I]	10
⑩	10	[10]	10	Ⓙ	10	[J]	10
⑪	10	[11]	10	Ⓚ	10	[K]	10
⑫	10	[12]	10	Ⓛ	10	[L]	10
⑬	10	[13]	10	Ⓜ	10	[M]	10
⑭	10	[14]	10	Ⓝ	10	[N]	10
⑮	10	[15]	10	Ⓞ	10	[O]	10
⑯	10	[16]	10	Ⓟ	10	[P]	10
⑰	10	[17]	10	Ⓠ	10	[Q]	10
⑱	10	[18]	10	Ⓡ	10	[R]	10
⑲	20	[19]	10	Ⓢ	10	[S]	10
⑳	10	[20]	10	Ⓣ	10	[T]	10
㉑	10	[21]	10	Ⓤ	10	[U]	10
㉒	10	[22]	10	Ⓥ	10	[V]	10
㉓	10	[23]	10	Ⓦ	10	[W]	10
㉔	10	[24]	10	Ⓧ	10	[X]	10
㉕	10	[25]	10	Ⓨ	10	[Y]	10
				Ⓩ	10	[Z]	10

Linotype—Miscellaneous Sorts

6 point Linotype Sorts

↙ ℔ ℔ £ ¢ % ○ † ‡ ‡ ← Ψ ⅄ ⅄ ○ ∿ ‰

7 point Linotype Sorts

‰ ℔ ‡ † £ [ ] ‖ @

8 point Linotype Sorts

√ ↙ ⌣ ∨ ∧ ○ ◂ ▸ ○ ⅋ % ‰ ¢ † # °

8 point No. 4 Horizontal Figures

١ ٢ ٣ ٤ ٥ ٦ ٧ ٨ ٩ ٠

9 point Linotype Sorts

% £ Æ ‰ = /

10 point Linotype Sorts

PRINTED IN U.S.A. ¢ £ « » ∨ ∧ = √ ↙ % ℔ @

[ ] ¶ / ‡ †

10 point No. 1 Cancelled Figures

1̶ 2̶ 3̶ 4̶ 5̶ 6̶ 7̶ 8̶ 9̶ 0̶

12 point Linotype Sorts

£ £ | / PRINTED IN U.S.A. √ ¢ ¢ † ‡ @ @

« » ↙ Æ Œ # ‖ ▦

14 point Linotype Sorts

▦ | ↙ = √ £ « » ‡ † ¢ ¢ /

@ ℔ #

Linotype—Miscellaneous Arrows

6 point (Linotype)

7 point (Linotype)

8 point (Linotype)

9 point (Linotype)

10 point (Linotype)

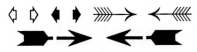

12 point (Linotype)

14 point (Linotype)

Linotype—Mathematical Sorts

CHEMICAL

Symbol	Name	Sizes
/	Single Bond	8 10
		Single Bond	8 10
\	Single Bond	8 10
		Single Bond	8 10
//	Double Bond	8 10
‖	Double Bond	8 10
\\	Double Bond	8 10
‖	Double Bond	8 10
⋮	Triple Bond	8 10
/	Broken bond	8 10
\	Broken bond	8 10
⇋	Equilibrium reaction beginning at right	8 10 11 12
⇌	Equilibrium reaction beginning at left	8 10 11 12
⇌	Reversible reaction beginning at left	8 10
⇋	Reversible reaction beginning at right	8 10
⇋	Reaction begins at right and is completed to right	8 10
⇌	Reaction begins at left and is completed to left	8 10
⇋	Reaction begins at right and is completed to right	8 10
⇌	Reaction begins at left and is completed to left	8 10
⇒	Reversible reaction	8 10
⇐	Reversible reaction	8 10
⇅	Equilibrium reaction	8 10
⇅	Reversible reaction	8 10
⇲	Reversible reaction	8 10
⇗	Reversible reaction	8 10
↔	Reaction goes both right and left	10
↕	Reaction up and down	8 10
⊂	Ring opening	8
↯	Electrolysis	8
⌒	Repositioning	8
⇑	Elimination	8
⇓	Absorption	8
○	Ring Cycle	8 10

MATHEMATICAL SCRIPT LETTERS

Symbol	Sizes
A	10
B	10
C	10
D	10
E	10
F	10
G	10
H	10
I	10
J	10
K	10
L	10
M	10
N	10
O	10
P	10
Q	10
R	10
S	10
T	10
U	10
V	10
W	10
X	10
Y	10
Z	10
F	Cap F	10
E	Cap E	10
Q	Cap Q	10
P	Cap P	10
C	Cap C	10
S	Cap S	10
U	Cap U	10
ℓ	Lower case ell	8 10
k	Lower case k	8 10
ℓ	Superior lower case ell	8 10
k	Superior lower case k	8 10
ℓ	Inferior lower case ell	8 10
∀	Inverted Aye	10
∃		8 10
∈		8 10

MATHEMATICAL—330

Symbol	Name	Sizes
+	Plus	6 8 10 11 12 14
−	Minus	6 8 10 11 12 14
×	Multiplied by	6 8 10 11 12 14
÷	Divided by	6 8 10 11 12 14
=	Equal to	6 8 10 11 12 14
±	Plus or Minus	6 8 10 12 14
∓	Minus or plus	8 10 12
≏	Difference between	10
≡	Identical with, congruent	8 10
≢	Not identical with	8 10
≠	Not equal to	8 10
≉	Not equivalent	8 10
≈	Nearly equal to	8 10
≅	Equals approximately	8 10
<	Less than	6 8 10 11 12 14
>	Greater than	6 8 10 11 12 14
≷	Greater than or less than	8 10
≶	Less than or greater than	8 10
≮	Not less than	9 10
≯	Not greater than	9 10
≤	Less than or equal to	8 10
≥	Greater than or equal to	6 8 10
≦	Less than or equal to	8 10
≧	Greater than or equal to	8 10
≦	Less than or equal to	8 10
≧	Greater than or equal to	8 10
⊂	Included in	8 10
⊃	Excluded from	8 10
⊃		8 10
∩		8 10
∪		8 10
∼	Difference	8 10 11 12 14
⊥	Perpendicular to	8 10
⊢	Assertion sign	8 10
⊣	Assertion sign	8 10
‖	Parallel	8 10
∠	Angle	8 10 12
∟	Angle	8 10 12
∡	Angles	8 10
⊿	Angle	10
△	Triangle	6 8 9 10 11 12
◬	Triangles	8 10
/	Rising diagonal	8 10
\	Falling diagonal	8 10
//	Parallel rising diagonal	8 10
\\	Parallel falling diagonal	8 10
⫴	Triple vertical	8 10
⫶	Cancelled vertical	10
⫼	Cancelled verticals	8 10
⌢	Segment	10
○	Circle	6 8 10
□	Square	6 8 10 12 14
▭	Rectangle	8 9 10 11
⌒	Arc	8 10
∴	Hence, therefore	6 8 10 12 14
·	Multiplied by	6 8 10 11
:	Ratio	6 7 8 9 10 11 12 14
::	Proportion	6 7 8 9 10 11 12 14
∷	Geometrical proportion	8 10
′	Minute	6 8 10
″	Second	6 8 10 12 14
°	Degree	6 7 8 10 11 12 14
°	Centered degree mark	6 8 10
⊙	Center degree mark with dot	8 10
⸴	Dotted minute	8 10
″	Dotted Second	8 10
°	Dotted degree	8 10
⸴	Cancelled second	8 10
‴	Triple prime	8 10

Linotype—Mathematical Sorts

√	Radical	8 10 12
√¹	Root	8 10
√²	Square root	8 10
√³	Cube root	8 10
√⁴	Fourth root	8 10
√⁵	Fifth root	8 10
√⁶	Sixth root	8 10
√⁷	Seventh root	8 10
√⁸	Eighth root	8 10
√⁹	Ninth root	8 10
√ⁿ	Nth root	8 10
√²ⁿ	2nth root	8 10
∝	Variation	8 10
∞	Infinity	8 10
∂	Differential	8 10
∂	Differential	8 10
∫	Integral	8 10
∿	Cycle sign	8 10
≃		8 10
◆	Diamond	6
ℵ	Hebrew symbol Aleph	10

MATHEMATICAL—200

≐	8 10
≒	8 10
∞	8 10
△	8 10
▽	8 10
≪	8 10
≫	8 10
≧	8 10
≦	8 10
∧	8 10
∨	8 10

⊇	8 10
⊒	8 10
⊧	8 10
≢	8 10
≠	8 10
≨	8 10
⇒	8 10
⟋	8 10
⫫	8 10
⫽	8 10
⩘	8 10
⩙	8 10
∮	8 10

MATHEMATICAL—526

+	Plus	8 10
—	Minus	8 10
×	Multiplied by	8 10
÷	Divided by	8 10
=	Equal to	8 10

MATHEMATICAL GREEK

Γ	Gamma	6 8 10
Δ	Delta	6 8 10
Θ	Theta	6 8 10
Λ	Lambda	6 8 10
Ξ	Xi	6 8 10
Π	Pi	6 8 10
Σ	Sigma	6 8 10
Υ	Upsilon	6 8 10
Φ	Phi	6 8 10
Ψ	Psi	6 8 10
Ω	Omega	6 8 10
α	Alpha	6 8 10

δ	Delta	6 8 10
ζ	Zeta	6 8 10
β	Beta	6 8 10
γ	Gamma	6 8 10
ε	Epsilon	6 8 10
η	Eta	6 8 10
θ	Theta	6 8 10
ι	Iota	6 8 10
κ	Kappa	6 8 10
λ	Lambda	6 8 10
μ	Mu	6 8 10
ν	Nu	6 8 10
ξ	Xi	6 8 10
ο	Omicron	6 8 10
π	Pi	6 8 10
ρ	Rho	6 8 10
σ	Sigma	6 8 10
ς	Sigma	6 8 10
τ	Tau	6 8 10
υ	Upsilon	6 8 10
φ	Phi	6 8 10
χ	Chi	6 8 10
ψ	Psi	6 8 10
ω	Omega	6 8 10

Supplemental:

ε	Epsilon	8 10
ⱸ	Epsilon cancelled	8 10
σ̃	Sigma with tilde	10
φ	Open Phi	10
ϑ	Open Theta	8 10
ϝ	Digamma	8 10
∂	Partial derivative	8 10
ϭ	Open Beta	10

Porson Greek

6 point (Linotype)

Α Β Γ Δ Ε Ζ Η Θ Ι Κ Λ Μ Ν Ξ Ο Π Ρ Σ Τ Υ Φ Χ Ψ Ω

α β γ δ ε ζ η θ ι κ λ μ ν ξ ο ρ σ ς τ υ φ π φ χ ψ ω

8 point (Linotype)

Α Β Γ Δ Ε Ζ Η Θ Ι Κ Λ Μ Ν Ξ Ο Π Ρ Σ Τ Υ Φ Χ Ψ Ω

α β γ δ ε ζ η θ ι κ λ μ ν ξ ο ρ σ ς τ υ φ χ ψ ω

ὰ ά ἀ ἄ ἐ έ ἔ ἒ ῐ ἰ ἱ ἲ ἴ ῑ ὸ ό ὀ ὄ ὅ ἤ ἠ ἢ ῃ ἦ ῆ ἥ ἡ ὐ ὒ

ῦ ὺ ύ ὠ ὦ ὤ ώ ϝ

10 point (Linotype)

Α Β Γ Δ Ε Ζ Η Θ Ι Κ Λ Μ Ν Ξ Ο Π Ρ Σ Τ Υ Φ Χ Ψ Ω

α β γ δ ε ζ η θ ι κ λ μ ν ξ ο ρ σ ς τ υ φ χ ψ ω

ὰ ά ἀ ἂ ἄ ἆ ἀ ἁ ᾳ ἔ ἐ ἒ ἕ ἓ ἐ ῆ ἤ ἢ ἦ ἠ ἥ ᾐ ῃ ἢ ῄ ἥ ἦ ῇ ἥ ἡ ῐ ῑ

ῖ ῑ ἲ ἱ ἴ ῒ ἶ ό ὸ ὀ ὄ ὅ ὂ ὅ ὀ ὁ ρ ὔ ὒ ῠ ὺ ὐ ύ ὐ ὑ ὒ ῦ ὔ ὖ ῧ ὦ ὠ ὢ ᾦ ὣ ὤ ὡ ὥ ϝ

5 point Superior (Linotype)

d ABCDEFGHIJKLMNOPQRSTUVWXYZ
d ABCDEFGHIJKLMNOPQRSTUVWXYZ
d abcdefghijklmnopqrstuvwxyz
d abcdefghijklmnopqrstuvwxyz
d 1234567890
d 1234567890
d ΑΒΓΔΕΖΗΙΘΚΛΜΝΞΟΠΡΣΤΥΦΧΨΩ
d αβγδεζηιθκλμνξοπρστυφχψω
d .,◊!‴△□○◎\ ⁄×⊙⊕/+=−±∓÷&√∞∝″′≗°●
d ×+●■★↓✚♯▲♦

10 point Superior (Linotype)

d ABCDEFGHIJKLMNOPQRSTUVWXYZ
d ABCDEFGHIJKLMNOPQRSTUVWXYZ
d abcdefghijklmnopqrstuvwxyz
d abcdefghijklmnopqrstuvwxyz
d 1234567890
d 1234567890
d .,-[]/()%−•′⅛¼⅜½⅝¾⅞⅛¼⅜½⅝¾⅞ḅçḍ eḥ p r ş y
d −÷×+=∓±∞
d ≥<⊂⊃⊇∩∪≦≋\ #→←≤≡✕√∅∞∝/″′∫∼
d ⊙±:∓±>%°∅∓≠

5 point Inferior (Linotype)

d ABCDEFGHIJKLMNOPQRSTUVWXYZ
d ABCDEFGHIJKLMNOPQRSTUVWXYZ
d abcdefghijklmnopqrstuvwxyz
d abcdefghijklmnopqrstuvwxyz
d 1234567890±∓≡\
d 1234567890
d ΑΒΓΔΕΖΗΙΚΑΜΝΞΟΠΡΣΤΥΦΧΨΩ
d αβγδεζηθικλμνοπρστυφχψω

6 point Inferior (Linotype)

d ABCDEFFGHIJKLMNOPQRSTUVWXYZ
d ABCDEFFGHIJKLMNOPQRSTUVWXYZ
d abcdefghijklmnopqrstuvwxyz
d abcdefghijklmnopqrstuvwxyz
d 1234567890
d 1234567890
d .,′″°+−×=÷±∓≡!‴?∞\ ⁄!()

8 point Inferior (Linotype)

d ABCDEFGHIJKLMNOPQRSTUVWXYZ
d ABCDEFGHIJKLMNOPQRSTUVWXYZ
d abcdefghijklmnnopqrstuvwxyz
d abcdefghijklmnnopqrstuvwxyz
d 1234567890
d .,:;!'‘-/()[]%'″°−×÷+=÷∞&†•
d ⅛¼⅜½⅝¾⅞⅛¼⅜½⅝¾⅞ ½ ¼ ¾ ⅛ ⅜ ⅝ ⅞

9 point Inferior (Linotype)

d ABCDEFGHIJKLMNOPQRSTUVWXYZ
d ABCDEFGHIJKLMNOPQRSTUVWXYZ
d abcdefghijklmnopqrstuvwxyz
d abcdefghijklmnopqrstuvwxyz
d 1234567890
d 1234567890
d .,:;!?'‘-°•$&()[]½%'−=÷+⊥×

10 point Inferior (Linotype)

d ABCDEFGHIJKLMNOPQRSTUVWXYZ
d ABCDEFGHIJKLMNOPQRSTUVWXYZ
d abcdefghijklmnopqrstuvwxyz
d abcdefghijklmnopqrstuvwxyz
d 1234567890
d 1234567890
d ΑΓΒΔΕΖΗΘΙΚΑΜΝΞΟΠΡΣΤΥΦΧΨΩ
d αβγδεζηθικλμνξοπρστυφχψω
d .,-′≡%[]()/−∓±+×÷=∞
d ′″±°⊃⊇∪∩⊂⊆\/≡→←#∝≠∫≥><≤≋∼∞
d ±⊙∅✕%√∞⅛¼⅜½⅝¾⅞⅛¼⅜½⅝¾⅞

12 point Inferior (Linotype)

d ABCDEFGHIJKLMNOPQRSTUVWXYZ
d ABCDEFGHIJKLMNOPQRSTUVWXYZ
d abcdefghijklmnopqrstuvwxyz
d abcdefghijklmnopqrstuvwxyz
d 1234567890
d 1234567890
d .,'‘-?!:;-/*$&[]×÷+−=∞°‡†'″()½¼%

Linotype—Miscellaneous Fractions

PIECE FRACTIONS

6 point Piece Fractions (Linotype)
1 2 3 4 5 5 7 8 9 9
1 2 3 4 5 6 7 8 9 0
1 2 3 4 5 6 7 8 9 6
1 2 3 4 5 6 7 8 9 0
¼ ½ ¾ ¹¹⁄₁₆ ²⁴⁄₆₀ ¹²⁰⁄₂₀₀

8 point Piece Fractions (Linotype)
1 2 3 4 5 6 7 8 9 9
1 2 3 4 5 6 7 8 9 0
1 2 3 4 5 6 7 8 9 6
1 2 3 4 5 6 7 8 9 0
¼ ½ ¾ ¹¹⁄₁₆ ²⁴⁄₆₀ ¹²⁰⁄₂₀₀

10 point Piece Fractions (Linotype)
1 2 3 4 5 6 7 8 9 0
1 2 3 4 5 6 7 8 9 0
1 2 3 4 5 6 7 8 9 9
1 2 3 4 5 6 7 8 9 0
¼ ½ ¾ ¹¹⁄₁₆ ²⁴⁄₆₀ ¹²⁰⁄₂₀₀

6 point No. 1
1 2 3 4 5 6 7 8 9 9
1 2 3 4 5 6 7 8 9
¼ ½ ¹¹⁄₁₆ ¹⁵⁄₁₆ ²⁴⁄₃₂ ¹²⁄₁₀₀

8 point No. 1
1 2 3 4 5 6 7 8 9 9
1 2 3 4 5 6 7 8 9
¼ ½ ¹¹⁄₁₆ ²⁴⁄₃₂ ¹²⁄₁₀₀

10 point No. 1
1 2 3 4 5 6 7 8 9 9
1 2 3 4 5 6 7 8 9
¼ ½ ¹¹⁄₁₆ ¹⁵⁄₁₆ ²⁴⁄₃₂ ¹²⁄₁₀₀

CASE FRACTIONS

8 point No. 362
$\frac{1}{16}$ $\frac{3}{16}$ $\frac{7}{16}$ $\frac{9}{16}$ $\frac{11}{16}$ $\frac{13}{16}$ $\frac{15}{16}$ $\frac{7}{32}$

9 point No. 362
$\frac{1}{16}$ $\frac{2}{16}$ $\frac{3}{16}$ $\frac{4}{16}$ $\frac{8}{16}$ $\frac{9}{16}$ $\frac{27}{64}$

10 point No. 362
$\frac{5}{7}$ $\frac{1}{9}$ $\frac{4}{9}$ $\frac{7}{9}$ $\frac{8}{9}$
$\frac{1}{10}$ $\frac{3}{10}$ $\frac{7}{10}$ $\frac{9}{16}$ $\frac{11}{16}$ $\frac{7}{32}$

PIECE FRACTIONS—SAN SERIF

6 point No. 3
1 2 3 4 5 6 7 8 9 9
1 2 3 4 5 6 7 8 6 6
¼ ½ ¹¹⁄₁₆ ¹⁵⁄₁₆ ²⁴⁄₃₂ ²⁷⁄₁₀₀

8 point No. 3
1 2 3 4 5 6 7 8 9 0
1 2 3 4 5 6 7 8 6 6
¼ ½ ¹¹⁄₁₆ ¹⁵⁄₁₆ ²⁴⁄₃₂ ²⁷⁄₁₀₀

10 point No. 3
1 2 3 4 5 6 7 8 9 0
1 2 3 4 5 6 7 8 6 6
¼ ½ ¹¹⁄₁₆ ¹⁵⁄₁₆ ²⁴⁄₃₂ ²⁷⁄₁₀₀

12 point No. 3
1, 2, 3, 4, 5, 6, 7, 8, 9, 0,
1 2 3 4 5 6 7 8 9 0
¼ ½ ¹¹⁄₁₆ ¹⁵⁄₁₆ ²⁴⁄₃₂ ²⁷⁄₁₀₀

14 point No. 3
1, 2, 3, 4, 5, 6, 7, 8, 9, 0,
1 2 3 4 5 6 7 8 9 0
½ ¼ ¹¹⁄₁₆ ¹⁵⁄₁₆ ²⁴⁄₃₂ ²⁷⁄₁₀₀

MISCELLANEOUS FRACTIONS

6 point No. 362
$\frac{1}{16}$ $\frac{3}{16}$ $\frac{5}{16}$

7 point No. 16
⅛ ¼ ⅜ ½ ⅝ ¾ ⅞

8 point No. 98
⅛ ⅓ ⅜ ⅔ ⅝ ⅞

8 point No. 362
$\frac{1}{16}$ $\frac{3}{16}$ $\frac{5}{16}$ $\frac{7}{16}$ $\frac{9}{16}$ $\frac{7}{32}$ $\frac{4}{5}$

10 point No. 1772
⅛ ¼ ⅜ $\frac{3}{16}$ $\frac{5}{16}$

PIECE FRACTIONS—SAN SERIF BOLD

6 point No. 3
1 2 3 4 5 6 7 8 9 9
1 2 3 4 5 6 7 8 6 6
¼ ½ ¹¹⁄₁₆ ¹⁵⁄₁₆ ²⁴⁄₃₂ ²⁷⁄₁₀₀

8 point No. 3
1 2 3 4 5 6 7 8 9 9
1 2 3 4 5 6 7 8 6 6
¼ ½ ¹¹⁄₁₆ ¹⁵⁄₁₆ ²⁴⁄₃₂ ²⁷⁄₁₀₀

10 point No. 3
1 2 3 4 5 6 7 8 9 9
1 2 3 4 5 6 7 8 6 6
¼ ½ ¹¹⁄₁₆ ¹⁵⁄₁₆ ²⁴⁄₃₂ ²⁷⁄₁₀₀

12 point No. 3
1, 2, 3, 4, 5, 6, 7, 8, 9, 0,
1 2 3 4 5 6 7 8 9 0
¼ ½ ¹¹⁄₁₆ ¹⁵⁄₁₆ ²⁴⁄₃₂ ²⁷⁄₁₀₀

14 point No. 3
1, 2, 3, 4, 5, 6, 7, 8, 9, 0,
1 2 3 4 5 6 7 8 9 0
½ ¼ ¹¹⁄₁₆ ¹⁵⁄₁₆ ²⁴⁄₃₂ ²⁷⁄₁₀₀

PIECE CASE FRACTIONS

10 point No. 10
1 2 3 4 5 6 7 8 9 0
1 2 3 4 5 6 7 8 9 0
$\frac{1}{4}$ $\frac{1}{2}$ $\frac{11}{16}$ $\frac{15}{16}$ $\frac{27}{32}$ $\frac{27}{100}$

12 point No. 2
1 2 3 4 5 6 7 8 9 0
1 2 3 4 5 6 7 8 9 0
$\frac{1}{4}$ $\frac{1}{2}$ $\frac{11}{16}$ $\frac{15}{16}$ $\frac{24}{32}$ $\frac{27}{100}$

Linotype's complete, authoritative system of phonetic transcription is based upon the phonetic alphabet devised by the International Phonetic Association. In addition to the characters approved by the Association, the list includes the most widely used signs and letters used internationally in influential scholarly works.

Detailed consideration has been given not only to the chief works in general phonetics in *Teutonic* (English, German, Scandinavian, etc.), *Romanic* (French, Spanish, Italian, etc.), *Slavic* (Russian, Czech, etc.), but also in the remoter tongues, such as the Bantu and Sudanic in Africa, and many languages in Asia. Note the group of independent diacritical marks or modifiers. These are to be placed immediately before or after the main character. This practice simplifies the problem of composition and greatly reduces the number of characters needed, while still offering broad, readable transcription under the principle of the phoneme.

NO.		NO.		NO.		NO.		NO.		NO.		NO.		NO.		NO.		NO.		NO.		NO.		NO.		NO.	
1	p	16	r̂	31	c	46	ļ	61	ş	76	x̧	91	i	106	ɨ	121	ū	136	ş	151	ż	166	ː	181	‗	195	ĵ
2	b	17	ř	32	ɟ	47	ɫ	62	s̱	77	ķ	92	e	107	ʉ	122	ɛ̃	137	ţ	152	ṡ	167	ˈ	182	ʹ	196	š
3	t	18	s	33	q	48	ḷ	63	z̧	78	g	93	ɛ	108	ɪ	123	œ̃	138	p̧	153	ë	168	×	183	ʼ	197	ž
4	d	19	v	34	G	49	ɹ	64	z̧	79	ɣ	94	a	109	ʊ	124	ɔ̃	139	ķ	154	ï	169	ã	184	ˋ	198	ɜ˙
5	k	20	w	35	ʔ	50	ʎ	65	ẕ	80	χ	95	ɑ	110	ʊ	125	ʌ̃	140	ẹ	155	ö	170	ĕ	185	ˎ	199	ɝ˙
6	m	21	ʍ	36	ŋ	51	ʎ̧	66	ʃ	81	ħ	96	ɔ	111	ʏ	126	ã	141	ǫ	156	ü	171	ĭ	186	ˆ	200	ǀ
7	n	22	z	37	ɳ	52	ɾ	67	ʒ	82	ʀ	97	o	112	æ	127	æ̃	142	ę	157	ɔ̈	172	ŏ	187	ˇ	201	ǁ
8	l	23	t̪	38	ɲ	53	ʈ	68	σ	83	ʕ	98	u	113	ɵ	128	ɒ̃	143	ǫ	158	ɛ̈	173	ŭ	188	˧	202	‖
9	f	24	ţ	39	ŋ	54	R	69	ǫ	84	ɦ	99	y	114	ə	129	ʒ	144	ţ	159	ï	174	ļ	189	˩		
10	h	25	ɫ	40	ŋ̧	55	ɸ	70	ʠ	85	ɥ	100	ø	115	ɜ	130	ḅ	145	ḍ	160	ä	175	m̥	190	˨		
11	g	26	ţ	41	ṇ	56	β	71	ẓ	86	ʊ	101	œ	116	ɐ	131	ḍ	146	ḷ	161	ü	176	ņ	191	T		
12	g	27	ḍ	42	N	57	θ	72	ç	87	ɭ	102	ɒ	117	ɑ̃	132	ǧ	147	ṇ	162	ü	177	ŗ	192	˃		
13	j	28	ḍ	43	ɫ	58	ð	73	ș	88	C	103	ʌ	118	ẽ	133	ǧ	148	ş	163	ʻ	178	ˈ	193	˂		
14	r	29	ḓ	44	ḥ	59	ɪ	74	ẓ	89	ɔ	104	ɣ	119	ĩ	134	ʏ	149	ẓ	164	ʻ	179	ˌ	194	č̌		
15	r̩	30	ḍ	45	ḷ	60	ș	75	x	90	ʯ	105	ɰ	120	õ	135	z̧	150	ṇ	165	ʼ	180	‐				

Index

Index

Index

Index